MEGAMERGERS

MEGA-MERGERS

CORPORATE AMERICA'S
BILLION-DOLLAR
TAKEOVERS

KENNETH M. DAVIDSON

Ballinger Publishing Company
Cambridge, Massachusetts
A Subsidiary of Harper & Row, Publishers, Inc.

International Standard Book Number: 0-88730-058-8

Library of Congress Catalog Card Number: 85-4025

Printed in the United States of America

Library of Congress Cataloging in Publication Data

Davidson, Kenneth M.
   Megamergers : understanding corporate acquisitions.

   Bibliography: p.
   Includes index.
   1. Consolidation and merger of corporations—United States.
I. Title.
HD2746.5.D38   1985   338.8'3'0973   85-4025
ISBN 0-88730-058-8

This book is dedicated
to the memory of my mother,
the late
Dr. Claire D. Davidson,
and her lifelong love of learning

and

to my father,
Alfred E. Davidson,
who has made public issues a fit
subject for dinner conversation

CONTENTS

ACKNOWLEDGMENTS

This book has benefited from the time and talents of many people, only some of whom are mentioned below. Without their generous help and encouragement I could not have written the book. I thank them all.

Dean Michael Kelly and the University of Maryland Law School in Baltimore provided me with an exceptionally congenial setting in which to write. The atmosphere of friendliness and respect among faculty, students, and staff more than made up for the long daily commute from Virginia. Several faculty members—David Bogen, Daniel Goldberg, Robert Keller, William Reynolds, and Marc Steinberg—kindly gave me their comments on drafts of chapters. Maxine Grosshans of the law library, tracked down books from other libraries for me and made sure replacements were available before they had to be returned. My research assistants, Charles Goldstein and Vivian Lipkey, made it possible for me to concentrate on writing. My secretary, Sandralee Palmer Morris, who cheerfully typed the entire text through its many revisions, also deserves much credit.

Dean Howard Glickstein and the University of Bridgeport Law School afforded me the opportunity to prepare for writing the book. The weekly commute by train offered ideal seclusion for reading materials I had assembled with the help of my research assistant Patrice Noah.

The Federal Trade Commission also helped make this study possible. James Miller, Chairman of the Federal Trade Commission, and his directors of the Bureau of Competition, Thomas Campbell and Timothy Muris, approved the leaves of absence during which I wrote the book. Former FTC Chairman Michael Pertschuk and his appointees, Alfred Dougherty, Daniel Schwartz, Alan Palmer, and Perry Johnson, assigned me a succession of projects that introduced me to the complexities of corporate mergers. My ability to handle those projects and prepare for this book was a result of the education I received from them and other FTC colleagues, including: Dana Abrahamsen, Roberta Baruch, Richard Duke, Alan Fisher, Albert Foer, Jonathan Groner, John Kirkwood, Robert Lande, Kenneth Miller, Robert Reich, Steven Salop, and Walter Vandaele.

John Huber and Joseph Connolly of the Securities and Exchange Commission patiently explained some intricacies of securities regulation to me.

Several chapters benefited from the comments of John Kirkwood, Martin Lybecker, Dennis Mueller, and Lawrence Sullivan.

Nancy Dunn provided timely help in completing the book after my leave of absence from the FTC had expired. The encouragement of Lynn Taylor and the Greenwood Press first persuaded me to undertake this book.

Finally, the book would not have happened without contributions from my family. My daughter, Alice, who likes the story about Liederkranz cheese, let me write at home. My daughter Claire, who was born March 10, 1984, knowing how to sleep through the night, has permitted me to do the same. My wife Ellen was there when I needed her.

July 12, 1984
Arlington, Virginia

MEGAMERGERS

M*egamerger* has become part of our business lexicon. With the help of T. Boone Pickens, Carl Icahn, and major American corporations, billion dollar mergers have become common. When Chevron pays $13 billion for Gulf Oil, or Capital Cities takes over the American Broadcasting Company for $3.5 billion, or General Motors buys the Electronic Data Systems computer service company for $2.5 billion, or R. J. Reynolds tobacco company acquires the Heublein conglomerate firm for $1.3 billion, or Santa Fe Industries combines with the Southern Pacific in a deal worth $5.2 billion, the transactions have only one feature in common: scale.

Megamergers are new. The term refers to the acquisition, merger, consolidation, or combination of already large firms. It also describes transactions in which well-known and successful firms buy each other for no obvious reason other than they have the resources to undertake the acquisition. It is the size of these transactions and their unexplained frequency that are phenomenal.

We have had large mergers before. The first billion dollar merger occurred in 1901 when United States Steel was formed by combining the Carnegie Steel Corporation with its leading rivals. But turn-of-the-century mergers were intelligibly motivated by the prospects of monopoly profits or production efficiencies. Since that time giant mergers have occurred sporadically and have been understandable, if at all, by the circumstances of the particular firms.

The current wave of large mergers is unprecedented. A few mega-mergers may resemble earlier transactions because the firms have achieved practical objectives by combining. But there have been too many other unexplained large mergers in the past decade to believe that these mergers represent the pursuit of a common, coherent economic objective. At the same time, too many large mergers are taking place to believe they are entirely unconnected.

This book began with one question, which then led to others. Why are all these mergers happening now? Apart from the federal budget, these are the largest annual spending decisions in the United States, amounting to $82 billion in 1982 alone. Who gets this money? And what are the consequences for our society?

No single theory can provide answers to these questions. Mega-mergers are a mixed bag for companies, shareholders, and society alike. While I believe a common trigger precipitated the megamerger wave—the combination of a tax law which provides incentives for corporations to retain their earnings and a lack of corporate spending opportunities other than mergers—the acquisitions are affected by many other influences and have many important consequences. The results affect stockholder profits, employee welfare, consumer choice, technological innovation, the economic base of communities, and the new capital investment plans of the nation. Congress regularly holds hearings on the impact of these large transactions and not infrequently has passed laws because of them.

Too often Congress and the public have been hurried in their judgments about mergers because of the imminence of a large takeover. Experts called in to analyze such transactions offer instant analysis based on the knowledge of their profession. Since many professional business analysts—economists, accountants, lawyers, and investment bankers—see the process from a number of different vantage points and since even within a single profession many disagree, it is hard to arrive at a complete, much less a consistent, picture of the mega-merger trend. This book provides a less hurried, broader discussion of these issues drawing upon the insights of many professions.

The purpose of the book is descriptive. Although my personal views no doubt color that description, my first intention is to paint a picture of what is happening rather than argue for any particular viewpoint. I have, therefore, tried to clarify the issues involved and areas of dispute rather than insist on the proper resolution. But where conclusions seem clear to me I have said so.

The focus of this story is sometimes on corporate executives or their investment bankers but as often it is on debates between people who have tried to understand mergers—business consultants, Congressmen, and economists. Sometimes the issue is whether "risk arbitrageurs" are good guys or bad guys, but other times the issue is whether mergers promote efficiency and why people disagree over the answer. Some debates over the virtues and vices of mergers are as lively as the corporate takeover contests themselves.

The book is organized into five parts. The opening section deals with the takeover process—who maps the winning strategies, how these strategies work, and whether they are fair. The second part then provides some historical perspective on merger waves and the role of antitrust. The third part examines the decision to merge— why firms merge and how the decision to do so relates to the choice of merger partner. The incidence of so many large mergers in the late 1970s and 1980s is explored in part four. The final section considers a series of public policy questions raised by the advent of megamergers, concluding with a chapter on government regulation of mergers.

In drawing these portraits of megamergers and the arguments surrounding them, I have used scholarly, legal, and historical sources, but for characterizations of contemporary mergers I have relied on the working press—especially, *Fortune* magazine, *Business Week*, the *Wall Street Journal*, the *New York Times*, the *Washington Post*, and the *American Lawyer*. Short deadlines sometimes make reporters less accurate on details than scholars, but collectively the business press provides the fullest picture. As a consequence, the contemporary picture I paint is, as often as not, with their words.

PART ONE

THE ACQUISITION PROCESS: TAKEOVER BATTLES, MERGER MERCENARIES AND SHAREHOLDER RIGHTS

Apart from the 1984 record-breaking oil mergers, the most visible megamergers have been titanic takeover contests. Billion dollar takeover attempts were fought off by Warner Communication, Disney Corporation, Mead Corporation, McGraw-Hill, and others in highly publicized battles. Even more dramatic were the takeover contests in which two or three firms bid against each other to gain control of a target firm. The bidding contest for Conoco among Mobil, Seagram, and Du Pont greatly increased the price paid to Conoco shareholders. It also demonstrated in 1981 that even the fourteenth largest industrial firm in the United States could become a takeover target. To understand megamergers it is necessary to understand the acquisition process: who gains from a contested takeover, why, and how.

Hostile takeover attempts have never amounted to more than 5 percent of the total number of mergers and acquisitions in any one year. Nevertheless, the 50 to 100 takeover battles waged each year have had a profound effect on corporations and their managers. By 1982, the *Wall Street Journal* reports, 1,500 companies had amended their corporate charters or by-laws to provide income protection for their managers in the event of a hostile takeover.[1] A great deal of time, effort, and energy has been expended to make companies less likely to be chosen as takeover targets or more difficult to take over if targeted. The prevalence of these takeovers has thus shaped the merger process. Some "friendly" mergers would have never happened absent the potential for the takeover to turn hostile. Other firms have felt impelled to make acquisitions to rid themselves of "excess" cash or to create antitrust conflicts in hopes of becoming less attractive takeover candidates.

While not typical of all mergers, acquisition battles dramatically illustrate methods of merging and the legal restrictions on takeover tactics. These unfriendly mergers also raise important questions about the value of mergers to shareholders and to society at large.

Although all corporate business is nominally conducted on behalf of shareholders, their role in the acquisition process is largely passive. The shareholders of acquiring firms do not buy the shares of target firms; the shares are acquired "for them." The shareholders of target firms are frequently cajoled, stampeded, or coerced into selling their shares and end up dancing to the tune of the takeover battle.

The battle is orchestrated and conducted by merger professionals, not corporate executives. Investment bankers, lawyers, and public relations experts compose the takeover and defensive strategies which determine he outcome of merger wars. They manipulate the federal and state laws to accomplish their objectives. Or, as Martin Lipton, a leading merger lawyer put it, "Corporate takeovers are analogous to feudal wars, and the lawyers are the mercenaries."[2]

These acquisition specialists operate in an arena that is separate from the corporate decisions to merge or the business consequences of mergers. The following chapters will describe the people and rules that control the battle in that arena. It will also explore the fairness of the acquisition process to the shareholders of target firms.

Although it sometimes appears that the shareholders of acquired firms are clear beneficiaries of takeover battles, the issue is more complicated. First, it is difficult, if not impossible, to determine whether shareholders are being offered a fair price for their shares. Second, current takeover rules permit acquiring firms to force shareholders to sell even when they believe the price offered is inadequate. Consequently, it is frequently unclear how much, if at all, these shareholders have benefited from a particular transaction.

Merger transactions are structured by highly paid bankers and lawyers who specialize in mergers. They and other professionals exploit the rules of the takeover process to win for their clients. That process creates personal incentives for professionals that are distinct from the interests of their clients. These personal interests can further distort acquisition rules that were designed to make the takeover process fair.

CHAPTER 1

TARGET SHAREHOLDERS

If a book of stock market maxims were being written, many people's favorite might be "Always invest in takeover targets." The benefit of holding shares in a firm targeted for takeover is that takeover bids (offers to buy a controling interest in a firm from current shareholders) are always at a premium—typically between 40 and 50 percent more than the current market price of the shares.[1] Do such premiums reflect a firm's true value? How can anyone know what a firm is truly worth?

A great deal of money can be made by investing in firms targeted for takeover. Judith McQuown's book, *Playing the Takeover Market*, is a guide for investors on how to profit from takeover transactions.[2] She notes that in 1980, 23 out of the 100 best performing stocks rose in value as a result of a rumor or an actual takeover attempt. The value of shares in each of these firms increased more than 100 percent during 1980, and in one firm, Shearson Loeb Rhoades, stock values rose 257 percent before being taken over by American Express.

The Supreme Court's recounting of the experiences of Vincent Chiarella describes the lucrative possibilities of investing in takeover targets:

> [Mr. Chiarella] is a printer by trade. In 1975 and 1976 he worked as a "markup man" in the New York composing room of Pandick Press, a financial printer. Among the documents that [he] handled were five announce-

ments of corporate takeover bids. When these documents were delivered to the printer, the identities of the acquiring and target corporations were concealed by blank spaces or false names. The true names were sent to the printer on the night of the final printing.

[Mr. Chiarella], however, was able to deduce the names of the target companies before the final printing from other information contained in the documents. Without disclosing his knowledge, [he] purchased stock in the target companies and sold the shares immediately after the takeover attempts were made public. By this method, [he] realized a gain of slightly more than $30,000 in the course of 14 months.[3]

While Chiarella and others who sold their shares to the acquiring firm made a profit, they did not necessarily receive full value for their shares.

Business economists describe the value of shares as the present value of a stream of future earnings, meaning a company is worth what it will earn. This, of course, permits a wide variation of value estimates. One person might expect consumer demand for the product to increase substantially. Another might disagree and expect demand for the product to be stable, or might expect, despite an increase in the number of products demanded, that the firm's sales will not increase because of growing competition. Other estimates might include differing expectations about the future costs of raw materials or advertising, and about work stoppages due to employee strikes, natural disasters, or lawsuits enforcing the public's interest in safety, pollution, and so forth.

Consider, for example, the value of Belridge Oil which was acquired by Shell Oil in 1979. The $3.6 billion purchase price was at that time the highest ever paid in a corporate acquisition. The $3,665 offered for each share represented a profit of over $5 million for the Over-the-Counter Securities Fund, which according to *Business Week* had been purchasing shares at one-fifteenth that price (an average of $287) since 1974 in anticipation of a takeover.[4] The Shell bid was also twice the amount of a joint bid submitted by Texaco and Mobil Oil.

Why did Shell offer such a high price for a firm that earned only $44 million the previous year, and why was Shell's bid so much higher than the prevailing stock market price or the joint bid of the competing oil firms? *Business Week* suggested four factors to help explain the high price: first, Shell's desire to obtain Belridge's proven reserves of U.S. oil (given the then-perceived world oil shortage);

second, Shell's greater expertise in recovering Belridge's large reserves of heavy crude oil; third, Shell's expectation of further technological breakthroughs, which would make it profitable to recover Belridge's very deep light oil reserves; and fourth, Shell's estimate of what it would take to outbid competitors in the auction process set up for Belridge Oil shares.[5]

Was Shell wrong and were Texaco and Mobil right? Had there been dissenting shareholders who placed a still higher value on Belridge, would they have been wrong? Doubts about the "true" value of shares exist because shares are valued by persons who evaluate a firm's prospects differently and because different owners operate a business differently, and thereby earn higher or lower profits. Thus, a takeover bid may be made at a price that is lower than, higher than, or equal to the true value of the shares, or a bid may be perceived as all three by different persons.

These different valuations are particularly significant because the laws that regulate corporations can "force" a shareholder to sell shares even at a price below his estimate of their value. A shareholder who refuses to sell at the premium price is likely to receive even less for the shares if the acquiring firm obtains control of the target. Once in control, the acquiring firm can require minority shareholders to sell their shares at designated "fair prices." These forced sales are invariably at a price lower than the takeover offer. Shareholders are therefore sometimes stampeded into accepting offers for fear of receiving much less than their estimate of the shares' full value.

Forced sales are based on the right of holders of a majority of the corporate shares to sell or merge the entire business of a corporation. This democratic procedure enables those majority shareholders to gain what they believe is the greatest value for their shares. Inevitably, the procedure disappoints the minority of shareholders who believe the price too low.

This right to sell the business may also frighten a majority of shareholders into selling their shares at less than full value if they believe others will sell and leave them as minority shareholders in a corporation about to merge. They would then be forced to accept the lesser amount paid in that merger.

These fears are not unfounded. The sequence commonly occurs and is explicitly stated in an acquiring corporation's initial takeover bid. Martin Marietta Corporation, for example, offered $75 a share for 50.3 percent of the shares in Bendix. Its tender offer also stated that after obtaining control of Bendix that corporation would be merged into Martin Marietta. The 49.7 percent minority shareholders would then receive Martin Marietta shares valued at $55 in exchange for each Bendix share.[6]

Is this takeover process a problem? Is it unfair to the 49.7 percent minority shareholders who are "frozen out" or to the 50.3 percent majority shareholders who are frightened into selling? Are the prices they receive for their shares unfairly low? Or is the first impression more accurate? Bendix shares had been selling for $50 each prior to the takeover bid. Are target shareholders the great beneficiaries of this takeover binge? We could answer these questions directly if we knew how much corporate shares are worth. Unfortunately, we have no way of accurately determining the value of corporate shares.

We can explain the difference in price paid to minority and majority shareholders, and we can describe the value of corporate shares. But we cannot measure whether an offer is fair because the value of shares is determined by the future success of the business. Moreover, there is nothing in the takeover process that forces acquiring firms to pay full value.

Economists like to say value is determined by whatever an item commonly sells for. If an individual wishes to purchase a few shares in a corporation, he can get an idea of their value and his probable cost by looking in a daily newspaper for the price at which those shares were traded on the previous day. That methodology, however, is not helpful for takeovers. You cannot buy a majority of the voting shares for the price of one share multiplied by a number equal to one half the firm's outstanding shares. The price at which one share trades does not include the major element acquired in takeover transactions: control of the target firm. Moreover, the assumption that some shareholders would be willing to sell a few shares for about the price of yesterday's transactions does not hold when applied to most shareholders. It is likely that many of those shareholders did not trade because they valued their shares much higher than the stock markets. So some other method must be used even to estimate the cost.

These two elements—"the value of the business" and "the value of the right to control and direct the business"—are distinct and have separate costs. In megamergers, where the acquiring firm automatically gains control by purchasing a majority of the shares, the separate acquisitions may be less obvious, but both elements are there. We might even imply a price for control in the Martin Marietta bid for Bendix. Martin Marietta was willing to pay $75 for shares that had sold for $50 a share in order to gain control of Bendix (with 50.3% of its shares) but only $55 a share for the remainder. One way of viewing this bid is that Martin Marietta valued Bendix at $5 a share more than the market, but it valued control at $20 a share more than that.

Federal law tries to ensure that all shareholders will have an opportunity to participate in this control premium by requiring that acquiring firms make tender offers to all shareholders, not a select few. As a result, if all Bendix shareholders had accepted the Martin Marietta offer, each shareholder would have received $75 a share for half his shares and $55 for the remainder, or an average of $65 a share.

The separate value of control can be seen more distinctly when it is sold by holders of less than a majority of the shares. Most large corporations are owned by so many people that the shareholders have little control over a corporation. Instead, control is exercised by the corporation's chief executive officer or board of directors who typically select their own successors. It is common practice for a person who buys a substantial, but minority, block of shares to include an agreement to have his nominees appointed to a majority of the seats on the board of directors.

The courts have upheld premium payments for agreements to purchase stock which include the resignation of current directors and their replacement by persons designated by the purchaser.[7] Courts have refused to permit payment for this sale of control only where it is totally divorced from ownership. For example, the New York courts set aside a transaction in which lawyer-financier Roy Cohn "sold" Lionel Corporation.[8] Cohn, who never owned more than 3 percent of Lionel shares, was the dominant force in the corporation and effectively appointed its board of directors, even after he had pledged all his shares to a bank in return for a loan. Cohn was able to sell these pledged shares for $350,000 (despite the bank's claim against them) because he also promised that he and other members of Lionel's board would resign and elect in their place persons designated by Mr. Sonnabend, the buyer. Courts refuse to permit the sale of control without ownership because of the dangerous probability that nonowning buyers will loot the corporation, not because courts resist the idea that control has a separate value from share ownership.

Is control worth a large premium? The value of control, as opposed to ownership, depends on whether the buyer has plans to change the business. A new owner's plans could greatly increase the value of the business, making whatever shares the owner holds much more valuable. This kind of ownership value cannot be obtained except when combined with control. A takeover that improves the target, can benefit everybody: Shareholders in the target company are paid some of the expected new value; the acquiring firm obtains a profitable new business opportunity; and the public benefits from a more productive use of business resources.

It is, however, unlikely that Martin Marietta's $75 bid was based on plans to increase the value of Bendix by altering the latter's operations. Martin Marietta made its takeover bid, after only a few days' consideration, as a way of preventing Bendix from obtaining control of Martin Marietta. Another view is that the $75 bid reflected the inherent value of Bendix, a value that already existed but was unrecognized by the stock market. The premium bid in this second view merely induces target shareholders to sell by raising the price to equal the value they placed on their shares. The takeover thus provided the target shareholders with an opportunity to receive the full value of their shares, which was denied them by the stock markets.

There is, however, no reason to believe that Martin Marietta's offer equaled the value of Bendix. To the contrary, Martin Marietta would have benefited most from purchasing at the lowest possible price. In fact, it immediately resold the Bendix shares at a higher price to the Allied Corporation.

A third view of takeover prices maintains that price has no necessary relation to the value of the company. Shareholders sell out because they fear receiving less for their shares. In 1982, after the much publicized takeover battles for Marathon Oil and Conoco, the trade periodical *Mergers and Acquisitions* held a roundtable discussion with investment bankers on how to value companies. After various methods were discussed, Jeffrey Henning of the investment banking firm of Shearson/American Express commented:

> The key question was not, "What's Conoco worth, what's Marathon worth?"
> The breakup value of those companies was far in excess of the values [i.e.,

takeover bids]. But everybody's offer was structured to beat the next guy's, not to deal with the matter of what it's worth. . . . Value is determined in the real live marketplace.[9]

As Henning's remarks indicate, that marketplace can force shareholders to sell for less than the liquidation value of a company even when there is competition to take over the target firm. The benefits of such takeovers are solely to the acquiring firm.

Hindsight provides yet another vantage on the adequacy of takeover bids. Do takeovers commonly pay full value? Not surprisingly, the answer is that sometimes the price seems to have favored the shareholders of the target firm, sometimes not. Merger lawyer Martin Lipton, in his spirited defense of the right of management to resist takeovers, compared takeover offers with subsequent stock market price of notable target firms that avoided being acquired. He found that the shareholders in Dictaphone, Sabine, Sterndent, and Universal Tobacco Leaf did substantially better by holding on to their shares than they would have done by selling out at the offer price.[10] On the other hand, the shareholders in Foremost McKesson, Marshall Field, Gerber, and Mead would have gained by selling at the takeover price: The size of the premium in these cases in no way corresponded to the eventual price of the shares. Dictaphone, which had been selling at $7 a share, was subject to a bid of $12, but rose on the stock market to $28 a share, whereas Marshall Field, which had sold as low as $22, refused a bid of $42 and ended up at $18 a share. Overall the scholarly studies suggest the acquiring firms more often than not pay too much for target firms. Thus, on average, target shareholders probably benefit from takeovers.

But in some transactions, like Marathon or Conoco, the price seems too low despite large premiums. In those circumstances, the shareholder has no way to increase the price of shares unless the target management resists the takeover or encourages other firms to begin a bidding contest for the firm. It is to protect shareholders from being forced to sell at prices below full value that Lipton bases his contention that corporate managers have the right to resist takeovers.

If a takeover price is to be raised, the decision to increase must be made first by the target management. They must decide to oppose the bid. They use the target's economic resources to hire investment bankers, merger lawyers, and other professionals. These professionals conduct the defense by obstructing the takeover, finding buyers willing to pay more, or forcing the acquiring firm to pay a higher price for the acquisition.

In theory, shareholders are the source of all power in a free enterprise system because they are the owners. In practice, however, the modern corporation is run by its executives. Shareholders are more like fans at a boxing match who have placed a bet. They can make a quick profit from takeover contests, but target shareholders are merely interested bystanders in a fight for corporate control that is fought by acquisition professionals.

CHAPTER 2

THE ACQUISITION PROFESSIONALS

B ruce Wasserstein, Ira Harris, Stephen Friedman, Joseph Flom, Martin Lipton, Gershon Kekst, Guy Wyser-Pratte, Richard Rosenthal, Robert Rubin, Ivan Boesky, and Carl Icahn all earn their living from merger transactions. They are investment bankers (Wasserstein, Harris, Friedman), merger lawyers (Flom and Lipton), a corporate publicist (Kekst), and risk arbitrageurs (Wyser-Pratte, Rosenthal, Rubin, Boesky, and Icahn). Each of these professionals plays an important role in mergers, especially in contested takeover transactions, and if they are on the winning side the spoils of victory can be enormous.

In principle, most of these professionals are facilitators of transactions on behalf of corporate clients. However, with so much money at stake in fees and earnings, they frequently take on a more activest role to foster, initiate, or alter transactions. Whether this added role is consistent with their traditional responsibilities is a matter of growing dispute.

INVESTMENT BANKERS

In January 1983, *Fortune* magazine devoted a ten-page pictorial essay, entitled "The Dealmakers," to investment bankers at eight firms.[1] What might attract a reader's attention to this almost textless

11

article spaciously decorated with color portraits? Money. In 1982 alone, these investment bankers participated in takeover transactions that cost their clients more than $20 billion and earned their firms over $100 million. Bruce Wasserstein, and his investment banking firm, the First Boston Corporation, participated in four of the five largest transactions. From these four mergers they earned over $31 million in 1982.

Merger departments of investment banking houses have been booming, and First Boston's merger and acquisitions department, codirected by Joseph Perella and Bruce Wasserstein, has set the pace. It grew from a one-person operation in 1970 to a staff of forty-four in 1983.

What do investment bankers do to justify these earnings? How are their fees fixed? Are they worth the cost?

The Role of the Investment Banker

In principle, investment bankers and other financial intermediaries perform four kinds of agent or broker functions for clients seeking to merge. First, they search for and identify a target or an acquiring firm (depending on who is their client). Second, they value the target firm or the corporate shares that are to be offered by the acquiring firm. Third, they advise on the structure of the merger—for example, whether the merger should be a hostile tender offer or a friendly stock swap. And fourth, they may supervise the execution of the transaction by underwriting a stock issue or formulating a tender offer.

Finding the right buyer or seller for the client is of course the essence of the transaction. The banker must understand the operations and objectives of both buyer and seller. To be effective the banker must know who is in the market to buy and who can be bought. Much of this expertise is gained by following annual reports, corporate statements, acquisition patterns, and stock market performance. But critical knowledge is often learned only by trying deals on corporate managers and listening to their reactions. An investment banker must be able to articulate why a deal makes sense so that the transaction is credible to both parties.

For the client, the key factor is often the value of the target firm. Naturally, the target wants as much for its shares as possible. Equally natural is the desire of the acquiring firm to conserve its own funds. To persuade a target firm that a client's demands are credible, the banker uses the target's annual reports, projected earnings, tax benefits, industry prospects, competitive advantages, and merger synergies to arrive at a single dollar figure. This dollar amount is then presented as the "fair" sales price. But investment bankers have expressed great skepticism about the accuracy of valuation methodologies,

> Edouard le Marie (E.F. Hutton): In principle, if . . . you have 10 investment bankers trying to value a company for a possible sale, normally they should all come out with the same absolute value, more or less.
>
> Stephen Waters (Lehman Bros. Kuhn Loeb): But they don't.[2]

Nevertheless bankers probably agree that personal credibility is their most important credential and concur with Gerald Rosenfeld's (of Salomon Brothers) characterization of their primary concern: "What will it take to buy or sell this business in the context of the marketplace? That is really what the investment banker brings to the table." So according to the *American Lawyer*, the great Bendix/ Martin Marietta takeover battle ended after Allied outbid Martin Marietta's offer for Bendix by $20 a share because Wasserstein said that was the price necessary to make the deal.[3] Allied believed him because they had worked with him before and had faith in his judgment.

But advising on price is only one aspect of the banker's role. Perhaps more central, especially in takeover battles, is the structuring of the deal. An initial judgment must be made whether the merger can be friendly, that is, whether the target management should be approached at the outset in hopes of achieving a good future relationship. Friendly approaches risk giving the target management an opportunity to successfully resist a takeover. If a hostile tender offer is to be made, other tactical issues must be faced: How much stock can be bought before announcing a public tender offer and at what price? What percentage should be sought: a majority, less than a majority, or all of the outstanding shares? At what price will shareholders sell, will they sell their shares for other than cash, and will the bid be high enough to discourage other potential competitors from competing for control of the target? Similar questions must be faced by the investment banker who is advising a target firm that resists a takeover attempt.

As we shall see in Chapter 4, bankers often work with lawyers, accountants, publicists, and others to devise their strategy. Even in friendly deals the merger of two large corporations is a complex transaction which will require technical professional services to calculate the impact on earnings, taxes, and so forth. Simply devising the overall strategy is often a difficult and expensive process. United Technologies, for example, paid investment bankers at White, Weld & Company $20,000 for presenting a plan for the takeover of the Babcock & Wilcox Company.[4]

In addition to devising a plan and offering strategic advice, the investment banker can also play a key role in implementing the transaction. They can underwrite new stock or bond issues needed to finance a merger. They also have the contacts to establish the underwriting group and the credibility to establish a price for the new issue. For hostile takeovers they have the personnel to buy the target shares on the open market and the experience to direct the tender offer for the target's shares.

In theory, anyone can act as a financial intermediary in merger transactions because formal credentials are not required to perform most of the necessary functions. Nevertheless, most substantial mergers are handled by a dozen or so firms located mostly in New York (Ira Harris of Salomon Brothers is a Chicago exception). These leading firms include major brokerage firms as well as private banking houses such as: Morgan Stanley; Goldman, Sachs; First Boston Corporation; Salomon Brothers; Lazard Freres; Merrill Lynch/White Weld; Shearson Lehman/American Express; Dean Witter Reynolds; Prudential/Bache; Kidder, Peabody; and Bear, Stearns.

The New Investment Banker

Until the 1970s, the role of investment bankers was more passive in merger transactions. Their participation was largely derived from their specialized role as underwriters. They were needed for their contacts and marketing techniques in the sale of new stock and bond issues. In 1974 this began to change when Morgan, Stanley represented the International Nickel Company (INCO) in its hostile acquisition of ESB, Incorporated. For an investment banking firm such as Morgan, Stanley to participate in an unfriendly takeover was as much a departure as it was for a blue chip firm like INCO to make the hostile tender offer in the first place. ESB's management fought back by threatening antitrust actions and by enlisting the aid of a rival bidder. Only when INCO raised its offer to more than twice the prebid selling price of its share did ESB's management agree to the takeover.[5]

Investment banking has not been the same since then. In his book, *The Takeover Barons of Wall Street*, Richard Phalon's investment bankers are the takeover protagonists, not the chief executive officers of the acquiring firms.[6] The investment bankers were the ones who identified Becton, Dickinson & Company as the target. The bankers searched for and found a buyer (Sun Company), and they planned and carried out the surprise takeover strategy.

At the invitation of Fairleigh Dickinson, the soon-to-be ousted board chairman of Becton, Dickinson, Salomon Brothers and Eberstadt & Company looked for a firm to buy Becton, Dickinson. When they found a possible acquirer, American Home Products, the Becton, Dickinson board (no longer chaired by Fairleigh Dickinson) declared it had no interest in being taken over by any firm. American Home Products was uninterested in attempting a hostile takeover and could not be persuaded by the Salomon group that the takeover would be friendly given the dissension at Becton, Dickinson.

Undaunted by the fact that they no longer represented either buyer or seller, investment bankers at Salomon Brothers and Eberstadt set out to find a buyer because they believed the price of the shares and the dissension made Becton, Dickinson ripe for takeover. Using all their contacts they approached numerous firms— Warner Lambert, Ciba-Geigy, Hoffman-LaRoche, Monsanto, Eastman Kodak, Procter and Gamble, and 3M—and finally won the interest of the Sun Company, which was a Salomon Brothers client on other matters.

With the help of attorneys and their stock trading staff, Salomon Brothers then devised an intricate plan for an immediate takeover. This plan was designed to skirt the requirements of the federal securities laws which would have delayed the takeover attempt and permitted the management to fight the acquisition of its shares. So delicate was the transaction that on the day that the Becton, Dickinson stock was bought each stock trader at Salomon Brothers had a lawyer close by to guarantee correct wording of the deal.

So seven months of hard work, mostly without a client, paid off for Salomon Brothers and Eberstadt. They picked the right dollar price and an effective strategy, and they had the necessary contacts and the ingenuity to devise a plan that would locate big shareholders who would sell. Consequently, Sun Company was able to get all the shares they wanted. The investment bankers earned several million dollars in fees. Unfortunately for Sun Company, however, the stock purchase plan was held to be too clever, and the court ruled it an unlawful evasion of the federal securities laws.[7]

Investment Banking Fees

The fees investment bankers earn are generally figured as a percentage of the cost of the acquisition. The fee normally ranges from one-half to 1 percent, but this amount may be split among several banking firms. The percentage basis for an investment banker's fee derives from the banker's traditional role as underwriter for new stock and bond issues. As guarantor of the price of a new issue, any potential liability (if no one wants to buy the issue at the offered price) is directly related to the size of the transaction. For example, First Boston Corporation, as underwriter, was stuck with over a quarter of the 2.1 million shares of Cities Service that it hoped to sell at $37 a share. In merger transactions, on the other hand, the banker is not open to such liability, although payment of the fee is often contingent upon success. If the takeover does not succeed, payment may be comparatively little, if at all. Felix Rohatyn of Lazard Freres & Company has estimated that a bid promising between $2 and $3 million would probably earn an investment banker $250,000 if unsuccessful.[8]

The fees earned by successful investment bankers can be enormous. *Fortune* magazine estimated that Salomon Brothers and Merrill Lynch split a $46 million fee for advising Gulf Oil when it was acquired by Chevron for $13.4 billion.[9] First Boston earned $17 million rescuing Marathon Oil from Mobil and delivering it to U.S. Steel and $15 million by outsmarting the other bidders for Du Pont in the contest for Conoco. Morgan, Stanley earned $14 million for engineering Shell Oil's $3.5 billion successful bid for Belridge Oil and another $14 million for representing Conoco in its acquisition by Du Pont. The median fee for *Fortune's* top fifty transactions of 1982 was $3.3 million.[10] Are the bankers worth the fees? Did Morgan, Stanley give Shell good advice? Shell's bid was reportedly twice as high as the next lowest bid, but Shell got a valuable oil field at a time when U.S. oil properties were scarce.

Types of Investment Bankers

Whether or not the fees are warranted, they are clearly high enough to make for very aggressive business practices. As the assault on Becton, Dickinson shows, investment bankers will operate without a client and push hard to make a deal happen. According to *American Lawyer*, Bruce Wasserstein offered his services several times to both sides in the Bendix/Martin Marietta contest knowing each already had investment advisors.[11] When things went badly for Bendix they called in Wasserstein, and he did, in fact, engineer a better deal for Bendix with Allied Corporation. His assertion that Bendix had other alternatives pressured Allied into making a high bid that closed the deal. Similarly, Salomon Brothers, which had been searching for months to find a buyer for Becton, Dickinson, warned the Sun Company they would have to act quickly because three other firms were interested in making a takeover bid.[12]

Wasserstein's reputation for inventiveness in structuring deals to eliminate bids by competing firms and pressure target shareholders to sell is well known. He helped Pullman avoid a takeover attempt by McDermott by having Pullman sell certain divisions to Wheelabrator-Frye, a more favored bidder. Without these divisions, Pullman's "crown jewels," McDermott was no longer interested. In the three-cornered fight to obtain control of Conoco, Wasserstein structured Du Pont's tender offer to pressure shareholders to sell to Du Pont by making it known that the remaining shareholders would be paid substantially less in subsequent merger with Du Pont. The possibility of this lower payment if Du Pont won made it risky for shareholders to hold their shares or tender them to Mobil Oil, Du Pont's principal bidding competitor.

Not all investment banking firms participate in the high-pressure takeover tactics used in representing acquiring firms. Goldman, Sachs & Company, one of the three largest merger and acquisition investment banking houses, refuses to represent the buyer in hostile tender offers. It's hallmark is trust. Clients have such confidence in Goldman, Sachs that in two of the largest transactions of 1982—Connecticut General Insurance's merger with the Insurance Company of North America and Morton-Norwich's merger with Thiokol—it represented and collected fees from both sides in both transactions, totaling $13 million. According to the *Wall Street Journal*, Stephen Friedman, executive in charge of mergers, believes the firm's refusal to represent firms in hostile tenders has gained the firm clients overall.[13]

Some bankers play a different kind of activest role in mergers and acquisitions. The merchant banking firm of Kohlberg, Kravis, Roberts & Company (KKR), for example, specializes in the leveraged buyout, in which a company is bought primarily through the issuance of debt by a newly formed corporation. Three of KKR's leveraged buyouts made *Fortune's* list of 50 Biggest Deals of 1981.[14] Such transactions use the financial strength of the corporation (its assets and growth prospects) and the competence of its management as security for the new debt. Continuity of management is often a prerequisite for such deals in order to persuade lenders that profits will not deline, because debt repayment must come from current income. Accordingly, such transactions are most suited to management taking a company private or the sale of a subsidiary to its managers.

These transactions are much more complex than takeovers based on cash tender offers or stock swaps, and KKR charges substantially more for its services (1% of the transaction price).[15] For example, *Barron's* has described how KKR pieced together $306.5 million in debt to finance management's leveraged buyout of Houdaille Industries in 1979: $60 million was raised in bank loans with repayment of principal to begin in 1983; $215 million in subordinated debt from sixteen insurance and other financial companies whose repayment of principal was to begin after the banks had been paid off; and $31.5 million in junior debt subscribed by another ten institutions.[16] In addition, KKR raised $23.5 million of the $48.1 million in new equity from the sale of preferred stock and a substantial portion of the rest from the sale of nonvoting common shares. For $7 million invested by two KKR limited partnerships they ended up with 37 percent of the voting stock. Houdaille management, which put up $2.1 million, obtained 11 percent of the voting shares.

Leveraged buyouts have become increasingly popular as alternatives to takeovers. Metromedia structured the largest such deal in 1983 when its management took the company private for $1.1 billion. Other leveraged buyouts have included Wometco for $970 million and Dr. Pepper for $620 million. The Dr. Pepper deal was put together by Forstman Little & Company, a new investment banking firm started by Theodore Forstman after he left KKR in 1978.[17]

In the typical takeover transaction, however, it is not necessary to be a banker. Salim Lewis, managing partner of the S.B. Lewis arbitrage firm, put together the American Express Company/Shearson Loeb Rhoades merger. He knew the chairman of American Express, presented the idea to the two firms, and earned $3.5 million.[18]

The "merger" investment banker bears little resemblance to the stereotype of a banker as a conservative, long-term guardian of the client's financial future. The merger banker is an entrepreneurial middleman for acquisitive firms engaged solely for a particular transaction. Ira Harris of Salomon Brothers is typical of the new merger banker. Beginning in 1969, he studied closely the businesses of firms headquartered in Chicago and cultivated their managers. According to *Business Week*, three years of "breakfast meetings" with the president of Esmark gave Harris the insight to put together the sale of Playtex to Esmark.[19] A similar combination of tenacity and business savvy was responsible for his role in selling Avis to Norton Simon, and McCall's to the Pritzkers. According to one observer, "[Harris] succeeded despite his style, which includes a degree of self-assurance bordering on arrogance."[20] The magazine attributed Harris's success to his ability to "fit" proposed transactions within the acquiring firm's concept of its business, to his driving a hard bargain on price, to his finding creative ways to finance an acquisition, and to his working twenty-hour days to pull together the deals.

It is to the investment bankers that we owe most of our newly coined merger vocabulary. Their shorthand labels are often metaphors drawn from war and athletics, as well as romance, bedtime stories, and pop culture. Thus, we have "target" firms fought over in "takeover contests" and "merger wars." Sometimes the takeover is avoided by a "scorched earth defense," which would make the target firm worthless if the takeover succeeds. At other times the target is saved from the "hostile raider" by a friendly "white knight" who buys the target. The white knight can be helped to defeat the bid of a raider by a "lock up" tactic such as selling it the target's "crown jewels," without which the target is unappealing. But a hostile tender, a "bear hug," avoids most "defenses" because it is an offer that cannot be refused (that is, one the target shareholders will probably accept). In such circumstances, only the "Pac-Man" defense (where the target acquires the acquirer) or a complete "show stopper" (for example, an antitrust lawsuit) offer any hope to the target firm's management. But the financial well-being of such managers is probably protected by a "golden parachute," which ensures them a healthy income for several years if they are fired.

The slang of Wall Street bankers contrasts with their three-piece suits and the enormous sums of money at issue in these takeover contests. This slang is a reflection of the close community of experts who direct them. Their vocabulary is then broadcast by the business press where it lends an aura of glamour, daring, gamesmanship and even frivolity to undertakings that bankers and corporate managers would prefer the public to believe are entirely serious endeavors.

Investment bankers do not necessarily possess formal credentials. Some, like Kenneth Lipper, who played a major role for Salomon Brothers in the Becton, Dickinson deal, and Bruce Wasserstein, do have degrees from prestigious universities in law, business, or economics. But others, like Richard Rosenthal, another major participant at Salomon Brothers, are high school drop-outs. Regardless of educational background, successful investment bankers share in two characteristics: they are young and they are winners. The hostile takeover sector of investment banking is democratic, and it respects winners, not credentials.

MERGER LAWYERS

Although Bruce Wasserstein is a lawyer and began his career at the prestigious Wall Street law firm of Cravath, Swain & Moore, he is not a merger lawyer. According to takeover lore, there are only two merger lawyers: Joseph Flom, the senior partner at Skadden, Arps, Slate, Meagher & Flom, and Martin Lipton, senior partner of Wachtell, Lipton, Rosen & Katz. That is an exaggeration of course since many other law firms represent companies in merger transactions. But the exaggeration is testimony to the highly visible role Flom and Lipton have played in takeover contests.

Like investment banking houses, law firms have been riding a crest of fees generated by the merger wave since the mid-1970s. And like the merger and acquisition departments of banking houses, the number of law firm merger specialists has also grown dramatically in size and importance. The Flom firm, for example, with 40 lawyers in 1970, expanded to become the nation's eleventh largest firm in 1982 when they employed 274 attorneys.[21] In the same period, Lipton's firm grew from 18 to 67 lawyers. This pattern of growth has been fed by merger work, particularly from hostile and contested takeovers.

Both firms have aggressively sought to shape the development of merger law, through the personal involvement of their principal partners in the largest, most innovative, and most combative takeovers of the merger wave, and by molding public opinion on merger issues. Martin Lipton, for example, is author (with his partner, Erica Steinberger, and contributions by other members of his firm) of *Takeovers and Freezeouts*, a two-volume guide for lawyers to merger wars.[22] Lipton has also written extensively in legal journals and the public press in defense of incumbent management's right to resist takeovers. In 1980 he participated in a New York University Graduate School of Business symposium entitled "Mergers and Acquisitions" and an academic study of merger motives contracted by the Federal Trade Commission.[23] He was also a member of the Securities and Exchange Commission 1983 panel of experts who studied government regulation of takeovers.[24]

Although Flom participated in the SEC panel, he has more often relied on members of his much larger firm to represent the firm's interests in contexts other than takeover battles. His partner, James Freund, author of the legal text *Anatomy of a Merger*,[25] joined Lipton in the FTC study of merger motives, and Stephen Axinn, Blaine Fogg, and Neal Stoll have written *Acquisitions Under the Hart-Scott-Rodino Antitrust Improvements Act*,[26] the most comprehensive guide to the premerger notification rules imposed by the antitrust laws. Axinn, the senior antitrust partner at the firm, also writes a regular column with Stoll in the *New York Law Journal* on general developments in antitrust law.

Legal Fees

These publishing activities have not only influenced merger law; they have also brought in large legal fees. According to *Fortune*, the minimum fee in a merger case at Wachtell, Lipton, Rosen & Katz was between $50,000 and $100,000 in 1982, and over 200 firms pay a

$75,000 annual retainer to Skadden, Arps in case they need representation in a takeover battle.[27] The fee for lawyers' work during a contested takeover can climb to between $400 and $600 an hour, and these hours mount up quickly during battle. In resisting a takeover bid by Occidental Petroleum, the *Wall Street Journal* reported that Mead Corporation used seventy-five lawyers during the nine-month seige.[28] The journal also estimated that Skadden, Arps and the other law firms representing Conoco during its contested takeover would submit fees totally $20 million.[29] But the *American Lawyer* placed the Skadden, Arps fee in a more modest range—$4 million.[30]

Although this lower figure is considerably below the $14 million fee earned by Morgan, Stanley, Conoco's investment banker, it is high enough to attract the interest of the large and prestigious law firms throughout the country, all of whom are searching for new sources of fees. According to *Fortune*, national law firms have ended their rapid growth patterns of the 1970s and now find themselves overextended with expensive, underutilized European and Washington offices.[31] A decline in regulatory work combined with increased competition from other firms and in-house corporate counsel have reduced earnings. Firms have therefore sought growth in new legal specialties, such as pollution, energy, equal employment, and merger law.

Of these specialties, only merger law has turned into a bonanza. In billion-dollar contested takeovers the corporate combatants do not squawk over a few million dollars more or less in banking and legal fees, if paying more contributes to victory. In the Conoco fight, Conoco was represented over the course of three months by five law firms all working nights and weekends. Flom, assisted by forty lawyers from his firm alone, was reported by the *American Lawyer* to have taken off only one day during twelve weeks.[32] The intensity of the lawyers' involvement is illustrated by a remark from another Conoco lawyer, Peter Bator, partner at Davis, Polk & Wardwell: "It was so exciting that you'd call in on Saturday, or go to a meeting, because you couldn't stand to be away from it. It was always on your mind."[33] From this cauldron of lawyer and banker conferences came the superheated legal fees totaling as much as $20 million.

The implications of merger work for law firms are more profound than the chance for a large, one-shot fee in a spectacular merger battle. Mergers and takeovers have become standard transactions for prosperous corporations able to afford highly paid legal assistance. Mergers, especially hostile takeovers, are complex and rapid-moving and require expertise in federal securities, tax and antitrust law, as well as state corporate law and other legal specialties. The steady procession of sizeable transactions that must be processed quickly without error is work ideally suited for big national law firms that employ cadres of specialists who can grind out answers to the many legal questions raised by even the most routine transactions.

In addition, the use of a law firm's tax and antitrust specialists, among others, enables clients to observe the firm's competence in these areas. And corporate clients that come for merger help may also stay for tax or trademark problems. The Skadden, Arps $75,000 annual retainer intentionally encourages clients to use the firm's talents more broadly. Although paid as "takeover insurance," that is, access to Flom in case of an attempt, the retainer may be applied to hourly work performed by any member of his well-diversified firm. It is no wonder many other major firms have developed merger specialties to keep and to attract corporate clients.

The Role of Merger Lawyers

The work of merger lawyers falls into two categories. The first ensures that the transaction complies with the technical requirements of the relevant statutes. The second takes advantage of the legal structure to achieve the corporate client's objectives. The former duty can be routine, exhausting, and exacting, while the latter frequently calls for more creative work, from discovering tax loopholes that convert a potentially hostile takeover into a friendly deal, to altering corporate charters to discourage takeover bids.

The Lawyer as Merger Technician

Ensuring compliance with a host of statutory provisions relevant to a merger transaction requires a knowledgeable and experienced group of lawyers. They must determine, for example, whether the merger is lawful, whether the transaction is properly structured to achieve its business objectives, and whether all the procedural requirements preceding merger have been met.

To determine the lawfulness of the merger, attorneys must examine the corporation's charter and by-laws, as well as the state law where the firms were incorporated. They must also determine whether the proposed combined firm will have increased monopoly power in violation of antitrust laws, or whether the merger requires and has received permission from government regulatory agencies. The answers may be obvious or routine, but some cases require a more sophisticated judgment. As we shall see, shifting antitrust enforcement standards encouraged Mobil Oil to enter the bidding for Conoco and Marathon Oil, but they had not changed sufficiently to permit Mobil to prevail.

Frequently more complex is the question of whether the merger agreement or takeover plan is properly formulated to achieve the client's objectives. Will the Internal Revenue Service agree that the transaction is (or is not) taxable? Will they permit a tax loss carry-over? Will the acquirer obtain sufficient stock to include profits and losses of the target on its income statement? Sun Company, for example, wanted to make sure it obtained at least 20 percent of Becton, Dickinson shares in order to include a proportionate amount of the latter's earnings on Sun's annual report. Does the merger agreement protect the client's options? Negotiations that would have resulted in Seagram owning 35 percent of Conoco, but not participating in Conoco management, foundered. This failure resulted in a hostile takeover free-for-all solely because the firms could not agree whether after fifteen years Seagram would be allowed to increase its Conoco holdings.

Finally, there is a series of actions that must be performed prior to mergers. Statutory mergers require approval at a shareholders meeting and state law and federal securities law prescribe the form and content of proxy statements to be mailed to shareholders. When making tender offers, federal securities law requires a similar disclosure of information to target shareholders. Also, federal antitrust laws require prior notification to the Justice Department and the Federal Trade Commission. Lawyers review these documents to make sure they include all necessary items, that the information contained in them is accurate, and that the client waits the required period after notices have been delivered before consummating the merger.

The Lawyer as Merger Tactician

The steps outlined above are necessary to complete merger transactions and each provides employment for legions of lawyers, but these do not compose the essence of the merger lawyer. His art like that of the investment banker, is to find the element in every transaction that will allow a client to prevail. Sometimes the work consists of hard bargaining or finding an economic key to the transaction in obscure tax provisions. At other times the work may center on litigation or amending corporate charters or by-laws. In all cases, it is strategic use of legal and other tactical resources for the client.

Joseph Flom's most famous antitakeover ploy, for example, was not a legal maneuver at all. When Sterndent, a dental supply firm, was subject to a takeover attack by the Magus Corporation, Flom suggested to the media that the firm's largely Jewish dentist clientele might cease doing business with the firm if it were taken over by an Arab financial corporation like Magus. The "Jewish dentist" defense worked.[34]

More typical of the attorney's role was a lawsuit initiated on behalf of Texasgulf to stop a July 24, 1973, tender offer by the Canadian Development Corporation (CDC). The day after the tender offer was announced, according to the U.S. District Court, the Texasgulf board determined to fight the takeover and gave its attorney, Tom Phillips, "a blank check including authority to institute legal proceedings if he found grounds to do so and by all means to stop the clock."[35]

A lawsuit was duly filed on July 27, 1973, alleging that CDC failed to disclose in its notice to target shareholders various matters required by SEC rules, including: that a takeover by a foreign corporation might violate a Texas statute; that the takeover would violate federal antitrust laws; and that a host of other horribles would occur. The court, in a barely restrained opinion, disposed of each of these contentions and pointed to a fundamental obstacle to establishing an antitrust complaint—CDC was not a competitor of Texasgulf. It also noted that the Texas statute that allegedly would be violated by the takeover did not apply to Texasgulf, and that if it did the statute probably would have been violated by Texasgulf itself prior to the takeover, would have conflicted with other state statutes, and would have been in violation of the federal and state constitutions. Nevertheless, the lawsuit must be counted as a success. It "stopped the clock" until September 14, 1973—long enough for the Texasgulf management to come to an agreement with CDC to limit CDC holdings to a minority interest.

Of course not all defensive legal actions are found to be baseless. Some actions are clearly pursued for more than their tactical value. Consider Becton, Dickinson's lawsuit to reverse Sun's takeover. Despite careful planning by two law firms (Watchell, Lipton, Rosen & Katz, and Cleary, Gotlieb, Steen & Hamilton) and their supervision of the telephone calls made by the Salomon group, the acquisition was held to be a "tender offer." It was therefore unlawful under the federal securities laws because of a failure to comply with disclosure requirements and a lack of opportunity for all shareholders to participate in the Sun offer. The "brilliantly designed lightning stroke" by which Sun acquired 34 percent of Becton, Dickinson was for nought: Sun was required to divest itself of the shares.[36]

In defensive strategy, the usual key for the lawyer is delay. For example: Make a claim under the securities acts on which a judge will have to hold hearings, take evidence, and consider a decision. Charge the acquiring firm in a lawsuit with being a "racketeer" because of securities law violations under the Racketeer Influenced and Corrupt Organizations Act.[37] Convince the Justice Department or the Federal Trade Commission to invoke its antitrust authority to stop the transaction pending submission of additional premerger information. If the lawyers can secure a delay, any number of changes may occur to help the target's incumbent management:

- They may find a "white knight" (a firm they prefer as an acquirer);

- They may buy a firm to create an antitrust conflict;

- They may sell their "crown jewels" to make the acquisition pointless; or

- They may change the target's corporate by-laws to stagger the terms of directors and thus delay for years giving the acquirer full control of the target.

Legal Advice

Accurate legal advice is critical to the implementation of both the acquirer's and the target's strategy. Dome Petroleum, as part of the Canadianization program mentioned in connection with Texasgulf, sought Canadian oil properties held by Conoco. It conceived of a plan that would force Conoco to sell, but at an attractive tax-free price. According to the *American Lawyer*, the plan was for Dome to buy a large chunk of Conoco and swap the shares for the properties.[38] However, the tax angle was questionable and became more so when it was discovered that the Canadian properties were not held by Conoco but by one of its subsidiaries. This made the tax-free exchange even less probable.

Equally important is the development of innovative legal approaches, because a tactic used once may not be successful a second time. For example, the sale of Pullman's crown jewels was an effective device in avoiding McDermott's takeover attempt, but Marathon Oil's attempted sale of its valuable Yates oil fields was held to violate the securities laws.[39] The "front-end-loaded, two-tier tender offer" successfully pressured target shareholders in Du Pont's acquisition of Conoco and Martin Marietta's defensive bid against Bendix. Shareholders, fearing they would be squeezed out at a lower price (in the second tier) if the takeover attempt were successful, rushed to sell at the higher first tier tender price. The SEC has tried to lessen the pressure of such two-tier offers by extending the time during which shareholders may accept two-tier offers.

Lawyers for acquiring firms must also make sure that their client is not trapped by the terms of its tender offer into buying shares for a deal that has already gone sour. Normally, an offer will contain escape clauses allowing the bidder to withdraw an offer if the antitrust agencies attempt to prevent the merger. Despite such a clause, Cities Service sued when Gulf withdrew its offer because of concerns expressed by antitrust officials. Almost always an acquirer wants to be assured at least a minimum percentage (often a majority, sometimes 100%) of the target's shares. In bidding contests, bidders do not want to end up being squeezed out in the second tier of someone else's more successful bid. (Contrary to the usual view, Seagram appears to have been quite content to have exchanged its Conoco shares for the lesser valued Du Pont stock.)

PRINTERS, PUBLICISTS, APPRAISERS, BANKERS, AND INSURERS

The proliferation of takeovers has created or expanded many supporting industries. For example, it has been a boon for the financial printers, such as the Pandick Press and Browne & Company, whose fees range from $10,000 for a routine shareholder proxy statement in a friendly merger, to over $1 million for lengthy stockholder notices in a contested takeover. Some of the other notable participants and their roles are briefly described below.

Publicists

Public relation firms have been prime beneficiaries of the megamerger trend. For example, Mead Corporation hired Gershon Kekst's firm to help them fight off the tender offer made by Occidental Petroleum in August 1978.[40] Normally, it is difficult to avoid a takeover once a tender offer has been made at a substantial premium over the prevailing market price of the target's shares. Defensive tactics may delay the takeover, permit the entry of a white knight into the bidding, or lead to negotiations for a better deal; but generally the target is acquired by someone. Mead, however, was adamant that they would fight off the takeover and used Kekst's publicity as their major weapon.

In principle, Mead's takeover defense was like many others that rely on lawsuits. The completeness of the tender notice to Mead shareholders was challenged under the federal securities law, the acquisition was alleged to violate the Ohio takeover law, and the merger was claimed to violate federal antitrust law. Such claims, unless they are upheld, normally only slow the acquisition. However, in this transaction the tactics caused Occidental to withdraw its offer. As a companion to its lawsuits, Mead broadcast the sins of Occidental to the world through Kekst & Company. They reminded the public of Occidental's illegal campaign contributions to reelect President Nixon, of illegal bribes given to foreign officials, and of the potential liabilities of Occidental's subsidiary, Hooker Chemical, for pollution at Love Canal. These were all relevant to the tender offer, because Occidental proposed to pay the target shareholders in

Occidental stock. However, the facts of these incidents were known and presumably already reflected in the value of that stock. The effect of the repetitions was to damage the public image of Occidental and also to put pressure on law enforcement officials and Congress to prevent this "good" company from being swallowed up by this "bad" company. By December 20th, after four months of the publicity barrage, Occidental withdrew its tender offer even though it had already disposed of two of the three legal challenges.

Richard Phalon has described in graphic detail a similar campaign in the defense of Becton, Dickinson.[41] The firm brought together Richard Cheney of the Hill & Knowlton public relations agency (who worked on eighty-nine takeovers during the 1970s[42]), Theodore Sorenson, President Kennedy's lawyer and speechwriter, and their own publicity people. But unlike Mead, the Becton, Dickinson shares had already been purchased, so the objective had to be a legal victory. In pushing for that victory it was important to portray the management of Becton, Dickinson as good guys and to simultaneously portray the Sun Company, Salomon Brothers, and their allies as cheating target shareholders of their opportunity to participate in the takeover premium guaranteed by the Williams Act. If this could be done, Sun would be forced to divest its Becton, Dickinson stock.

The publicity campaign succeeded. Most of the press sided against Sun, as did members of Congress, who were subjected to a companion lobbying campaign. Senior members of Congress put pressure on the Securities and Exchange Commission to bring an action to require Sun to divest its shares.[43] The lawsuit was instituted and won. Whether the SEC and the courts were convinced by public relations, Flom's legal arguments, or the merits of the case is more difficult to evaluate. Sun's purchases were a novel tactic and certainly not an obvious violation of the law. On the other hand, while the wording of the law was vague, its purpose was clear, and the method Sun used, if permitted, would have clearly created a large loophole. This was dramatized by the publicity.

Business Publications

The merger wave has also been a spur to the information industries, greatly increasing the readership of trade publications such as *Mergers and Acquisitions* and W. T. Grimm & Company's yearly *Merger*

Summary. Because W. T. Grimm publishes totals of merger volume and specifically $100 million mergers, their numbers became the unofficial scorecard tracking the progress of the merger wave. Grimm's yearly publication was transformed by the addition of a hard cover in 1982 into a longer annual volume, *Mergerstat.* Many other reporting services have developed. For example, in 1978 *The Yearbook on Corporate Mergers, Joint Ventures and Corporate Policy* was first published. It parallels *Mergers and Acquisitions'* quarterly listings of completed transactions and helps those companies contemplating mergers with a lengthy, descriptive list of commercial banks offering merger assistance services. In the same year, the *Acquisition/ Divestiture Weekly* began printing its newsletter for those who wished to follow more closely the progress of completed, impending, or rumored transactions and for other information relevant to mergers. *Fortune* magazine joined the trend in January 1981 by inaugurating an annual listing of the 50 Biggest Deals during the preceding year.

Consultants

Financial consultants, such as W. T. Grimm, have also done well by providing advice on targets from their business information data base. To take advantage of the demand Dun & Bradstreet formed a specially focused business information subsidiary—Mergex. Surprisingly, management consulting firms, who have been very influential in developing theoretical justifications for corporate growth through acquisitions, such as the Boston Consulting Group, appear to play little role in the takeover process itself. Perhaps their role ends with the decision to merge or the selection of the industry or target firm. Arthur D. Little Company, which advised Seagram on acquisition policy prior to its takeover bids for St. Joe Minerals and Conoco, appears not to have suggested targets. Rather, *Fortune* reports, in return for $500,000 they provided Seagram with information on more general business trends and factors to consider in selecting a target.[44]

Accountants and Appraisers

The merger boom has also enlisted the services of accounting firms and appraisers. The appraisers, like American Appraisal and Manufacturers Appraisal, help the accountant and tax specialist figure out how much the parts of the merged firms are worth. With over $30 million in annual fees at stake in 1980, merger business was important enough to American Appraisal to sponsor, by themselves, an all-day conference on merger developments for dozens of corporate executives. The conference, which featured leading investment bankers, lawyers, and government officials, was repeated for other potential customers in six metropolitan areas throughout the country. According to the *Wall Street Journal*, the demand for appraisal services grew so fast in 1980 that clients were placed on waiting lists several months long.[45]

Banks and Insurance

Commercial banks have benefited by syndicating loans to finance mergers, because the prevalence of cash tender offers has required acquiring firms to borrow staggering sums of money from banks. For example, at the time of the Conoco takeover battles, merger-based loans were arranged for prospective bidders totaling more than $20 billion.[46] However, Federal Reserve regulations severely restrict the amount American banks can lend to a single customer. Consequently, the $3 billion credit lines obtained by Seagram, Du Pont, and Conoco were syndicated loans in which a number of American and foreign banks participated. Syndication can be more profitable than the actual loan. The lead bank, which puts the loan package together, can earn up to one-half of 1 percent of the total as a management fee, or $15 million on a $3 billion loan.[47]

Beginning in 1980, Lloyd's of London began to offer takeover insurance. For an annual premium of $35,000 to $100,000 or more, a target under seige was entitled to up to $5 million to hire lawyers, investment bankers, and publicity experts.[48] Corporate managers insure themselves by obtaining "golden parachutes," long-term employment contracts that can be canceled but require the full payment of the promised salary.

ARBITRAGEURS

Risk arbitrageurs, like their fellow investment bankers in the merger and acquisition departments down the hall, can make enormous profits for their firms from a takeover transaction. Four arbitrageurs netted an estimated $30 million from the takeover contest for Babcock & Wilcox according to *Fortune*, and earned themselves a four page feature article with color photographs: Richard Rosenthal of Salomon Brothers, Guy Wyser-Pratte of Prudential/Bache, Robert Rubin of Goldman, Sachs, and Ivan Boesky, who heads his own arbitrage firm.[49] But as the name of their profession suggests, arbitrage has its risks. Ivan Boesky & Company, which earned $7 million from its Babcock & Wilcox shares, is alleged by *Barron's* to have lost $12 million on Delhi International Oil shares.[50]

Risk arbitrageurs are described here separately from other merger professionals because their principal earnings are not fees from the acquirer the target, or their advisors. Nevertheless they have had a profound affect on some takeover contests.

Risk arbitrage, which bears almost no relation to other arbitrage transactions, is possible when a tender offer is announced at a price higher than the shares are selling for on the market. The risk is that if the offer is called off then the price of the shares will probably fall to their preoffer level. For example, the price of McGraw-Hill shares, which had been selling for $26, rose dramatically when American Express proposed a tender offer of $40. A few days after the announcement, according to the *Wall Street Journal*, Guy Wyser-Pratte bought almost 50,000 shares for about $30 each.[51] Unfortunately for his firm, the deal did not go through so Bache lost about $200,000. Had American Express won and accepted all of Wyser-Pratte's shares, his firm would have earned half a million dollars.

Risk arbitrageurs thus profit from takeovers in much the same way as any other corporate shareholder, but risk arbitrageurs, or "arbs," are very much unlike other shareholders. They do not invest in the firm; they invest in the transaction. They have extensive information-gathering networks. They use vast amounts of borrowed money. They have lower transaction costs because they use their own firm's brokerage services. They sometimes collect additional fees from the acquiring firm for soliciting shares in response to the tender offer.

And in some cases, they can individually or collectively determine the outcome of takeover contests.

Predicting Takeover Battles

The key to making money as a risk arbitrageur is predicting whether a takeover bid will succeed and at what price. Unlike investors, or speculators in takeovers such as the Over-the-Counter-Securities Fund which bought Belridge Oil years before its sale, arbs normally do not buy target shares until a takeover is announced. Once the tender price is announced the arbs must determine how high they should bid. Babcock & Wilcox, for example, had been selling for about $34 a share in 1977 prior to a tender offer by United Technologies for $42 a share. As a result of arb purchases, the price rose quickly to $45 a share in obvious anticipation of a higher bid by United Technologies or a competitor. The arbs were right. McDermott obtained control for $65 a share. Similarly, when Seagram offered $45 a share for St. Joe Minerals, the stock moved from $28 to $52 a share. Again, optimism was rewarded by a competing offer, this time from the Fluor Corporation which offered $60 a share. By limiting stock purchases to sales at less than the initial tender price, an arb would have been unable to fully participate in profits from either of these takeovers.

Of course, the flow of takeovers is not always so smooth. In May 1982 Mesa Petroleum made a takeover bid for Cities Service Company. It offered $50 for shares that had been selling at $35. That was wonderful news for the First Boston Corporation, which was holding 570,000 shares it had been unable to sell when it underwrote the sale of 2.1 million shares at $37 earlier that year.[52] Based on Table 2-1, consider when First Boston should have sold its shares.

First Boston's $20 million underwriting mistake was eventually saved by the Occidental $50 bid. Note how much better off First Boston would have been if it had sold in the market to arbitrageurs around June 23rd, when a *Wall Street Journal* article reported that Gulf's bid was underpriced. Arbitrageurs who purchased expecting the $63 per share bid to prevail lost money. *Business Week* estimated before the Occidental bid that the losses to arbs could have been as high as $400 million if the price of a Cities Service share fell below $30.[53]

Table 2-1. Cities Service Takeover Chronology.

Date	Event	Cities Service Stock Prices
June 1	Cities Service files counter bid for Mesa Petroleum	$38.2
June 2	Cities Service rejects Mesa $3.9 billion bid	37.0
June 3	Suit alleges Mesa unable to complete bid: Suit alleges stock manipulation in take-over bid	36.7
June 12	Boosts offer for Mesa to $21 for 51 percent	34.6
June 16	Asks Court to block Mesa 15 percent bid	37.6
June 17	Mesa bid enters decisive stage	42.0
June 18	Gulf Oil to buy 51 percent of Cities for $5 billion: Gulf to buy for $63 per share	53.1
June 23	Gulf's bid seen as underpriced	55.1
July 3	90 percent of shares tendered to Gulf	54.6
July 6	Gulf takeover delayed by FTC antitrust review	53.4
July 30	FTC blocks takeover: Court delays acquisition 10 days	Trading suspended
August 6	Gulf acquisition hits new tax law snag	37.2
August 10	Gulf withdraws offer: Allied seeks to acquire Cities	32.1
August 12	Phillips Petroleum may acquire Cities: Union Pacific may acquire Cities	31.4
August 14	Occidental Petroleum makes $4 billion friendly offer for Cities	33.2
August 17	Cities rejects Occidental friendly offer	37.5
August 18	Cities sues Gulf for breach of contract	No trading
August 19	Occidental makes $50 a share unfriendly offer	42.5
August 24	Cities rejects $50 offer as inadequate	45.0
August 26	Cities accepts Occidental $4.05 billion bid	46.4
August 27	FTC clears takeover by Occidental	47.2

Source: *New York Times* and *Wall Street Journal.*

Each of the news reports in the Cities Service chronology bore on the outcome of the takeover battle for the arbs. Each news item contributed to a daily decision to buy more shares, hold, or sell. By June 2, 1982, when Cities rejected the Mesa bid and made a counter-bid for Mesa, a takeover fight was in the works. If Cities had won, Mesa might never pay off to those who tendered Cities shares. Worse yet, as an acquiring firm the value of Cities shares would be likely to fall below its $35 premerger level. The arbs, therefore, ought to have been wary of buying Cities shares. Of equal concern were the lawsuits reported on June 3rd and 16th, because they might have delayed or even prevented the transaction. Since arbitrageurs use borrowed money, interest payments can become an important factor and can force arbs to liquidate their holdings before an outcome is clear.

Arb Lawyers

Litigation is considered such a key concern to the arbs that they employ attorneys to advise them on the probable outcome of defense legal tactics and others' legal issues.[54] The arbs, whose business is prediction, demand answers in a form that is uncongenial to most lawyers: They want to know the *odds* on a target firm's winning a lawsuit. Lawyers would prefer to hedge on their advice and explain the factors that might influence a judge's decision. However, lawyers like Tim Waters of Peabody, Lambert & Meyers, or Charles Nathan of Cleary, Gottlieb, Steen & Hamilton, who have frequently advised arbs, will give advice on takeover legal issues in response to telephoned questions.

Because time and timing are so important to the arbs, the arb counsel must be continually available. Thus, the arb will expect a lawyer, a seasoned partner (not a junior associate), to be in the courtroom to follow the proceedings and report on the demeanor of judges or juries and the probable outcome of the case. If the arb needs to unload shares or decides to buy more, action must be taken before the stock markets have absorbed the impact of the courtroom events. Because arbs' firms often own seats on the stock exchanges, the information advantage can be translated into market transactions almost instantly. For the same reason, the arb requires a basis for acting prior to a final decision. For example, the arbs bailed out of the Pan Am/Eastern battle for National Airlines as soon as the Civil

Aeronautics Board barred a joint bid by Continental and Western Airlines on grounds that they were both large domestic airlines.[55] With the help of their lawyers, arbs correctly guessed the CAB would prevent the takeover of National by Eastern, the largest domestic air carrier.

The Arb Advantage

The arb's "feel" for the transaction explains why arbs are often viewed with a mixture of awe and mistrust. They sometimes even seem to receive treatment normally reserved for a prima donna. When millions of Bache (now Prudential/Bache) dollars were committed to the Babcock & Wilcox transaction, Guy Wyser-Pratte went on vacation, first to Martha's Vineyard and then to Maine. He kept in touch with his office by phone. His reward, based on a percentage of the arbitrage department's earnings, has been an annual salary upward of $1 million, or more than five times the salary earned by the firm's chief executive officer.[56] The respect held for arbs probably explains why Salomon Brothers called upon Richard Rosenthal to leave his arbitrage desk and aid the merger department in setting the price Sun bid for Becton, Dickinson shares.

The pitfalls of risk arbitrage, however, are numerous. Even if an arb chooses the winners in a takeover contest and predicts the final takeover price, money can still be lost if the tender offer is for less than all of the target shares. A *Fortune* article provides two examples. Fluor offered $60 a share for 45 percent for St. Joe Mineral's shares. The other 55 percent were to be exchanged for Fluor shares in a second tier of the offer. However, because more than 45 percent of the shares were tendered to Fluor the shareholders who tendered received a package of cash and the less valuable Fluor shares, worth about $56 each. During the takeover battle for St. Joe, its shares had traded as high as $55 a share, making the margin of profit for persons who bought at the top exceedingly slim. For arbs or would-be arbs with high transaction costs (due to brokerage fees, interest payments, or information costs), this may have resulted in a loss. For the professional arbs whose transaction costs are usually less because they use in-house brokerage services and can spread their other costs over larger investments, the margin might be profitable. But even that profit would have disappeared if a larger number of shares had been tendered. When, for example, Allegheny International bought Sunbeam, it had almost twice as many shares tendered as it requested. As a consequence, the $41 per share offer was ultimately worth only $35, less than the $36 Sunbeam traded at during the tender offer period. Even so, shareholders were much better off in both cases if they tendered their shares to the winner rather than exchanged their shares in the second tier of the offer: The Fluor shares were worth $44 at the time of exchange; the Allegheny shares were worth only $29.[57]

Of course, the arbs and their imitators do not always guess right. The arbs sold out for an estimated loss of $30 million when Penn Central delayed its planned $600 million acquisition of GK Technologies in order to determine the target's liability for the MGM Grand Hotel fire. It was no consolation to the arbs, who could not hold the shares because of interest costs, that the deal was consummated in 1981, the following year, at a higher price.[58] And some deals never go through. The prospective acquisitions of Delhi International Oil, the Grumman Corporation, Colt Industries, Mead Corporation, and McGraw-Hill resulted in rising stock prices which fell when the acquisition failed. Those who lost included the arbs.

Because of the risks a great many investors, including corporate stockholders and investment institutions, sell their shares (to arbs and speculators) after a tender offer rather than follow the complex procedures and tendering in a takeover battle. The sell strategy can be very profitable. Chevron's unsuccessful bid for Amax, which temporarily doubled the value of the target's shares to about $80, is not unusual. The lucky investor can profit from a quick sale without the trouble and expense of following the battle. However, if an investor sells too quickly he may miss the bidding contest. As noted above, United Technologies' bid for Babcock & Wilcox of $42 a share was ultimately surpassed by McDermott's $65 bid. Seagram's $73 bid for a share of Conoco was not close to the $98 received by shareholders who tendered to Du Pont. There are risks in selling and in tendering. Many, perhaps most, of those willing to sell, sell to arbs because it is simpler, and it protects them from losing the gain already possible from the takeover bid.

Dangerous Arbs

Because they have so much money at stake arbs can be sore losers. Wyser-Pratte, for example, went to a Gerber Products Company annual meeting to complain that its board had unfairly opposed a tender offer by Anderson Clayton and Company.[59] He also sought to force McGraw-Hill to submit the American Express offer to its shareholders.[60] In neither case was he successful, but the publicity generated by his efforts contributed to a sinister image of the arbs as fomentors of takeovers without regard to the welfare of the business. The feared scenario is as follows:

> Good Corporation is selling at below its true value despite wonderful management. Raider Corporation makes a tender offer substantially above market value but below true value. The tender offer is defeated (for any reason) and the arbs are stuck with 38% of the target shares. The arbs then find a new acquirer and force the sale of the target to reduce their losses.

Arbs operate primarily on borrowed money; therefore, they must sell as quickly as possible without regard to the fundamental value of the firm or the quality of new or old management. Can arbs hold on long enough to bring in a new buyer?

One risk arbitrageur who can hold on long enough and who specializes in aggressive moves is Carl Icahn. Icahn's methods differ in one major respect from his mainstream arb colleagues: He does not wait for a tender offer to be made. Rather, in principle, he looks for a firm that is likely to be taken over because its stock is undervalued. Icahn then buys the stock and *makes* the takeover happen. In practice, Icahn and his associates are equally happy to oblige the management of the target by selling their shares to the target at a premium over the cost of the shares.

Icahn began his distinctive career in risk arbitrage buying shares in the Tappan Company.[61] A takeover appeared probable because Tappan had excellent prospects and its shares were selling for 40 percent of book value. After purchasing 10 percent of Tappan's shares, no acquirer appeared, so Icahn encouraged a friendly merger with Walter Kidde and Company. When management rejected that deal, Icahn decided on a proxy fight. He ran for the board of directors on a platform that he would find a high-price buyer for Tappan, won, and then pressured the board to find an acquirer. *Forbes* reported that Icahn and his associates profited $2.8 million from a $2.9 million investment when A.B. Electrolux of Sweden bought Tappan in 1979.[62]

By far, Icahn and his associates profited most from Marshall Field & Company—$30 million according to the *Wall Street Journal*.[63] This transaction is worth a closer examination because it provides some greater support for Icahn's claims that his actions serve a socially useful function.

By the time Icahn went after it in 1982, Marshall Field had spent a dozen years avoiding takeovers. According to *Fortune*, in 1970, to avoid a possible takeover by Associated Dry Goods, Marshall Field pursued a twofold strategy recommended by Joseph Flom: It increased its size to raise takeover costs and it bought firms in competition with likely purchasers to set up antitrust obstacles.[64] In 1977, when Carter Hawley Hale offered a $42 per share merger, the management felt the bid was too low and deterred the takeover by more defensive acquisitions to create antitrust problems. Marshall Field shareholders brought suit against their board. They were angered because the board's rejection of Carter Hawley Hale's offer caused Field shares to drop from a preoffer level of $20 to $13 a share. Although the lawsuit failed, it was generally agreed that most of the defensive acquisitions harmed the company. Some of these acquisitions, in fact, were later divested.

Consequently, in 1982, when Icahn began accumulating Marshall Field stock at $20 a share on the grounds that it was undervalued, some shareholders applauded even though it was widely rumored that he intended to not only break up the conglomerate, but liquidate some of its prime assets, such as the flagship store, a city landmark in downtown Chicago. Again, Marshall Field management tried to avoid takeover, arguing in court (still represented by Skadden, Arps, Slate, Meagher & Flom) that Icahn was barred by the RICO statute. Claims that Icahn was a racketeer were based on a consent decree he had signed with the Securities and Exchange Commission concerning alleged law violations when purchasing Hammermill Paper Company shares. Such legal tactics, however, only delayed the outcome. Marshall Field's antitrust tactics could not work on Icahn, and *Fortune* reported it hadn't enough cash or debt capacity to buy him off. So it used the time to find a white knight. BATUS, Incorporated bought the firm for $30 a share.

It is certainly arguable that Marshall Field had bad management. That management had shown no signs of being dislodged through conventional means of corporate governance, that is, by shareholder vote. Further, it seems clear that Icahn's actions did precipitate a change in management. It is not clear, however, that such takeovers are a desirable method of change.

Forcing a firm to seek a white knight does not ensure that able new managers will be installed. The speed with which such mergers typically are arranged precludes careful consideration. The white knight is equally likely to buy because it also perceives the shares to be undervalued, and its favor by the target may be based on nothing more than personal benefit to the target's managers. Moreover, where the target is a well-managed, single-product firm, such as Tappan, forcing a conglomerate merger may even reduce the efficiency of the firm by imposing the control of less knowledgeable managers.

Carl Icahn's 1982–83 takeover battle with Dan River, Incorporated, chronicled in a dozen or more articles in the *Wall Street Journal*, resulted in a long editorial by that newspaper arguing for changes in the securities laws to reduce such noninvestment profiteering.[65] They noted that many others have seen this as a profitable path, citing Victor Posner of Sharon Steel and Saul Steinberg of the Reliance Group. They could have included other small arbitrage firms such as O'Conner Securities, which went after the Trane Company in 1982, or large professionals like Ivan Boesky & Company, who used its 10 percent stake to push ERC corporation into a merger with Getty Oil.

The path blazed by Icahn showed how vulnerable large companies are to a takeover assault by a smaller but determined organization, or even a few individuals. Those who have followed this path have justified their assaults, like Icahn, on grounds that the target's management policies are unsound. Their claims of serious takeover intent have had additional credibility because these new investors include operating companies, conglomerates, or even corporations in the same industry as the target. The result in most cases, however, has been not a takeover, but a buyback of the assaulters shares—"greenmail" paid by the target company in exchange for the assaulter's shares and an agreement not to buy more shares.

Nineteen eighty-four was a banner year for greenmail. T. Boone Pickens, Jr., chairman of Mesa Petroleum, for example, led an attack on Gulf Oil, claiming the giant oil firm could be made much more

Table 2-2. Greenmail Profits, 1984.

Investor	Target	Profit ($ million)	Days that Shares were held by Investors
Mesa Partners	Phillips Petroleum	$89.0	45
Saul Steinberg	Walt Disney Productions	59.8	76
Bass Bros. Enterprises	Texaco	280.0	49
Rupert Murdock	Warner Communications	49.8	137
Sir James Goldsmith	St. Regis Corporation	51.2	25
Coastal Corporation	Houston Natural Gas	42.1	18

Source: "Leading Deals and Deal Makers in the First Half of this Year," *New York Times*, July 3, 1984, p. D-6.

valuable by breaking it up. When Pickens and his group accumulated 13 percent of Gulf's shares they provoked the biggest merger in history—Chevron's (then Standard Oil of California) $13 billion takeover of Gulf. Pickens's group made a half billion dollar profit when they turned in their Gulf stock to Chevron. Rupert Murdoch, the Australian newspaper, magazine,and television entrepreneur, was paid a profit of almost $50 million by Warner Communications to go away.

Table 2-2 covering leading examples of greenmail during 1984 shows that whatever the original intent, the large profits from quick sales were sufficient to sway investors to abandon their takeover plans.

If risk arbitrage in any of its manifestations is a problem, it is not limited to abuses by a few. The problem, if it is one, is that the profit comes from the transaction rather than from the performance of the target firm. For the present, however, arbs seem to be more envied than condemned.

INSIDER PROFITEERS

Unlike risk arbitrage, insider trading is almost universally condemned. It is also widely practiced. Federal securities laws make it illegal for corporate officers or persons hired by them such as their lawyers, accountants, and bankers, to buy or sell securities on the basis of information that is not yet public. For violating the restrictions an individual can be forced to surrender any profits and may be liable for criminal penalties. However, these laws, designed to prevent individuals from taking unfair advantage of secret knowledge and preserve honesty in the stock market transactions, are violated continually.

Mergers have become the most important source of inside information because takeovers have become plentiful and takeover attempts almost always result in a dramatic rise in the value of the target's shares. Vincent Chiarella's operations provide a classic illustration of the value of nonpublic information. He knew, before it was announced, that certain firms were targeted for a takeover and that their price would rise in response to the announcement. He could, therefore, buy shares from an unknowledgeable individual and then sell them for a profit after the announcement.

Chiarella, who worked on tender offers as a printer at the Pandick Press, had to break codes to identify target firms. But others have obtained their information much more easily. Carlo Florentino, working as an attorney at Wachtell, Lipton, Rosen & Katz, learned of firms that were about to become takeover targets, and between 1977 and 1981, he profited $450,000 by purchasing shares in nine targets prior to the public announcement of the takeover attempt. Several officials in Morgan, Stanley's merger department were also convicted of using the firm's information for personal profit. Through secret Swiss bank accounts, they had hoped to hide their pretakeover transactions.[66] Morgan, Stanley itself was accused of profiting from the use of nonpublic information about the Olinkraft Corporation. The accusation, denied by Morgan, Stanley and never proven, was that this information was given to Morgan, Stanley's merger department and passed on to its arbitrage department. The firm then allegedly bought a very large amount of Olinkraft shares after a takeover announcement by the Texas Eastern Company because its confidential information showed Olinkraft was worth more than the bid. A higher competing bid then emerged.[67]

Sources of inside information can be less direct. Father and son, Frank and Frederick Wyman, profited from secret information on takeover targets passed on to them from an employee of Skadden, Arps. The informant, a paralegal at Skadden, Arps was, according to the *Wall Street Journal*, "romantically involved with Frederick

Wyman" and "didn't know the Wymans would trade on the information she provided."[68]

Usually, those who profit are the insiders themselves or their friends and relatives. For example, an American navy official bought shares in a firm just before announcing he had awarded it a lucrative contract.[69] Directors and employees of Sante Fe Industries profited from advance knowledge that Kuwait Petroleum Company was to buy Santa Fe International for $2.5 billion.[70] And Deputy Secretary of Defense Paul Thayer was accused in January 1984 of unlawfully passing to friends inside information he learned as chairman of LTV Corporation and a director of the Anheuser-Busch Company.[71]

Trading on the basis of insider information is pandemic, particularly in cases of mergers and acquisitions. An academic study published in the *Journal of Finance* by Professors Keown and Pinkerton confirmed what has long been known on Wall Street—purchasing in target shares almost always begins before the public takeover announcement. The professors' survey of 194 targeted firms revealed that the price of target shares and trading volumes began to move upward twenty-five days, on average, before the public announcement.[72] Three weeks preceding an offer, the price of many shares increased dramatically, and by the final week the normal trading volume of almost 80 percent of the firms in the survey tripled, even though prices continued to increase. Clearly, many people knew or guessed that good news was imminent.

Can insider trading be stopped? As a matter of law, only "corporate" information must be disclosed before buying or selling shares, and only certain individuals are barred from trading unless they disclose. It is often difficult and costly to detect and prove insider trading. Moreover the penalties for insider trading tend to be light and persons convicted of insider trading are not shunned by the business community.

Much information is available, but may be perceived by the general public not to have an impact on the value of certain corporate shares. For example, the increasing elderly United State population may provide significant new markets for producers of baby products such as soft foods and diapers. Such information is not considered "corporate" information and subject to insider disclosure restrictions, even though the transaction occurs because a seller does not understand the significance of demographic changes. Rather anyone, including insiders, who can figure out the significance of such "market" information is free to profit from it.

On the other hand, corporate officials have a special opportunity to learn about impending mergers and other important non-public corporate information. Section 10(b) of the Securities Exchange Act and Rule 10b-5 make it unlawful for persons who are responsible to the shareholders, corporate officials, their agents, or people they have tipped off, to buy or sell shares unless they reveal the information.[73] Others, such as Chiarella, who have no relationship to the shareholders, may also learn important information, but the Supreme Court has held that they are not barred from using this knowledge in trading stocks. The Securities and Exchange Commission responded to the unfairness of this trading by creating a rule directed solely at information about impending tender offers. Rule 14e-3 declares trading on the basis of such information unfair regardless of the way in which it was received.[74] Consequently, for tender offers at least, the law clearly prohibits all persons from trading on inside information.

The detection of general insider trading prior to takeover announcements is rather simple, as the Keown and Pinkerton study illustrates. It is more difficult, however, to isolate the individuals who had inside information from those who suspected the possibility of a takeover and jumped on the bandwagon when they saw the target's price and trading volume begin to move. Nevertheless, the SEC enforcement director, John Fedders, was quoted in a 1982 *Wall Street Journal* article on the sale of Santa Fe International that "we can catch anyone."[75] By investigating brokerage records and tracing phone calls, the SEC was able to identify violators despite the use of secret Swiss bank accounts. The SEC had even tracked down an accountant who deduced the merger from his client's questions about the tax effect of an increase in the value of Santa Fe's stock.

If it is possible to detect and prove individual violations, prosecutions are oftentimes ineffective. The civil penalty for insider trading usually consists of relinquishing the unlawful profits (though the SEC recommended to Congress in September 1982 that the penalty be increased to three times the insider's profit). Criminal penalties (of up to five years in prison) are rarely handed down. Florentino received a suspended sentence. Other violators have also received small fines and short or suspended sentences. One individual was jailed for thirty-nine weekends.[76] The four-year jail sentence received by Paul Thayer in 1985 was a significant departure from past practice.

Moreover, the impact of such prosecutions seems not to have had any effect on the premerger movement of prices. Nor are the SEC prosecutions considered serious offenses by Wall Street. Rather, according to *Fortune* magazine, "The man who walks into a cocktail party and announces that he has made a bundle on a tip is unlikely to be handed over to the gendarmes. Indeed he is apt to get inquries about other corporate secrets he knows."[77]

Part of the reason for this tolerance of what seems to be deceitful "bargaining" is that it resembles acceptable investor behavior. Not only is the object the same—profit—but the investment reward is greatest if based on information that is not generally available. Where an investor has ferreted out a new source of value (for example, understood the implications of a new invention or a change in demographics), that investor is rewarded for encouraging the market to continue investing in needed products. Unlike the use of advance knowledge, the investment based on insight helps create new value. Unfortunately, the distinction between advance knowledge and forward thinking is not always easy to make.

Should we have insider trading rules then? At least one business analyst believes we should not. Henry Manne, a well-known proselytizer for the free market and an opponent of government regulation, has argued against existing restrictions. He believes that persons selling to insiders would have sold at that price to anyone and thus have not been harmed.[78] In addition, he argues that insiders who benefit are as often as not managers reaping a reward for their services in adding to the value of the firm (or sharing that reward with their friends).[79] So, for example, if the premium prices for the target were justified by the activity surrounding the merger, Manne might argue that the executives of the acquiring firm created that new value through their decision to merge and ought to be able to participate in the value they have created.

Perhaps. But the general view is that such self-dealing violates the trust shareholders of an acquiring firm place in its manager. If there is an opportunity for profit, current legal standards maintain that it belongs to the firm, not the manager. In addition, there is a consensus that the insider is unfair to the target shareholders who are ignorant of the basis of the transaction, and that the public's faith in the stock market as a reliable and fair institution is being undermined. Despite the difficulty of the task and its uncertain, long-term effectiveness, attempts to eliminate insider trading continue.

C H A P T E R   3

TAKEOVER LAWS

In boxing, contestants must stay in the ring, and they may not kick, bite, butt, or hit below the belt. The rules for takeover contests are similar. The ring, or more properly, rings (for there are three principal arenas) are circumscribed by three sets of laws. First, there are the rules of the state in which the target company is incorporated. These determine when and how control of the target may be exercised and transferred. Second, there are the federal securities laws, particularly the Williams Act, which establish disclosure requirements and the minimum offering period which must be satisfied before an acquisition may proceed. Finally, there is the Hart-Scott-Rodino Antitrust Improvement Act of 1976, which stipulates its own set of premerger waiting periods and notification requirements. In other words, before an acquiring firm can buy target shares it must wait until the two statutory premerger time periods have expired, then it must buy enough shares to obtain control over the target. Within the context of these laws almost any tactic designed to pressure target shareholders to sell or to delay expiration of a premerger waiting period is legal (apart from lies). Just as precise timing is important in a boxing match, so, too, in a contested takeover battle, strategic timing is often the key to victory.

THE OLD RULES

To appreciate the game-like qualities introduced by these rules, it is helpful to compare takeover strategy prior to the passage of the Williams Act in 1968. Previously, a firm seeking control could simply instruct its broker to start buying shares of the target without disclosing its intention. Or, if the acquiring firm was concerned that it might purchase a great many shares and yet fail to obtain control, it might make a tender offer. The discretion of the acquirer determined how long the offer remained open, whether withdrawal rights existed for tendering shareholders, and what information beyond offer price and timing was disclosed. Unless constrained by New York Stock Exchange rules, the offer to purchase 51 percent of target shares, although open for perhaps ten days, would be available on a first-come, first-served basis. Thus, if a shareholder delayed and 51 percent of the shares were tendered, the shares might be rejected even though they had been submitted within the necessary ten-day period. (Only New York Stock Exchange rules then required all shares submitted within the ten days be accepted on a proportionate or "prorata" basis.)

Samuel L. Hayes and Russell A. Taussig, Harvard Business School professors, writing in 1967, considered whether an acquiring firm ought to approach the management of a target firm if the former suspected its approach might be rejected. Hayes and Taussig responded: "Our answer is emphatically *no.* The reason is that the incumbents can take a variety of defensive measures that are successful in direct proportion to the speed of their execution."[1] Secrecy in planning the takeover and speed in acquiring the shares were the preferred strategies for the acquiring firm.

Target firms had few defenses against an all-out, overnight raid on their shares other than the inertia of the market. They could and often did resist disclosing lists of their shareholders to gain time to implement more permanent defense strategies. Finding shareholders willing to sell seems to have been a major problem in the cash tender offers of the 1960s. Brokers (including investment bankers and arbs) were paid a special commission to tender shares on behalf of themselves or clients that often equaled or exceeded the tender offer premium. Special commissions are now uncommon, perhaps because the larger current takeover premiums—50 percent versus 16 percent over the preoffer stock price[2]—have eliminated the need for an added incentive to tender.

In the past, if the target had time to fight a takeover, the strategies recommended by Hayes and Taussig could include major defensive moves that continue to this day: defensive mergers, issuing new shares, lawsuits, negative publicity campaigns, repurchasing shares, and raising dividends. However, with tender offers of shorter duration—frequently, the tender offer was open for only ten to fifteen days or as few as four days—and with terms that favored those who tended first, the takeover dynamic favored the acquiring firm. When faced with a tender offer of short duration and with little time to decide and little information to go on about the acquiring firm, or its plans, many shareholders felt compelled to opt for the short-term profits from the takeover bid, rather than hold on to a longer range investment in a changing firm.

THE WILLIAMS ACT OF 1968

The Williams Act[3] was designed to change the framework of the tender offer. Its provisions were modeled on those of earlier securities acts, and its principal provisions ensure that investors have access to information needed to make intelligent decisions. The object of the act was to prevent practices that stampeded shareholders into acting out of ignorance, and the offering period and disclosure requirements were aimed at enabling shareholders to act after delibereration. The purpose was to enhancing the stock market's overall reputation for fairness and honesty. Confidence in the market, it was thought, would attract more people to invest more money in equity securities.

The Williams Act established the following rules of behavior:

Offerors must disclose when making a tender offer who they are, where they will raise the money to pay for the tendered shares, what plans they have if any to change the target company and any special agreements they have concerning the takeover with other shareholders or the target management.

The Offeror's disclosures must be made to the SEC, the target company, other bidders for the target company, national stock exchanges *and* owners of the target's shares.

Target management may support, oppose or not comment on the tender offer. If they support or oppose the offer, they are also required to make a disclosure statement of their interests and objectives in the transaction.

During the 20 day minimum offer period the acquiring firm must accept any shares tendered during the first ten days (on a prorata basis) but any person tendering may withdraw shares tendered through the fifteenth day.

All persons are forbidden from encouraging or discouraging the sale or tender of shares through the use of *false or deceptive statements.*

Persons who acquire more than 5% of another firm's voting shares through "open market" or negotiated purchases (that is, not through a tender offer) *must disclose* within ten days of reaching 5% much of the same *information* required of a tender offeror.

The act does not define its central term—the tender offer—nor has the SEC. The failure to issue a definition may have caused some confusion, but the consequence has been to warn would-be avoiders of the act that its procedures cannot be escaped through technicalities. As the Sun Company discovered in its acquisition of Becton, Dickinson shares, neither giving their brokers a scripted purchase speech nor the watchful eye of their lawyers was sufficient means to sidestep the act when Sun's intent to purchase a fixed percentage of shares had been made clear.

Disclosure

One of the securities law's central concerns is the transference of corporate control, not just tender offers. Thus, even in situations where no tender offers are made, any person obtaining more than 5 percent of a firm's shares must disclose who they are and their intentions. The rules are careful to include as "one person" any group that is cooperating in a takeover plan. When control is obtained, there are further disclosure requirements upon the appointment of new corporate directors.

Disclosures are intended to provide information on which investors might tender (sell) shares in the target firm, buy shares in the resulting merged firm, or oppose the transaction. Most important to the shareholder is the question of control. If the buyer's intention is to obtain control, the fortunes of the firm might be affected in many ways. New management may intend to have the target reorient its business, for example, to supply the acquiring firm's corporate needs, or the acquiring firm may help the target by offering freer access to developmental capital from the acquiring firm. In choosing between tender offers from competing bidders, assurance that the funds to pay for the tendered shares are immediately available may be of crucial concern.

Although the disclosed information is useful to shareholders, the target's management, or competing bidders, the disclosure requirement is also a fruitful source of litigation for purposes of delay and confusion. Details about the identity, background, and future plans of the acquiring firm are frequent subjects of litigation. When successful, the results of such litigation are more disclosure and a better-informed stock market. However, the purpose of litigation is often delay, not disclosure. For those who typically initiate the lawsuits— target management or competing bidders—delay is used to gain time to pursue other defensive strategies.

By requiring the target firm to cooperate in notifying its shareholders of the terms of the tender offer, the Williams Act has to some small degree forced target firms to aid acquirers in soliciting shares. However it is not clear whether these communications to shareholders, usually through the mails, are fast enough in contested takeovers to keep shareholders adequately informed to exercise their various rights throughout the tender offer waiting period. As noted earlier, most investors whose shares are tendered sell in the market to arbs.

The Williams Act Offering Period

The terms of tender offers and the various deadlines for tendering make it difficult for average investors to understand their rights, especially in a contested takeover bid. The Williams Act and SEC regulations have established the following complicated set of rules for tender offers.[4]

All tender offers must be open for at least twenty days.

This means that the acquiring firm *must* accept all shares tendered during the twenty days (up to the number of shares included in the offer) but *may not* actually buy any of the shares until after the twenty-day period expires. Tender offers may be open for longer than twenty days, and many acquiring firms extend the period to encourage a larger number of shareholders to act.

> *Any shareholder who tenders in the first ten days of the offer is guaranteed participation in the offer on at least a prorata basis.*

If a shareholder tenders after the tenth day and the acquiring firm has already received all the shares it requested, the shares will be returned (if the acquiring firm doesn't want the extras). However, if too many shares were received during the first ten days, then the acquiring firm must accept an equal proportion of the shares tendered by all persons during that ten-day period. Thus, if the firm's offer was for 10 percent of the target's shares and 20 percent were tendered during the ten-day period, then the acquirer must accept half of the shares tendered by each shareholder.

> *Any shares tendered may be withdrawn by the person tendering during the first fifteen days of the offer.*

In other words, a shareholder can, without risk, immediately send shares to the acquiring firm to avoid any possibility of missing out on the ten-day proration rights. The shareholder may then consider the terms of the offer and the disclosures and, through the fifteenth day, change his mind and withdraw the tendered shares.

> *If at the end of twenty days (or longer if stated in the offer) the acquiring firm has been tendered the number of shares it requested, it must pay the tendering shareholders in accordance with its offer.*

If the acquiring firm does not reach its goal, it may, but it is not obliged to, buy any of the tendered target shares. This is one of the major advantages of using a tender offer. The acquirer is only bound to pay if it has won control or whatever amount it requested. Typically, a tender offer will also include other escape clauses for the acquiring firm. For example, Gulf Oil claimed it was relieved of its obligation to buy Cities Service shares because antitrust authorities started an investigation of the acquisition.

> *If, during the offering period, another firm makes a competing tender offer for the target, shareholders are guaran-*

teed ten days in which to decide if they wish to leave their
shares tendered with the first firm, or wish to withdraw
them.

In the normal sequence, after day fifteen, shares that have been tendered cannot be withdrawn; both shareholders and the acquiring firm are bound by the terms of the offer. The acquiring firm is assured after fifteen days that no shares then tendered can be withdrawn. However, if on day nineteen of a twenty-day tender offer a competing offer were announced, then a person who had tendered to the first firm would be given until day twenty-nine to withdraw that tender. The first firm's offer would be automatically extended for another nine days. The intention of the additional withdrawal period, like that of the initial waiting period, is to guarantee investors an adequate period of time to study the offers before deciding. Should there be a series of bidders, each would start a new ten-day withdrawal period.

While the additional withdrawal period reinforces the act's goal of considered investment decisions, the purpose of having proration and withdrawal periods less than the length of the offer is still unclear. These complex rules, consequently, often pressure shareholders to tender early in the process and to lock in their shares while the offer is still technically open.

Williams Act Loopholes

The pressure to commit early in the process and become locked in can be increased by making the tender offer part of a two-tier offer. U.S. Steel's successful tender offer for Marathon promised $125 a share for the 51 percent of Marathon shares included in the first tier, but the other shares (49%) were to be exchanged in the second tier for notes valued at $83. The success of two-tier offers like U.S. Steel's demonstrated how the structure of the rules could be bent to greatly reduce the period set aside for consideration of a tender offer's merits. In December 1982 the SEC, to reduce investors' fears of being left in the second tier, established a new waiting period rule.

For two-tier tender offers the proration period is a mini-
mum of twenty days and not shorter than the life of the
offer.[5]

The intent is to guarantee participation in the first tier for anyone who tenders and to slow the overall rush to tender.

For all its detailed concern about target shareholders, the act does have one large loophole. Acquiring firms can and do buy up to and beyond the 5 percent reporting mark for purchase of target shares on the open market without a prior announcement of their intent to obtain control or the use of a tender offer. Firms like McDermott, when it entered the tender offer bidding contest for Babcock & Wilcox, typically begin by making a substantial (and secret) purchase of target shares for which they pay no takeover premium.[6] This move is completed before the tender offer is made.

Williams Act Tactics

Once the Williams Act offering period begins, its limits become the focus of strategic action. A tactical lawsuit that challenges the acquiring firm's disclosure statement too early would not delay a rival bidder if it is dismissed before the offering period expires on the twentieth day. The same lawsuit, if brought on the eighteenth or nineteenth day of the offering period, might induce a judge to prevent the acquisition of tendered shares for a few days beyond the waiting period in order to resolve the issue. Big-city judges familiar with merger strategies may have become skeptical of such blatant attempts at delay, but some judges are still sympathetic to the tactic.

The object of delay is to find a better way out for the target or its management. Delay may pressure an acquiring firm, or arbs with faltering lines of credit. Delay may also allow the target to get a stronger strategy in place, for example, a competing bid from a friendly "white knight." If the white knight's bid is made before the twentieth day, the offering period is automatically extended ten days from the time of the bid. If a bid is merely rumored between the fifteenth and the twentieth day, it may have no effect because tendered shares are frozen.

On the other hand, if the rumor of a second, higher bid surfaces before the fifteenth day, that may induce the arbs and other shareholders to withdraw their shares from tender. As the contested battle for Babcock & Wilcox showed, when the investment community is convinced that a credible and substantially higher competing bid will arise, the arbs will take the tender offer away from the acquiring firm. Babcock & Wilcox avoided, in May 1977, a United Technologies tender offer at $42 a share when it was rumored that McDermott would make a tender offer. The arbs bid the shares up to $44 a share in May. Thus, anyone wishing to sell Babcock & Wilcox shares would have sold to McDermott rather than tendering to United Technologies. Finally, in August United Technologies raised its bid to $48 a share, and McDermott quickly responded with its first public offer at $55 a share.[7] A rumored second bid is effective but only if it is generally believed and if the timing is right—before shares are locked in after the fifteenth day.

The Williams Act establishes the timing of the battle, and any tactics employed must be fit within the proration, withdrawal, and expiration limits set by the SEC. While greater resources, greater insight or imagination, and better luck may ultimately determine the outcome of a takeover contest, the framework of the transaction is set by an act designed to help the target shareholder make a reasoned decision.

The clear congressional intent to protect the shareholder's considered choice during a takeover contest has led some federal courts to impose more than tender offer disclosure and timing obligations. These courts have interpreted the Williams Act prohibitions to include any defensive tactic used by target management that would usurp the right of shareholders to consider and accept a hostile tender offer. This interpretation does not prohibit a target management from seeking a white knight or delaying, so long as a fair bidding process results. It is aimed at tactics, such as "selling the crown jewels," that make a victory pyrrhic for the hostile bidder. For example, Marathon Oil gave U.S. Steel an option to buy at a fixed price its interest in the Yates oil field, which was exercisable only if Marathon were taken over. This option would have made it pointless for Mobil to try to outbid U.S. Steel for Marathon, when U.S. Steel already had Marathon's most valuable asset locked up at a bargain price. To ensure that Marathon shareholders would have the benefit of an open bidding contest, the court invalidated the option.[8]

This direct regulation of defensive tactics is new and seemingly departs from a more conventional approach that allows individual states to determine whether target management has acted properly on behalf of its shareholders. The court in the Marathon case, however, was persuaded that the purpose of the Williams Act offering period and disclosure requirement could not be achieved if a shareholder's opportunities to consider competing bids were defeated by tactics that eliminated the basis for tender offers from other firms.[9] The court, without judging whether Marathon's defensive tactics properly protected its shareholders, held that the Williams Act gave those shareholders a right to benefit from an open tender offer bidding process.

If the result of the Marathon case is contrary to a tradition of deference to state regulation of corporations, it is consistent with the spirit of the Williams Act which displaced state regulation of tender offers as inadequate. Congress created a procedure not to protect the target's management or any prospective acquiring firms, but to safeguard the interests of the shareholder.

THE ANTITRUST WAITING PERIOD

The premerger notification requirements of the Hart-Scott-Rodino Antitrust Improvements Act of 1976[10] were passed to give federal antitrust authorities in the Justice Department and the Federal Trade Commission an opportunity to review proposed mergers and acquisitions. If transactions were likely to violate the antitrust laws by reducing competition or creating a monopoly, then a lawsuit could be instituted to forbid the merger. The premise of the notification requirement and waiting period is that it is easier and more efficient to prevent an unlawful merger than it is to "unscramble" the corporate "eggs" after the transaction is completed.

The Hart-Scott-Rodino act requires acquiring firms to notify the federal antitrust agencies and the target firm of the proposed acquisition or merger and file certain information about the volume and kind of business the acquirer conducts and the business of the target. The target is required to file similar information. Antitrust officials are then given fifteen days in the case of a cash tender offer (otherwise 30 days) to determine whether the transaction might violate the antitrust laws. If the transaction is to be challenged, the investigating antitrust agency will usually issue a "second request" for more detailed information. After receiving the requested material (in a tender offer), officials are allowed ten more days of analysis before the antitrust waiting period ends. A lawsuit must then be instituted if a decision is reached to stop the transaction.

The significance of the Hart-Scott-Rodino legislation is that it imposes procedural and time constraints on almost all transactions over $15 million regardless of antitrust concerns. For example, had Sun's acquisition of Becton, Dickinson occurred later in 1978, after the act's notification requirements had gone into effect, a surprise takeover would have been impossible. Sun would have had to notify the Department of Justice, the Federal Trade Commission, and Becton, Dickinson at least fifteen days before it tried to buy any of the target's shares. Although the antitrust agencies may shorten the fifteen-day period—it may be shortened if the transaction does not pose any antitrust problem and the acquiring firm requests early termination of the waiting period—the tactical element of total surprise has been eliminated. The "midnight merger" is gone. On the other hand, the hostile bidder, once the fifteen-day notification period has begun, has an advantage over potential rivals, whose waiting period begins later.

The difference in waiting periods—twenty *working* days under the Williams Act versus fifteen *calendar* days under the Hart-Scott-Rodino Act, plus ten calendar days to review second request information—could determine a takeover contest. Probably most crucial is the issuance of the second request by antitrust officials. The request is a strong indication that officials will seek to stop a transaction by legal means, and it represents a lengthy delay in the running of the waiting period while both target and acquiring firm gather complex and detailed information. An early FTC study showed the median response time to second requests to be twenty days.[11]

It is therefore common for an unwilling target to emphasize to antitrust officials all conceivable antitrust violations in hopes of triggering a second request. A target firm may even try to favor a white knight in a contested takeover by filing its transaction quickly in order to minimize any possible antitrust problems. It may, at the same time, drag its feet in filing a notification with a hostile firm. Although enforcement officials are well aware of the thinking behind such tactics, they are, to a significant extent, dependent upon the speed with which firms make information available.

The possibility for delay under the existing statutes has made for a number of different tactics. If the target is able to foster a second request that favors a friendly white knight, the hostile bidder might be able to balance that time advantage with a carefully timed Williams Act ten-day delay based on a new tender offer. While shareholders consider this new offer, the hostile bidder may in the interim convince the antitrust authorities that its concerns over reducing competition can be resolved.

In some instances the Hart-Scott-Rodino Act can disadvantage one bidder in a contested takeover, and this is not entirely inappropriate. The act is supposed to prevent anticompetitive mergers. Consequently, where it is likely that an acquisition will violate the law the transaction may be delayed some weeks while the transaction is being examined. Indeed, if a lawsuit is brought to prevent a merger, years may pass before the antitrust issues are resolved. In other instances, the antitrust waiting period becomes only another arena in which all merger contenders must do battle.

STATE LAWS

State law provides a third arena for control battles. Corporations are created under state law and therefore the powers of corporate managers and directors are those permitted by the states. That permission, as enacted by state legislatures and interpreted by state courts, has been very generous. States generally give a target corporation discretion to take any action its managers think is in the corporation's (as opposed to their personal) best interest. This permissiveness has freed managers to make acquisitions or fight takeovers with whatever resources their corporations command.

Four kinds of corporate actions have been particularly important elements in takeover battles: fighting takeovers, favoring white knights, freezing out shareholders who did not tender, and providing defeated managers with "golden parachutes." State court decisions have upheld the right of corporate management to take each of these actions except in cases where the sole object is to preserve or obtain control of the corporation. In other circumstances, courts have refused to second-guess managers' decisions. Instead, even when an action is arguably contrary to the interests of shareholders, the courts have generally deferred to management on the grounds that the actions are matters of "business judgment." The business judgment rule leaves unhappy shareholders with two options: either throw the managers out at the next board of directors election or sell their shares.

Fighting Takeovers

Managers of target firms have been permitted a very broad range of tactics to resist takeovers. They may, for example, raise the price of their shares above the price stated in the tender offer. Hayes and Taussig pointed out that target firms frequently declare special or higher dividends in hopes the market will revalue the shares at a price the acquiring firm is unwilling to pay.[12] Or, if others are unwilling to pay a price higher than the bid, the target corporation may buy its own shares. Hi–Shear Corporation, for example, did just that and successfully defeated a 1975 takeover attempt.[13]

Managers at a target firm may also try to protect their jobs by buying the corporation themselves. The leveraged-buyout techniques described in Chapter 2 have developed to the point where they provide a plausible alternative for even the largest firms undergoing a takeover seige. During the battle that resulted in the largest merger ever—Chevron's $13.4 billion takeover of Gulf Oil—one of the options presented to the Gulf board of directors was a leveraged-buyout package put together by Kohlberg, Kravis, Roberts & Company.[14]

If the firm cannot hope to raise the price out of the range of the hostile bidder, it may try to frustrate the takeover attempt by issuing more shares. Matthew Josephson, in *The Robber Barons*, described how the "Erie" gang successfully used this device to prevent Cornelius Vanderbilt, head of the New York Central Railroad, from buying control of its rival, Erie & Lackawana Railroad. Each time Vanderbilt came close to buying a majority of the shares, Erie issued a large new batch of stock.[15] This device can still be used today, although to a more limited extent. Given state and federal securities laws, targets are generally limited to selling treasury stock (shares previously repurchased) or already authorized but unissued shares.

Or the target might try the Pac-Man defense: "buy the acquiring firm before they can buy you." Heublein scared off General Cinema using this tactic.

The ultimate corporate transformation was effected by Martin Horowitz, chairman of U.V. Industries, to raise stock prices and avoid a takeover by Sharon Steel. According to *Fortune*, when U.V.'s board of directors voted in January 1979 to sell all of its assets and distribute the proceeds to its shareholders, U.V. stock jumped from $19 to $30 a share.[16]

If the tender offer cannot be defeated directly, the target may make itself either undesirable or indigestable to the acquiring firm. For example, state law normally permits a corporation to sell its most valuable assets, and thereby become unattractive, or it may deliberately reduce its cash assets. One reason McDermott entered the bidding contest for Babcock & Wilcox is that McDermott had an excessive amount of cash and liquid assets. It was concerned that if it did not invest the money it would become a takeover target.[17] The target can also change its position by buying other firms which will create antitrust conflicts with a would-be acquirer, as Marshall Field did to avoid a tender offer by Carter Hawley Hale. The court upheld Marshall Field's defensive mergers, even though they may not have benefited shareholders. According to the court's business judgment standard:

> When [directors] act in good faith, they enjoy a presumption of sound business judgment, reposed in them as directors, which courts will not disturb if any rational business purpose can be attributed to their decisions. . . . Corporate directors have the duty to oppose a takeover offer which they have determined would be detrimental to the interests of the corporation and its shareholders. . . . [They] had not only the right "but the duty to resist by all lawful means persons whose attempts to win control of the corporation, if successful, would harm the corporate enterprise."[18]

In addition, a number of corporate by-laws can be written to impede or discourage a takeover. Some by-laws, such as a right of a corporation to repurchase its shares, are too restrictive for widely held corporations traded on national exchanges. Other by-laws more acceptable to stock exchanges may greatly delay the acquiring firm from asserting control even after obtaining a majority of the voting shares by staggering the terms of directors, eliminating the right of shareholders to call special meetings, requiring that directors be removed only for cause, and requiring super majorities before directors can be removed.[19] In general, these kinds of provisions may discourage takeovers because it will take so long to obtain actual control (the provisions may also be undesirable because they may pose the same barrier to friendly transactions). In a particular transaction, such as the Bendix/Martin Marietta fiasco, such by-laws can have strategic value. The final battle in this "Pac-Man" war turned on which of the two firms could obtain control of the other's board first since both owned a majority of the other's shares.

The object of takeover bids is frequently complete ownership of the target, but this is typically not achieved through a tender offer even in the few cases where the acquiring firm seeks 100 percent of the target's voting securities. More common is a tender offer for a majority of the voting securities or for "working control" (ownership of enough shares to dominate the board of directors). After control of the target is established, a shareholder vote is then held directing that the target be merged into the acquiring firm in exchange for shares of the acquiring firm.

By-laws can impede this absorption process. It may be possible to require a super majority of 70 or 80 percent to approve this second part of a two-tier merger. Or a majority of votes other than those of the acquiring firm can be required. By-laws can also specify that any shareholder who wishes must be paid an amount equal to that paid to shareholders who tendered their shares. Such provisions can backfire, though, by deterring friendly mergers or by preventing rapid rescue by a white knight. Furthermore, the validity of the many by-law provisions has not been fully tested, and is likely to vary from state to state.

Other state-imposed barriers have not fared well. Antitakeover statutes, which impose cumbersome procedures to examine the impact of a proposed takeover on the state and its residents, have been held unconstitutional as undue burdens on interstate commerce.[20] It remains to be seen whether by-law provisions of the Control Data Corporation, which also require the evaluation of the community impact of a proposed merger, will be more successful than the state laws.

Favoring White Knights

Where it is clear that a firm cannot escape a takeover, it is common for the target's management to seek a white knight, a more congenial firm with which to merge. The search for a more generous acquirer poses no problem under federal or state law for the entry of a competing bidder almost always raises the final sales price of the target, thus benefitting shareholders.

Problems arise when the target sells shares or assets to the white knight at a price below their potential value. Carl Icahn, for example, objected when Marshall Field gave its white knight an option to buy its flagship store in Chicago and a large block of treasury stock. The Marathon decision showed that these "lockup" transactions can also violate the Williams Act. In addition, lockups can be attacked under state law if a shareholder can show that the low sale price is a giveaway of corporate property.

But the business judgment rule makes it particularly difficult to attack under state law the decisions of directors that favor white knights. Where directors are resisting takeovers, their actions may be suspect on the grounds that they are protecting their own jobs. Suspicions are especially raised if a majority of the board is composed of or dominated by corporate officers. However, even when a white knight succeeds, the corporate officers lose their independence and not infrequently resign or are replaced. Consequently, the suspicion of personal interest does not attach so easily to actions that help white knights.

Not surprisingly, white knights sometimes demand lockup deals because of the cost of takeover battles and the disadvantage to entering the contest late. For example, to entice Wheelabrator–Frye and avoid a takeover by McDermott at $28 a share, Pullman gave Wheelabrator an option to buy Pullman's crown jewel—its engineering and construction division. Wheelabrator eventually prevailed at $52 a share, but had both bidders dropped out, Pullman would have remained independent (minus its prize asset). The *Wall Street Journal* report of the transaction posed the following question: "Should Pullman have placed itself and its shareholders in such a position? 'If Pullman hadn't,' argues First Boston's Mr. Wasserstein, 'it would have been bought by McDermott for $28 a share.'"[21]

Freezeouts

If state law is permissive toward target management resisting takeovers, it is equally generous to its successors after the acquiring firm has obtained control. The ability of the acquiring firm to gain complete control of the target and at a far reduced price per share is almost assured. This second level of a two-tier offer is reserved for those who did not tender. The acquiring firm can use its majority vote to accomplish a merger to squeeze out any remaining dissenters by forcing a swap of its shares for target shares at the then prevailing price.[22] Typically, the price of the target shares falls below their pre-tender offer price.

In some states shareholders who do not like the terms of the freezeout merger can require payment according to a statutory appraisal procedure. This is rarely invoked because the shareholder must waive the right to the acquiring firm's freezeout offer and accept the appraised value even if the appraisal is lower than the second-tier merger offer (which it usually is). As a consequence, statutory appraisal serves only a very limited purpose. According to University of California law professor Melvin Eisenberg,

> The appraisal right presents many difficulties from the shareholder's perspective: It is always technical; it may be expensive; it is uncertain in result, and, in the case of a publicly held corporation, is unlikely to produce a better result than could have been obtained on the market; and the ultimate award is taxable. It is, in short, a remedy of desperation—generally speaking, no shareholder in a publicly held corporation who is in his right mind will invoke the appraisal right unless he feels that the change from which he dissents is shockingly improvident and that the fair value of his shares before the change will far exceed the value of his shares after the change.[23]

Nor are the remaining shareholders left with many rights if the acquiring firm decides to wait until the shareholders are willing to sell at a low price. Specifically, shareholders are unlikely to be able to force the target firm to declare dividends even if it is very profitable. For example, the Tidewater Oil Company announced in 1960 that it would not pay dividends over the next five years. This announcement was allegedly to depress Tidewater's stock prices to help J. Paul Getty, the firm's president, purchase its stock at reduced prices. The court rejected the relevance of Getty's motives since Tidewater's generous earnings were being reinvested in new projects.[24]

Golden Parachutes

A "golden parachute" is an employment contract provision that guarantees compensation to key corporate executives if the firm is taken over. An executive becomes entitled to this compensation after the takeover if the executive is fired or quits because his or her authority has been reduced (which is inevitable for chief executive officers), or if someone has gained control of a stated percentage of the firm's shares. The provisions are golden because they are generous. William Agee, chief executive officer of Bendix, was protected by a $4 million parachute. Ralph Bailey, head of Conoco, had a slightly softer landing on $4.1 million.[25]

Golden parachutes are justified as the only way, given the number of corporate takeovers, to offer job security to senior management officials. Job security, it is argued, serves two functions. First, corporations, and especially those subject to takeovers, could not attract talented executives without these inducements. Second, when subject to a takeover bid, it is argued, a corporate manager can determine more dispassionately whether the offer is in the best interests of the corporation. Because of the parachute, it is supposed, an executive will not resist a merger merely to maintain his corporate perquisites.

As in all other matters, state law grants a great deal of discretion to a board of directors in setting the salaries and terms of employment for corporate officers. The business judgment rule applies to such decisions. It is also a common part of friendly mergers to stipulate the compensation and employment rights of the target's senior management. In North American Phillips' takeover of Magnavox, a hostile takeover was converted to a friendly transaction after the bid was raised and new employment contracts were arranged for the sixteen senior officers of the target.[26] Except in cases where compensation is patently absurd, courts normally hold that parachutes or other compensation plans are valid. Whether they are needed to attract able executives or whether they improve the takeover process is less clear.

Although state law obviously favors incumbent management, there are limits to what managers are entitled to do. Consequently, to get into court requires only an assertion that the actions of target or acquiring firms are unlawful. In a particular case such lawsuits may at least delay a takeover or defensive manuever, but in extreme cases lawsuits can be determinative. For example, the Delaware courts held that North American Phillips could not throw out (by a merger) minority shareholders of one of its subsidiaries simply because it wanted to eliminate dissent.[27]

CHAPTER 4

MERGER WARS

The takeover battles of the late 1970s and early 1980s involved great sums of money, many contestants, lots of business action and suspense over who would win and why. Three of the largest and most notorious of these merger wars will be examined here because they illustrate, on a grand scale, distinctive characteristics of the megamerger wave. They are the acquisitions of Conoco, Marathon Oil and Bendix.

THE CONOCO PLAY: OR, YOU CAN WRIGGLE BUT YOU CAN'T GET FREE

To understand the events that took place between May 4, 1981, when Dome Petroleum made a tender offer for 20 percent of Conoco's shares, and August 6, 1981, when Du Pont obtained control of Conoco, the cast of companies involved in the transaction should be introduced.

The Cast (in order of appearance)

Conoco was the target. Conoco was the ninth largest integrated oil company and second largest coal company in the United States. In 1980, when it had sales of $18 billion and assets of $11 billion, Conoco ranked 14th on the *Fortune* list of 500 largest industrial companies. In early May 1981, its shares had an estimated value of $150 apiece but were selling for less than $50.

Dome Petroleum, a small Canadian oil company, offered $65 a share for 20 percent of Conoco's stock. Dome wanted to purchase Conoco's majority interest in the Hudson Bay Oil & Gas Company with the help of financing by Canadian banks. These banks were implementing a national policy to reassert domestic control over Canadian natural resources.

Cities Service Oil negotiated a friendly merger with Conoco that failed. Cities, the nation's 44th largest industrial firm, also felt itself to be a potential takeover target because its shares were undervalued at the time. Its fears were later realized when Mesa Petroleum made a tender offer for Cities, which was eventually taken over by Occidental Petroleum.

Joseph Seagram & Sons was first a friendly, then a hostile bidder for Conoco. Seagram, a giant Canadian liquor firm, was ranked only 220 on the 1980 *Fortune* list. It was in search of an investment for the $2.3 billion it received when it sold its subsidiary, Texas Pacific Oil, to the Sun Company. Seagram had previously tried to take over St. Joe Mineral, but lost out, in an acrimonious battle, to St. Joe's white knight, the Fluor Corporation.

E. I. Du Pont de Nemours & Company (Du Pont) was Conoco's white knight. Du Pont, the nation's leading chemical company and number 15 on the *Fortune* list, entered the bidding, with Conoco assistance, to obtain Conoco shares at a bargain price.

Mobil Corporation was a hostile bidder. It is the nation's second largest integrated oil company and ranked second behind Exxon on *Fortune's* list of largest industrial firms. Mobil is known as a highly aggressive firm in part because of its television and newspaper editorials. Its $1.4 billion acquisition of Marcor in 1974 had set a precedent which helped make large hostile takeovers acceptable behavior for "blue chip" firms. (Ironically, Marcor had been the product of a 1971 defensive merger between Montgomery Ward and Container Corporation of America, a merger designed to prevent such takeovers.[1]) Mobil was interested in acquiring Conoco at a bargain price in order to extend its oil business.

Act I: Prologue

Scene 1: Tempest in a Dome Pot

When Dome Petroleum made its $65 a share tender offer for Conoco shares on May 5, 1981, it had no idea that Conoco would oppose the offer. Because of Canadian tax discrimination against foreign-owned (the U.S. in this case) natural resource companies, Conoco had earlier asked investment banker Robert Greenhill of Morgan, Stanley to find a Canadian buyer for its subsidiary, Hudson Bay Oil & Gas. According to *Fortune*, Greenhill located a buyer willing to pay $1.7 billion.[2] Conoco's chairman, Ralph Bailey, rejected the offer as being too low.

While Morgan, Stanley was searching for another buyer, Bailey was approached by Dome's management with a tax-free plan to buy the Canadian subsidiary by swapping (then unbought) Conoco shares. For reasons that remain mysterious, Bailey did not comment when Dome presented the plan to him, nor did he tell Greenhill about the approach from Dome. Dome assumed Bailey's reticence to explicitly approve the plan was based on an understanding that the deal would be more likely to receive favorable tax treatment if there had been no negotiations between Dome and Conoco prior to the purchase of Conoco shares. So when Dome made a tender offer for not less than 13 percent and not more than 20 percent of Conoco shares, it expected to trade them for control of Hudson Bay Oil & Gas in a bargain that would benefit both firms.

When Greenhill learned of the tender offer, he immediately took steps to have it stopped: first, by calling Dome and asking them to negotiate, and second, by having Conoco hire Skadden, Arps, Slate, Meagher & Flom. Greenhill realized there was a danger that the $15 a share premium would attract more than 20 percent of Conoco's shares. If it did, Conoco would become an obvious takeover target. According to the *Wall Street Journal*, over 60 percent of Conoco shareholders were bank trust departments, insurance companies, and mutual funds.[3] These institutional investors were most likely to jump at the opportunity to sell even though the offer was still greatly under book value for the shares. The end to the world oil shortage, the concentration of Conoco oil reserves in unpredictable Libya, and strikes against its coal subsidiary all provided reasons for knowledgeable investors to take a quick profit and reinvest elsewhere.

Headed up by Joseph Flom, lawyers from Skadden, Arps and from two other Wall Street firms, Dewey, Ballantine, Bushby, Palmer & Wood, and Davis, Polk & Wardwell, planned litigation to stop the tender offer. Despite what the *American Lawyer* described as "good ammunition" (Dome's tender offer had some clear mistatements) and "performing masterfully in arguing,"[4] the team was unable to convince the federal judge in Oklahoma who presided over the case.

Having failed to stop the tender offer, Greenhill sought to sell the Canadian subsidiary—to Dome or anyone else in order to eliminate the reason for Dome's offer—but Bailey was dissatisfied with the prices.

As a result, on May 27 the whole financial world found out what Ralph Bailey had refused to believe: 53 percent, not just 13 percent, of the Conoco shareholders were willing to sell their shares for $65 each. Dome's bargaining position was greatly enhanced because, had it chosen to, it might have altered its tender offer and taken control of Conoco. Nevertheless, because its tax-free swap failed, it eventually paid $1.68 billion in stock and cash to Conoco for the subsidiary, or about twice what it had hoped to pay. Even so, this was less than the amounts Conoco had been offered by other firms.

Not only did Conoco not profit from the tender offer, it had made clear that for a modest premium anyone could take over the company. Something had to be done if Conoco was to remain independent.

Scene 2: Wriggling Free

Conoco immediately tried to make sure Dome would not buy all the shares tendered. In this they succeeded. The danger of Dome taking over Conoco seems to have been greatly exaggerated. Not only was Dome unlikely go have been able to raise the money to pay for 53 percent of Conoco, but the Securities and Exchange Commission almost surely would have required Dome to begin the tender process all over again. Dome's Williams Act disclosure stated it wanted only a small portion of Conoco shares for a short period of time. Because "control" is the central concern of the Williams Act, this is the kind of change of purpose by an acquiring firm that the SEC would find unlawfully misleading if not disclosed. In other words, if Dome had decided it wanted control it would not have had an advantage over anyone else who saw Conoco as ripe for takeover.

In fact, everyone posed a danger. Even after scooping up 20 percent of the shares from Dome in exchange for Hudson Bay Oil & Gas, there were still at least 33 percent of Conoco shares with willing sellers. With that number of shares assured, it was clear to everyone inside Conoco and in the financial community that a higher dollar bid would easily bring in a majority of Conoco shares. So Conoco began a search for a desirable merger partner, and this it found in Cities Service. At the same time, Conoco was approached by Edgar Bronfman, chairman of Seagram.

Bronfman proposed on May 31 that Seagram buy 35 percent of Conoco as an investment at a price of $70 to $75 a share.[5] This would remove from the market all the shares that were known to be seeking a bidder. To assure Conoco that it had no intention of controlling the firm, Seagram was willing to sign an agreement pledging to vote its shares with management for the next fifteen years and not to increase its holdings during that time. To demonstrate its friendly intentions, Seagram hired Goldman, Sachs (which has refused to represent acquiring firms in hostile acquisitions) to represent its investment banking interests and promised that it would not make a hostile bid if the negotiations failed.

Fortune suggested that the deal with Seagram foundered on the question of what was to happen at the end of the fifteen-year period. Conoco's board is reported to have believed that Seagram was buying control (albeit delayed) and that $75 was too low a bid for a takeover. The *American Lawyer* suggested that Conoco never wanted a deal with Seagram, and that the negotiations were being held only in case a noncontrolling white knight was needed suddenly.[6] It is hard to determine which version is more accurate. The premium Seagram offered was substantially higher than Dome had offered, and the fifteen-year "standstill" agreement is precisely the arrangement Seagram alter worked out under similar circumstances with Du Pont. On the other hand, the Conoco board had a majority of independent directors who knew the book value of the firm was twice Seagram's offer.

In any case, something better did come along. Conoco and Cities Service agreed to a merger on June 25. Martin Lipton negotiated on behalf of Cities Service a noncash merger based on the value of shares in the two companies. That merger agreement became impossible when Conoco's stock rose above that agreed value in response to the announcement of a tender offer by Seagram for Conoco.

Act II: Battle of the Giants

Scene 1: The Opening Bell

Seagram, contrary to Bronfman's promise, began buying shares without Conoco's knowledge (much less approval) on June 18, 1981, the day after the Conoco board rejected its offer. In making these purchases, Seagram took advantage of Williams Act provisions that permit the acquisition of less than 5 percent without disclosure and the Hart-Scott-Rodino Act's "investment only" exemption for acquisitions of up to 10 percent. This produced sufficient stock market activity on the following day for the New York Stock Exchange to suspend trading in Conoco shares until Conoco explained that the trading was probably based on rumors of a cash tender offer, that Conoco had declined that offer but was currently considering a stock-swap merger.

Then, on June 22, Seagram filed its Hart-Scott-Rodino notification with the Federal Trade Commission and the Department of Justice of its intention to acquire Conoco. From this point on Conoco was on notice that a tender offer could come at any time because the Seagram filing had to certify that it had already given a copy of its notification papers to Conoco. Nevertheless, Conoco appears not to have expected the tender offer because Flom and Lipton proceeded to work out the Cities Service merger. They finished their work on June 25.

On that same day, the Seagram board met and voted to make a hostile cash tender offer for 41 percent of Conoco shares at $73 a share. Why the Seagram board broke its promise and whether it was justified in doing so by an absence of "good faith" bargaining by Conoco later became the focus of litigation. At Seagram, the major impact of the hostile bid was Goldman, Sachs' resignation as Seagram's investment banker for this transaction. Seagram then turned to two more aggressive firms, Shearson Loeb Rhoades (now Shearson Lehman/American Express) and Lazard Freres.

With the Cities Service merger gone and facing the tender offer time clock, Conoco had to move in two directions at once. First, it had to fight off Seagram, and second it had to find a white knight. Escape was too late.

The Seagram lawyers at Simpson, Thatcher & Bartlett cleared the way for the tender offer by knocking out three state antitakeover statutes and overcoming various legal obstacles raised by Flom and his platoon of lawyers. These legal matters included a new Conoco by-law forbidding control by a foreign company like Seagram, and a novel state liquor law claim that Seagram, a liquor manufacturer, could not buy Conoco because beer was sold in some of Conoco's Florida filling stations. Flom's variant on the "Jewish dentist" defense here was to have a letter wonder publicly whether anti-alcohol Muslim Arab countries would be happy to supply oil to a Jewish liquor manufacturer. The *American Lawyer* depicted these and other courtroom defense tactics used by the lawyers in these proceedings as less than admirable.[7] For example, while meeting with Seagram lawyers in New York Conoco obtained an injunction in another state court without even giving notice to the other side. They then told them of the injunction but not who granted it. In the end none of those tricks mattered except to raise the lawyers' fees.

On the other side Morgan, Stanley's search for a white knight for Conoco met with more success. On June 26 Conoco's board officially rejected the Seagram tender offer on the grounds that it was too low and unfair to most shareholders, given that Seagram intended to accept only 40 percent of the shares. Expressions of interest then followed from Mobil, Texaco, and Du Pont. Texaco, the nation's third largest oil company, was reported by *Fortune* to have offered $85 a share in cash for 100 percent of the Conoco shares.[8] But the board rejected this indisputably more even-handed and greatly improved offer over the Seagram bid because of antitrust concerns. Instead, Conoco chose a very complex merger proposal from Du Pont that was designed by Bruce Wasserstein.

Scene 2: The Clock is Ticking

On July 6 Du Pont announced an offer for Conoco at $87.50 a share, which was endorsed by the Conoco board. The offer included a lockup option for 18 percent of the shares from treasury stock held by Conoco. Du Pont sought a total of 40 percent for cash. The remaining Conoco shareholders were to receive 1.6 shares of Du Pont. The offer was conditioned on obtaining a minimum of 51 percent of Conoco shares.

As an initial matter, the Du Pont bid on July 6 stopped Seagram because the stock market price immediately rose above Seagram's tender price of $73. Seagram had made its cash tender offer on June 25. The Hart-Scott-Rodino antitrust fifteen-calendar-day waiting period would be over at the latest (assuming no problems) on July 10, but the Williams Act would not let Seagram buy until the expiration of a 20-business-day period on July 24. The critical date was the fifteen-business-day withdrawal period, which was not to expire until July 17. No one was locked into Seagram. Even had anyone been locked in, the entrance of a new bidder (Du Pont) would have reopened withdrawal rights for ten days, that is until the 16.

That advantage was vulnerable to a counteroffer from Seagram. Du Pont, unlike Seagram, had not made a purely cash tender offer, so it faced both the twenty-business-day Williams Act period (which would expire on August 2) and a thirty-calendar-day antitrust waiting period (which would expire on August 6, thirteen days after Seagram would be permitted to buy). All Seagram had to do was raise its $73 bid before the 17th to lock in shares it would purchase on the 24th. In the meantime, Du Pont would have to stand by doing nothing.

Scene 3: The Clock is Stopped

So Conoco went to court to eliminate Seagram from the bidding. Federal Judge Edward Weinfeld characterized the Conoco claim:

> The . . . claim, based on promises made by Seagram to Conoco's directors during the course of negotiations, should not deprive the stockholders of an opportunity to exercise their individual judgments to accept or reject the Seagram offer, particularly since Seagram disputes the viability of the promise in light of the charges of duplicity by Conoco.

> What is sometimes lost sight of in these tender offer controversies is that the shareholders, not the directors, have the right of franchise with respect to the shares owned by them.[9]

On July 16, 1981, Judge Weinfeld ruled in favor of Seagram. By that time, Seagram had countered Du Pont's cash offer of $87.50 for 40 percent with an offer of $85 for 51 percent, hoping the earlier acceptance date and higher percentage of cash would tempt shareholders to tender. Du Pont responded with a new cash offer for 40 percent at $95 a share. The market price for Conoco was hovering around $85 a share on the 16th, so it was possible, if the institutional holders and the arbs got tired of waiting or nervous, that Du Pont would not reach its overall minimum of 51 percent. The market was poised to jump to Seagram.

Instead, something bizarre happened. Mobil entered the bidding on July 16 with a hostile cash tender offer for 50 percent of Conoco's shares at $90 a share, or $5 per share less than Du Pont. Of course, Mobil would have paid cash for a larger percentage, so the chances of being paid were greater if all shareholders tendered. Unlike Du Pont, Mobil offered nothing to shareholders who were not to receive cash, so the average price would likely be less if the offer were oversubscribed. In addition, it was inevitable that shareholders would worry that the Mobil bid would have antitrust problems. At the time, however, it did not matter that no one would tender to Mobil. The Williams Act commanded that everyone's withdrawal period stay open for ten business days—until July 30.

Why Mobil should have bid so low is completely baffling, but the rest of its strategy is understandable. Mobil was sure it could outbid Seagram, which did not have the money to get into a real bidding war. The problem, if Mobil was going to have one, was to establish its credibility as a contender. Doubt in this regard did not center over money, but whether antitrust officials would sue to prevent the merger.

Mobil was confident, however, that even though it would mean the largest amalgamation in history, the transaction did not violate traditional antitrust merger guidelines, much less fail the more friendly review expected from President Reagan's conservative Assistant Attorney General for Antitrust, William Baxter. Mobil, in fact, expected to be able to prove the full legality of the merger. It had filed for a cash tender offer so the fifteen-day antitrust waiting period would be over five days before Du Pont's thirty-day noncash offer. This would more than make up for the fact that the Williams Act would not permit Mobil to buy any shares until August 13. Or if the Antitrust Division were to decide to make a second request (because this was such a big merger), then it would make a request for additional information to Du Pont also and both firms would come out of the antitrust review process together. Armed with a greater bankroll, Mobil could then grind up any Du Pont offer.

Act III: Denouement

Scene 1: The Mills of Gods Grind Exceeding Slow

Conoco and Du Pont had good reason to fear defeat by Mobil and were left with only one real possibility for victory, an antitrust "show stopper." Joseph Flom, using the public relations firm of Kekst & Company, screamed antitrust throughout the business community. Flom was successful. Mobil tried to counter the propaganda by bringing in the arbs and a number of institutional investors for a meeting with Mobil's lawyers (including Sanford Litvak, Baxter's predecessor as Assistant Attorney General for Antitrust before joining Donovan, Leisure, Newton & Irvine, and Professor Richard Posner of the University of Chicago Law School, a leading antitrust authority later appointed to the U.S. Court of Appeals). But the session was unconvincing, perhaps because the investors were not allowed to bring their own lawyers to question the Mobil experts.

After Seagram increased its bid to $92 a share for 51 percent, Mobil was forced to respond and raised its bid to $105 for 50 percent. Du Pont, which had previously raised its bid to $95 for 40 percent, studiously ignored Mobil's raise to conform to its position that Mobil was not a serious bidder because of its antitrust problems.

On the antitrust and related political issues, Mobil was both correct in its analysis and wrong on the practical consequences. Attorney General William French Smith stated, with respect to antitrust, that "bigness does not necessarily mean badness." [10] Even so, letting the second largest industrial firm buy the fifteenth would not have looked good, especially because both were giant oil companies. It would have also looked like the end of antitrust, even though a dozen or more huge oil companies remained.

Mobil seems to have believed that if the Reagan administration took this attitude, it would apply to Du Pont as well. It did, but Du Pont was ready. Modern antitrust litigation is mostly made up of economic analysis of individual product markets, not grand theory or rhetoric. Du Pont force-fed cartons of documents to attorneys at the Justice Department in response to the latter's questions and quickly resolved a potential problem of the merger—creating an arguably unlawful Du Pont/Monsanto joint venture—by quickly buying out Monsanto before the waiting period ended. Mobil took a less aggressive attitude toward the antitrust review. Because of this, at the end of its waiting periods, Mobil was served with a "second request" for additional information, and Du Pont got a green light.

At this point, the pace was accelerated because Du Pont would become free to buy in five days' time. Mobil raised its bid to $115 for 50 percent. Du Pont's modest response was to raise its bid to $98 for 45 percent. Mobil then increased its bid to $120, but to no avail. The stock market refused to go above Du Pont's tender price; instead, it fell almost to Seagram's $92 level.

Mobil next asked the Securities and Exchange Commission to start a new ten-day withdrawal period because of all the new bids. The SEC would not because it does not consider a new offer to have been made when only the price offered changes. The alteration must be more fundamental—the introduction of a new bidder or a change from a noncontrol to a control bid.

Mobil went to court to argue that it was unfair to Conoco's shareholders to let Du Pont buy Conoco. What could Mobil say that Du Pont had not said when it tried to stop Seagram's tender offer? Nothing.

Scene 2: The End Game

So in the end, Mobil was waving money at people who sold their shares elsewhere. They went to Du Pont first and then to Seagram because of the way each structured its offer.

Du Pont had made a front-end-loaded, two-tier offer. In normal circumstances, this kind of offer is designed to pressure investors to tender early to collect the higher cash offer and avoid the less valuable subsequent stock exchange. While Du Pont's offer had some of that intent, the second tier was also designed to benefit those shareholders who wanted a tax-free stock swap. Consequently, Du Pont established separate pools for those who wanted cash and those who wanted stock. If the separate pools worked, it had the additional benefit of keeping up the price received by those who preferred cash. Without the separate pools, or if everyone had opted for cash proration, the result would have been a much lower average price for tendered shares because part of it would have been paid for in less valuable Du Pont stock. The *Wall Street Journal* reported that less than 2 percent of the shares tendered were forced to take Du Pont shares.[11] The offer worked well.

The offer also worked well because of Seagram's unconditional tender offer. At $92 a share it was worth considerably more, for those wanting cash, than the Du Pont shares which were worth only $72. Du Pont could not have accommodated all those who wanted the higher price cash portion. It also gave Seagram, which put no conditions on its acceptance, 32 percent of the Conoco shares.

Seagram eventually exchanged its shares in Conoco for 20 percent of Du Pont stock and signed an agreement not to buy any more shares for fifteen years and to support management during that time. Seagram won three seats on the Du Pont board of directors.

Who Won and Why?

The investment bankers received fees of more than $35 million; lawyers may have been paid as much as $20 million. Ralph Bailey, chairman of Conoco, became eligible for his $4.1 million parachute. The arbs, institutional investors, and speculators of all stripes made a great deal of money.

The holders of Conoco shares could have made a lot more money if they had tendered to Mobil. Why they did not is still something of a mystery. According to one influential Wall Street arbitrageur:

> Mobil, how can you ask me about Mobil? . . . They're clowns. A total joke. They come into this thing two weeks late with a half-assed offer, then raise it like mad, while all of us ignore them. They're morons, weirdos. All those raises they did later on to make up for their antitrust risks, while they said they had no antitrust risks, were hysterical. We were laughing so hard we were crying. We never gave them a thought. Clowns! The only thing not funny is that they happen to be the second largest company in the capitalist world. That's scary.[12]

To be sure antitrust complications posed a problem for Mobil, but the most likely problem was delay. It would have taken awhile for the Justice Department to sort out the many oil product markets to find if any monopoly power were being created, and then to require some minor divestitures. It is almost sure that the Antitrust Division would not have tried to block the merger completely.

Had the arbs held the balance of power, delay might have been crucial. Their interest costs might have pressured them to take the one bird in the hand (although they had waited patiently for a second bidder to emerge in 1978 for Babcock & Wilcox and other transactions). But here the size of the transaction was too large. The role of the arbs was minor, albeit lucrative. A solid majority of the shares was held by institutional investors who did not face the pressure to sell immediately.

The answer may be found in the structure of the takeover offers. The terms of the offers created a tip-over or bandwagon effect. All investors might have wanted, for example, to tender to Mobil. They might have all been willing to take the small antitrust risk that Mobil could not buy Conoco because they perceived the potential profit (once Mobil started its serious raises) to be much greater than the risk. However, each investor might have been afraid that the others would tender to Du Pont. If a majority did so, then those tendering to Mobil would receive nothing (from Mobil) because Mobil's offer, like Du Pont's, was conditioned on receiving a majority of Conoco shares. Instead, those tendering to Mobil would have been forced to accept the lower payment of Du Pont shares in the second tier of its offer. So the problem for Mobil may have been not antitrust but the widely shared belief that Du Pont would win.

Mobil could have eliminated this problem by following the terms of Seagram's offer, that is, not to condition its acceptance of tendered shares on receiving a majority of Conoco shares. If it had done so, there would have been no reason not to tender to Mobil because the money would have been guaranteed and tendering to Du Pont would then have become the risky move.

Why didn't Mobil make an unconditioned offer? One reason might be that despite its protestations about antitrust risk, Mobil believed there was a risk and it was unwilling to take it. Mobil preferred to impose the risk on the tendering Conoco shareholders. If so, Mobil deserved to have everyone believe the antitrust problem would prevent the merger.

The *American Lawyer* quotes Mobil's lawyers as having considered several means of reducing the risk for shareholders tendering to Mobil, but they thought of it after the tender offer had been made and were concerned that they would lose because of the additional delay inherent in a change.[13] If that was their thinking, it would support the *Wall Street Journal's* assessment that the relative inexperience of Mobil advisors at Merrill Lynch was the problem (investment bankers at Morgan, Stanley; First Boston; Lazard Freres; Shearson Loeb Rhoades; and Salomon Brothers were all taken, as were merger lawyers Joseph Flom, Martin Lipton, and Arthur Fleischer).[14] Mobil was already at a time disadvantage because its Williams Act period did not expire until August 13, a week after Du Pont was free to buy Conoco and two weeks after Seagram was free. So being late was not the problem; that was inevitable.

Mobil's main problem was that they did not have enough credibility to win a conditional tender offer battle with Du Pont. Mobil could not bridge the credibility gap and did not change the terms of the battle. They lost. As a consolation prize, Mobil asked the Justice Department to complete its antitrust analysis of Mobil's purchase of Conoco. The Justice Department refused: Its Antitrust Division does not give advisory opinions on mergers.

Did Du Pont win? At the end of the day on August 4, 53 percent of Conoco's shares were in Du Pont's hands. In gaining control of Conoco, Du Pont more than doubled its size. The $3.9 billion it borrowed to pay Conoco shareholders also increased Du Pont's long-term debt almost fivefold. Du Pont stock fell in value, and for the first time in its history, Du Pont had its bond rating lowered.[15] In addition, as a result of the Conoco stock swap, Seagram now owns 20 percent of Du Pont and has three seats on its board of directors.

Did Conoco win? The company is now a wholly owned subsidiary of a company smaller than itself. The Bronfmans of Seagram now sit on the board of Conoco's parent, Du Pont, with a fifteen-year standstill agreement similar to the one Conoco rejected.

Will Conoco be better run by Du Pont than it was by Bailey?

Did Seagram win? It sold its Texas Pacific Oil Company for $2.3 billion and bought 20 percent of Du Pont for $2.6 billion. Texas Pacific had a negative cash flow according to *Fortune*, whereas Du Pont will add more than $100 million a year to Seagram's income.[16] But putting $2.3 billion in the bank would easily earn twice that amount. Furthermore, Seagram paid $92 for Conoco stock and received in exchange Du Pont stock worth $72. Within three months Seagram's total investment in Du Pont, $2.6 billion, fell in value to $1.8 billion.

Who won?

THE RACE TO MARATHON: OR CROWN JEWELS AND THE SHOW STOPPER

There are many parallels between the takeover of Marathon Oil and the takeover of Conoco. Both oil firms were undervalued in 1981 when they began defensive maneuvers prior to a hostile bid. Both sought to sell Canadian oil properties and merge with U.S. oil firms. Mobil Oil failed to obtain control of either firm despite being the high bidder in each contest. In both battles, the target firms favored their white knights who held desirable stock options. In both, shareholders were pressured to accept tender offers from the white knights by front-end-loaded, two-tier tender offers.

Despite these similarities, the significance of the two takeover battles is very different. The contest for Conoco can be characterized as a promerger adventure story in which the tactics of all parties appear primarily as comic relief. Beginning with the misunderstanding between Dome and Conoco, to the friendly/hostile relationship with Seagram, the hide and seek lawyering by Flom for Conoco, and the obtusely low and late initial bid by Mobil, the whole chronology looks like low comedy. But the story has a happy ending with all the players getting something they wanted except for Mobil, whose failure was its own doing. Like the Northern Lights, the Conoco battle transfixed the financial scene and then disappeared.

In contrast, the takeover of Marathon was fought out principally in the courts and may result in permanent changes in the way tender offer battles can be conducted. The court decisions have greatly restricted the way in which target firms may favor white knights. The courts also adopted a more aggressive role in deciding antitrust issues, at least for oil mergers. Finally, the courts faced for the first time the issue of whether loading only the front end of a two-tier tender offer is lawful.

It cannot have come as a surprise to Marathon Oil on October 30, 1981, that it was subject to an $85 per share cash tender offer by Mobil. As early as June 1981, the Marathon board of directors began planning its takeover defense. The *Wall Street Journal* reported on July 10, 1981, in the midst of the Conoco battle, that Marathon shares had jumped from $49 a share on June 12 to $69 a share because of takeover speculation.[17] The article also contained denials from Marathon that it intended to sell or spinoff its crown jewel— a 48 percent interest in the Yates Field, a Texas oil property—in order to raise the price of Marathon shares and thus avoid a takeover. Marathon was publicly viewed as a much more undervalued integrated oil company than Conoco, with oil and gas reserves estimated by *Newsweek* to be worth $210 per share.[18]

Nevertheless, by July 23 Marathon had arranged for a $5 billion line of credit, and later that summer it hired the investment bankers at First Boston to sell its Canadian holdings and advise the company on acquisition matters.[19] On October 29 Bruce Wasserstein informed Marathon that Mobil was buying Marathon shares and that a tender offer would probably follow soon.[20] It did. On October 30, 1981, Mobil bid $5.1 billion for Marathon. The Marathon board rejected the Mobil $85 per share offer on the grounds that it was "grossly inadequate" and because the merger would be likely to violate the antitrust laws.

The Williams Act and Hart-Scott-Rodino Act premerger periods initially established a time framework for the Mobil offer. It put pressure on Marathon to obtain a white knight immediately. According to the *Wall Street Journal*, First Boston had difficulty in finding a friendly bidder because Marathon was so big, the 39th largest industrial firm on the *Fortune* list, and because it was reluctant to undermine its antitrust lawsuit by favoring another oil company.[21]

Only Allied Corporation, Gulf Oil, and U.S. Steel entered into serious negotiations. The successful negotiations with U.S. Steel were frequently in doubt.

U.S. Steel wanted to make an offer equal to $100 per share, with other conditions including an option on the Yates Field for $2 billion. Finally, a bargain was struck: U.S. Steel would offer an average of $106 a share (in a tender offer of $125 cash for 51% and notes valued at $86 for the remaining 49%) but would receive 10 million shares from Marathon at $90 per share and an option to buy the Yates Field for $2.8 billion if a third party (that is, Mobil) gained control of Marathon.

The framework established by the securities and antitrust waiting periods was quickly superseded by court orders as a result of litigation by Marathon and Mobil. Marathon claimed the takeover would violate the antitrust laws. Its claim was preliminarily upheld, and this provided U.S. Steel the margin for victory. Mobil claimed that the lockup options granted to U.S. Steel violated federal securities laws. Its claim was completely upheld but did not help Mobil. [22]

The Crown Jewels

U.S. Steel demanded and was given by Marathon an option to purchase the Yates Field for $2.8 billion, which would become exercisable if Mobil's tender offer succeeded. This tactic is referred to by several names. It is a "scorched earth" policy because it ruins the target business if the hostile bidder wins. It is also selling the "crown jewels" because it disposes of the target's most attractive asset. Finally, it is a "lockup" because it guarantees that only the holder of the option can benefit from the takeover.

The lockup guarantee most concerned the court ruling on Mobil's challenge to the option granted U.S. Steel. There is little question that the crown jewels option was worth less than the Yates Field. While selling corporate property at less than full value may violate state law, the federal courts were concerned that the option would eliminate the bidding process guaranteed by the Williams Act.

Consider this simplified example: Target firm has an approximate value of $100 with a crown jewel worth about $50. Target gives an option to white knight to buy the jewel for $25 if the hostile bidder wins. Assuming the option is valid, target is now worth about $75 to hostile bidder, because if it takes over the firm, it will get money worth half its value, instead of the crown jewel. With the crown jewel locked up by the white knight, the bidding for target will be somewhere between $75 and $100. Most likely it will be close to $75, because after the option is granted the firm is worth more than $75 to only the white knight. In other words, the option will eliminate bidding competition over the firm's true value.

As a result, the price per share offered to the target shareholders will be less. Instead of two or more firms bidding $90, $100, $110 for the target (depending on their individual estimates of its value), firms other than the white knight will be bidding on the value of the remainder of the target's assets plus the amount to be paid for the crown jewel. This prevents shareholders from having a chance of receiving full value for their shares.

In fact, the bidding process is undermined even if the white knight pays a "fair value" for the crown jewel. Suppose, in the simplified example just described, that the white knight were required to pay $50 to exercise the crown jewel option. Although the price is "fair," it will nevertheless avoid the auction bidding process required by the Williams Act. If, for example, any firms other than the white knight valued the crown jewel at more than $50, the option would prevent that higher valuation from being reflected in the bid. The option price defeats the bidding process by placing a ceiling on the value of the crown jewel.

Another way to understand the damage to the Williams Act bidding process of the crown jewel lockup is to suppose that, instead of giving the white knight an option on the crown jewels, the target offers an option on all of its assets. This "heads I win, tails you lose" option would clearly displace the bidding process entirely. Any winner other than the white knight would receive only the proceeds of the sale to the white knight. The crown jewels option provides an identical end-run to the Williams Act for a designated portion of the target.

The terms of the Yates Field option made it obvious that its sole purpose was to deter bidders other than the white knight: It became effective only if someone other than U.S. Steel took over Marathon Oil. So, in order to preserve the Williams Act bidding process, the courts tore up the option Marathon had given U.S. Steel to buy the Yates Field.[23]

For similar reasons, the courts also voided the option Marathon gave U.S. Steel to buy 10 million unissued shares at a cost of $90 a share. The damage to the bidding process resulting from this option may be less obvious, especially since it was agreed upon at a time when Mobil's bid was for $85 a share, or $5 less than U.S. Steel would pay. The effect of the option, if exercised, would be to increase the number of shares outstanding from about 60 to 70 million, to guarantee U.S. Steel 10 million shares, and to reduce U.S. Steel's average cost per share below that of its rivals in a bidding contest.

One way to view the problem with the share option is to draw a direct parallel between it and the crown jewels option: The target is selling a corporate asset (shares) without bidding, and therefore the corporation and its shareholders receive less than full value. Another way is to imagine the impact of issuing shares if the target sold 60 million shares at $90, thereby giving the white knight control. This would also completely eliminate the bidding process because control would be transferred solely through the option at the agreed price. Regardless of the bid, the hostile firm could not obtain control. In these circumstances, the shareholder would participate, if at all, in a subsequent freezeout after control was established.

Sales of smaller percentages of unissued shares have similar but less dramatic effects. Such sales can block a takeover by transforming a minority opposed to a takeover into a majority, or by preventing a bidder from reaching the necessary percentage of control to achieve some business objective (such as changing by-laws or conducting a short-form merger). These sales also allow the white knight to outbid rivals on a smaller outlay of money, with an even smaller portion of the money going to the shareholders.

Consider the following simplified example: Target has 80 shares outstanding and gives white knight an option to buy an additional 20 shares at $5 a piece. If the winning bid will pay $10 per share up to 50 percent of the 100 shares, the costs will be as follows:

> White Knight $400
> (30 shares at $10 + 20 shares at $5)
> Rival Bidder $500
> (50 shares at $10)

The rival bidder has to pay more for the same amount of control and is therefore discouraged from entering the bidding contest at all. (This disadvantage increases as the price is bid up higher.) Also, the percentage of shares held by investors that benefit from the Williams Act bidding contest are reduced by the issuance of new shares. If the new shares had not been issued, 40 shares held by investors would have had to participate in the control premium, whereas with 20 shares issued at $5, only 30 shares need be included.

Because the issuance of new shares can block the Williams Act process and reduces the benefit of the bidding process to the shareholders, the courts found the share options to be unlawful as well.

If these decisions appear convincing, consider that U.S. Steel said it would not have entered the bidding without the options. Allied Corporation and Gulf Oil demanded similar options as security in their discussions with Marathon. The entrance of a new bidder raised the price for Marathon shares from $85 a share to an average payment of $106 a share. In a *Wall Street Journal* article on the impact of the court's decision, Bruce Wasserstein, the lockup innovator, said, "The next time around, a Mobil might win at $85."[24]

Perhaps it would, but why? U.S. Steel eventually won without the advantage of either option. Once bids have been made, the high bidder will win in a fair fight.

The Show Stopper

The outcome of the Williams Act litigation was a surprise. Even more surprising was the antitrust litigation. As a general matter, lawsuits to prevent mergers under section 7 of the Clayton Antitrust Act are brought either by the Antitrust Division of the U.S. Department of Justice or the Bureau of Competition in the Federal Trade Commission, but they can also be brought by target firms, as Marathon did, to stop a takeover.

Although an antitrust lawsuit is frequently referred to as a "show stopper," that is, a tactic that will immediately and completely defeat a takeover attempt, it need not have that effect. The show stopper is normally the issuance of a preliminary order (or injunction) by a federal judge on the grounds that: one, the merger is likely to violate the antitrust laws; and, two, because it is difficult to disentangle firms once merged ("unscramble the eggs"), it is better to prevent the merger pending the outcome of the litigation. But where the acquiring firm is willing, it is often more sensible to execute a "hold separate" agreement, which allows the takeover but forbids integration of the operations of the two firms. This procedure was used, for example, when Exxon purchased Reliance Electric. This procedure is particularly desirable in acquisitions like Reliance Electric where the government ultimately abandons legal action or in instances where the merger will require only minor adjustments of the resulting firm's business ventures.

Mobil expected in the Conoco transaction that the Justice Department would argue that the antitrust laws required some changes in Conoco's business as a result of the merger, as it did to Du Pont. Mobil also expected to have some antitrust conflicts that might require it to sell some small parts of Marathon. These expectations were confirmed by the Federal Trade Commission which obtained jurisdiction over the Marathon merger. According to the *Wall Street Journal*, the FTC would have required, at most, disposition of some Marathon transportation, marketing, and refining assets.[25] At worst, Mobil should have been able to buy with a hold separate agreement. It would have then resolved which operations had to be spun off after it bought the Marathon shares.

It did not work out that way. U.S. Steel won the race for Marathon in a walk, despite its loss of the lockup lawsuit, because Mobil was barred from buying any Marathon shares. The courts enjoined Mobil from buying any shares, even though Mobil agreed to sign a hold separate agreement and agreed to sell all the Marathon assets that worried the Federal Trade Commission. Why? No completely satisfying answer can be offered, but the following factors were all likely to have been influential.

Size. Although current antitrust laws are most often stated in economic terms, they were passed in response to still evident fears of the power of big business. As the nation's second largest industrial firm, and its most outspoken, a multibillion dollar purchase by Mobil could only renew those fears. These fears were no doubt aggravated by the fact that the purchase of Marathon was the fourth multibillion dollar oil transaction in two years. Had Mobil won, it was widely felt that many more might follow.

Oil Profits. Since the oil embargo of 1973 and the resulting oil shortage, profits of American oil firms had increased greatly. In the debate over the taxing of windfall profits, oil companies had argued that these profits were needed to locate new oil reserves. The acquisition of Marathon Oil and the Yates Field would have added no new reserves to American control.

Oil Industry Structure. The structure of the oil industry is unique and perplexing to economists and antitrust lawyers. It has a large number of firms which antitrust considers "good," but many of these firms engage in a very large number of joint ventures which might be "bad." As a result the courts looked at some special factors for hints on the antitrust issue. They noted, for example, that Marathon seemed to be a price discounter. That is, it benefited the consumer by often selling gas for a lower price than Mobil. The courts also surprised Mobil by suggesting an anticompetitive reason for its willingness to sell off the Marathon refineries and gas stations, which had worried the FTC. The courts further suggested that Mobil was unconcerned about competition from selling these Marathon facilities because they would no longer have been able to discount without their own inexpensive oil reserves.

Ohio. Marathon Oil had its headquarters in Findlay, Ohio, and it was represented by a Cleveland law firm before a federal court located in Ohio. Had Mobil, rather than U.S. Steel, succeeded in taking over Marathon, the corporate headquarters would probably have been dissolved, with a resulting loss to Ohio of executive jobs, supporting services, charitable contributions, and the like. As a result, the case looked different than if it had been brought by government lawyers arguing economic effects in specific geographic markets or New York lawyers using the latest tactics to delay or double cross their opponents to further their client's financial gain.

By the time Mobil lost its second takeover contest, it had learned a great deal. It had won a significant victory against lockup tactics. It had learned not to condition its tender offers. Mobil also learned that the courts were not going to permit it to make a large purchase of an integrated oil firm without a long and expensive trial.

The court's implicit message—the promise of a lengthy trial—also trumped Mobil's final ace. When all else had failed, Mobil started to buy U.S. Steel shares. Whether the intent was to scare off U.S. Steel, to buy a large percentage and swap the shares for the Yates Field, or to buy U.S. Steel is not known. Once the implications of the antitrust case became clear, Mobil abandoned its efforts.

In the end, the courts only delayed takeovers in the oil industry. Two years later, after Texaco and Chevron had broken the antitrust barrier, Mobil was able to buy a $6 billion oil company, Superior Oil.

Aftermath

One effect of the public discussion surrounding Mobil's takeover attempt of Marathon was to create discontent among Marathon shareholders about the amount were paid. Shareholders were particularly incensed at receiving $86 a share in the second tier of an offer approved by the Marathon board of directors when that same board had branded the Mobil tender offer of $85 a share as "grossly inadequate." The unhappy shareholders argued that the board should, at minimum, have disclosed the valuation studies done for it by the First Boston Corporation showing per share values between $189 and $323. However, their main complaint was the two-tier offer itself, which forced shareholders to sell control and paid them less than full value for the remainder of their shares.

The court rejected the shareholders' argument entirely. It upheld the two-tier tender offer, and it accepted the board's explanations that it had approved not the $86 second tier but the $106 average price if all shareholders tendered. The board's decision not to disclose the high "selling valuation" of Marathon shares was also upheld by the court. If the shareholders objected to their freezeout payments, the court suggested they look to state court appraisal remedies.[26] Although these shareholders received short shrift from one federal court in Ohio, other courts will have to face the issue of fairness.

THE BENDIX AFFAIR: PAC-MAN AND THE DOOMSDAY MACHINE

Although the takeover of Bendix did not involve sums nearly as large as the acquisitions of either Conoco or Marathon, the battle received widespread media attention and may well result in a more lasting impact on takeover tactics. Public reaction to the battle was so adverse that the SEC altered one of its tender offer rules and empaneled an advisory group to examine the entire tender offer process.

Part of the reason for the great public attention to the Bendix affair in 1982 was that the public and the working press had become educated about corporate acquisitions. The merger wave beginning in 1978 increasingly featured very large mergers. Also, there had been a spate of contested takeovers including the battles for Conoco and

Marathon during the preceding year. The public had become aware of the dramatic possibilities of corporate acquisitions and the press was prepared to interpret the intricacies of takeover tactics.

Another reason for the attention given this transaction is that Bendix's chief executive officer, William Agee, had been involved in several highly publicized incidents in the two years leading up to the takeover battle. These incidents provided embellishment for those who portrayed this takeover as a billion dollar melodrama.

Strategies at Bendix

According to a prebattle *Fortune* article, featuring William Agee's problems at Bendix, Agee was brought to Bendix by former chief executive officer, Michael Blumenthal.[27] Blumenthal thought so highly of the thirty-eight-year-old Agee that he recommended Agee to succeed him in 1976 when Blumenthal left to become Secretary of the Treasury. Agee was determined to have Bendix grow by merger. In particular, he sought to buy a high-tech firm. He positioned Bendix for acquisitions by selling off a substantial portion of its operating divisions and accumulating over $500 million in cash.

Agee's promising beginning at Bendix was to become frustrated by his own actions. His rapid promotion of Mary Cunningham (now Agee's wife), a reputedly brilliant, albeit recent, graduate of the Harvard Business School, created a corporate scandal. Cunningham was hired as a special assistant to Agee for strategic planning in 1979. Within two years she became a corporate vice president for planning. But the promotion was not without a cost to Bendix. Its president and vice president for corporate planning resigned, and there was a loss of corporate morale. The Cunningham promotions were not simply a sex scandal. It was argued the personal relationship, whatever its basis, was so intense that it excluded those who should have been consulted on corporate planning. The appearance of impropriety existed and media interest was being fed by statements of unhappy Bendix executives. Thus, in October 1980, the Bendix board, over Agee's strenuous objection, required Cunningham to resign.

Throughout the incident much was made by Agee and his defenders of the evident business talents of Cunningham and her value to Bendix in planning corporate acquisitions. But during her tenure, at least, no major acquisitions were actually made. Indeed, the only sizeable acquisition by Bendix during this period was the purchase of $285 million worth of its own shares.

A contemporaneous incident, unpublicized until the *Fortune* article, seems to have also been related to Agee's desire to increase his corporate power. Upon learning that Secretary Blumenthal was to be appointed head of the Burroughs Corporation when he left the Treasury Department in 1979, Agee sought to persuade a Bendix board member (who was also a director of Burroughs) that he, Agee, should be chosen instead. Previously, Agee had (unsuccessfully) explored the willingness of Burroughs to merge with Bendix. While nothing came of Agee's extraordinary proposal to become simultaneously chief executive officer of both corporations, the plan suggested enmity toward his former patron or continuing designs on Burroughs.

Subsequent events would seem to confirm either hypothesis. After Cunningham's resignation, Agee pressured two Bendix directors who also served on the Burroughs board to resign in early 1981 on the grounds that Bendix was about to make a bid for a large high-tech firm. Although the target was not named, Burroughs seemed a possible choice. In addition, Agee pressured a former Burroughs director, known to be friendly with Blumenthal, to resign. Each of these freed positions was filled by individuals more supportive of Agee. But Bendix did not bid on any high-tech corporation during 1981, nor was a bid proposed to the board of directors.

Because he subsequently also refused to reappoint a long-time board member who questioned the basis for forcing the directors to resign, it appears that Agee's aims included consolidating his influence on the board. Having confirmed his power over the corporation, Agee made some changes in the Bendix corporate structure. He moved his executive offices from the headquarters in Southland, Michigan, to the nation's financial hub, New York City, where Cunningham had become a strategic planner for Seagram. But no large takeover plan emerged until March 1982, and then the target was not a high-tech company.

The takeover attempt, if it was one, was a flop. The target was RCA. Initially, analysts predicted Bendix would have little trouble taking over the once powerful communications and electronics firm. RCA had lost its technological leadership in electronics, its television and radio network, NBC, had slipped in the ratings, and its other major ventures, Hertz and CIT Financial, were in trouble. As a result, the firm was heavily burdened by debt. Nevertheless, *Business Week* concluded that RCA might be an attractive target for Agee, a financial expert, who might make a profit by selling off large chunks of the RCA conglomerate.[28]

After buying 7 percent and filing a notification of an intent to buy up to 9.9 percent of RCA stock, Agee met with RCA's chairman Thornton Bradshaw and his attorney, Martin Lipton. What transpired in this meeting is not known, but Agee seems to have agreed not to buy any more RCA stock. One RCA executive was quoted at the time as saying: "Mr. Agee has not demonstrated the ability to manage his own affairs, let alone someone else's."[29]

So the acquisition strategy that was presumably planned in 1979 and 1980 with Cunningham and threatened in 1981 (forcing four Bendix directors to resign) did not occur until March 1982. The attempt did not fit the announced strategic design nor did it succeed. The abortive takeover attempt was probably embarrassing both professionally and personally to Agee. Moreover, it posed a danger to the Bendix Corporation.

Bendix's cash reserves made it a likely takeover target. It had accumulated for a substantial period of time a large portion of its assets in cash—over $500 million—to finance a major acquisition. Although high interest rates gave Bendix adequate earnings on this money, the existence of a large cash balance made the firm vulnerable to a takeover bid. An acquiring firm could use Bendix's own cash reserve to pay off its cost of buying Bendix.

Chasing Pac-Man

The August 20, 1982, Bendix offer to buy 45 percent of Martin Marietta for $43 a share fit "the strategy." In fact, *Fortune* magazine reported that in a Barbara Walters interview taped earlier in August, Mary Cunningham (by then married to William Agee) "was bubbling over about 'The Strategy'. She told ABC crew members to watch the newspapers."[30] Martin Marietta is both a high technology firm, best known as a defense and aerospace contractor, and a diversified manufacturer of products ranging from aluminum and dyestuffs to data systems and construction products. Along with much of the economy and the stock market, Martin Marietta shares in 1982 were depressed below its recent prices and below its book value.

In July Agee asked the investment bankers at Salomon Brothers to analyze a hostile takeover of Martin Marietta by Bendix. Salomon Brothers advised that a takeover probably could succeed at a reasonable price. Martin Marietta, number 130 on the *Fortune* list in 1982, with annual sales totaling $3.2 billion and $2.5 billion in assets, was slightly smaller than Bendix, which was ranked 86th with $4.3 billion in sales and $3.2 billion in assets. Nevertheless, Salomon Brothers cautioned that Martin Marietta might try a then recent defensive tactic to make a countertender offer for Bendix shares. According to the *American Lawyer*, the bankers discounted Martin Marietta's ability to use this tactic on the grounds that it did not have the financial resources to make a credible counteroffer.[31]

In August final preparations for a Bendix takeover bid, scheduled after Labor Day, were made. Arthur Fleischer of Fried, Frank, Harris, Shriver & Jacobsen was brought in to direct the legal side of the transaction. Fleischer planned certain Bendix by-law changes to remove a Martin Marietta takeover time advantage. These were not implemented because there wasn't enough time. The failure to amend Bendix by-laws became the deciding factor in the outcome.

The takeover timetable was moved up because while Bendix was accumulating allowable percentages of Martin Marietta shares prior to filing under the Williams and Hart-Scott-Rodino Acts, the price of Martin Marietta shares began to rise rapidly. On Friday, the 13th of August, the shares closed at $24. By the following Wednesday they reached $27 a share and closed the week at $30. The day before Bendix's tender offer, the following Tuesday, Martin Marietta shares sold for $33. Whether the price rise was due to the general upsurge in the August 1982 bull market or the common insider/speculator run-up in share price preceding a tender offer, it pressured Agee to make the bid before his tender offer premium evaporated.

The Pac-Man Defense

The hostile tender offer by Bendix did not find Martin Marietta unprepared. Like a great many other firms, it had a takeover defense plan. Martin Marietta had established an internal defense committee that included the chairman of the board, president, chief financial officer, chief public relations officer, and general counsel. In addition, it had hired an investment banker (Kidder, Peabody & Company), a law firm (Dewey, Ballantine, Bushby, Palmer & Wood), a public relations firm, and a proxy solicitation firm. Ironically, the newly established takeover defense procedures were scheduled to be tested during the week of August 23.

According to Frank Menaker, general counsel of Martin Marietta, defensive plans began after *Newsweek* listed Martin Marietta as a possible target in March 1982.[32] An analysis was undertaken at that time which concluded that an antitrust defense was unlikely to stop a takeover.[33] This early alert, however, gave the corporation time to develop more formal defensive procedures.

These procedures worked, and in the week before the tender offer, Martin Marietta picked up rumors that its stock activity was due to an impending takeover by Bendix. An attempt by Kidder, Peabody to check out the rumor produced false reassurance until the morning of August 25, when Bendix called to notify Martin Marietta of the tender offer pursuant to its obligations under the Williams Act and the Hart-Scott-Rodino Act.

On August 30 the Martin Marietta board of directors met to consider the recommendations of its defense committee and the advice of its lawyers and bankers. The board made three decisions that day: It determined that the offer was inadequate; it rejected any attempt to seek a white knight; and it decided to make a tender offer for control of Bendix. In other words, the board and its chief executive officer, Thomas Pownall, were determined to keep the corporation independent.

It is not hard to understand why the board considered Agee's offer grossly inadequate. Agee's $900 million cash offer on the front end, with a $600 million noncash second tier, totaled $1.5 billion (or $200 million *less* than Martin Marietta had invested in capital improvements between 1977 and 1982). The tender offer premium was $10 over the $33 current price of Martin Marietta shares but not even over that year's high. Finally, the price offered was insufficient when measured against projected Martin Marietta income.

By bringing in a white knight, Martin Marietta might have raised the takeover price and fought off the Bendix offer. Conoco and Marathon Oil were able to greatly increase the takeover premium through this strategy. However, choosing a white knight is not a defense to a takeover; it is the target choosing the place of "surrender."

Instead, the board decided to make its own tender offer for Bendix. Since it had established takeover response procedures, the defense committee was able to present the board with a full range of options ready to go on August 30. Kidder, Peabody was able to assure the board that money could be raised to finance the counter-tender, a possibility that Salomon Brothers had doubted. Most im-important, the lawyers at Dewey, Ballantine had already identified the legal flaw in Bendix's attack. Bendix was likely to get Martin Marietta shares five days before Martin Marietta could buy Bendix shares, but differences in state law would allow Martin Marietta to exercise its ownership more quickly. In other words, instead of a five-day handicap, Martin Marietta might have a five-day advantage.

The possible advantage came from the difference between Mary-land law, where Martin Marietta was incorporated, and Delaware law, where Bendix was incorporated. Under Maryland law, changing the board of directors would have to be done at a shareholder meeting, and ten days' notice had to be given before such a meeting could be held. Under Delaware law, holders of a majority of shares can act without a meeting. Although these rules could have been altered by corporate by-laws, statutory procedures were in effect for both firms and seemed to give the advantage to Martin Marietta.

Legal snags could have upset this optimistic scenario. If Bendix owned a majority of Martin Marietta shares, then Martin Marietta would become a subsidiary corporation, barred by both Maryland and Delaware law from voting shares of its parent corporation. Menaker says the board was assured that these statutes would be held not to prevent voting in a takeover contest.[34]

Whether the board was completely satisfied that it would win on these technical legal issues (which it did) was probably not decisive on August 30. Although the board had to be convinced that the take-over tender offer for Bendix would be good for Martin Marietta if it succeeded, it is doubtful the board expected the transaction to succeed, or if it did that the initial Williams Act timetable would remain in effect. The directors more likely expected Bendix and Martin Marietta to call off their tender offers (which was possible under the terms of both offers).

Immediately after the board meeting, Martin Marietta lawyers went into action. They brought suit (using Maryland lawyers at the federal court in Baltimore) challenging the adequacy of Bendix's disclosures under the Williams Act. (Although they lost on this claim, the lawsuit established a home court advantage for the other matters litigated.) They then announced the tender offer for Bendix and filed the notifications required by the Williams Act and the Hart-Scott-Rodino Act. In the next few days they successfully challenged state takeover laws that might have delayed purchase of the shares.

The offer, like the one made by Bendix, was a front-end-loaded, two-tier tender offer. Martin Marietta offered $75 in cash for 50.3 percent of the Bendix shares and $55 worth of securities for the remainder. Bendix was then selling for $50 a share.

The Gray Knight

Bendix's response on August 31 to the countertender offer was mild. Its board of directors voted "golden parachutes" for Agee and other key executives after voting to oppose the Martin Marietta offer. In addition, it voted to submit charter and by-law amendments to shareholders to eliminate the Martin Marietta time advantage. Agee felt particularly secure because a large chunk of Bendix stock (23%) was held by the employee stock option plan. Bendix took precautions against the offer, but clearly did not think it serious enough to abandon the takeover attempt.

Nor were financial observers convinced by Martin Marietta's efficient defense. The stock market's tepid response to the offer was to raise the price of Bendix shares to the mid-$50's. Apparently, the arbs doubted Martin Marietta would ever get a chance to pay off on a tender offer that had a minimum value of $65 a share. By September 4, its proration deadline, Bendix had been tendered 58 percent of Martin Marietta's shares. *Business Week* described Martin Marietta as "gone" and predicted Bendix could only gain from the contest, either by obtaining control or by selling its Martin Marietta shares at a profit to a white knight.[35]

To bolster the credibility of its tender offer, Martin Marietta entered into an agreement with Harry Gray, chairman of United Technologies Corporation. On September 7 United Technologies announced it was making a backup tender offer for Bendix which would become effective if the Martin Marietta offer failed to receive the 50.3 percent it had requested. In any case, Bendix was to be split between the two corporations. United Technologies would receive the $500 million in cash, the automotive parts division, and other divisions that would not present an antitrust conflict. The remainder of Bendix would go to Martin Marietta. In order to ensure against antitrust problems for United Technologies, Martin Marietta promised not to seek a white knight or drop its bid for Bendix.

The alliance with United Technologies, quickly dubbed the "gray knight" by the press, altered the psychology of the battle. The price of Bendix shares jumped six points the next day to $62.75. In a *Wall Street Journal* profile, Agee suddenly became "Bendix's beleaguered chairman . . . according to some, outgunned, outmanned and outmaneuvered in the climactic struggle of his career."[36] (Agee had just raised the Bendix offer for Martin Marietta from $43 to $48 a share to preempt a bid by a white knight that never came.)

The psychological impact of Gray's entry is understandable. As chairman of United Technologies, he presided over its growth from the 59th largest industrial firm to number 20 on the *Fortune* list. The firm, which includes Pratt and Whitney aircraft engines, Sikorsky helicopters, Hamilton Standard aircraft controls and propellers, Otis elevators, and Carrier air conditioners, was forged in the 1970s by Gray's aggressive program of corporate acquisitions. Although he lost Babcock & Wilcox to McDermott and ESB to INCO, those were exceptions. More typical was his pursuit of Carrier Corporation which tried to avoid capture by merging with Jenn-Air Corporation. United Technologies promptly bought them both.

It was at this point that Bendix should have negotiated a peace agreement with Martin Marietta and United Technologies. Once it became clear that the Martin Marietta takeover threat was credible, the risk of continuing the battle was enormous. Even if Bendix won, and it couldn't be sure it would, it would have been vulnerable to a takeover. But it persisted, guided by its new investment banker, Bruce Wasserstein at First Boston, Arthur Fleischer from Fried, Frank, and the determination of William Agee (and volunteer Mary Cunningham) to implement "the strategy."

The day after the announcement of the United Technologies offer, Bendix received another psychological setback. Citibank, trustee for the Bendix employee stock plan, tendered its shares (23% of the total outstanding) to Martin Marietta. This reversal of the bank's initial intention and Agee's assumption was induced by Martin Marietta lawyers who stressed to the bank its legal obligation to maximize the return to its beneficiaries.[37] Specifically, they warned that if Citibank did not tender before the end of the proration period the bank might be liable for up to $100 million to beneficiaries forced to exchange their stock in the unloaded second tier. The bank, after warning Agee, tendered the shares over his protests. The pressure applied by the two-tier offer was too great.

A complicated series of maneuvers then followed: an amendment to the employee plan requiring withdrawal of the shares, a court order leaving the withdrawal option to the individual employees, and a "unity" day at Bendix (complete with balloons) pressuring employees to withdraw their tendered shares. Although eventually most of the employee shares were withdrawn, it made no difference in the outcome, but on its proration day Martin Marietta could say that it had been tendered 70 percent of Bendix's shares.[38]

The Doomsday Weapon

Strategic theory maintains that a deterrent is effective only when the attacker believes the target will use its ultimate weapon.[39] The two necessary elements are: possession of an ultimate weapon and convincing an attacker that the target has the will to use the weapon even though use might destroy the target as well as the attacker. Martin Marietta had the weapon in the form of the countertender offer, but apparently Bendix did not believe it would be used.

Bendix seems to have believed either it could prevent Martin Marietta from buying or voting the shares tendered to it or that good sense would prevent Martin Marietta from going through with its counteroffer. The reason for Bendix's doubt was that if Martin Marietta won it would have to assume an enormous debt. Prior to the tender offers, each firm had very healthy balance sheets. But victory by Martin Marietta would have, in the words of *Fortune* magazine, "convert[ed] two perfectly normal companies with reasonable debt-to-equity ratios of 1 to 3 into a single corporate mutant with a $2.7 billion debt load on a $1.1 billion equity base."[40] Victory would mean Martin Marietta would have to pay off both the money it borrowed to buy Bendix shares and the money Bendix borrowed to buy Martin Marietta shares. Bendix strategists labeled this the "Jonestown defense" (after the cult that committed suicide drinking poisoned Kool-Aid) but did not seem to believe Martin Marietta would use it.

To make its threat credible, Martin Marietta created a "doomsday weapon." In Stanley Kubrick's classic 1960's movie "Dr. Strangelove" the Soviet Union had invented a retaliatory doomsday missile that would automatically launch if nuclear warheads were detonated over Soviet cities. This made surrender by the Soviets after a nuclear attack impossible even if they wanted to. Even an accidental attack would set off the nuclear doomsday weapon. The purpose of this end-of-the-world weapon was to deprive the United States of any incentive to initiate a surprise or preemptive attack because mutual destruction was assured.

Martin Marietta's doomsday weapon was the term of its tender offer. On September 13 the board of directors at Martin Marietta voted to drop all of the conditions in its offer (that is, all of the escape clauses) except two. Martin Marietta would buy Bendix unless Bendix withdrew its tender offer or unless Bendix passed amendments to its charter that would wipe out Martin Marietta's five-day advantage. In other words, if Bendix bought the shares tendered to it, Martin Marietta bound itself legally to buy Bendix unless Martin Marietta lost its time advantage. Martin Marietta gave up its power to back out of buying to make its doomsday threat credible. Of course, the whole point of a doomsday weapon is that it will never be used. Once it is in place, the other side, if it is rational, has to back off. Bendix did not quit.

Showdowns

Fortune and *American Lawyer* both reported that Bendix strategists simply did not believe Martin Marietta would buy.[41] Arthur Fleischer, with the active support of Bruce Wasserstein, persuaded the Bendix board that Martin Marietta was not legally bound to buy Bendix shares and that, should Martin Marietta try to do so, there was a good chance that the courts would stop Martin Marietta from buying the shares or from voting the shares. The Bendix board voted to go ahead despite the risks.

On September 17 Bendix bought the 52.7 percent of Martin Marietta shares tendered to it and continued buying until it had 70 percent of the shares. The plan was to overwhelm the opposition at Martin Marietta and the courts before the 23rd of September (when Martin Marietta could buy Bendix) with the fact that Bendix owned almost all of Martin Marietta. It was not a bad plan, but it did not work. Nothing worked.

The Martin Marietta directors refused to resign voluntarily and be replaced by a Bendix-nominated board. The Delaware courts did not block Martin Marietta from voting its proxies prior to the Bendix shareholder meeting, so the vote on charter amendments was not held. The federal district court in Baltimore refused to forbid Martin Marietta from buying Bendix.

The argument made by Bendix in federal court had some strength, at least at first glance. They argued that because Bendix owned 70 percent of Martin Marietta, the latter's board was obliged not to do anything contrary to the interests and desires of its shareholders' wishes, namely buy Bendix. Martin Marietta's attorneys replied that its board had an irrevocable commitment to pay the Bendix shareholders who had tendered their shares. In resolving these confused notions of duty to Bendix shareholders, the federal court took a more direct business approach in its decisions on September 22:

> This Court finds, that in refusing to halt Marietta's offer, Marietta's board has acted in a manner reasonably believed to be in the best interests of Bendix shareholders. . . . [I]t is the considered view of Marietta's board that Bendix' current management has little managerial competence or experience in Marietta's business and, as a result, Marietta's management would be more competent to manage the combined Bendix-Marietta entity. . . . [T]his Court cannot, in keeping with the Maryland business judgment rule, say that it is unreasonable for Marietta's board to adhere to its view.[42]

Having a Maryland court make the decision may have helped Martin Marietta, but the essence of the decision seems right. In the end, the issue was which management should run the business. That is clearly not a matter the courts should decide.

The White Knight

In the closing days before the September 23 deadline, Agee and his wife, Mary Cunningham, along with other members of the Bendix team, flew to Maryland to try to persuade Martin Marietta to give up. It is not known what Agee offered, but it was not enough. By the 22nd of September, it was clear that Martin Marietta would buy the Bendix shares tendered to it. Faced with the possibility of losing to Martin Marietta and having part of his firm sold to United Technologies, Agee turned to a white knight, the Allied Corporation.

Under the agreement with Allied, the disparate elements of Bendix remained "intact." William Agee received the face-saving title of president of Allied. He soon pulled the rip cord on his golden parachute. Allied, who was a bridesmaid at both the Conoco and Marathon mergers, finally won the right to wear the winner's ring.

The Bendix agreement with Allied came too late in the day of the 22nd to prevent Martin Marietta from buying Bendix. Had the agreement been made a few hours earlier, the Williams Act would have reopened withdrawal rights for ten days, thus preventing Martin Marietta from buying the shares tendered to it. Martin Marietta bought Bendix on the 23rd. It then traded Allied its Bendix shares in return for a portion of the Martin Marietta shares held by Bendix and a standstill agreement. Martin Marietta was heavily in debt but still free. Its board's decisions to resist were quickly vindicated by the stock market. Within a year, its shares rose above the $48 per share offered by Bendix.

As usual, the lawyers, the arbs, and many others made a great deal of money. And because of the timing, the investment bankers got paid for three deals—the acquisition of Martin Marietta by Bendix, the acquisition of Bendix by Martin Marietta, and the acquisition of Bendix by Allied—for an estimated combined fee of almost $20 million.[43]

After Words

The Bendix offer for Martin Marietta was carefully researched. It fit a strategic plan. Shareholders oversubscribed the offer at the tender price. However, Martin Marietta remains independent and Bendix was sold on one afternoon to a corporation that seems to have been looking for any big purchase. There were too many bidders and too many deals arranged too quickly to believe this was all sensible business behavior. The result may be for the best but the process is worrisome.

Tender offers do not seem to have provided a mechanism for the expression of corporate democracy. For example, Martin Marietta shareholders who favored the merger with Bendix because they thought the combined firm would be more valuable were put in a quandary. If they sold their shares to Bendix, the merger was more likely, but they would not participate. On the other hand, if they held on to their Martin Marietta shares (to exchange them for Bendix or Allied shares), they implicitly voted against the merger.

The conundrum for the Martin Marietta shareholders who opposed the offer was even greater if they thought (1) that the offer was inadequate, (2) that Bendix's management was poor, but (3) believed Bendix had a good chance of succeeding in its offer. If shareholders held on to their shares and Bendix won, they received the lower, second-tier payment of Bendix shares and Bendix's possible poor management of Martin Marietta resources. If they tendered to Bendix, shareholders sold at less than what they believed to be full value and helped bring about the opposed takeover.

Is it relevant to the objectivity of Bruce Wasserstein that his advice to ignore the doomsday weapon coincided with the interests of First Boston? First Boston's payment was contingent on the purchase of Martin Marietta stock. Is it relevant that, as a result of following Wasserstein's advice, First Boston earned substantial fees even though Bendix was taken over by Allied? Do the hourly legal fees paid to Fried, Frank provide an incentive for Arthur Fleischer to be optimistic about the consequences of continuing the takeover battle?

It was clear after the Bendix affair that something was wrong with the takeover process. The *New York Times* and the *Washington Post* published articles blaming the egos of corporate executives, blaming the rapaciousness of investment bankers and merger lawyers, blaming the arbitrageurs, and blaming the two-tier tender offer.[44] The Securities and Exchange Commission voted to change the rules for two-tier tender offers and established an advisory panel to review the entire tender offer process.

The SEC's Advisory Committee on Tender Offers was a blue-ribbon panel dominated by active participants in merger transactions. The lawyers included Joseph Flom and Martin Lipton, and the investment bankers included Bruce Wasserstein of First Boston and Robert Greenhill of Morgan, Stanley. Edward Henessy, chairman of the board of Allied, fresh from his white knight experiences taking over Bendix, was one of the chief executive officers on the committee. Robert Rubin, the chief arb at Goldman, Sachs participated, as did senior officials from an accounting firm and a major commercial bank. The committee recommended that Congress and the SEC:

(1) Establish a single minimum time framework in which competing offers will expire at the same time;
(2) Keep proration and withdrawal rights open until the minimum offer time expires; and
(3) Extend an expiring offer period if a bidder raises or otherwise changes its offer.

The committee's recommendations to encourage multiple bids and eliminate confusing timing and bidding procedures were designed to make it easier for the unsophisticated investor to participate in the benefits of a takeover battle. If these recommendations were enacted the investor would no longer be faced with separate deadlines for proration and withdrawal or reopening of withdrawal rights. And if faced with a flurry of last minute bids, such as Mobil made for Conoco, the investor would have an additional opportunity to consider them. These recommendations would thus complete the changes initiated by the SEC with its December 1982 rule for two-tier offers.

By extending the proration period to equal the length of the offer, the new rule is simpler and puts the average shareholder on a more equal footing with the arbs and institutional investors, but it would change only slightly the dynamics of takeover battles by providing for a common expiration date of the Williams Act time periods. Neither the committee in its July 1983 report nor the SEC in its May 1984 recommendations to Congress suggested that tactics such as front-end-loaded, two-tier tender offers or defensive lockup agreements be prohibited. Instead, they focused more on the unseemliness of greenmail and golden parachutes. The SEC recommended forbidding the target's board of directors from approving golden parachute contracts during tender offers and forbidding payment of greenmail unless other shareholders were offered repurchase at the same price (or unless a shareholder vote approved payment of the greenmail).

Despite the advisory committee report, the SEC recommendations, and renewed fears of takeovers at giant corporations, no new laws governing mergers were enacted in 1984.

PART TWO

MERGERS PAST AND MERGERS PRESENT

W hy do we have so many large mergers? Why aren't they stopped by antitrust laws? The second question is easier to answer so it is dealt with here first. Why there are so many large mergers is only partially answered in Chapter 6 and throughout this book.

Antitrust laws have not prevented the hundreds of megamergers that have taken place since 1974. To the surprise of some, these laws have never made specific reference to corporate size. The longstanding tradition in antitrust against large size, and especially against mergers between giant firms has in recent years diminished, nearly to the vanishing point. Instead, antitrust has become almost purely an economic set of rules designed to prevent corporations from obtaining or exercising monopoly power. The goal of this newer antitrust is to reduce consumer prices and increase business efficiency by promoting competition.

With preservation of competition as its objective, antitrust continues to forbid mergers between rival firms that would reduce overall competition in a particular industry. As the economic foundations of antitrust legislation have become more explicit and better communicated, the laws have become largely self-enforcing. Only a handful of the thousand or so mergers that are screened annually by antitrust officials result in lawsuits. Most enforcement takes place within the offices of corporations and their lawyers by preventing mergers that might be challenged.

Perhaps because of this transformation antitrust has ceased to be the scourge of the business community. On the contrary, it has become a model of how corporate executives believe regulation ought to work. Public goals are encouraged with minimal dictation by government officials. When obeyed, the antitrust laws, and the competition they foster, are thought to pressure firms to offer better products and service at the lowest profitable price.

How effective antitrust is in achieving any of its objectives is largely a matter of conjecture. Nevertheless, support for antitrust continues to grow. For example, the European Economic Community and West Germany have, in recent years, copied large portions of the American laws. This widespread support for antitrust seems to rest on the unarguable benefits of its objectives, the plausibility of its economic theory, and the lack of organized opposition in the business community.

Megamergers take place then within an antitrust framework that has been fully accommodated for by corporate planners. When executives risk antitrust prosecution for a merger, it is done knowingly. Antitrust objections are usually over matters of detail that can be resolved through negotiation.

As Chapter 5 makes clear, this cozy relationship between large mergers and antitrust is very new. Antitrust's traditional antagonism toward mergers influenced the direction of corporate growth for almost a century. In doing so, it helped to change corporate organization so as to include megamergers.

Why have antitrust attitudes changed so radically? Is the change permanent or merely the product of particular presidential administrations. Chapter 5 concludes that, although politics have played a role, the changes reflect more complex factors. These factors are not unalterable, but the current orientation of antitrust has been developing for at least two decades and is unlikely to disappear quickly.

The departure point for Chapter 6 is the peculiar propensity of mergers to occur in groups or waves. We are in the midst of the fourth such wave in the past hundred years. Although we can identify certain leading characteristics of each of these merger waves, we do not have conclusive evidence of why they occur. One motive behind the periodic popularity of merging may simply be the perception that everyone else is doing it. The precipitating factor for a merger wave may be a new business idea, but the intensity may also reflect group psychology.

CHAPTER 5

MERGERS AND THE WORLD OF ANTITRUST

Antitrust has changed. It is no longer an angry and frightened populist movement fighting the growing power of big business. Today, it is a bureaucratically enforced set of legal rules which approved the $6.6 billion acquisition of Marathon Oil by U.S. Steel but trimmed a few hundred million dollars of anticompetitive fat from Chevron's $13 billion acquisition of Gulf Oil.

Antitrust merger law has become pervasive. No company can consider undertaking a large acquisition without consulting its antitrust lawyers. Prior to a merger, packets of documents must be sent to the antitrust offices at the Department of Justice and the Federal Trade Commission. In large complex transactions these packets may grow to cartons, or crates, or even carloads. But as Attorney General William French Smith told a corporate audience in 1982, the close scrutiny of large transactions by modern antitrust does not rest on an assumption that big means bad.[1]

Modern antitrust law shapes the kinds of mergers a firm may undertake. Its aim is to prevent monopoly power, not the growth of corporations by merger. As its enforcement has become more effective, antitrust has altered the acquisition patterns of large corporations. We do not see all the firms in the tobacco industry or all the firms in the sugar industry combining to form a monopoly. Such consolidations, common at the turn of the century, no longer occur. Instead, the urge to merge must now be satisfied by the combina-

103

tion of firms in totally unrelated businesses. Such mergers became typical in the 1960s and continue today as megamergers.

Pervasive antitrust has helped alter the concept of a corporation by encouraging conglomerate mergers. Instead of being one organizational form for conducting a single line of business, the corporation has become an independent entity that conducts any number of businesses. The Greyhound Corporation, for example, earns most of its income from businesses other than its bus service.[2] The Penn Central Corporation has long been out of the railroad industry.[3] Esmark sold its Swift Meats subsidiary before Esmark was taken over by Beatrice Foods.[4]

Corporations no longer necessarily have a continuity of business purpose, ownership, or management.

Blocked by modern antitrust and competitive considerations from expansion within an industry, successful corporations thus acquire unrelated firms in order to broaden their field of investment. This kind of expansion, unlike monopoly mergers at the turn of the century, has no natural limit. There is no signal to corporations that they have accomplished their purpose, so they continue to grow by merger and internal expansion. It is ironic that antitrust, whose original concern was corporate size, should have helped form a corporate viewpoint of unbounded growth.

The evolution of antitrust from a broad-based, political movement to narrowed law enforcement should be understood historically and not merely from the standpoint of legislative intent or economic doctrine. To trace this transformation, therefore, we must first understand when and why antitrust strayed from its origins.

THE FEAR OF POWER: 1890

Antitrust grew out of the fear of corporate power. Toward the close of the nineteenth century, huge enterprises were formed from many previously separate businesses. Typically, these new firms dominated a single industry, such as oil, tobacco, steel, whiskey, or sugar. The unprecedented size provoked widespread fear of the power that lay unchecked in the hands of these corporate giants.

Senator John Sherman, author of the 1890 antitrust act which bears his name,[5] declared: "If we will not endure a king as a political power we should not endure a king over the production, transportation and sale of any of the necessaries of life.''[6] And he went on to warn Congress:

> The popular mind is agitated with problems that may disturb social order, and among them none is more threatening than the inequality of condition of wealth and opportunity that has grown within a single generation out of the concentration of capital into vast combinations to control production and trade and to break down competition. . . . You must heed [the] appeal or be ready for the socialist, the communist or the nihilist.[7]

These new business entities inspired awe, admiration, fear and hatred. If the humble origins of the new captains of industry made for success stories in the American tradition, their creations, the giant enterprises, destroyed forever the original character of America. Since the War of Independence, we had had no king, no aristocracy, no dominant landowners, no established church. Richard Hofstadter, the Pulitzer Prize-winning historian, has written:

> From its colonial beginnings through most of the nineteenth century ours was a nation of farmers and small town entrepreneurs—ambitious, mobile, optimistic, speculative, antiauthoritarian, egalitarian and competitive. As time went on Americans came to take it for granted that property would be widely diffused, that economic and political power would be decentralized. The fury with which they could be mobilized against any institution that even appeared to violate these expectations by posing a threat of monopoly was manifest in the irrational assault on the Bank of the United States during the Jackson Presidency.[8]

The fear of the nineteenth century corporate giants was rational. They had monopoly power. They used the resources at their disposal to maintain and expand that power. Henry Frick, for example, sent in hundreds of armed Pinkerton agents to break the strike he had provoked by lowering wages at Carnegie's Homestead steelworks. When that failed, he persuaded the government to bring in soldiers to end a five-month seige of the factories and break the union.

At times businessmen were given a choice of either joining the new enterprises or being driven out of business. Matthew Josephson's flamboyant historical account, *The Robber Barons*, describes John D. Rockefeller's method of building Standard Oil. [Rockefeller] would say:

> "You see, this scheme is bound to work. There is no chance for anyone outside of Standard Oil. But we are going to give everyone a chance to come

in. You are to turn over your refinery to my appraisers, and I will give you Standard Oil stock or cash, as you prefer, for the value we put upon it. . . ."

Now a sort of terror swept silently over the oil trade. In a vague panic, competitors saw the Standard Oil officers come to them and say (as Rockefeller's own brother and rival, Frank, testified in 1876): "If you don't sell your property to us it will be valueless because we have got the advantage with the railroads."

The railroad rates indeed were suddenly doubled to outsiders, and those refiners who resisted [Standard Oil] came and expostulated; then they became frightened and disposed of their property.[9]

As these examples suggest, the outcry against corporate power was not limited to complaints of monopoly profiteering. Indeed, as Robert Lande's legal review of the goals of the Sherman Act shows,[10] consumers benefited from a general decline in the cost of living from the end of the Civil War to 1890. Part of that decline may have been due to the more efficient production methods of the larger, threatening business enterprises. In any case, Lande, like the careful historians of this period—Hofstadter, Letwin, and Thorelli[11]—concludes that groups favoring the Sherman Act wanted to prevent the "accumulation of power by large corporations and the men who controlled them."[12]

The antitrust sentiment in 1890s congressional debate went beyond the power over prices:

Representative Mason: Some say the trusts have made products cheaper, have reduced prices; but if the price of oil, for instance, were reduced to 1 cent a barrel it would not right the wrong done to the people of this country by the "trusts" which have destroyed legitimate competition and driven honest men from legitimate enterprises.[13]

Senator Hoar: The complaint has come from all parts and all classes of this country of these great monopolies, which are becoming not only in some cases an actual injury to the comfort of ordinary life, but are a menace to republican institutions themselves.[14]

The initial outcome of this widespread feeling was passage of the Sherman Antitrust Act which only purported to condemn "every combination in restraint of trade" and "attempt to monopolize." The Sherman Act of 1890 was unenforced for almost a decade. Revisionist historian Gabriel Kolko has argued that a cynical Congress intended no effect,[15] but Hofstadter's opposing view is more persuasive:

[T]he problem of big business and the threat of monopoly were still so new that it was hard to get one's bearings. Bigness had come with such a rush that its momentum seemed irresistible. No one knew when or how it could be stopped. . . .

Since it had been widely assumed that competition, being "natural," would be largely self-perpetuating the [American traditional] had not reckoned with the possible necessity of underwriting competition by statute.[16]

The problem for Congress and the courts—how to eliminate the power of big business without losing the benefits of competition and mass production—is still not resolved. Nevertheless, by the turn of the century the Sherman Act had gained authority. And with the support of Presidents Theodore Roosevelt and William Howard Taft, major antitrust lawsuits were instituted that resulted in the break up of two of the most notorious trusts—Standard Oil and American Tobacco.

The Supreme Court, although unequivocal in its condemnation of Standard Oil and American Tobacco, did not declare any of their individual actions, such as buying out competitors or selling products below cost, to be illegal in and of themselves. Rather, the Court announced a "rule of reason" in which the totality of circumstances were to be considered in determining legality. Only when mergers were undertaken for the purpose of monopolizing an industry were they clearly unlawful and then perhaps only if accompanied by bad acts.

These decisions issued in 1911, angered supporters of antitrust because its restrictions on business were vague and loose, and because they did not provide any means to reduce the power of large corporations. Dissatisfaction with the Court's rulings spilled over into the presidential campaign of 1912 and the following sessions of Congress.

In 1914 two new laws were passed, the Clayton Antitrust Act[17] and the Federal Trade Commission Act.[18] These two laws represented different philosophies about how to curb corporate power. The former reflected a belief that Congress could write specific rules outlawing bad corporate behavior, while the latter held that only an expert agency could develop rules separating the good from the bad. Section 7 of the Clayton Act prohibited mergers that "lessened competition" or "tended to create a monopoly." The FTC Act forbade "unfair methods of competition." Neither of these laws resulted in a clear code of business behavior, and neither addressed the issue of corporate power directly. And because of the wording of the Clayton Act antimerger provision (it made no reference to acquiring the assets of other firms, only their stock), the law of mergers was left essentially unchanged.

By the mid-1920s, when merger activity heated up again, large firms had discovered they could buy out competitors without violating the Clayton Act if they purchased a rival's assets (factories, offices, inventory, etc.) instead of its stock.[19] The omission of asset acquisitions was not accidental. Congress wanted to preserve economic freedom and thought it necessary only to include stock acquisitions. The bad trusts had been established by "the development of holding companies and [by] the secret acquisition of competitors through the purchase of . . . stock."[20]

However narrow the legislated remedy, the purpose of these new laws remained as broad as those of the Sherman Act. Again, Hofstadter described the motives:

> The . . . case against business organizations was not confined to economic considerations, nor even to the more intangible sphere of economic morals. Still more widely felt was a fear founded in political realities—the fear that the great business combinations, being the only centers of wealth and power, would be able to lord it over all other interests and thus put an end to traditional American democracy. . . .[21]

Despite the asset loophole, no serious attempts were made to pass a new antimerger law. A number of reasons would explain this seeming indifference. First, by 1914 the wave of mergers which began in the 1890s was over, so public attention was not aroused by ongoing giant mergers. Second, when a new merger wave began in the mid-1920s, the transactions created large competitors, such as Bethlehem Steel, which challenged the existing dominance of monopoly firms like U.S. Steel. Third, it was 1934 before the Supreme Court had decided unequivocally that neither of the two new laws could be used to oppose mergers that were not stock acquisitions.[22] And fourth, big business in the United States had become commonplace and thus less frightening to the public mind.

By the 1920s and 1930s, it became apparent that corporate growth did not, once begun, continue to accelerate. The first merger wave had come and gone and so had a second. Although they had altered American life, large-scale acquisitions had not established a business oligarchy. Moreover, many Americans were benefitting from big business. The enormous productivity of the large enterprises introduced a new range of products—the automobile, the sewing machine, the telephone, the radio—within the economic means of millions, and offered badly needed jobs to both the skilled and the unskilled workers. According to historian Louis Galambos, from the 1880s to 1940 Americans "slowly and unevenly came to accept giant enterprises as a necessary element in their urban industrial system. The people gradually adopted organizational values."[23] Acceptance and recognition did not, as we shall see, entirely eliminate the fear of big business however.

For all their shortcomings, the Sherman and Clayton Acts had a substantial impact on corporate mergers: They eliminated the most blatant abuses of corporate power; they established that competitors could not join together to monopolize an industry; and they set up a standard which allowed firms to complain if they had been driven out of operation by "unfair" business practices. These were significant accomplishments and no doubt did much to secure public acceptance of large corporations.

POWERFUL ANTITRUST: 1950

The fear of big business was reawakened during World War II. In Nazi Germany and Imperial Japan, Americans believed, the leaders of huge, concentrated industries supported and encouraged the militaristic policies of their governments. It was though that had Germany and Japan been more pluralistic, democratic nations, their citizens would have resisted both tyranny and war. So to prevent the concentration of industry and preserve the American way of life, Congress passed an aggressive antimerger law: the Celler-Kefauver Act of 1950.[24]

Representative Emanuel Celler was explicit on the lesson of recent history.

I want to point out the danger of this trend toward more and better combines. I read from a report filed with [the Secretary of War] as to the history of cartelization and concentration of industry in Germany: "Germany under the Nazi set-up built up a great series of industrial monopolies in steel, rubber, coal and other materials. The monopolies soon got control of Germany, brought Hitler to power and forced virtually the whole world into war."[25]

Senator Estes Kefauver explained the rationale behind the act in terms that echoed the fears expressed by Senator Sherman sixty years earlier.

> Through monopolistic mergers the people are losing the power to direct their own economic welfare. When they lose [that] power they also lose the means to direct their political future. I am not an alarmist, but the history of what has taken place in other nations where mergers and concentrations have placed economic control in the hands of a very few people is too clear to pass over easily. A point is reached, and we are rapidly reaching that point in this country, where the public steps in to take over when concentration and monopoly gain too much power. The taking over by the public through its government always follows one or two methods and has one or two political results. It either results in a Fascist state or the nationalization of industries and thereafter a Socialist or Communist state.[26]

Kefauver's equation of mergers and economic concentration was based on a 1948 report of the Federal Trade Commission that announced its conclusions in equally apocalyptic terms. The FTC reported that between 1940 and 1947 over 5 percent of all manufacturing assets in the United States had disappeared through acquisitions of small firms. The report warned:

> [N]o great stretch of the imagination is required to foresee that if nothing is done to check the growth in concentration, either the giant corporations will ultimately take over the country, or the Government will be impelled to step in and impose some form of direct regulation in the public interest.[27]

The problem in 1950, as it had been in 1890 and 1914, was how to write a law that responded to those political concerns without destroying the productive economic system. The solution adopted was to amend Section 7 of the Clayton Act (which dealt with mergers). The Celler-Kefauver Act eliminated the asset loophole, prohibited mergers that reduced competition "in any line of commerce" (not just mergers that reduced competition between the merging firms), and outlawed mergers that "*may* substantially lessen competition" (not just those where the anticompetitive effects are certain). Although the legislation still made no mention of corporate power, the statutory changes were substantial. The new law eliminated all obvious means for avoiding the restriction on acquiring competitors. And for the first time the law applied to the acquisition of noncompeting firms (for example, a manufacturing corporation buying out its suppliers) if the merger was likely to reduce competition.

Equal in importance to the statutory changes, according to the Supreme Court in the Brown Shoe case,[28] was the clear intent Congress had expressed throughout its legislative history. That history showed that "the dominant theme . . . was a fear of . . . a rising tide of economic concentration in the America economy."[29] The Court further explained that "Congress saw the process of concentration in American business as a dynamic force; it sought to assure the Federal Trade Commission and the courts the power to brake this force at its outset and before it gathered momentum."[30] The law provided "authority for arresting mergers at a time when the trend to a lessening of competition was still in its incipiency."[31]

The intent to enact a strict antimerger law was clear, but it was up to the Court to fashion the standard of illegality because "Congress neither adopted nor rejected specifically any particular tests for measuring . . . the anticompetitive effects of a merger. . . ."[32]

In Brown Shoe and subsequent cases, the Court, under Chief Justice Earl Warren, developed an economic analysis that seemed to implement the political ideals of Congress. In each case, the Supreme Court used its discretion to search every line of commerce for any probability of a lessening of competition or any trend toward concentration, and in every case found against the mergers. This provoked a dissent by Justice Potter Stewart in the Von's Grocery case:

> [T]he Court pronounces its work consistent with the line of our decisions under [Section 7 of the Clayton Act] since the passage of the 1950 amendment. The sole consistency I can find is that under section 7, the Government always wins. . . . The merger between Von's and Shopping Bag produced a firm with 1.4 percent of the stores and 7.5 percent of the grocery sales and resulted in a 1.1 percent increase in the market share enjoyed by the two largest firms in the market. . . . [Those] figures are hardly [an] "undue percentage" of the market, nor are [they a] "significant increase in concentration."[33]

There is no doubt that the Celler-Kefauver Act fundamentally altered corporate acquisition patterns. It eliminated almost all large-scale mergers between competing firms and between giant firms and their suppliers or customers. The assets acquired in such mergers declined from about half of all mergers in 1950 to about 20 percent in the mid-1960s.[34]

But the act had little effect on the acquisition of unrelated firms. In fact, in 1967 and 1968, following the Von's Grocery decision, the

United States experienced a sudden surge in mergers. Despite its expressed concern with corporate growth, the statute had been interpreted to require some showing of harm to competition. So, like the Clayton Act of 1914, the 1950 Celler-Kefauver Act proved effective in stopping the mergers of the past, but not the mergers of the future.

THE ECONOMICS CONSENSUS: 1968

The development of a powerful antitrust law after passage of the Celler-Kefauver Act was based in part on an activist judiciary and on a political and academic consensus regarding the merits of antitrust. Academics, especially economists, fashioned arguments that courts could adopt in striking down mergers.

Since the late 1930s economist Gardiner Means and others at the congressionally created Temporary National Economic Committee (TNEC) had argued that the American economy performed poorly because it was dominated by big business. For example, the TNEC concluded in 1941 that economic concentration was a major problem that required the passage of new antimerger legislation.[35] But neither the TNEC nor economists since have been able to explain with any precision just how much big business hurts the economy or which mergers threaten competition.

Hofstadter has summarized the views of Edward Mason, Carl Kaysen, Joel Dirlam, Alfred Kahn, John Kenneth Galbraith, and other leading economists of the 1950s and 1960s who supported aggressive antitrust enforcement:

> What makes it possible to institutionalize antitrust activities . . . is not a consensus among economists as to its utility in enhancing economic efficiency, but a rough consensus in society at large as to its value in curbing the dangers of excessive market power. As in the beginning, it is based on a political and moral judgment rather than economic measurement or even distinctively economic criteria.[36]

This consensus, begun under Democratic administrations, was furthered by the Eisenhower administration in 1955. Attorney General Herbert Brownell's National Committee to Study the Antitrust Laws unanimously endorsed the antitrust laws that had been strengthened by the Celler-Kefauver Act.

Given this broad support, it is not surprising the Supreme Court declared that the Celler-Kefauver Act required only "probabilities, not certainties,"[37] of economic harm when challenging a merger. Economic theory was usually able to sustain this light burden. The strongest antitrust economic theory was based on the following proposition: The smaller the number of competitors, the less the competition between them. When few enough, rival firms will sell their products at the monopoly price set by explicit agreement or by mutual recognition of the benefit of not competing on price. When more firms compete to sell the same product, coordination becomes impossible. Then prices fall since all firms are forced to compete for sales by producing the best product at the lowest profitable price.

This theory, which remains at the heart of antitrust economic analysis to this day, suited antitrust perfectly. It not only provided a rationale for stopping a merger, the act of stopping that merger reduced prices for consumers, preserved the independent existence of the smaller firm, prevented increased concentration of economic power, and promoted production efficiency and product innovation. These points were all part of the ideal state Congress sought to re-establish through the antitrust laws.

But as Justice Stewart's dissent in the Von's Grocery case illustrates, even if one accepts the theory, there can be disputes over how many firms are needed to maintain an ideal state of competition. Moreover, even if valid as a generalization, the theory does not necessarily describe the effects of a particular merger. A merger might increase competition by creating a stronger rival to the leading firms in that industry. The merged firm operating on a larger scale of production might have lower costs, might have the resources to be more innovative, and might sell products for a lower price. Even explicit price-fixing agreements might not be less likely with more competitors. Facing "ruinous" competition from too many firms might force competitors to agree on prices. The merger might also have no effect on economic concentration or might even reduce concentration if the merging firms would have been unable to survive separately.

Notwithstanding these weaknesses, the economic theories condemning mergers of direct competitors (or horizontal mergers as they are called by antitrust lawyers) were stronger than the theories that condemned mergers between customers and suppliers (vertical mergers) or mergers between unrelated firms (conglomerate mergers). Vertical mergers are harmful if a manufacturer buys all of its possible raw-material suppliers or all possible retailers. Such acquisitions would violate the Sherman Act's prohibition on monopolization. Under the Clayton Act, however, vertical mergers were said to be suspect even without the danger of monopolization. If a large manufacturer bought a small retailer, this might shift the structure of the industry in an anticompetitive direction. The acquisition, for example, could initiate a series of imitative vertical acquisitions that would eliminate suppliers for independent retailers and thereby make it difficult for new firms to start operating because they would have to start as both manufacturer and retailer. Conglomerate acquisitions by large firms might also reduce competition. By using the greater economic resources of the acquiring firm, it might be possible to drive competitors of the target firm out of business by lowering prices or by saturation advertising.

All theories calling for antitrust enforcement against the threat of horizontal, vertical, or conglomerate mergers are necessarily speculative. That is inherent in the Celler-Kefauver Act, which was designed to prevent an anticompetitive effect by requiring a court decision before a merger takes place. Furthermore, because the statute was intended to stop a *trend* toward lessening competition "in its incipiency," the anticompetitive effect need not occur directly as a result of the challenged merger. Even in the case of horizontal mergers, there is no direct way to prove that if the challenged acquisition were permitted the remaining firms would conspire or coordinate their actions to set monopoly prices for their products.

The relatively greater weakness of the nonhorizontal theories was that they depended on other acts occurring after the merger. The cumulative effect would be anticompetitive. In contrast, horizontal theory presumed competitors always want to fix prices and will do so when the number of rival firms becomes small enough. Some vertical merger theories require that a series of acquisitions occur or that the acquisition be imitated before there is any danger of economic harm. The harm projected to result from conglomerate mergers is often based on the assumption that the acquiring firm will choose particular anticompetitive strategies for its new enterprises.

Of course, the harm to competition from conglomerate or vertical mergers may be as likely, or even more likely, than harm from horizontal mergers. No one knows, because firms do not advertise their anticompetitive intentions and mergers that are prevented have no effects. So the empirical evidence to support any of the above theories has been indirect and subject to many attacks.

A direct theoretical connection exists, however, between reduced competition and price fixing. A smaller number of competitors makes it less complicated to negotiate agreements and probably easier to monitor them. Horizontal mergers, which necessarily eliminate at least one competitor, are therefore logical transactions to stop. A vertical or conglomerate merger has no such direct theoretical link with economic harm.

In a 1960 article, Derek Bok, then a law professor (now president) at Harvard, argued for a practical way to combine economic learning with the legal standards of the Celler-Kefauver Act.[38] He suggested that because the current state of economic knowledge made it impossible to judge the individual effects of a merger, the courts should adopt a series of rules based on the number of competitors selling a product. The courts would assume that if few competitors sold a product, a merger between large firms would reduce competition. This general approach has been adopted. Antitrust litigation in merger cases does not, by and large, consider the specific economic impact of the challenged merger; rather, the litigation centers on defining the product, how many firms sell the product, and the percentage of sales belonging to the merging firms.

Even these items of basic information can be difficult to identify. If, for example, cold breakfast cereal is the product market in question, there are a certain number of obvious competitors. But should we not also include in the same product market makers of hot cereals and sellers of bacon, eggs, milk, and juice? Should we not include all food producers or all firms that *could* provide cold cereal or potential providers of breakfast foods in general? Common sense suggests that cereal is a distinct product market, but competition is a matter of degree and opinions vary on both facts and interpretation of facts, as merger cases usually demonstrate.

The plausibility of all these theories for the courts was probably aided by the fact that there was no organized opposition to the antitrust laws within the economics profession. Economists who viewed the business behavior very differently endorsed antitrust including Joe Bain's structural economics and George Stigler's neoclassical price theory economics.

The highwater mark of antitrust enforcement theories was probably reached in 1968. In that year, President Johnson's assistant attorney general for antitrust, Donald Turner, a Harvard law professor with economics training, announced a comprehensive set of merger guidelines. The guidelines summarized the criteria the Department of Justice would use in deciding whether to challenge announced mergers. In that same year, a presidential *Task Force on Antitrust Policy*, chaired by University of Chicago law school dean Phillip Neal, recommended strengthening antitrust with new legislation.[39]

The Department of Justice merger guidelines described a wide variety of horizontal, vertical, and conglomerate theories drawn from case law and economic theory. In addition, the guidelines tried to define more precisely the circumstances under which the Justice Department's Antitrust Division would challenge mergers based on each theory. For example, it was well known that the division would challenge even quite small mergers between competitors in highly concentrated product markets. The guidelines added illustrative numbers: A highly concentrated market was defined as one in which four firms made 75 percent of the products sold. A firm making 10 percent of those products would be sued if it tried to buy a firm making as little as 2 percent of the total production. In a less highly concentrated market, the 10 percent firm would likely be permitted to merge with a firm having a market share of up to 4 percent. Lest even these strict rules promote a spate of smaller mergers, the guidelines warned:

> Because changes in enforcement policy will be made as the occasion demands ..., the unamended guidelines should not be regarded as barring ... any action ... deem[ed] necessary to achieve the purposes of §7.[40]

The antitrust concern with concentrated markets and conglomerate mergers was confirmed by the *Neal Report*. The report called for new legislation granting antitrust officials the authority to break up large firms solely on the grounds that they dominated concentrated industries. It also advocated new legislation barring large firms from merging with even small firms in unrelated markets if the small firm controlled a large share of its product market.

These documents, although not universally endorsed, purported to reflect a broad consensus within the antitrust community. Long before E. F. Schumacher wrote his book, *Small is Beautiful*,[41] antitrust experts had agreed. Although President Nixon's antitrust chief was even more aggressive in attacking large conglomerate mergers based on theories of general economic concentration and although Senator Phillip Hart introduced deconcentration legislation in Congress, neither of these later efforts succeeded. The consensus that had looked so firm in 1968 dissolved soon after.

THE NEW LEARNING: 1974

By 1974 academic consensus on antitrust had collapsed. At the same time scholarly opinion was shifting, the antitrust bureaucracies were moving from enforcement policies supported by political theory to policies based on economic theory. And by the end of the decade claims were being made for a new consensus that greatly reduced the role of antitrust. Certainly by the 1980s in the administration of President Ronald Reagan the Department of Justice and the Federal Trade Commission have adopted much less aggressive enforcement policies.

Almost before the ink was dry on the Justice Department's "Merger Guidelines" and the *Neal Report*, President-elect Richard Nixon appointed George Stigler to chair a Task Force on Productivity and Competition.[42] The report cast doubt on the need for the deconcentration and antimerger legislation advocated by the Neal commission and for the enforcement of antitrust laws against conglomerate mergers.

The Chicago School

George Stigler was a persuasive individual to repudiate the Neal Commission's recommendations. Stigler, an economist at the University of Chicago who received the Nobel Prize for Economics in 1982, is, with his economist colleague and fellow Nobel Prize-winner Milton Friedman, a leader in the "Chicago School" of economics. The Chicago School is noted for its strong reliance on pure price theory. Its adherents believe that the behavior of individuals in business can best be predicted by assuming that all actions are based on personal economic interests, that individuals know their own economic preferences, and that individuals can identify the goods and services that will satisfy those preferences. They also believe that the interaction of individuals in voluntary transactions will automatically create the best possible distribution of goods because parties will not agree to transactions unless benefits accrue from the transaction. The free marketplace, which is the sum of all such transactions, benefits society by rewarding hardworking producers of well-made, affordable goods with many customers and punishing producers of shoddy, overpriced items. Like Adam Smith before them, these neoclassical economists believe the individual pursuit of selfish interests ("profit maximizing behavior") best promotes the public interest. Although many Chicago School economists admit that the theory does not hold up perfectly in actual marketplace operations, they maintain that the theory is a fair description of events and that, in general, the market will resolve issues better than government regulation.

Despite the bias against government interference implicit in pure price theory, Stigler had been a stalwart of antitrust enforcement throughout the 1950s and 1960s. He and other members of the Chicago School found antitrust to be one of the few acceptable forms of government regulation because, they believed, it reinforced the self-regulating character of the marketplace. Their view of the free market paralleled in important ways the antitrusters' small-business ideal of a self-regulating society.

It was thus not surprising that the relatively conservative Neal commission took comfort, when making its recommendation for de-concentration legislation, in quoting Stigler:

> In the manufacturing sector there are few industries in which the minimum efficient size is as much as five percent of the industry's output and concentration must be explained on other grounds.[43]

Because few major industries had anywhere near the twenty competitors efficiency seemed to permit, the implications of the *Neal Report* for big business were ominous. The disassociation of Stigler and the Nixon administration from that view must have been comforting.

The object of the dissident antitrust movement was not Stigler. His position had been perhaps an embarrassment because the dissenters were also committed Chicago price theorists. Their primary opponent was economist Joe Bain of the University of California, Berkeley.

In the 1950s, Bain had published studies that provided a theoretical and empirical foundation for aggressive antitrust policy.[44] Bain found that profit rates were higher in concentrated industries (which he defined as industries in which eight or fewer firms produced at least 70% of the goods). This smaller number of producers could reduce their competition and thereby earn some monopoly profits. Like Stigler, Bain found evidence that these product markets could support a larger number of efficient producers. But unlike Stigler, Bain concluded large firms could and did do many things that created barriers to new competition. In other words, unless antitrust intervened, the large producers in a market would continue to earn monopoly profits.

Bain was less trusting in the romantic antitrust ideal of a self-regulating market than the Chicago School was. Bain and other industrial-organization economists did not believe the free market, if left to itself, would produce desireable results for society. He saw that the market was imperfect and thought it would get worse unless adequately policed by antitrust.

To implement their views Bain and others developed the structure-conduct-performance theory: Bad structure (few manufacturers) facilitated bad conduct (price fixing or price leadership) which produced bad performance (high prices and monopoly profits). The presence of any one of these three elements implied the existence of the others. High profits, for example, implied an anticompetitive structure (that is, too few competitors and barriers preventing new competitors). Use of economic power—tying the sale of one product to the sale of another (paper for a photocopy machine, for example)—implied a bad market structure. This approach provided a rich source of proof for any number of antitrust cases.

The Chicago School had argued that most of antitrust law was unnecessary because the free market could cure the alleged competitive problem. Worse yet, some antitrust enforcement actually hurt competition by prohibiting business practices consumers wanted.[45] By 1974 the Chicago School was ready for a more comprehensive attack on structural antitrust. A heads-on confrontation occurred at a conference sponsored by Columbia University.

Issue-by-issue attackers and defenders of structural antitrust paired off in sessions at Airlie House in Virginia.[46] John McGee, an economist from the University of Washington, took on Bain's structuralist successor and then director of the FTC's Bureau of Economics, F. M. Scherer, on the question of minimum efficient size. McGee, who had made his reputation "proving" that the Standard Oil Trust had not sold products below cost in its drive for control of oil, maintained that larger firms can achieve greater production efficiencies. Yale Brozen of the University of Chicago, squared off with H. Michael Mann, another former Bureau of Economics director, on the question of barriers to entering product markets. Brozen, whose research had "proven" that concentrated industries did not display persistent high profit rates, maintained that advertising did not erect barriers preventing new firms from entering high-profit industries, thus competing away the monopoly profits. Advertising was instead the means by which new firms were able to break into an established product market. Harold Demsetz, a UCLA economics professor, took on Leonard Weiss' defense of the concentrated-industry, high-profit correlation. Demsetz held that only the largest firms earned higher profits. From the fact that only some firms earned the high profits he concluded those profits must be a result of greater efficiency, not price fixing. If more were needed, Demsetz's UCLA colleague J. Fred Weston had maintained elsewhere that competition was too complex to make tacit price-fixing agreements workable, so the only problem for competition was overt, detectable price-fixing conspiracies that could be prosecuted under the Sherman Act.

The attack on structural antitrust could not have been more direct. Big business was not bad, it was the epitome of good. Large corporate size was the reward for efficiently satisfying consumer wishes. Continued growth was proof of that efficiency. Monopoly price fixing was unlikely even with few competitors because coordination was difficult and easily detected. If successful, the profits of price fixing would quickly entice new producers who would increase the supply of the product and thereby drive down the price.

While McGee, Brozen, Demsetz, and Weston failed to convince their structuralist counterparts with their "new learning," the attack fundamentally altered the debate over antitrust issues. For the first time in twenty years, powerful antitrust was on the defensive. No longer could antitrust supporters assert without contradiction, that enforcement would implement political, social, and economic goals. The new learning suggested that achievement of these goals of antitrust did not necessarily move in the same direction. Counterarguments quickly followed from antitrust supporters in an attempt to preserve the structuralist position. McGee's views on the efficiency of large size were largely unsupported by empirical evidence, and Brozen's evidence on the deterioration of high profit margins might be explained by other theories. (Nobel Prize-winner Herbert Simon's "satisficing" concept, for example, suggested that the managers and workers could absorb the monopoly profits in personal benefits.)[47] Demsetz's evidence of the high profits of market leaders could be explained by product differentiation. But any such refutations were met by stepped-up methodological arguments, differing interpretations, and more debate.

Antitrust enforcement had assumed consensus and had not shouldered the burden of proving specific harm in a particular case because it was enforcing multiple goals. If efficiency were not improved by stopping a merger, it had been assumed efficiency would not be hurt and political diversity and entrepreneurial opportunity would be preserved. Now the assumed compatibility of those goals were under attack. Of course, the new learning was at least as uncertain as prior generalizations about the effects of a particular merger transaction, but the former consensus on the nature of those effects was now gone.

At this same time, the political basis of antitrust was under attack from other Chicago hardliners. Judge Robert Bork, a dissenting member of the Neal commission and member of the Yale law faculty, had written in the 1960s a tour-de-force history of the Sherman Act that concluded that the "real" purpose of Congress in these matters was to prohibit monopoly restrictions on production output and not to prevent the centralization of political or social power or even to prevent transfers of wealth resulting from monopoly prices.[48] While this article made little impact initially, by 1978, when Bork included his interpretation as part of his widely read book *The Antitrust Paradox*,[49] it helped undermine preexisting confidence in congressional intent.

Donald Turner, author of the 1968 "Merger Guidelines," for example, modified his views. Writing in 1960 with Carl Kaysen, he had concluded that antitrust "rests basically on a political judgment,"[50] but by 1978 his multi-volume antitrust treatise with Harvard law colleague Phillip Areeda stated:

[P]olitical forces are too numerous, diverse and confusingly countervailing to permit any satisfying conclusions about the political effects of market concentration or economic size. If anything, it is the number of people whose interests are directly involved in a particular economic activity, rather than the structure of the market, that primarily determines political impact; and that is an inseparable feature of democratic government.[51]

Stanford University law professor William Baxter, later assistant attorney general for antitrust under President Reagan, wrote in 1977, "As one of the initial drafters and authors of the deconcentration act which first appeared in the Neal Report . . . , it seems particularly appropriate that I recant. The state of economic art has changed somewhat since 1968."[52]

By 1978 University of Chicago law professor, now Judge, Richard Posner was able to claim at an antitrust symposium that Chicago analysis had won its basic points:

> No longer is it such a simple thing to identify a Harvard or a Chicago position on issues of antitrust policy. Partly this is a matter of growing consensus; partly a shift from disagreement over basic premises, methodology and ideology toward technical disagreements of the sort that would be found in a totally nonideological field.[53]

The shift Judge Posner identified was all in the direction of the Chicago school Antitrust had to be justified in economic terms. Robert Pitofsky, now dean of the Georgetown University Law School, in defending "The Political Content of Antitrust"[54] at the same symposium, conceded that use of congressional purpose would be appropriate as a tie-breaking consideration in doubtful cases if it were clear that economic efficiency would not be harmed. In short, antitrust enforcers would have to shoulder the burden of proving economic harm in antitrust lawsuits.

The disintegration of the politically based antitrust consensus cannot be attributed solely to the Chicago School. By the 1970s World War II and Nazi Germany were long past. Despite aggressive antitrust enforcement, American corporatioans had grown by merger and internal expansion. That growth had not resulted in a fascist state. The fear of concentrated power may have also receded and thereby undermined the remaining cement of antitrust consensus. The two decades following World War II, even more than the 1920s, were years of unparalleled economic growth in America. Big business had played a leading role in the rising standard of living by providing jobs and low-cost products.

The Antitrust Bureaucracies

Bureaucracies have their own logic imposed by the continuity of their activites and their organizational structure. These have also helped transform antitrust. They have changed the enforcement agencies from crusaders in an antitrust army to cops on the beat enforcing business traffic regulations.

Both the Antitrust Division in the Department of Justice and the Federal Trade Commission have permanent offices of economic analysis. The economists in these agencies were expected to provide support for the antitrust enforcement process. The result has, however, been to create an internal constituency arguing against prosecutions. Part of the reason for this bias can be traced to the Chicago training and beliefs of many government economists. Part of the reason is bureaucratic. The economists are asked whether a merger or other business action will cause or is causing economic harm. It always has been a matter of speculation to declare harm will result from a merger, and remains so.

Chicago analysis has some advantages in speculative debates about the harm that may result from a merger because the data surrounding an impending merger can never be complete. Chicago-trained economists generally believe mergers will improve efficiency. Because the free market favors economic survival of the fittest, they reason, managers can decide to merge only to increase profits. This Chicago presumption about purpose is based on theory, not on evidence of profits. It is always possible that a merger might improve profits by improving efficiency. It is also possible a merger will cause no economic harm because the product market has been defined too narrowly and should include more potential producers. These and other possibilities must be overcome to prove a merger will cause economic harm. If economists want to avoid being incorrect, they can simply list reasons why a case for potential harm is not proven.

Moreover, the professional economists cannot rely on general political values to bolster their analysis. Economists are not experts in political matters, and even if they were inclined to include political or social factors in their recommendations, the reception they would receive is uncertain. Appointees who run the agencies with different political views may distrust all advice from economists who incorporate noneconomic criteria.

Much the same is true of career lawyers in the two agencies. Professionalism is a way to escape charges of personal bias. Once political ideology becomes a source of contention, it can no longer be relied upon as a basis of analysis.

Bureaucrats base their judgments on objective terms, and "objective" here tends to translate into those criteria that everyone agrees on. For antitrust, the leading criteria have come to be economic harm and monopoly profits.

Professionalism also means developing knowledge and acting on the basis of new insights. The very general assertions of competitive harm that supported antitrust in the 1950s and 1960s were bound to be investigated. Those investigations would either confirm or not confirm the Supreme Court's speculative economic analysis. That subsequent analysis did not verify the Court's views does not mean the Court was wrong (it simply means we have no proof they were right), but it does limit the ability of professionals to rely on those decisions and retain their personal credibility.

As professionals, antitrust lawyers and economists developed ways to measure more precisely matters that had previously been determined by theory and speculation. This did not mean necessarily an abandonment of enforcement. It did mean, however, a much more restrictive framework for argument.

Robert Lande's work during his five years at the FTC is illustrative of the new professional. Lande a 1978 graduate from Harvard with dual degrees in law and public administration, joined the FTC's antitrust enforcement unit as an attorney. His economics work at Harvard's Kennedy School of Government had already led to publication of an article in a highly technical economics journal, the *Public Utilities Fortnightly*.[55] Before he left the FTC in 1984, he published two further articles arguing against Chicago positions. The first not only disputed, with extensive historical citations, Bork's premise concerning the purpose of antitrust laws, it also developed an analysis showing in sophisticated economic terms why Bork's concern with restrictions on output underestimated the damage caused by monopoly.[56] In the second article, Lande teamed up with Alan Fisher, an FTC economist, to argue against litigating the efficiency of individual merger transactions—a Chicago proposal.[57] The care and technical sophistication of this work prevented its being dismissed as merely the reflection of personal bias. In fact, the Chicago-oriented administration at the FTC promoted Lande and increased his responsibilities.

Lande's thinking, even if contrary to Chicago opinion, accepts the limitations agreed upon by Posner, Pitofsky, and Turner. It places economic efficiency as the arbiter of antitrust and uses history, Supreme Court decisions, and legislative intent as secondary sources of authority. Lande refines those elements that can be proven by economic analysis.

Many academic antitrust professionals have moved in the same direction as Lande. Instead of spinning grand theories of economic and political harm, Robert Harris and Thomas Jorde of the University of California (Berkeley) business and law schools, for example, have tried to design practical ways to prove that few firms compete in product markets. If accepted, their view, derived from analysis of business behavior, would also ease the government's burden of proof in antitrust cases and defeat the Chicago presumption that sufficient competition exists to permit almost any merger. Harris and Jorde have both worked for federal agencies. Their writing, which draws on a broader tradition of economic analysis, still respects the economic limitation on the terms of debate over antitrust policy.[58]

The professionalization of the antitrust bureaucracies and their academic counterparts has resulted in more precise methods of measuring potential monopoly power than were imagined in the 1950s. Instead of searching broad national markets or narrow product markets for possible injury to "any line of commerce," product markets are now commonly defined by statistical tests. The results of these methods might prevent monopoly prices, but they also limit the scope of antitrust to the problem of economic injury.

The Reagan Administration

There is no doubt that the administration of President Ronald Reagan brought with it a different attitude toward antitrust legislation. Consistent with Attorney General William French Smith's declaration about corporate size, the Justice Department and the FTC closed or settled the four largest matters pending before them. A ten-year-old monopolization lawsuit against AT&T, the nation's largest corporation was settled. An even older monopoly case against IBM, the world's largest computer company, was dropped. A case against the eight largest oil companies in the United States was abandoned just before the trial was set to begin. And an investigation of the major American automobile companies was closed. In their place the FTC sued a small group of attorneys who represent indigent criminal defendants in Washington, D.C., and started investigations of state boards that license taxicabs and optometrists and of labor unions that represent actors.[59] Such actions have been justified in economic terms by economist James Miller, the first nonlawyer chairman of the FTC.

Not surprisingly, when Assistant Attorney General for Antitrust William Baxter announced new merger guidelines in June 1982 they included only one theory of economic harm—monopoly price fixing between direct competitors.[60] Gone were the theories of corporate power based on size. Gone were the theories about concentration trends. The new standard for illegal horizontal mergers also seemed less strict: A more concentrated market, that is, fewer competitors, is probably required before enforcement is likely (although this is difficult to tell because the new guidelines use a different method of measuring product market concentration).

Although less obvious to those outside the agencies, these new guidelines did not represent a large shift in internal enforcement criteria from the more aggressive-sounding Carter administration. The new guidelines reflected much more closely the procedure by which the agencies had been screening the thousand or so mergers reported to them each year. Whatever the preferences of the Carter team, it too had initiated cases on the basis of economic harm within a single product market. The days were long past when a merger would be opposed on the basis of corporate size or even on "trend" analysis. The bureaucracy did not find appropriate mergers to challenge based on those theories.

There was one aspect of antimerger enforcement, however, that differed markedly from prior practice. Previously, lawsuits had been brought to stop mergers. But beginning with the contested takeover of Marathon Oil, the FTC launched a policy of opposing only the anticompetitive aspects of mergers.[61]

In the case of Marathon Oil, the FTC found reason to believe that because Marathon and Mobil (one of the firms trying to buy it) both had substantial market shares in certain local gasoline markets, the merger was anticompetitive. The FTC took the position that it would not challenge the merger if certain minor divestitures were agreed to. Although the FTC's position was rejected by the courts in the takeover of Marathon, the policy became central to the FTC's subsequent merger enforcement strategy.

In one sense, the FTC's strategy is merely a logical extension of its economic criteria for enforcement of antitrust law. A merger is unlawful only if competition is reduced. Therefore, it should be stopped only to the extent competition is damaged. Where the proof of economic harm falters, enforcement stops.

In another sense, this is a radical reversal of prior antitrust policy. In the 1950s and 1960s corporate growth by merger was assumed to be bad. The evidence of economic harm was known to be incomplete, but it was believed that more complete knowledge would reveal more anticompetitive consequences. In any case, economic analysis, such as it was, merely provided the trigger for accomplishing the greater goals of antitrust.

Chicago School analysis reverses this assumption. Mergers are good. They should, therefore, be permitted, except to the extent they can be proven harmful.

The result of this shift in thinking has been to eliminate antitrust restrictions on mergers between firms in unrelated product markets regardless of their size. It has also permitted the largest mergers in history and these between direct competitors. The record $13 billion takeover of Gulf Oil was permitted when Chevron agreed to sell some facilities in order to reduce its share in a few local gasoline markets. Antitrust laws no longer have any intentional impact on corporate size or growth. These policies also almost bring the antimerger prohibitions full circle, that is, back to where they were before the Celler-Kefauver Act.

This narrowing of antimerger laws by the FTC and the Justice Department has been accomplished by administrative decisions not to challenge mergers. Section 7 can however also be invoked by private parties, such as Marathon Oil, who are opposed to a merger. It remains to be seen whether the courts will follow the lead of the antitrust agencies or continue the broader tradition of antitrust.

Observations

There is great irony to the role the Chicago School has played in diminishing the political content of antitrust law. The distinctive price theory analysis the Chicago School holds was developed by Aaron Director and Henry Simons at the University of Chicago in the 1930s and 1940s. In an introduction to a collection of Simons's essays, Director said:

> Simons found his work . . . consisted of an even more powerful defense of the direct relationship between the "precious measure of political and economic

freedom" and the decentralization of power inherent in a freemarket system and an elaboration of the program requisite for survival and proper functioning of such a system.[62]

Simons formulated the elements required for survival of a free society in his "Positive Program for Laissez-Faire." They included:

1. No corporation which engages in the manufacture or merchandising of commodities shall own any securities of any other such corporation.
2. [Limit] the total amount of property which any single corporation may own. . . .
3. Corporate earnings shall be taxed to shareholders [including] undistributed earnings.[63]

Stigler's 1952 article in *Fortune*, "The Case Against Big Business,"[64] and even Milton Friedman's 1962 book, *Capitalism and Freedom,*[65] both urge policies to limit corporate size because of the link between a dispersion of economic power and personal freedom.

A greater irony lies in the role of powerful antitrust in encouraging corporate growth. To the extent that it was successful in the 1950s and 1960s, antitrust law pushed firms to buy unrelated businesses. Unlike mergers to achieve monopolization, these conglomerate mergers have no limit. Antitrust never developed an approach that would limit these mergers, which were common in the 1960s and are typical of the more recent megamergers. As a consequence, antitrust has encouraged the development of a managerial perspective that is consistent with unlimited corporate growth through unrelated mergers.

The broader approach to antitrust is not dead, but it is hiding in academia. Lawrence Sullivan of the University of California, Berkeley, Eleanor Fox of New York University, Louis Schwartz of the University of Pennsylvania and Hastings, Joseph Brodley of Boston University, John Flynn of the University of Utah, and others have been struggling with new formulations of antitrust policy that integrate the economic and political goals of antitrust.[66] As the last chapter of this book on merger policy will indicate, their concerns also have a continuing life in Congress.

CHAPTER 6

MERGER WAVES

L ike flocks of birds or of packs of wolves, mergers come in waves. Why mergers have bunched together periodically rather than spread themselves more evenly over the years is not fully understood. Theories which seem to explain one wave do not explain other waves. Only two characteristics unequivocally link the waves, their identifiable existence and the undistinguished profits record of merged firms.

On four occasions in the last one hundred years Americans have witnessed the business community engaging in intense merger activity. Each of these merger waves is often identified with certain characteristic transactions. The first wave, which peaked between 1898 and 1902, is remembered for mergers that created monopolies. The second wave, which crested from around 1925 to the late 1920s, was characterized by acquisitions of related firms, (suppliers, customers, and competitors), but these mergers did not create monopolies. From 1966 through 1968, a third wave produced large conglomerate firms composed of unrelated business. Finally, since 1974 the incidence of megamergers between large firms has dramatically increased and allowed these firms to diversify their holdings.

Our understanding of these merger waves is hampered by the absence of ongoing data, which would permit more detailed comparison of the merger periods. For example, the leading modern annual listing of mergers, the Federal Trade Commission's Large Merger Series, covers only the years 1948–1979. Corporate merger listings for prior years have had to be reconstructed from incomplete records. Because the FTC list includes only manufacturing or mining mergers, it excludes billion dollar transactions such as the Chessie System's railroad acquisition of the Seaboard Coast Line, Mobil's purchase of Montgomery Ward, or Manufacturers Hanover's acquisition of CIT Financial Corporation. More recent commercial merger information services, such as W. T. Grimm & Company's *Mergerstat*, began their time series in the late 1960s. Although *Mergerstat* provides more comprehensive annual totals than the FTC, it does not list individual transactions. It is therefore impossible to check the Grimm figures or compute other totals from *Mergerstat* data. While it is now possible to create more complete current data sources through computer services, such as *Compustat*, the process is costly and not readily available.

To understand the megamergers of the current wave it is helpful to contrast them with earlier takeover practices. We will therefore divide our discussion into two parts. The first deals with acquisitions of closely related businesses, which characterised mergers prior to passage of the Celler-Kefauver Act in 1950. The second part will treat mergers between unrelated businesses, beginning in the mid-1960s.

MERGERS BETWEEN RELATED BUSINESSES

The mergers that took place between 1887 and 1904 are generally considered to have been a widespread attempt to monopolize the American economy. That generalization, although true, does not tell the whole story about the mergers that succeeded as business ventures or the larger number that failed. Businesses that profited from mergers at this time created a new kind of organizational structure that has become typical of the modern corporation.

Following the Civil War, a single national market was created through the growth of railroads. This revolution in transportation, together with the equally revolutionary development of new products and production techniques, transformed American industry. Instead of large local or regional firms in control of separate markets, there were suddenly, in the late 1800s, firms with national produc-

tion capacities that faced the probability of intense, direct competition from distance rivals with equal capacities.

To avoid such competition the firms frequently merged. To succeed, the newly merged firms invented or adopted a new decentralized organizational structure, which permitted national corporations
to operate with greater efficiency.

The steel industry, the oil industry, the tobacco industry and
many other industries all grew rapidly in response to a thriving
American economy during the final quarter of the nineteenth century. But economic advance in the United States could also be
uneven, and periodically the new national industries were faced with
overcapacity during economic downturns. Even worse some inventions such as the Bonsack continuous-process cigarette machine provided the American Tobacco Company with the capacity to produce
cigarettes for the entire nation from as few as fifteen machines.[1]

Sometimes more efficient production techniques provided another
motive for mergers. The Standard Oil Trust began as a price-fixing
cartel to coordinate the production of oil refineries. By 1878 it could
regulate production to equal demand for oil because the Standard
Oil group of firms controlled over 90 percent of America's oil industry. But by the 1880s, with the construction of oil pipelines, Standard Oil was able to produce two-fifths of the world's total oil production from three huge refineries. To eliminate unnecessary plants
of the separate firms within the group required the greater central
control of a single legal entity.[2]

These national businesses, whether formed to increase efficiency
or reduce competition, faced new organizational problems. Previously, owners of businesses commonly supervised all operations. In
national enterprises such watchful supervision from a single source
became impossible. The owner or manager of a large firm could not
hire all the workers, buy the raw materials, or meet all the customers.
He could not even review reports on each of these.

Historian Alfred Chandler has described the organizational solution in *The Visible Hand*. His book, winner of the Bancroft and
Pulitzer Prizes, describes the development of the modern multidivisional corporation in the late nineteenth and early twentieth century.
The new business was decentralized. Owners or central managers of
multidivisional corporations did not approve or review the individual
decisions of "line officers," such as plant managers, regional sales
directors, or purchasing agents. Rather, the central "staff officers"

established production goals and allocated funds for each of the operating units of the business. The operating divisions were then run autonomously by their managers. If they met or exceeded the central staff's expectations, they could expect to be rewarded, and if they failed they were likely to be punished.[3]

For the modern corporation this method of operation was as revolutionary as any of the technological developments of the nineteenth century. Freed from reviewing the manufacture or sale of individual products, the central managers could coordinate more complex and varied operations using statistical reports. They could thus combine within a single enterprise the mining of raw materials, the transportation, manufacture, sale, and service of products, and also offer installment purchase terms to a national or international audience of consumers.[4]

Without the responsibility of managing the day to day operations of business, the corporate executive could plan the same way that a general deploys an army. The general, who fires no weapon and does not see the enemy, can, using reports, formulate strategies to defeat an army of the strongest and most skilled soldiers. The efficiency of internal coordination, according to Chandler, is why the modern corporation displaced the fragmented industries and multitudes of middlemen that characterized commerce earlier in the nineteenth century.

We think of the earliest wave of mergers as profitable because their monopoly objective was so blatant. But Samuel Richardson Reid's evaluation of the economic literature concludes: "If there is one dominant factor which emerges from [reviewing] . . . studies [of] the first great wave, it is the general lack of success of these mergers, which (in many cases) were designed to secure a high degree of market control and/or scale economies."[5]

It was not enough to succeed in most industries to buy out the competition. Competitors demanded high prices for their firms and soon were replaced by new competitors. Then the "monopoly" firm was at a competitive disadvantage burdened by a high debt incurred in achieving its temporary dominance.

Chandler has noted that unless the combined enterprise achieved some new economy of scale and greater efficiency by internal coordination, the monopoly was likely to fail.

> The success of those mergers . . . depended on two things: a shift from a strategy of horizontal combination to vertical integration and the creation of

a managerial hierarchy to run the various departments in and coordinate the flows through the integrated enterprises.[6]

Only certain industries seem to have the potential for these efficiencies, so only some succeeded.

Mergers came in every industry; the textile industry, for example, had twelve big mergers, although only one of these firms survived American Woolens — and that was never much of a success. Central Leather was the only firm that survived in the leather industry, and it was not successful either. For in these industries, as I have pointed out, size and integration gave few advantages. In oil and other industries with capital intensive production and economies of scale, however, there were many successes.[7]

One important group did not care if these mergers failed or succeeded: the bankers who promoted them. For the banker, the profits came from the merger not the business. Matthew Josephson describes the first billion dollar merger which consolidated the American steel industry in 1901:

Against tangible assets of $682,000,000 possessed by the "United States Steel Corporation," [J. P.] Morgan underwrote and offered for sale whole masses of new securities: $303,000,000 in mortgage bonds, $510,000,000 in preferred stock and $508,000,000 in common stock, making a grand total of $1,321,000,000. . . . In addition, the repeated fees to promoters . . . when added to Morgan's syndicate fee of $12,500,000 and subscription profits of $50,000,000 footed up to a grand total of $150,000,000 as the cost for launching the completed steel Trust.[8]

It is little wonder that a Harvard economist and former director of the FTC's Bureau of Economics, Jesse Markham, concluded that promoters were a significant influence on the formation of unprofitable mergers.[9]

Table 6-1 lists the number of mergers that occurred at the peak of the turn-of-the-century wave. The occurrence of such a large number of mergers during this period, and especially in 1899, is still something of a puzzle. Economists have hypothesized that increase in merger activity is related to the business cycle and that economic downturns promote takeovers because of overcapacity in an industry. But, on the whole, economists have rejected business cycle theories in favor of stock market theories. Markham concludes:

[B]etween 1897 and 1903 stock prices and mergers were subject to the same pronounced cyclical swings. Hence, merger activity . . . seems to have

Table 6-1.   Mergers 1897-1904.

Year	Number of Mergers
1897	69
1898	303
1899	1,208
1900	340
1901	423
1902	379
1903	142
1904	79

Source: Ralph L. Nelson, *Merger Movements in American Industry, 1895-1956* (Princeton: Princeton University Press, 1959), p. 60.

been tied more closely to stock price movements than to general business fluctuations.[10]

The stock price theory also lends support to Markham's conclusion that promoters played an important role in fostering mergers. Many of these mergers were financed by the issuance of new securities. Sale of these securities must have been easier during an optimistic stock market with rising prices.

If new production efficiencies, industry overcapacity, and managerial innovations created conditions favoring mergers and if promoters and rising stock prices provided an immediate impetus for takeovers, then some of the merger puzzle may be solved. We must still explain, however, why the wave subsided as quickly as it arose.

Several explanations have been offered. Chandler has pointed to the importance of antitrust after 1904 in stopping mergers that created monopolies:

> The meat packers were about to put together what was to be called the National Packing Company, which would be a holding company. They went to [the investment banking firm of] Kuhn, Loeb which said "Fine, we'll finance this merger." At that moment the *Northern Securities* [antitrust] case was decided; the Bureau of Competition started to make noises, and Kuhn, Loeb said, "We won't touch it," and the effort was dropped.[11]

Markham adds that the stock market collapse in 1903 made it more difficult to finance the large mergers. While both of these observations are important, the explanations do not seem complete. The structural forces favoring efficiency mergers remained and the stock market went up after the "panic" of 1903, but mergers dropped in popularity.

At least one other factor, therefore, seems likely: The wave was partly a business fad. Businessmen and investors never have complete knowledge of current events and their plans are ultimately based on guesswork about the future. They are therefore disposed to follow what looks like a good idea. Monopoly mergers, at the time, looked like the perfect idea. But, as Markham notes,

> the merger-creating industry did not thrive for long. Bankers, industrialists and the stock-buying public, on whose support the promoter relied, soon had their expectations shattered. In the eighteen-month period preceding October 1903, the market value of 100 leading industrial stocks shrank by 43.4 percent. Much of this shrinkage was undoubtedly a downward adjustment of stock prices to reflect the difference between *expected* and *actual* earnings. The result was the "Rich Man's Panic" of 1903, by which time the early merger movement had run its course.[12]

The fad ended because it lost its credibility.

The second merger wave, which peaked in the late 1920s, provides additional support to the above theories. Although blocked by antitrust laws from creating monopolies, the mergers of the second wave exploited the potential of Chandler's multidivisional firm. Promoters used the roaring stock market of the 1920s to finance these combinations. And if ever investors were led by their own enthusiasm, it was during the 1920s. Frederick Lewis Allen's classic, *Only Yesterday*, reminds us of the temperament of the times:

> Throughout 1927 speculation had been increasing. The amount of money loaned to brokers to carry margin accounts for traders had risen during the year from $2,818,561,000 to $3,558,355,000—a huge increase. During the week of December 3, 1927, more shares of stock had changed hands than in any previous week in the whole history of the New York Stock Exchange. One did not have to listen long to an after-dinner conversation, whether in New York or San Francisco or the lowliest village of the plain, to realize that all sorts of people to whom the stock ticker had been a hitherto alien mystery were carrying a hundred shares of Studebaker or Houston Oil, learning the significance of such recondite symbols as GL and X and ITT, and whipping open the early editions of afternoon papers to catch the 1:30 quotations from Wall Street.[13]

With the stock market crash in October 1929, the merger wave ended.

Because of the crash and the Great Depression of the 1930s, we do not have accurate information on how the merged firms would have fared. Nevertheless, Reid speculates they were no more successful than the turn-of-the-century mergers. For support, he cites a National Industrial Conference Board study released in 1929 which concluded that mergers "are far from being universally successful."[14] Reid adds:

> Some [merged firms] made high profits and grew in size and industrial importance correspondingly. But there were many that failed absolutely and passed out of existence. The majority did not achieve a conspicuous success as profit-makers . . . [and] the [Conference Board] study makes clear that industrial consolidations have not provided a safe, easy, and sure way to business success.[15]

The notable mergers of this period followed the path described by Chandler of creating large multidivisional firms. As Stigler noted, some of these mergers during the 1920s, created "oligopolies," thereby diluting the power of the monopolies created by the turn-of-the-century merger wave.[16] Bethlehem Steel, for example, became a formidable competitor to U.S. Steel after Bethlehem absorbed the third, fourth, sixth, and eighth largest steel producers. But many of these large mergers vertically integrated industrial manufacturers with their suppliers or their customers who made consumer products. Anaconda Copper, for example, bought American Brass and other finished goods producers.[17] Vertical integration provided the best opportunity to exploit Chandler's managerial efficiencies. Within the framework of a single firm, the flow of raw materials to finished product was coordinated more efficiently than by use of contracts between many independent firms.

The decentralized, multidivisional structure of corporations also made possible a new kind of firm in the 1920s—the multiproduct firm. In the chemical industry, Du Pont and Allied Chemical were able to acquire firms in different businesses and thus added new product lines without making the operation of their firms unduly complex. The integration of related, though noncompeting, product lines also may have afforded these corporations a greater number of manufacturing economies and further marketing benefits. The central staff of the multidivisional firm could manage these separate products in the same manner that they managed different divisions handling a single product at different stages—through statistical reports.

While organizational efficiency may have been the objective of some of the 1920s mergers, Markham states that this was not the key motivation:

> The most important single motive for merger at the peaks of merger movements seems to have been promotional profits. The waves of mergers in 1897–1899 and in 1926–1929 rode to their respective peaks with concomitant, rapidly rising stock prices. Both periods were marked by easy money and a securities hungry public. This environment gave rise to a new type of entrepreneur—the producer of mergers.[18]

And after the 1929 stock market crash, the role of stock market promoters led to a new legal environment for mergers.

Legislation in the 1930s tried to prevent a repeat of the runaway enthusiasm that characterized the previous merger waves through two kinds of regulation. First, the Securities Act of 1933 and the Securities Exchange Act of 1934 required disclosure of pertinent and accurate facts concerning the business firms and any relationship of those firms to promoters of the merger. Investors would, thus, know how much the promoters stood to gain from the sale of securities. Second, through the Glass Steagall Act of 1933, it became unlawful for a bank to promote a new issue of securities or use its depositors' funds to acquire those securities. The purpose of these laws was to minimize the conflict of interest between persons acting on behalf of the seller and the buyer of securities and to make sure that buyers knew who was who and what was what.

The turn-of-the-century merger wave produced the modern corporation and led to the Sherman Act's prohibition on creating monopolies by merger. The 1920s wave developed the potentials of the modern corporation and provoked the "truth in securities" legislation of the 1930s. With the passage of the restrictive, antimerger Celler-Kefauver Act in 1950, there was some reason to believe that the merger wave was a thing of the past.

MERGERS BETWEEN UNRELATED BUSINESSES

The two merger waves of the last twenty years share a number of common characteristics: Many were between firms in unrelated businesses, many were unprofitable, and many involved hostile takeovers. But the differences between the conglomerate mergers of the mid-1960s and the megamergers since 1974 seem at least as great as any similarity. Conglomerates rose out of obscurity through the merger process, riding the crest of the business cycle and a climbing stock market. Megamergers, in contrast, have been undertaken by already well-known, successful firms through periods of stagnant economic growth and a declining stock market. While much of the conglomerate wave may appear to be a sport of large-scale business, megamergers reflect a profound organizational transformation beyond the multidivisional corporation.

The conglomerate merger wave of the mid-1960s was a phenomenon. Given the strength of antitrust, the disclosure requirements of the securities laws, and the lessons of the 1920s for speculative investments, the conglomerate merger wave should not have happened. That it did happen must illustrate man's resistance to imposed constraints. Perhaps we believe "the grass is always greener on the other side of the fence," or, like mountain climbers, we will inevitably try to overcome obstacles "because they are there." In any case, obstacles to mergers were overcome and mergers became the business fad of the 1960s.

To many corporate leaders at this time, the obvious loophole in antitrust was conglomerate mergers. But who wanted to build or buy into corporations made up of unrelated businesses? How would such mergers be financed with the tight credit market that attended corporate expansion and the Vietnam War? University of Michigan economist Peter O. Steiner's analysis of the conglomerate merger wave offers the following answer:

> The mid-sixties provided an amazing constellation of "go" signals, particularly for conglomerate acquisitions. Capital was being rationed and interest rates were high. A bull market was developing, with growth stocks the darlings of investors imbued with a market outlook that was prepared to extrapolate growth in earnings per share without looking at the source (or the genuineness) of the reported growth. Some found that tax laws and accounting conventions made it easy to play the PE game and realize instant earnings from mergers. Many of those best able to detect the manipulative aspects of the transactions — the corporate insider, the manager of mutual funds and the leading brokerage houses — were in the best position to benefit and thus were slow to blow the whistle. Courts, which traditionally interpreted securities laws to protect stockholders . . . were reluctant to let these laws be used to stop mergers because such use might deprive stockholders of the opportunity to sell out at a premium. . . .

Like many self-reinforcing movements, the early market success of the conglomerate acquisition tended to justify the perhaps shaky assumptions being made about PE ratios, and reinforced a genuinely favorable speculative alimate.[19]

"PE" magic was the key to the wave of conglomerate mergers. It financed the mergers and made hostile takeovers possible. The PE ratio, or the price of a firm's shares (P) over its annual earnings (E), is a rule of thumb for making stock investments. If, for example, an average company normally sells for ten times its annual earnings, an investor who discovered the company's shares were selling for only five times its annual earnings would rush out and buy at the bargain rate. But if the price of the shares rose to fifteen times earnings, the investor would sell with quite a profit.

The PE ratio is a sensible investment guideline. The formula (stock price equals ten times annual earnings per share) is merely a shorthand way of expressing how many years it will take a corporation to repay an investment in its shares at the current rate of earnings. But because some companies are healthier or display better prospects than others, they should have different PE ratios. The next Xerox or Polaroid should have a PE ratio of 100 to 1, or better, in its early years, whereas the company facing bankruptcy should have a share price that is a fraction of one year's earnings (assuming it has any).

It is these expectations about future earnings that made PE magic possible. If a company with a high PE ratio (20 to 1), for example, merged with an equally sized company that had an average PE ratio (10 to 1), the resulting company ought to have a PE ratio of 15 to 1. But suppose the buying company were larger, then the investors in it would add the earnings of the smaller firm, but they might not reduce the stock price ratio. Why not? Perhaps because the impact of the target firm was too small to calculate, perhaps because they expected the target firm to improve through new management, or perhaps only because they wanted to believe.

If the magic worked—and for a time it did in the 1960s—all kinds of mergers suddenly became possible. A high PE company that issued new shares to pay off the shareholders of a low PE company could pay more than those shares had previously sold for and increase the value of its own shares at the same time. For example:

A high PE firm (20 to 1) has annual earnings of $1,000 and has issued 1,000 shares. Its shares sell for $20 each.

It then buys a low PE firm (5 to 1) that has annual earnings of $100 and has issued 100 shares, which sell for $5 a share.

To induce the shareholders of the low PE firm to sell, the high PE firm offers one of its shares for every two shares of the low PE firm.

The shareholders of the low PE firm accept because they are trading two shares worth $10 for one worth $20 — a 100 percent profit.

The shareholders of the high PE firm benefit from the issuance of the 50 new shares because their shares rise in value. With a 20-to-1 PE ratio the firm has annual earnings of $1,100 and 1,050 shares (or about $21 per share).

The high PE firm had merely to print new stock certificates and shareholders of both firms could make a profit. Obviously, it was magic.

This kind of magic also solved the financing problem, since no money had to be raised in a tight credit market. Anyone with a printing press and a reputation for success could do it. The acquiring firm needed "glamour," not experience or assets, to gain and maintain the high PE ratio. This meant that relatively obscure companies with "dynamic" executives could build empires by swapping their stocks for those of firms with low PE ratios.

And these "conglomerateurs" did not even have to be nice about it. They were buying shares from millions of shareholders in the anonymous stock market, not negotiating a deal with managers of other firms. Conglomerateurs would announce their willingness to trade high-priced stock "for a limited time only," and the shareholders of the low-priced stock would rush to get in on the bargain.

Steiner's list of the most active acquiring companies is headed by five previously little known firms — Gulf & Western, LTV, ITT, Tenneco, and Teledyne. Between 1960 and 1968 each of these firms acquired over $1 billion in assets through mergers of this kind. Gulf & Western alone bought assets of almost $3 billion in 67 transactions, while Teledyne's 125 mergers pushed its assets just over the $1 billion mark.[20]

Not surprisingly, the leaders of these new conglomerate enterprises were not well liked in the business community. Their takeover tactics were unfriendly, and they were not businessmen in the true sense: They did not operate their businesses; they manipulated reports. At best, they were financial wizards. At worst, they were snake oil salesmen or dream merchants riding the crest of a booming economy and soaring stock market, taking advantage of tax loopholes, gaps in accounting rules, and a gullible public.

Table 6-2. Merger Activity and the Dow Jones Average, 1960-1971.

Year	Dow Jones Average		Mergers of Firms, $10 Million and Above
	Low	High	
1960	566	685	51
1961	610	735	46
1962	536	726	65
1963	647	767	54
1964	766	892	73
1965	841	969	64
1966	744	995	73
1967	786	943	138
1968	825	985	174
1969	770	969	138
1970	631	842	91
1971	798	951	59

Source: *Statistical Report on Mergers and Acquisitions*, FTC (1979), and *The Dow Jones Investor's Handbook* (1980).

There is little question that the momentum of this particular merger wave was carried along with the help of the stock market. As Table 6-2 shows, the number of mergers followed close behind the price level of the Dow Jones Industrial average during the 1960s and early 1970s.

When the stock market fell in 1969, the "go-go" years were gone. "High flying" conglomerates were mostly affected because their price-earnings ratio contracted greatly. Litton Industries, which had a PE ratio of 45 to 1 in 1968, fell to 22 to 1 in 1969, and 14 to 1 in 1970. Teledyne dropped from 41 to 1 in 1967, to 13 to 1 in 1970. Gulf & Western went from 25 to 1 in 1965, to 7 to 1 in 1970.[21]

It seemed as if the secret was out about the emperor's clothes: Conglomerates were not real business organizations. Suddenly, everybody knew they were too complex to be well managed. *Fortune* magazine summarized the feelings of many in a 1973 article:

Probably the most damaging result of the conglomerate merger era was the false legitimacy it seemed to confer on the pursuit of profits by financial manipulation rather than by producing something of genuine economic value. Some conglomerates specialized in using adroit legal tricks to fatten their profits, and the example has been widely emulated. By temporarily seducing

Table 6-3.   Diversification of American Firms, 1949-1969.

Type of Business	1949	1959	1969
Single Business	34.5%	16.2%	6.2%
Dominant Business	35.5	37.3	29.2
Related Businesses	26.7	40.0	45.2
Unrelated Businesses	3.4	6.5	19.4

Source: Richard P. Rumelt, *Strategy Structure and Economic Performance* (Cambridge, Mass.: Harvard University Press, 1974), Table 2-2, p. 51.

much of Wall Street with earnings growth based on accounting gimmicks, conglomerates may have, in the long run, weakened public confidence in the securities market.[22]

Congress reacted with a series of laws. The Williams Act of 1968 was aimed at hostile takeovers. It extended the securities laws of the 1930s to slow down the takeover process by requiring disclosure of information before a takeover. The Tax Reform Act of 1969 eliminated the tax advantage of acquiring firms by replacing corporate shares with long-term debt. And in 1976 Congress passed, fifty years after it was first recommended by the FTC, a law requiring companies to notify the antitrust agencies prior to mergers.

If these measures were supposed to reverse the tide of conglomerate firms by stopping mergers, it was too late. The great conglomerates were only the most visible and active diversifiers. Everybody was doing it. In the two decades following the 1950 passage of the Celler-Kefauver Act, the composition of American industry had changed from predominantly single-business firms to predominantly multibusiness firms.

UCLA economist Richard Rumelt has traced this evolution using a more sophisticated classification system than the horizontal, vertical, and conglomerate merger categories described in Chapter 5. Table 6-3, which uses Rumelt's broader categories, shows that in 1949 70 percent of the 500 largest industrial firms in the United States earned most of their income from one business. By 1969 almost 70 percent did not. By merger or internal development almost all of these largest firms had diversified to the point where they no longer received 95 percent of their revenues from one business. Large businesses were continuing to develop in the direction begun during the merger wave of the 1920s, toward a firm made up of many different but related businesses. However, during the 1960s most of the change was in the direction of unrelated conglomerate firms.

Chandler's multidivisional firm can manage related businesses, but it has yet to be shown that the multidivisional structure works for conglomerates. The question is whether a central corporate management can understand a multitude of unrelated businesses well enough to make successful capital investment, marketing, and research decisions. This question, left unsettled by the conglomerate wave of the 1960s, is equally pertinent to the more recent spate of megamergers, for they too have been typically conglomerate.

Three prime characteristics mark the period of the megamerger as a distinct chapter in the history of American mergers: (1) the large size of target firms, (2) the equally large size, prior success and prominence of the acquiring firms, and (3) the use of hostile takeover tactics. I mark its beginning in 1974. Although 1974 recorded few large mergers, two of them were portents of things to come. Mobil made what was essentially a $1.6 billion hostile takeover of Montgomery Ward, and the International Nickel Company, with the aid of the investment banking firm of Morgan, Stanley, won a bitter takeover battle for ESB. From this point on, established companies would use the surprise takeover tactics of the conglomerate upstarts and the advantage of greater resources to outbid other firms. The day of gentlemanly, friendly mergers for America's business establishment and the investment banking community had passed.

Investment banking took on an even more aggressive promotional role in facilitating cash tender offers than it had as underwriters of securities to finance the acquisitions of the 1960s. Because they were no longer tied to corporate decisions to issue new shares, investment bankers could freelance in search of targets or acquiring firms regardless of the presence of a client. These megamergers seemed, at times, to usher in a new era in which all businesses were merely streams of future income to be bought and sold without reference to production technology, marketing channels, or any other unifying basis for operating a business.

W. T. Grimm & Company has chronicled this megamerger wave with its statistical summaries, and Figure 6-1 and Table 6-4 illustrate the rise in popularity of the megamerger and the increasing assets acquired through these mergers using Grimm's $100 million merger series as a guide. From only a handful of megamergers in 1974 and 1975, the number climbed to 40 in 1976 and to 80 in

Figure 6-1.   Acquisitions of $100 Million Firms, 1974-1983.

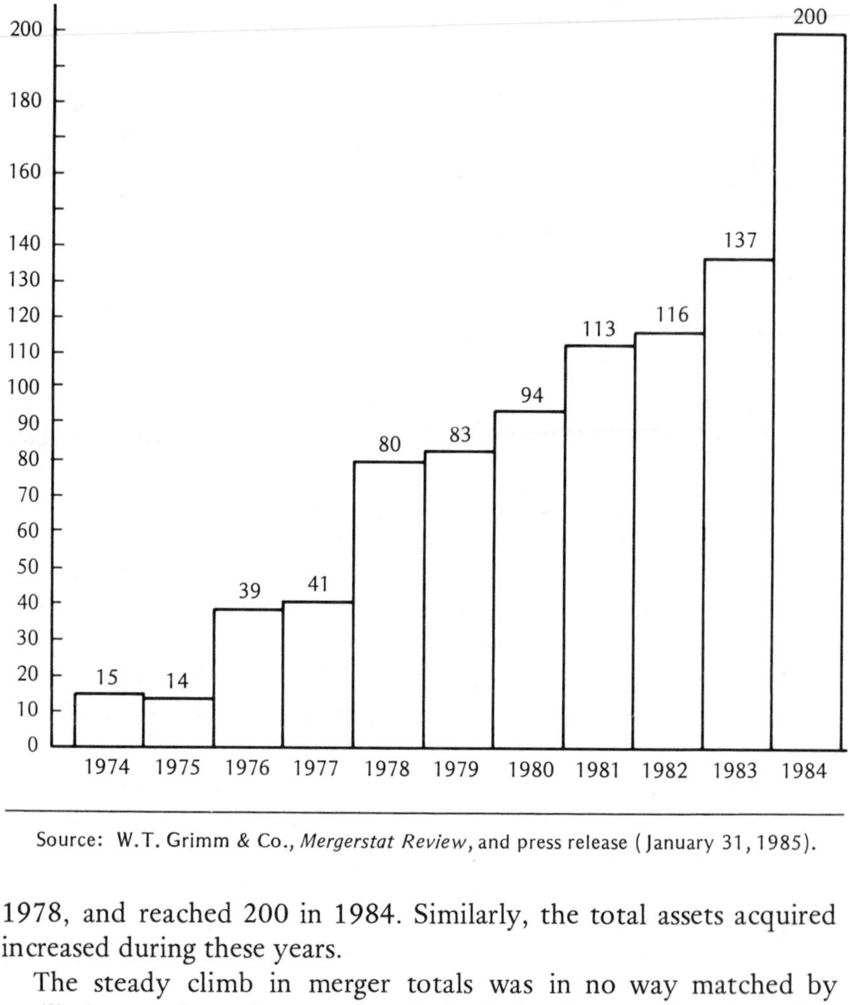

Source: W.T. Grimm & Co., *Mergerstat Review*, and press release (January 31, 1985).

1978, and reached 200 in 1984. Similarly, the total assets acquired increased during these years.

The steady climb in merger totals was in no way matched by vacillating stock market averages. Indeed, the depressed stock market seems to have abetted the large takeovers. Grimm's figures (Table 6-5) show that these firms used their ample reserves of cash, whereas conglomerateurs had had to depend on stock swaps.

Given the resources of these large firms, their takeovers appear at present unstoppable. Whether this takeover process is sensible, whether the decision to take over other firms makes business sense, and whether the takeovers help or hurt the public are questions to be dealt with in the following chapters.

Table 6-4. Total Dollar Value of Mergers, 1974-1984.

Year	Assets Acquired (in billions of dollars)
1974	12.5
1975	11.8
1976	20.0
1977	21.9
1978	34.2
1979	43.5
1980	44.3
1981	82.6
1982	53.8
1983	73.1
1984	122.0

Source: W.T. Grimm & Co., *Mergerstat Review* (1984) and Press Release January 31, 1985.

Table 6-5. Stock and Cash Takeovers, 1967-1982.

Year	Stock Takeovers	Cash Takeovers
1967	60%	36%
1968	62	29
1969	57	32
—	—	—
—	—	—
—	—	—
1977	26	54
1978	30	46
1979	26	53
1980	31	47
1981	34	42
1982	29	37

Source: W.T. Grimm & Co., *Mergerstat Review* (1983).

PART THREE

DECISIONS TO ACQUIRE: BRIGHT IDEAS, BARGAINS AND BLUNDERS

Why was there an unprecedented number of large mergers in the decade following Mobil's acquisition of Marcor in 1974? The answer offered here is that in the 1970s successful American firms accumulated excess profits for which they could find no use other than acquisitions. Once begun, these acquisitions set off a chain reaction which resulted in a wave of megamergers.

Like the answer of notorious bank robber Willie Sutton who responded to the question of why he robbed banks, "because that's where they keep the money," the excess profits explanation seems to border on tautology. Access to large pools of cash was a prerequisite to the major hostile tender offers of the 1970s. Moreover, common sense dictates that had such firms discovered better uses for their profits they would have taken advantage of them.

Analytic studies have so far failed to explain the megamerger wave. Most such studies have assumed that acquisitions are made either to obtain a desirable target firm (for example, because the target's shares are undervalued) or to obtain something the target has that will make the resulting firm more efficient and profitable (for example, a target's better marketing organization). But the perspective offered here suggests the reasons a firm chooses a particular target is secondary to the decision of an acquiring firm to make an acquisition in the first place.

If the determination to merge is internally generated rather than the result of external attractions, then there may be little pattern to the types of firms that are acquired. The crazy quilt of target firms and selection criteria can be better understood if one accepts the proposition that the choice of a target is a decision of lesser importance than the initial decision to acquire. Under such circumstances target selection criteria are likely to be highly variable.

The inconclusiveness of prior studies highlights this lack of consistent acquisition criteria. Two studies of this merger wave sponsored by the Federal Trade Commission illustrate the limits of previous inquiries. One study, an econometric analysis of the financial characteristics of merging firms, was undertaken by Willard Carlton and two associates at the University of North Carolina.[1] The second, by Wayne Boucher of the University of Southern California, employed in-depth interviews to determine the views of merger experts.[2]

The Boucher panel of fourteen merger experts included James Freund, a senior partner at the law firm of Skadden, Arps, Slate, Meagher & Flom, their archrival Martin Lipton of Wachtell, Lipton, Rosen & Katz, Steven Friedman of the Goldman, Sachs & Co. investment banking firm and Ira Harris of the Salomon Brothers investment banking firm. Boucher also included Willard T. Grimm, head of the firm which compiles statistics on merger activity and two Harvard Business School professors, Malcolm Salter, a specialist on merger strategies, and Michael Porter, another expert on business strategy. In addition, he interviewed the chief executive officer of a major firm, a senior officer of one of the major accounting firms, and the president of a public relations firm that specializes in contested takeovers.

Boucher's study is an incisive investigation of the merger process, but it failed to uncover why so many mergers were taking place in the late 1970s. The formal results of the study were a rank ordering of reasons corporations merged (mergers occurred to acquire (1) undervalued targets, (2) a rapid means of growth, (3) a new product, (4) a new business with fewer risks than starting from scratch, (5) etc.). This rank ordering reveals little of why mergers were accelerating in 1979. Given the overlapping definitions of merger motives the ranking process does not inspire confidence. All the motives are plausible and surely true of some transactions, but none suggest an intelligible pattern for the merger wave.

The Carlton report is similarly inconclusive. Their review of econometric studies of the 1960s showed little success in identifying distinguishing characteristics of merging firms, but it did expose one erroneous belief that had been circulating for at least fifteen years—that highly leveraged firms buy underleveraged firms. Carlton's one conclusion—that firms in concentrated industries tend to acquire firms in other concentrated industries—was tentative and explained only a small proportion of the transactions surveyed.

It is, of course, possible that no pattern emerges from such studies because mergers can be explained only on an individual basis. But while possible, this explanation seems unlikely given the sudden concentration of mergers.

Chapter 7 is an explanation of why mergers were a logical course of action for leading acquiring firms in the 1970s. The answer—that these firms needed investment outlets for excess profits—is a common sense conclusion based on the circumstances of those firms.

The term "excess profits" does not refer to an identifiable amount of accumulated earnings or an unusually high rate of return. Profits are considered excess if management believes that earnings cannot wisely be reinvested in a corporation's existing business. Because the cash to finance some takeovers rests on a credit rating rather than accumulated earnings, it might be more accurate to refer here to "excess lines of credit." The less precise term, excess profits, is used because this more specific source of extra funds is easier to visualize.

The relaxed definition of "excess" reflects the high degree of subjectivity that goes into business decisionmaking. Firms with identical balance sheets are frequently rated quite differently by members of the financial community. It is not surprising, therefore, that computer analysis of the financial standing of acquiring firms has yet to confirm an excess profits thesis.

CHAPTER 7

THE ACQUISITION
IMPERATIVE

Success poses a problem for businesses. Until it is successful the objectives of a firm are fairly obvious: obtain capital, market the product, keep costs low. Pressure from competitors and capital markets command all the attention and all the earnings of new ventures. But once the initial wrinkles are ironed out of the production process, once a market share is established for the product, and once profits and a positive cash flow materialized, corporate managers must look beyond their product and consider the disposal of excess profits. Apart from making acquisitions, the successful firm, may choose from five major alternatives. It can reinvest in the existing enterprise, distribute the profits to shareholders, start new businesses, invest in securities, or give the profits to employees. Although likely to be attractive, these alternatives to merging, are, for reasons to be discussed, frequently insufficient to absorb the profits of successful large firms completely. For that reason, many firms turn to mergers.

REINVESTING IN THE EXISTING ENTERPRISE:
PROBLEM PROFITS

The first instinct of a manager of a newly successful firm must be to reinvest profits to expand the business. To repeat his early success is

151

no doubt a matter of both pride and profit. Initially, at least, it has often been a successful strategy.

Alfred Chandler's prize-winning history, *The Visible Hand* describes early examples of reinvestment in the sewing machine, tobacco, and other industries. Even before the turn of the century, many firms that exploited new developments in mass production and mass distribution were able to finance their phenomenal growth though reinvested profits. Singer Sewing Machines marketed the first mass produced major home appliance. To do so, they developed a comprehensive marketing and distribution system. Their salaried sales people had to convince wives of the usefulness of this expensive machine, teach them how to use it and be available to repair it. In addition, Singer had to design a system to make sewing machines affordable to families—the installment plan—and, it had to carry the costs of both the sales and credit systems.

Its extraordinary success required Singer to build more and more production facilities. In 1874, it built the world's then largest sewing machine factory in New Jersey. In 1885, it opened an even larger facility in Scotland. Chandler has described how these were paid for:

> All Singer's capital facilities—its two great factories, a small cabinetmaking plant in South Bend, Indiana, and a foundry in Austria—were financed out of current earnings.
>
> Increased demand in these years caused Singer to expand and systematize its purchasing operations. By the 1890s the company had obtained its own timberlands, an iron mill and some transportation facilities. These purchases were also paid for from the ample cash flow provided by the sale of the machines. Indeed the company often had a surplus which it invested in railroad and government bonds, and even other manufacturing enterprises.[1]

Having achieved their initial goal of making the business venture viable, corporate managers have typically expanded the firm using operating profits instead of returning them to the shareholders.

James Buchanan Duke's direction of the American Tobacco Company also illustrates the use of operating profits as a means for corporate expansion. By 1890 American Tobacco had quickly dominated the nation's cigarette industry through the invention of the Bonsack continuous-process cigarette machine. Chandler describes Duke's subsequent strategy:

> The organization [Duke] had created and the profits it produced were to be used to conquer the rest of the tobacco industry. In the 1890s pipe tobacco,

plug or chewing tobacco, snuff and cigars still commanded much larger markets than cigarettes. Duke's plan was first to acquire factories making these other products. Then by driving prices down and spending heavily for advertising he expected to bring the leading producers in his orbit.[2]

Duke eventually had to supplement his war chest by resorting to the capital markets, but operating profits were the backbone of his campaign.

Although some of Duke's partners at American Tobacco objected to the elimination of current dividends, there is no legal impediment to reinvesting all corporate earnings. For example, the Ford Motor Company, originally capitalized at $100,000 in 1903, had by 1915 declared $41 million in dividends but retained and reinvested earnings of over $110 million. When minority shareholders sued to force distribution of a larger proportion of the company's earnings, the court upheld Henry Ford's right to retain and reinvest as much of the company's earnings as he wished.[3] The court forced disgorgement of a lesser amount ($19 million) only because the corporation had no specific plan to use these funds.

United States tax law takes a similar approach to retention of corporate earnings. The Internal Revenue Code provides for a punitive tax on corporate earnings that are not distributed as dividends if the earnings are accumulated "beyond the reasonable needs of the business." This standard is not designed to limit corporate growth, however. Its only purpose is to prevent the retention of earnings as a means by which shareholders can avoid personal income taxes. Thus, the tax law assesses no penalty where profits are retained to expand a corporation. Indeed, the tax regulations explicitly permit accumulation of earnings for the purpose of buying a completely unrelated business.[4] There is then no limit to the growth of firms through the use of retained earnings.

According to economist Lester Thurow, no new net capital was contributed to business during the years 1980 and 1981. He states that retained earnings supplied not only all new investment to business but also supplied the federal government with the cash to fund the increase in national debt.[5] Not surprisingly, retained earnings are the favorite source of capital funds for corporate managers, far surpassing the use of new debt or equity. Investment based on retained earnings lessens a firm's dependence on capital markets and, to some degree, frees corporate managers to pursue their own plans.

Some managers, such as those at Digital Equipment Corporation, have decided to pay no dividends at all and to reinvest all earnings. Digital's need to develop its products and markets and meet competition quickly absorbed the $2 billion cumulative profit earned by this very successful firm. The reinvestment paid off, and annual profits increased from $25 million in 1976 to $166 million in 1979 and to $400 million in 1982.[6]

Investment Limits

At some point, however, reinvesting all of a company's earnings ceases to be a sensible method of expansion. While the tobacco industry, for example, continues to be enormously profitable, it is no longer a growing market. Since the 1950s health warnings have held those Americans who smoke at a steady percentage. As a result, aggressive marketing activities by any cigarette company is unlikely to be successful. Price cutting or increased advertising by one firm would have been matched by its tobacco industry competitors. Thus head-to-head competition would result in higher costs and smaller profit margins for all. Michael Porter's insightful guide, *Competitive Strategy*, dictates that firms in such industries should narrow their strategies:

> [S]electing the right competitive move involves finding one whose outcome is quickly determined (no protracted or serious battle takes place). . . . That is, the goal for the firm is to avoid destabilizing and costly warfare, which spells poor results for all participants, but yet still outperform other firms.[7]

Following what might be called Porter's Law, however, leaves managers with the problem of how to dispose of tobacco profits that cannot be reinvested. Porter's Harvard Business School colleague Robert Miles has described the tobacco industry's solution. Beginning in the 1950s, and particularly since the Surgeon General's report on the dangers of smoking in January 1964, tobacco firms have diversified their holdings.[8] Liggett & Meyers, for example, attempted to move completely out of the cigarette business and into pet foods, liquor, soft drinks, and sporting goods by divesting itself of overseas tobacco operations and trying, unsuccessfully, to sell its domestic brands.

Phillip Morris, which bought Liggett's overseas operations (antitrust laws prevented it from buying the U.S. operations) has continued aggressively to claim a share of the home market for its own brands. Nevertheless, it too felt compelled to use its cash flow to diversify. Phillip Morris's notable acquisitions, the Miller Beer and 7-Up companies, were expensive acquisitions, costing over $600 million. Its earlier acquisitions, Clark Gum and American Safety Razor, were also costly and ended as mistakes.

R. J. Reynolds (RJR), the cigarette industry leader in market share and profits, made even more costly investments—in containerized shipping, oil, and food products, among others. Its investment in the sea-freight business alone exceeded $2 billion in the 1970s. Burmah Oil Company, purchased by RJR in 1976, cost $522 million and required an equal investment after the purchase. The RJR foods subsidiary was started in the 1960s with relatively small acquisitions, which included Hawaiian Punch and Chun King. Despite significant problems in making this unit profitable, Reynolds added Del Monte in 1979 at a cost of more than $600 million. In 1982 it bought the Heublein Corporation for $1.3 billion dollars.

As a group, the returns on these nontobacco investments were much lower than the cigarette profits of either Reynolds or Phillip Morris. Reynolds, for example, earned 70 percent of its profits from cigarettes, even though they only accounted for 50 percent of its net revenues.[9] The willingness of these firms to divert most of their earnings to less profitable industries is evidence that the firms felt further investment in tobacco would merely increase costs without increasing earnings. In other words, the profits used for acquiring new businesses were considered irrelevant to future operations of the tobacco business.

Excess Profits

Many other firms have earned profits they could not reinvest in their company without violating Porter's Law. For many the choice has been to use their profits to buy new businesses.

Coca-Cola is a typical example. Locked in head-to-head competition with Pepsi, Coca-Cola continued to battle for the cola market through innovative packaging, diet colas, and health promotions. But its flow of earnings has long exceeded the investment potential of this extremely lucrative but saturated market. Consequently, Coke bought, with their excess profits, noncola soft-drink companies, Minute Maid, a series of wine companies (since divested), and Columbia Pictures.[10]

Seagram's profits from the stagnating liquor industry not only financed its ventures in the oil business and ultimately its large share of Du Pont, but were also the source for its entry into the American wine business. With the advice of Mary Cunningham, Seagram's wine division added in 1983 Coca-Cola's wine subsidiary (which included Taylor Wines and Mogan David) to a collection that already featured Paul Masson Wines.[11]

Sears, Roebuck and Company, faced with barriers to expansion in the merchandizing field from Ward's, Pennys, discounters, mail order houses, and local department stores, has used its profits to enter more dynamic financial markets. Its ownership of Allstate Insurance has been complemented by acquisitions of the Dean, Witter, Reynolds stock brokerage firm, savings and loan companies, mortgage companies, and the Coldwell, Banker & Company real estate firm.[12]

General Motors' $2.5 billion acquisition of Electronic Data Systems (EDS) in the spring of 1984 quickly followed its announcement that at the end of the first quarter GM had $9 billion cash on hand.[13] The *Wall Street Journal* reported the views of Philip Fricke, a securities analyst at Goldman, Sachs, on the reasons for the acquisition:

[Fricke] said GM had only three things it could have done with all that cash: make acquisitions, raise its dividends or buy back some of its stock. The auto maker is already spending $6 billion this year on improvements to introduce new auto models and boost production efficiency. Mr. Fricke says there is "no unit growth in sight" in the auto industry so in going outside "GM must be seeking to restore prospects for real earnings growth."[14]

Even smaller companies may face the same problem. For example, California's intrastate airline, PSA, began buying hotels and other businesses it knew nothing about with its large profits in the late 1970s, rather than expand into head-to-head competition with regulated, interstate airlines.

In each of these instances, industry leaders have sought, through acquisition, a new outlet for their considerable profits. Success required that these firms look beyond their own industries. The nature of these acquisitions has varied, some, like EDS, are in high-growth, new technology markets, and others, like Del Monte or Conoco, are in more established lines of business. Some of these ventures have immediate profit potential; some do not. But what these acquisitions have in common is they require a large expenditure of corporate funds.

But why should R. J. Reynolds's managers have been allowed to invest billions of their shareholders' dollars in the sea-freight business? Why should Coca-Cola stockholders have financed ventures into the wine business? And why should the owners of Phillip Morris have had to bankroll the takeover of Miller Beer? Why should managers be permitted to speculate in new businesses using stockholders' money? Why shouldn't the excess profits be distributed as dividends?

THE DIVIDEND ALTERNATIVE

According to theory, business ventures should pay out all excess profits to shareholders in the form of dividends. But, as the history of Ford Motor Company illustrates, minority shareholders cannot compel corporations to declare dividends. So long as the earnings are invested in "the business," courts will not intervene. And because modern businesses are defined by their investments, rather than by some statement of purpose in the corporate charter, there is no occasion for intervention unless the excess profits are stored in a mattress.

Again, theory suggests that shareholders could band together as owners of a majority of the corporate shares and require that the profits be distributed. As a practical matter, it is extremely unusual for shareholders in large corporations, whose shares are usually dispersed among millions of holders, to undertake any concerted action against their managers' wishes. Such concerted actions are very expensive and rarely successful.[15]

More important, most shareholders do not object to corporations retaining earnings. Given the structure of corporate and personal income taxes in the United States, it is perhaps more surprising that shareholders want their corporations to declare any dividends.

Commentators, from economic theoreticians, like Milton Friedman, to practical business consultants, like Bruce Henderson, have traced this tendency of corporations to retain earnings to the structure of the income tax laws.[16] Corporations are taxed on their profits; those profits are then taxed again when received by shareholders as dividends. This double taxation of dividends makes it advantageous for shareholders that do not need the profits immediately for personal use to delay the second tax by having the corporation reinvest the profits for them.

For example, if a corporation earns $100 per share and the corporation and a shareholder are each subject to the maximum 50 percent tax on corporate and personal income, the shareholder will receive only $25 of the corporation's earnings:

$100.00 earnings
− 50.00 for corporate income tax, equals
50.00 dividend
− 25.00 for personal income tax
$ 25.00 cash available to the shareholder for
consumption or investment

On the other hand, if the corporation does not distribute the $50 earnings, a shareholder can have the $50 reinvested by the corporation without personal taxation. In this way a shareholder can delay taxation indefinitely, which is the equivalent of getting an interest-free loan each year on the amount that would be paid in taxes to the U.S. Treasury.

Furthermore, the shareholder can avoid high personal income tax rates on dividends forever by selling his shares. The shares (probably) will have risen in price to reflect the value of the retained earnings. When the shareholder sells more valuable shares, the tax will be based on the lower rate (20%) generally applicable to gains on the sale of capital assets by an individual in the 50 percent bracket. Even in the first year, this would represent a considerable tax savings:

$100.00 earnings
− 50.00 corporate tax
50.00 increased share value
− 10.00 capital gains tax on sale of share
$ 40.00 available for consumption or
reinvestment

Consequently, there is a strong bias in favor of retaining earnings to reduce and delay taxation.

Traditional corporate theory might provide another objection to this no-dividend scenario. To obtain any return from retained earnings, shareholders must reduce their control over the corporation, that is, sell some of their shares; whereas, when dividends are paid, all shareholders retain their proportionate control of the corporation. But few shareholders have any significant control or interest in controlling large corporations. Typically, the shares are so dispersed that shareholders exercise no control over the corporation's activities. More usually, shareholders express their satisfaction by buying, or dissatisfaction by selling, the corporation's shares.

Why then do corporations distribute dividends at all? First, there is a very strong tradition of successful firms declaring dividends. That tradition may have issued from the now less common concern of shareholders to maintain their proportionate control, or it may persist as a test of the performance of management. Some shareholders are skeptical of the accuracy of corporate reports concerning the investment value of retained earnings. They consider it crucial that corporations be required to dedicate at least a small portion of earnings to dividends.

Not all firms have committed themselves to regular dividends. Digital, for example, has not, but for those that do, the missing or even lowering of a dividend is frequently taken as a very significant sign of a corporation in trouble. Rather than face such stock market judgments, corporations, even on the brink of bankruptcy, have continued paying dividends. For example, the Penn Central Company, which went bankrupt in 1970, increased dividends from $1.25 in 1964, to $2 in 1965, and to $2.40 in 1967 and 1968. In 1969 the dividend finally dropped, but only to $1.80.[17]

Shareholders who pay little or no tax also pressure corporations to pay dividends. Low-income and retired individuals, nontaxable charitable organizations, pension funds, and even corporations (which pay less than 8% tax on intercorporate dividends) may depend on the income without fear of double taxation.

Individuals, for whom investment search costs are likely to be higher, will also tend to stay with a successful firm. If they need a current income and are in a low-tax bracket, they may choose a firm with a policy of regular dividends, but they will rely upon the firm to reinvest any additional profits. The costs of stock market transactions, as well as the costs of finding a better investment, further discourage shareholders from demanding full disgorgement of excess profits.

So investment search costs, transaction costs, and the double taxation of dividends all combine to permit corporate managers to retain control over most earnings, whether or not these earnings are required to conduct the firm's original business operations. The disposal of those profits is left to the decision of managers.

THE NEW BUSINESS ALTERNATIVE

Starting a new business from scratch can be an attractive option for a successful firm seeking an investment for its profits, but it usually is not. The unformed business alternative has two major disadvantages when compared with buying an existing business. Starting a business is risky because the product market and the production processes are unknown. Also, new businesses frequently cannot absorb very much money in their early stages, so they don't help dispose of "excess" profits.

The risks of starting new businesses are legion. First, even if the product is already accepted by consumers, the new firm cannot be sure that it will be able to wrest a market share away from more experienced established firms. Second, there are complexities in the production and distribution process which cannot be anticipated. Third, costs cannot be accurately projected until production and marketing methods are established and the production levels are fixed by demand for the new firm's product.

Even for successful firms, the survival rate of new products is very low. A study of 13,000 products introduced between 1968 and 1981 showed that in 1968 only 1 new product in 58 succeeded. While that ratio improved to 1 out of 7 by 1981, the lower failure rate on new products was a reflection of the more widespread use of tests of consumer reaction prior to formal introduction of a new product.[18] In other words, fewer new product ideas now reach the market.

Vivienne Marquis and Patricia Haskell recount a classic tale in *The Cheese Book* about Liederkranz cheese. It illustrates how risky it is to build a new production plant even when there is good reason to believe a manufacturing process is well understood. Liederkranz is an American cheese that was invented in 1882 in upstate New York for the New York City restaurant and delicatessen market. It was immediately popular and business grew. Some years ago, after the firm had been purchased by Borden, production was moved to Von Wert, Ohio.

The Liederkranz managers wished to make sure that the quality of the cheese did not suffer so they took precautions. They had the cheesemaking formula. They carried a "mother culture" of the bacteria that produced the cheese. They transported the original cheesemaking equipment. They even persuaded the cheesemakers to move to Ohio and paid for their move. Nevertheless, the cheese was not the same. Marquis and Haskell write:

> They tried again and again, but they simply could not duplicate the Liederkranz they had been making before. Finally, they took some of the Liederkranz cheeses made in the old plant and smeared them all over the new tile walls. That done, the cheeses came out right. No one had realized till then that the curds had been affected just as much by bacteria floating free in the air as by cultures that were mixed directly into them.[19]

The particular problems of cheesemaking are unique, but the unforeseeable risks surrounding any new kind of business venture are typical. R. J. Reynolds decided in 1957 to expand its cigarette-packaging division, Archer Products, to include the manufacturer of gift wrapping and aluminum-foil products. According to Miles:

> Almost as soon as the integrated Archer subsidiary had been assembled, it was dismantled. First, Reynolds managers found that the seasonal nature of the gift wrapping business created more problems than benefits. . . . Next, the household aluminum-foil line was divested because . . . Reynolds managers had begun to recognize they could not compete against fully integrated competitors. . . .[20]

New ventures may be unlikely to receive approval from large, bureaucratic corporations which employ stated return-on-investment criteria for their capital allocation decisions. Even if the idea for a proposed venture is conceded to be novel and exciting, allocations may be withheld because it is impossible to predict costs, consumer demand, and competition with sufficient accuracy. In contrast, acquisition of an existing firm in an established product market provides more easily identifiable benchmarks for evaluating a proposal.

New ventures are unsatisfactory means of disposing of excess profits for another reason. Unless the venture is involved in the production of steel, autos, or oil, the start-up costs of even a major new venture are unlikely to be significant to a large successful firm. Exxon Corporation, with earnings of $5.7 billion in 1980, distributed $2.35 billion in dividends that year. It has nearly $26 billion in retained earnings and, according to the New York Times, a yearly capital allocation budget of $10 billion.[21] Exxon entered the office automation market with its Qyx, Qwip, Zilog, and Vydec products in the 1970s, and in 1977 it invested a total of $9 million in the research and development of information systems, peanuts compared to the research budgets of established office automation leaders such as IBM, Xerox and Digital. Only after much experience in this field was Exxon able to develop projects (many of which were questionable) that absorbed greater amounts of capital.

It is not surprising, then, that when Exxon thought it had a revolutionary design for electrical motors, it decided to take a bigger plunge. According to *Fortune*, it rejected a plan to make a $40 million start-up investment. And instead of buying a $10 million electric-drives business, Exxon purchased the Reliance Electric Company for $1.2 billion.[22]

The risks of committing a billion dollars to a new business in an uncharted product market are too great. However, even with the data available from established companies, mistakes are possible. Exxon, it seems, made mistakes in both the prospects it held for its "new" design of an electric engine and in its confidence in Reliance Electric. But even if *Fortune* is correct in reporting that the Exxon purchase represented a $600 million mistake, recovering fifty cents on the dollar is better than RCA did when virtually the entire $500 million investment it had put into an internal expansion of its computer operations had to be written off.[23]

THE PASSIVE INVESTMENT ALTERNATIVE

Clearly then it is risky to enter a new business at a scale that will absorb a significant flow of earnings. It is often safer, to place these corporate profits in the capital markets which have an unlimited capacity to absorb funds and an array of risk levels to suit investors. Such "passive" investments, therefore, provide another outlet for accumulated profits.

Almost all large firms hold securities. Efficient use of cash reserves requires that corporations invest their money rather than let it sit in a bank until the money is redeployed in the business. As a consequence, corporations hold all kinds of securities, ranging from shares in other corporations to home mortgages. But such investments pose two dangers to the corporation if they generate more than a small percentage of the firm's revenue: tax liabilities and takeovers.

If a corporation reinvests its profits in passive investments, it is subject to the punitive rates of the accumulated-earnings tax. As mentioned above, the tax law does not require that a firm invest in any particular business, only that it continues to actively manage the businesses it owns. Thus, the provision is unlikely to affect a successful company unless its managers intend to transform it into an investment company.

Even Bendix, which had substantial undistributed earnings in its $500 million acquisition hope chest—in cash and securities—did not face tax problems. Its passive investments were permitted because the earnings were accumulated for the purpose of buying a new company.

Bendix's cash and securities could have created a more immediate problem for its corporate managers. Having so many assets in cash and securities made Bendix an attractive and vulnerable takeover target. In a stock market where corporate shares had been generally undervalued, a corporation with a large number of liquid assets is easier to purchase. The acquiring firm can pay part of the price to target shareholders using the target's cash.

Selling some of the target's assets is always a possible tactic to partially finance a takeover, but it is much less convenient. Bendix's attempted takeover of RCA, for example, was reported to be based on a plan to sell one or more of the target's operating divisions. The expectation was that Bendix would sell RCA subsidiaries—Hertz or CIT Financial—at a premium and thereby recoup a substantial portion of the purchase price.[24]

But selling off operating assets is apt to be slow and may not be profitable, as Du Pont discovered after buying Conoco. It had been assumed that Du Pont would reduce the debt used to buy Conoco by selling some of the target's oil or coal assets. Because of the fall in energy prices, few of these assets have been saleable at the price Du Pont paid. One of the few sales was a leveraged buyout by managers of a coal division.[25]

In contrast, an acquiring firm can immediately value and use liquid assets of a target to defray takeover expenses or reduce its debt. As a consequence, an undervalued $4 billion firm like Bendix, with over $500 million cash, had to fear a takeover attempt if it didn't make use of the cash.

Utilizing cash resources can therefore become a compelling reason to merge. McDermott was reported to have bought Babcock &

Wilcox to reduce its liquid assets,[26] and Hiram Walker avoided an attempt to tap its liquid profits by a quick merger with an oil company.[27] When the Disney Corporation was reportedly ripe for a takeover, it also rapidly disposed of excess cash by making acquisitions.[28] Consequently, even if there were no potential tax penalties for passive investments, a firm's increased vulnerability to takeovers would deter managers from accumulating too many profits in a liquid form.

THE SALARY ALTERNATIVE

Even before a corporation's main business has become saturated by investment of retained earnings, corporate managers and employees claim the profits of successful firms. There is evidence to suggest that they succeed in capturing a portion of these profits, but like other uses for retained earnings, salaries, bonuses, hourly wages, and fringe benefits are unlikely to eliminate the excess.

Salaries of chief executive officers of large corporations are impressive. In its annual survey of executive compensation, *Business Week* reported that the top two earners of 1982 were Frederick W. Smith, chairman of the innovative Federal Express, and Charles P. Lazarus, chairman of the Toys "Я" Us Company, whose discount marketing concept saved its faltering parent corporation, Interstate Stores, from bankruptcy. Including stock options, bonuses, and salaries, Smith earned over $51 million and Lazarus earned $43 million in 1982.[29]

To be sure, these two figures are exceptional. They reflect the unique contributions of these chief executive officers to the overall achievement of the two companies. Their total compensation, including exercised stock options, is a one-time payment rather than an annual salary. Even so, *Business Week* also found twenty-five executives who earned more than $1.8 million in 1982 when bonuses and long-term income were included in the figuring.

Lazarus's annual salary of $315,000 was more typical of the base pay of chief executive officers, which generally ranged between $250,000 and $500,000. Executive salaries seem to be more related to the industry sector and firm size than to corporate profits. For example, the survey showed that the salary of a chief executive at a leading bank or bank holding company was normally between

$400,000 and $500,000, despite profits ranging between $80 million and $440 million. Salaries for airline chief executives ranged between $320,000 and $380,000, although Eastern lost $75 million and Delta and United made money in 1982. Automobile chief executives earned at least $350,000. Executives at the larger firms, Ford and GM, received $446,000 and $549,000 in salaries, even though Ford lost $600 million in 1982 and GM made almost $1 billion.

Executives are not the only ones to benefit from the success of large firms. The hourly wage of unionized employees in the automotive, steel, and airline industries, for example, are higher than the national average. According to J. K. Galbraith in *Economics and the Public Purpose*, the wages do not reflect the productivity of the workers. Rather, these industries (when they were successful) shifted the burden of inflated wages onto consumers and gave these "profits" to the workers.[30]

That these wage rates are based on profits rather than on productivity is illustrated by the declining profitability of the steel and auto industries. Wage "give-backs" have therefore helped rescue Chrysler from the brink of insolvency in 1981 and have become a common bargaining issue in the faltering American steel industry in the 1980s. Efforts to sell Ford's River Rouge steel plants to a Japanese firm failed because of union wage demands, and a complete shut down of the facilities was averted in 1983 only after the union agreed to a large "give-back."[31]

Similarly, in the newly deregulated airline industry, Continental Airlines sought to break what it claimed was an uneconomic salary structure in order to compete with nonunion air carriers. By going through bankruptcy proceedings, Continental's management sought to reduce the $83,000 a year salary negotiated by the pilot's union to $43,000.[32]

To what extent, then, may employees claim a share of corporate profits? As a general matter, courts uphold compensation plans, regardless of the amounts involved when it can be argued that compensation payments encourage higher levels of production and efficiency. Courts have usually declared employee compensation to be an unauthorized gift of corporate funds only in cases where additional compensation is planned after completion of the work. Only under the most extreme circumstances would courts limit compensation. As a practical matter, courts have not declared that a compensation system awards too great a share of profits to hourly workers or corporate managers. The limits on compensation are more likely to be set by prevailing wages within an industry and a firm's size.

It is important for a firm to stay within industry compensation standards so as not to exceed rivals' costs. A larger firm may have more flexibility in the area of executive salaries because they are spread over greater revenues. On the other hand, there is little incentive to lowering worker or executive salaries below prevailing industry wages. If managers cut wages, morale will suffer and the best workers will probably leave. In 1982, when the Intel Corporation lowered salaries by 10 percent, seventeen top managers and scientists resigned.[33] Even if managers do lower wages, competing firms may do the same, and then any competitive advantage is lost, as recent events within the airline industry will attest.

Because labor costs tend to be uniform, and because little advantage can be gained by lowering those costs, a company paying high wages is unlikely to be at a competitive disadvantage (from U.S. competitors). Nor are they especially likely to become takeover targets, since new owners will not win any leverage by reducing wages. The free market works very slowly unless foreign competition, new products, or deregulation force wages to correspond more closely to production levels.

How industry labor costs are established is poorly understood. Worker skills and training, productivity, and industry profitability all play a role in setting hourly wages. Executive salaries are, according to Nobel price winner Herbert Simon, derived from a hierarchical rule of thumb in which each layer of managers must earn some fraction greater than the group below them.[39] Consequently the largest firms with the greatest number of managerial levels and highest paid hourly workers are likely to pay their chief executive officers the most.

While Simon's analysis makes it easier to raise, than lower, salaries it also contains limits. Firms still have to have profits to satisfy investors. Thus even allowing for comfortable corporate headquarters and custom jet liners the successful large corporation is unlikely to exhaust a firm's excess profits.

THE MERGER SOLUTION

Mergers provide a practical alternative for successful corporations that need to place their excess profits. Mergers solve the problems posed by other uses of profits.

Foremost, the acquisition of other firms can absorb almost limitless amounts of money. Chevron's acquisition of Gulf Oil for $13 billion, Seagram's acquisition of Du Pont shares for $2.6 billion, GM's acquisition of EDS for $2.5 billion, Exxon's acquisition of Reliance Electric for $1.2 billion, Mobil's purchase of Marcor for $1.6 billion, R. J. Reynolds investment of $2 billion in the sea freight business and Phillip Morris's purchase of 7-Up for $500 million each illustrate the potential of mergers as repositories of profits.

The motive behind these megamergers is often quite explicit. The Sun Company's decision to buy Becton, Dickinson is a good example of a firm's desire merely to deploy funds, rather than base an investment on exciting profit opportunities. The court that reviewed that transaction summarized the thinking behind the takeover:

> Harry Sharbaugh, Sun's chief executive, had determined in 1977 that Sun needed to diversify by investing in institutions outside the energy field. Sun sought the acquisition of no less than a 20% interest and not more than a 50% interest in 3 or 4 companies over the succeeding two or three years by investing some 300–400 million dollars in each organization. Sun's corporate development committee was given responsibility for developing major acquisition opportunities. . . .[34]

The decision to acquire a firm serves another important function; it is a decision capable of rational defense. Compared with the creation of a new business, a merger is a much less risky venture for corporate executives to enter. The target's history of product acceptance, production costs, and profits provides managers of the acquiring firm with a basis for projecting the future value of the target. Even if they are wrong and overestimate the value, managers are usually saved from writing off the entire cost of the investment, as is frequently not the case with new ventures. At a minimum, those undertaking the acquisition can point to the verifiable data of a target's history to justify to a board of directors, stockholders, or financial analysts that a failure had been a reasonable prospect.

The reduced possibility of failure may explain the recent choices of targets, such as R. J. Reynolds's purchase of Del Monte. Reynolds earns very high profits in the tobacco industry yet paid $600 million for a firm of average profitability with no obvious prospects for growth. Del Monte was already the largest seller of canned goods, a steady market but not one slated for rapid expansion. Reynolds's attraction may have been based on the safety of the investment. This consideration was especially important to Reynolds, given the high costs and low short-run returns of its other acquisitions.

Acquisitions also have the potential to increase profits. They can become showcases for managerial talent and corporate prestige. The reputation of the Phillip Morris management, for example, benefited from their success with Miller beer.

Success through merger has special rewards for managers. There are more opportunities within larger firms for middle rank executives, and top executives tend to be paid more money in larger firms. Also, larger firms seem to confer more managerial status to members of the business community.

Mergers also offer an opportunity for substantial tax benefits. Investments in new ventures are treated less favorably by the tax laws than investments in ongoing businesses. The courts have held that

> even though a taxpayer has made a firm decision to enter into business and over a considerable period of time spent money in preparation for entering that business he [cannot deduct those expenses from the corporation's profits] until such time as the [new] business has begun to function as a going concern. . . .[35]

In contrast, investments to expand current businesses or the operations of a target firm can be deducted immediately. A major marketing project, such as Phillip Morris's introduction of Miller Lite beer, could require an independent firm to seek new equity or debt. However, under within a corporate umbrella, the new venture's tax deduction can defer the taxes of currently profitable operations. Those untaxed profits can then be used to finance the venture instead of the twice-taxed funds of the capital market.

In addition, the acquisition offers an occasion to distribute corporate earnings without shareholders paying the higher rate applicable to dividends. When the acquisition is for cash, the sale of shares to the acquiring firm will be taxed at the lower capital-gain rates. For the target shareholders, this means they will (or may) realize the increased value of their shares attributable to retained earnings without having to pay the higher tax that would be levied if the corporation distributed those profits.

Mergers, therefore, provide an attractive solution for the successful corporation possessing excess profits. By combining the interests of shareholders and management in pursuit of further profits (while avoiding major risks), mergers can promote corporate growth and accommodate as much investment as a firm has at its disposal. Mergers have become in our day the logical, although not inevitable, result of corporate success.

That logic seems to be reflected in the recent megamergers of successful firms. Their acquisitions rather than those of "high flying go-go" conglomerate firms, have made the notable purchases of the 1980s using hard cash rather than paper securities. These acquisitions are likely to continue.

CHAPTER 8

STRATEGIC INVESTMENT THEORIES

B usiness strategists have developed rationales for every type of investment option open to executives. And if these strategists were not directly responsible for the popularity of megamergers in the latter half of the 1970s they at least actively promoted the belief that acquisitions were beneficial to corporations and their shareholders. Recent business literature, however, has suggested that the advantages to merging were often overstated or implemented too freely.

Strategic investment theories that justified mergers rested on a series of premises: (1) Successful firms have a life cycle; (2) during their "mature" phase, firms generate excess earnings that should then be used to acquire other firms; (3) appropriate acquisition targets can be identified; and (4) corporate executives can manage the conglomerate firms resulting from such acquisitions.

The Boston Consulting Group (BCG) is noted for its synthesis of these business strategy axioms and for transforming them into a handy investment matrix. Bruce Henderson, BCG chief executive during the 1970s, popularized the matrix through a series of influential essays.[1] These essays provided a simple investment guide for managers with excess earnings and suggested criteria on which to base acquisitions (and divestitures) that would solve management's problems.

The matrix divided a firm's businesses into quadrants (see Figure 8-1). In order to produce a continual growth in corporate earnings,

171

Figure 8-1.   BCG Cash-Cow Investment Matrix.

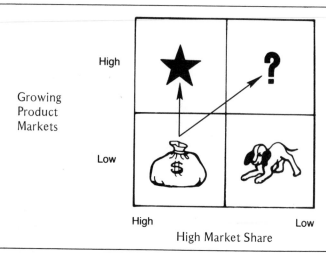

managers were advised to invest profits from their mature businesses ("cash cows") in growing product markets if: (1) those businesses were already the largest producers ("stars"), or (2) those businesses could grow to become the largest producers ("question marks"). The leading producers were bound to become large cash cows as the growing business matured. Firms that did not succeed in becoming leading producers (question marks) or that were not in growing product markets ("dogs") were to be divested.[2]

If a firm did not have an appropriate complement of stars and question marks the investment guide became a merger matrix. The BCG matrix distinguished itself as a method of making "smart" acquisitions in the 1970s, unlike the discredited "go-go" acquisitions of the 1960s. Through mergers, the matrix could become the key to eternal growth and everlasting profits.

Investing profits from stagnant industries in growing product markets is a good idea. The idea was communicated effectively through concise and seemingly concrete advice. However, the advice may have been too simply put or managers may have been too eager to read into it what was not meant.

To be fair, business strategists did not develop the matrix as a means of choosing merger targets. The purpose of the matrix was to provide a coherent approach to internal capital investments. Nor have business consulting firms played a major role in selecting targets for acquiring firms. Rather, firms with resources to acquire other firms have used the strategic framework to organize or justify their selection of targets.

CORPORATE MANAGERS AS GENERALISTS

The single most important message carried to executives by the BCG matrix was implicit: You can manage a diversified corporation by numbers. If believed, that message freed managers from any restraints surrounding acquisition policy. Any firm could become a target. No firm resulting from mergers would be too large, too diverse, or too complex if the numbers—product market growth and market share—provided all the information necessary to good management.

Some reassurance to corporate executives was necessary after the reputation of conglomerate firms eroded following the merger wave of the 1960s. The collapse of the booming 1960's stock market had its greatest impact on the glamour stocks of newly created conglomerate firms. The value of these corporate empires (built by PE magic) vanished, and executives were blamed for buying companies they did not understand and creating firms they could not manage.

The good news that large successful firms could make profitable acquisitions may have been more important than the specific advice offered by BCG's matrix or by General Electric's more sophisticated "market attractiveness" matrix. Analysts of conglomerate failures were wrong. Conglomerate firms *could* be run well if only the right investment policy were followed. The problem was poor management, not mergers.

For executives who needed acquisitions to place earnings that could not be invested in current businesses, this was welcomed news. Mergers could be undertaken without raising fears that the firm would become unmanageable. Even if BCG were not exactly right in its prescription, the key to good management was in the numbers. And many executives were confident they could manage numbers.

Such confidence is not surprising. As we have seen, the development of the modern corporation rested on a transition from direct supervision of operations to management by reports. The multidivisional firm is controlled by professional executives, who manage by establishing performance objectives for line officers who supervise production operations. The central staff direct these complex firms by monitoring performance and allocating internal investments. In short, through numbers, corporate executives manage large and diverse businesses and buy and sell subsidiaries.

This, in turn, has given accountants, lawyers, and other financial experts an advantage in becoming corporate executives over individuals with production, sales, or engineering backgrounds. Harold Geneen's reknown as chairman of ITT was based on his phenomenal memory of performance statistics while grilling the managers of the conglomerate's numerous businesses. Harry Gray of United Technologies, William Agee, formerly of Bendix, and many others have found the fast track to corporate power through financial expertise.

In 1980 *Business Week* reported the results of a study by Theodore Barry & Associates that showed that "most executives have never participated in line management."[3] Another study, by Korn/Ferry International, revealed that almost half of the 1,700 corporate vice presidents surveyed (from whose ranks chief executives are usually chosen) began as either financial or marketing executives rather than production officers.[4]

The broad training inside business schools, with instruction based largely on case studies and statistical examples, has led to a new generation of business leaders less daunted by the prospect of making unrelated acquisitions. And careers no longer rest on a particular product market. Phillip Morris, for example, began its diversification strategy in 1957 when Parker McComas succeeded the tobacco supersalesman Alfred Lyon as chief executive officer. McComas spent twenty-seven years in the banking and finance industry before joining Phillip Morris. George Weissman, whose career started in Hollywood public relations and ended as CEO of Phillip Morris, was the moving force behind the Miller Beer acquisition.[5] These men, with financial or marketing backgrounds, have pressed diversification strategies. Their training, which transcended the tobacco industry, gave them the vision and confidence to move into unrelated businesses.

Financial experts have an advantage over other executives in pursuing top corporate positions, because financial reports have become the language of business. They are used by a corporation's central staff internally to direct activities and externally to interpret corporate health to the investment community. Depreciation schedules can determine the rate of profit for a division. Return on investment criteria can eliminate new project proposals from consideration by a firm's board of directors. Financing strategies can magnify a corporation's resources or shrink them. Because they are more familiar with the numbers and how they are set, financial executives can assume a role over executives whose expertise relates to narrower matters of production.

Financial Mergers

Financial executives are less likely to be concerned about differences in production processes or sales methods of merging companies and more likely to be concerned with the compatibility of cash flows. For example, a financial executive might favor a merger between a ski company and a tennis company to even sales income throughout the year, or the acquisition of an insurance company with large cash reserves to match the needs of a retailing company with large credit sales. The executive might be attracted by a company that had lost money or had unused tax deductions. After merger, these losses or unused deductions could be carried over and set off against the profits of the acquiring firm. Because financial officers tend to view businesses less as producers of goods and services, and more as streams of income and expenses, they have developed their own strategies for profitable mergers.

Testimony to the influence of financial analysis is provided by the fact that purely financial theories of mergers are taken seriously by corporations. At the time of its merger with Home Oil Ltd., the chairman of the distillery Hiram Walker was quoted by *Business Week* as saying, "We don't know a damned thing about oil."[6] The attraction of the oil company was its ability to soak up liquor profits. The merged firm's president, William Wilder, planned to use the liquor business as a cash cow to finance oil exploration. This merger also promised double tax benefits. Both exploration expenses and depreciation allowances could offset earnings from the liquor business. Of course, the world of business does not always cooperate with the plans of financial executives like Wilder. A year and a half later *Business Week* reported that Wilder may have made a $295 million mistake in buying a Denver oil property for $630 million.[7]

The Influence of Financial Analysis

The outlook presented by a cash-flow analysis is at least as important as the prescription it writes for profits. The analysis reinforces, through its assumptions, the view that profitable mergers can be selected according to the numbers without reference either to the personnel or to the production processes of the target. This management by numbers is consistent with the role of the central staff in the large modern corporation. The chief executive officer, the board of directors, or members of the central staff cannot be experts on the separate needs of the divisions of a major corporation. Decision-makers must, instead, rely on divisional managers to supply them with the facts of production costs and consumer demand. Only after these facts have been translated into expected expenses, cash flows, and predicted rates of return can the central administration reach its decisions. A merger proposal justified by the numbers may not appear to the generalist thinking of central management as being so very different from any other corporate decision.

LIFE CYCLES AND PORTFOLIO MANAGEMENT

The conclusion that diversification, through merger or internal investment, is an appropriate course of corporate action most often rests on two assumptions: (1) The principal business of a firm will reach a point when it can no longer absorb the profits generated by that business, and (2) the firm can profitably reinvest the excess profits. The first premise, known as the life cycle theory, is based on a widely accepted understanding of product demand. The second, sometimes referred to as portfolio management of business products, is a much more controversial topic and will be dealt with separately from life cycle theory.

Product Life Cycle

Harvard business professor Theodore Levitt has outlined four stages in the "life" of a successful product: market development, growth, maturity, and decline. He depicts this cycle as a curve of sales reve-

Figure 8-2. Product Life Cycle.

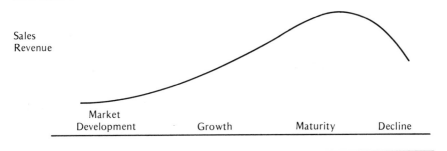

Source: Theodore Levitt, "Exploit the Product Life Cycle," *Harvard Business Review* (November/December, 1965): 81.

nue that rises as the product is introduced to consumers and accepted as a staple and falls as the product is displaced (see Figure 8-2).

The first stage is thought to be short but critical, since a high percentage of new products fail. If too few consumers buy the product, the firm will abandon production. For more favored new products, a critical mass of consumers "accepts" the product, that is, they decide that it fits a need not satisfied by other products on the market.

During the second stage the market for the new product grows. As more consumers learn of the existence of the product, sales build. Expenses also increase with the expansion of production facilities and the broadening of advertising campaigns. Advertising is particularly important at this stage to widen the public's awareness of the product and to gain public recognition of the firm's brand of the product. These costs often make this stage unprofitable, on a current basis, even for products with instant appeal.

The third stage, maturity, is typically the most profitable. Public acceptance of the product has been established and purchases are made at regular intervals by a predictable number of consumers. The firm's brand will have earned a stable share of the market so no new production facilities are required. Advertising costs will also level off. Production costs will drop because the firm will have the benefit of efficient manufacturing on a large scale.

The expectation that profits will increase as costs decline is based on the assumption that because the market shares of other firms' products are stable, these latter brands will not be in direct competition. Each firm will direct its own brand to a separate segment of the product market. Rival firms will compete directly only in accordance with Porter's Law—that is, when the outcome can be determined quickly and the advantage is clear. Otherwise, firms will continue to set prices so as to avoid the pressures of competition.

The fourth stage, decline, occurs when the introduction of a better product or a change in the public's taste makes a product no longer desirable. This stage may or may not be profitable, but any profit margin will typically be based on a reduced sales volume. Mass-marketed ballpoint pens and felt-tipped markers have, for example, left a lucrative low-volume product niche for Mount Blanc and other fine fountain pens.

Profits may even increase at the beginning of the fourth stage for the firm may no longer have to maintain and replace expensive production equipment. The firm may also be able to make substantial savings by abandoning expensive quality control or consumer service features. If the brand name is not to be continued, this quality "deception" can increase profit margins. But at some point, whether the product is buggy whips, radio tubes, hula hoops, or pet rocks, the product market will shrink or even disappear.

For managers with ambitions to maintain or increase the size of their firms, the lessons to be learned from this idealized description of the product life cycle are clear. Excess profits generated during the mature third stage should be invested in new or growing products. As current products decline in popularity, a new generation of products, with larger revenues, should be introduced to assume their market place.

Product Portfolio Management

The logic of the product life cycle gave rise to the BCG matrix and other capital-allocation theories. General Electric's "Market Attractiveness-Business Strength" matrix, for example, has the same objective as the BCG model: to transfer unneeded profits from today's goods to develop tomorrow's successful products.[8]

These strategic investment models were attractive to corporate managers. Their existing decision processes already required them to do much of the analysis, at least at the level of generality in the BCG matrix. Academic attempts to generalize the shape or duration of the product life cycle, though, have not been successful.[9] Nevertheless, corporations must still decide whether their product market is growing and, if so, whether new production facilities are needed. And the firm must decide if reinvestment of all profits in the existing business would violate Porter's Law by increasing costs without increasing profits. If some of these unneeded or excess profits are retained, the firm ought to invest them in tomorrow's products. Thus, as a practical matter, the firm decides implicitly where its products fit along the life cycle curve.

Growth and survival are the ultimate issues for managers, and survival means selling products people will want in the future. But the pretensions of product portfolio management are grander than any notion of mere survival. Bruce Henderson, of the BCG, said of the firm that produces many and diverse products.:

> Conglomerates are the normal and natural business form for efficiently channeling investment in the most productive use. If nature takes its course, then conglomerates will become the dominant form of business organization. . . .[10]

Henderson then added that

> internal reinvestment of capital] can be far more efficient and effective than the public capital markets. . . . [First] top management . . . is better equipped than an outside investor to appraise the potential and characteristics of a growing business. . . . [Second] any company which can treat its investments in growing businesses as an expense to be offset against other profits has a great [tax] advantage in terms of its cost of capital.[11]

Not everyone agrees, however, that a firm's retained earnings represent a source of low-cost capital, or if they are, that the lower cost can be used to increase earnings.[12]

Regardless of a manager's belief in the ultimate promise of portfolio management, the BCG matrix paralleled the annual financial analysis utilized to allocate the firm's capital. Managers can easily translate predictions of future earnings and investment needs to life cycle categories. The matrix is, therefore, a useful framework for discussing or justifying capital-allocation policy.

The only new decision required by the employment of strategic matrices pertains to the question of which businesses should be bought and which should be sold. Here the GE and the BCG models part. The GE matrix requires a very detailed analysis of the growth prospects of a product market and its profit potential, as well as an equally detailed analysis of the ability of the firm to operate the new business. (Criteria include firm size, market growth, market diversity, competitive structure, industry profitability, and technological, environmental, and sociopolitical factors.)[13] While such detailed analyses are recommended by business advisors such as Harvard Business School professors Kenneth Andrews or Michael Porter,[14] they are rarely performed. It is also very difficult to translate the many GE factors into a quantitative formula. Thus, even after making a detailed analysis, the basis for distributing capital may remain unclear. In contrast, by assuming that any new business can be operated by any firm, the BCG matrix defines future profitability solely in terms of high market growth and high market share.

The popularity of the BCG matrix may result from its conceptual simplicity. The factors—future market growth and market share—may be no more ascertainable than the complex of characteristics demanded by the GE matrix, but they are few enough to focus discussion. Even if they were less precisely knowable than the GE criteria, the implications to be derived from a discussion of market growth and market share can easily be understood.

The BCG model picks business winners. Investments should only be made in quickly growing product markets (markets that have grown more than 10% per year) and only in businesses that have the largest share of the product market. These criteria provide explicit direction as to how to dispose of conflicting claims for funds from different businesses within a firm. The needs of those firms owning the highest share in the fastest growing markets should be satisfied first.

This market growth/market share matrix is then the key to managing a large portfolio of totally different products. It is also suitable for buying and selling existing businesses, because the market criteria are comparable. On the other hand, evaluating a new business proposal under the BCG matrix is difficult because no market data exists. The less explicit GE matrix is less helpful than the BCG matrix because so many individual aspects of businesses are considered that their relative importance is unclear.

CHOOSING THE RIGHT TARGET

While the decision to invest in growing product markets was based squarely in life cycle theory, the targeting of a leading firm rested on an entirely different basis. BCG insisted that firms invest in only the number one manufacturer in a particular market because it believed the producer with the highest market share would eventually achieve the lowest costs and therefore the biggest profits.

According to Henderson, "Unit costs . . . decline 20 to 30 percent each time accumulated [production] experience doubles."[15] The emphasis Henderson placed on production totals was a significant extension of existing theories about firm size and cost reductions. If sound, it promised to simplify competitive analysis greatly and thereby facilitate capital-allocation decisions.

Prior to the enunciation of this "experience curve," business analysts and economists had discussed three relationships between size and cost: Larger production facilities lower unit costs; longer production runs lower unit costs; and labor costs fall as a firm's employees learn their jobs better.

The first two types of cost reductions, often referred to as "economies of scale," are based on physical properties. For example, a container that holds twice as much liquid does not require twice as much material to construct, because the volume of a container increases more rapidly than its surface area. Longer production runs permit other kinds of savings. For example, if a firm's machinery has to be set for making different sizes of product, the machinery is shut down between each run. The longer the production runs, the less down time. Also, if the runs are long enough, it may be possible to use specialized machinery that requires no setting alterations and thus no down time (except for maintenance).

In addition to these economies of scale, labor costs can be reduced by large-scale production. Northwestern University industrial organization economist F. M. Scherer describes the result:

> Output per hour of work rises, the number of errors tends to fall, and unit costs decline along a so-called learning curve with increases in the cumulative volume of a specific product manufactured. Studies of World War II aircraft production show that labor costs per unit fell by approximately 20 percent with each doubling of cumulative output.[16]

The pioneering industrial-organization economist, Joe Bain, believed that these scale economies were quickly exhausted, that is, firms would soon find that further increases in size would provide no lowering in costs. He further believed that many firms operating at maximum efficiency could coexist in any one industry. As a consequence, being first or being biggest was not likely to be a reliable predictor of a firm's relative costs or competitive success.

BCG disputed Bain's conclusions. Instead, they developed a dynamic theory of scale economies that was loosely based on the learning curve. BCG's experience curve declared that all costs, not merely labor costs, would decline as firms gained production experience. Overall costs would fall because, with experience, managers as well as workers would learn more about the product and its production. New insights would be generated by this learning, and costs per unit would fall. If one firm had more experience, it would display the lowest costs, and it would be almost impossible for any other firm to catch up and compete with a well-established leader.

BCG's claim that costs will decline 20 to 30 percent each time experience doubled was supported by a few statistical studies of industrial costs. The conclusion relied on lessons taught by the airframe industry during World War II and early experiences of Alcoa's aluminum production. The most dramatic confirmation of the theory, however, came from BCG's direct experience with the Texas Instrument Corporation.

While consulting with BCG, Texas Instruments (TI) entered on a marketing program for pocket computers. The key to the program was to grab market share and volume (that is, experience) by selling below current costs but above anticipated average total cost. It was a daring strategy that succeeded. TI's production costs fell, and it became the number one producer as profits poured in.[17]

If BCG were right and Bain were wrong, the key to competitive success would be simple: Be number one. And if success could be diagnosed so easily, then the investment policies of large, diversified firms was also easily determined: Invest in the number one firm and get out of everything else. Even if these prescriptions were exaggerations, they could provide central direction to management of complex firms.

The importance of being number one received added confirmation from Harvard's Marketing Science Institute and the Strategic Planning Institute's work on the PIMS (Profit Impact of Marketing Strategy) project.

By 1975 Robert Buzzell and his Harvard associates were confident that they had demonstrated the importance of market shares.

[T]he PIMS project . . . reveals 37 key profit influences, of which one of the most important is market share. . . . On the average, a difference of 10 percentage points in market share is accompanied by a difference of about 5 points in pretax ROI [return on investment].[18]

In other words, the higher the market share, the higher the profits. Buzzell's group claimed the PIMS data base provided statistical support for BCG's experience curve theories and seriously undermined Bain's assertions regarding the limits to economies of scale. They, therefore, went on to discuss the strategic implications of their findings in terms quite similar to the BCG matrix.

The sophisticated PIMS data base and the simple BCG matrix combined to dominate discussions of business strategies during the 1970s. Together they provided a basis for claiming that bigger firms are more productive and that diversified firms are not less manageable. Thus, corporate managers could reject the discredited experience with mergers during the 1960s. Those mergers failed because managers made mistakes in their acquisition and investment policies. All managers had to do was choose the right targets.

THE CRITIQUE OF MERGER STRATEGIES

As the merger wave began to swell in 1978 and 1979, American firms were rapidly losing market share to foreign competitors in steel, automobiles, electronics, computers, and other products. Some commentators, like Bruce Henderson, declared that Japanese successes were a result of their adherence to strategic theory. The Japanese, like Texas Instruments, had followed a strategy of building market share through low prices on high-quality goods. They were rewarded by an increase in sales and a decrease in costs and by profitability, if not dominance, in many industries.

But an increasing number of other observers agreed with a University of Chicago Business School professor, Edward Wrapp, who stated in 1980, "All kinds of companies feel they can acquire any kind of company and run it. . . . [The problem is] "the professional manager believes certain tools can be applied in any situation."[19] Professors Abernathy and Hayes of the Harvard Business School elaborated on these sentiments: "[T]he new management philosophy with its . . . preoccupation with strategists, master strokes and organizational processes should bear a large share of the blame.[20]

In 1980 national news weeklies joined the cry with features on the decline of the American economy. *Time* magazine asked, "Capitalism: Is It Working?"[21] *Newsweek* declared, "An Economic Dream in Peril."[22] And *Business Week's* special issue on "Revitalizing the U.S. Economy" singled out for censure the assumption that firms could be well managed by financial strategies.[23] These critiques spotlighted holes in business strategy theory that had previously escaped public attention. The premises on which strategic theory had been built were suddenly thrown into question.

Doubting the Experience Curve

The experience curve never worked especially well as theory because BCG could not explain why costs should fall with more experience and why lesser firms could not copy a leading firm's production techniques. Moreover, evidence of the relationship between experience and market share was still unconfirmed. In fact, there was even a possibility, mentioned by Buzzell's group in 1975 but left unexplored, that BCG had its causal factors backward:

> The simplest of all explanations for the market-share/profitability relationship is that both market share and ROI [i.e., profitability] reflect a common underlying factor: the quality of management. Good managers (including perhaps lucky ones) are successful in achieving high shares of their respective markets, because they are skillful in controlling costs and so on.[24]

Even if the experience curve did provide useful knowledge with regard to cost cutting, such knowledge would not protect a market leader if its experience were made irrelevant by changes in technology or consumer taste. For example, at the outset of the 1920s the Ford Motor Company produced over half the automobiles sold annually in the United States. It had a great cost advantage over General Motors and other manufacturers. Nevertheless, General Motors overtook sales of the Model T despite Ford's production experience by introducing a slightly more expensive car that had some additional features, most notably a hard roof. By 1927 the Model T had lost its market position. Ford shut down its entire operation for over a year to retool its very efficient but rigidly specialized plants to produce a new car, the Model A.[25]

An advantage can also be lost if the experience of one firm can be borrowed by a competitor. The so-called fast-second firm may learn from the mistakes of the innovator and thus begin further down the experience curve with lower start-up costs. IBM has not been a leader in introducing new computer products, but it has maintained dominance in the industry by quickly marketing more reliable versions of technology ushered in by its competitors.[26]

The cost advantages available from greater market share and experience seem to have been exaggerated. Buzzell, writing in 1979 and using more broad-based PIMS data, stated:

> [W]hile a competitor with a market share twice as large as his leading rival might have expected to have costs 20–30% lower than those of the rival, based on the typical slope of long run experience curves, the actual difference is likely to be 5–10%.[27]

In fact, the savings on direct production costs were found to be much less. Only when total costs, which include overhead, advertising, research, and interest expenses, were compared did the differences reach the 5 to 10 percent levels.[28]

Some studies contradicted even these modest claims. William Hall, of the Michigan Business School, found significant exceptions to the generalization that the largest producer will have the lowest costs.[29] Buzzell had noted that the cost/size pattern was more likely to hold in mature rather than growth industries. But Hall found after examining eight mature industries that the low-cost producer in four of these industries—steel, major home appliances, beer, and cigarettes—did not have the greatest sales volume.

In any case, the concept of high market share can be very misleading. Mercedes-Benz and Rolls Royce claim a very low share of the automobile market, yet both are very profitable. The results can be squared with the experience curve only by assuming that both of these firms have established their own market segments and thus became the largest (and only) firm in their market. But such examples suggest that segmentation has been the key to success for these firms, not production volume.

By 1981 even BCG had changed its mind. Alan J. Zakon, Henderson's successor as chief executive, was quoted by *Business Week:*

> The relationship between relative market share and profitability doesn't hold as much significance anymore. You can live as well as a small company or as a big company. And you can be as successful with a low-cost product or a high-value-added product.[30]

The most fundamental criticism of the experience curve was that large production volume does not automatically create any cost savings. If firms do not ride down the experience curve, if they have to fight their way down the experience curve, or if the relationship between market share and costs is tenuous in growth markets, then the BCG matrix does not provide a clear guide for corporate investment policies. If the key to lower costs is better management based on an intimate knowledge of each business, then the highly diversified firm is likely to be much more difficult to manage. If firms cannot be managed by the numbers, then corporate growth through mergers is a high-risk venture.

Doubting the Product Life Cycle

The product life cycle—the other building block of the BCG matrix—also has been severely questioned. Nariman Dhalla and Sonia Yuspeh, directors of economic research at J. Walter Thompson Company, have cited studies of over 100 products that do not conform to the life cycle progression.[31] Not only was it difficult to determine when a product had entered any one of the four phases of the life cycle, but growth and decline of product sales did not follow a regular pattern. The authors plotted numerous sales curves that were unlike each other and included periods of alternating growth and decline.

Some, like Richard Hamermesh and his colleagues, noted that investments in stagnant industries could be profitable if a growth segment could be identified. For example, while the total number of motion picture theaters was declining, General Cinema Corporation profited from opening new theaters in shopping malls.[32]

Both sets of authors condemn corporate policies that depend on the inevitability of the product life cycle. PIMS data show that research and development investments in stagnant industries are likely, in fact, to be profitable.[33] For example, General Foods profited from the development of "freeze-dried" instant coffee.[34] And Honda lowered the cost of motorcycles and opened up a whole new market segment for recreational cycles.[35]

William Hall's study presented the most direct challenge to the BCG matrix.[36] After examining eight mature industries (steel, tire and rubber, heavy-duty trucks, construction equipment, automobiles, major home appliances, beer, and cigarettes), his results showed that over a five-year period the well-managed firms in these industries outperformed well-known technology firms in growth industries, such as Xerox, Texas Instruments, or Digital Equipment, as well as leading professionally managed, diversified firms, such as General Electric or United Technologies. Hall's sample of mature firms had higher average returns on both equity and capital. Moreover, the traditional firms grew faster during the period than 3M, IBM, or Texas Instruments! The most profitable firms in Hall's industries—the low-cost producers and the quality or specialty producers—did not harvest profits from these mature industries. Contrary to the dictates of the BCG matrix, their profits were reinvested and the firms were rewarded with both growth and profits.

The life cycle critics would agree with Theodore Levitt's classic statement on this issue: "The reason growth is threatened, slowed or stopped is *not* because the market is saturated. It is because there has been a failure of management."[37] If management understands its customers and the potential of its product, there is no natural termination point for profits. If there is no natural point, then individual investments must be based on an understanding of individual industries. In other words, there is no sure guide to capital allocation for diversified firms.

Financial Analysis as Management

The idea that management is performed by matching cash flows or that efficiency is measured by quarterly ROI reports has been thoroughly criticized. Financial analysis and other statistical records are aids to good management, not substitutes for it. Good management requires an understanding of the product, the production process, the products, consumers, the firm's employees, and the possibility of change in any of these sectors.

Since the development of the modern corporation, there have been recurrent swings in styles of management between those who emphasize the numbers and those who emphasize the consumers, the product, and the employees. The reaction to economic stagnation in 1980 caused yet another swing away from management based on statistics.

By 1980 the collective diagnosis was that American business had become overly preoccupied with the appearances of success—meeting quarterly ROI objectives or growth in sales, for example—and had lost touch with the substance of business. Long-term research and development investments were being sacrificed to make short-term profit statements look better. The quality of American goods suffered because employees were apathetic. Businesses that looked to sales trends rather than customer needs or desires invested in the past rather than the future.

The key to international competitiveness was to emphasize the human side of business: Involve workers in decisions about production processes. Quality circles are beneficial not simply because they make employees feel a part of the organization. Employees know more than managers about certain aspects of the business and can contribute to designing more efficient production methods. The personal commitment of these workers makes the production system more efficient by increasing employee morale which, in turn, increases concentration on work. All of these improve quality and lower costs.

Service your customer's needs. The dominant message in Peters and Waterman's 1982 best-selling book on management, *In Search of Excellence*, is that successful firms see themselves as providing a service to their customers.[38] By adopting a service mentality, firms, even those that manufacture standardized products, get needed feedback on the quality of their product, the timeliness of their delivery systems, and the current needs of their customers. The needs of the customer provide a different, a more direct measure of a firm's performance and how it might be improved. Attention to customers therefore helps protect a firm from losing out to competitors.

Understanding customers' problems can also guide future investment policy. Peters and Waterman declare:

[The] excellent companies are better listeners. . . . Most of their real innovation comes from the market. . . .

Who in Levi Strauss invented the original Levi's jean[s]? Nobody. In 1873, for $68 (the price for filing the patent application), Levi's obtained the right to market steel-riveted jeans from one of its users, Jacob Youphes, a Nevada buyer of Levi's denim. And . . . Bloomingdale's invented faded jeans for Levis. Almost all early IBM innovations, including the company's first computer, were developed in collaboration with the lead customer—the Census Bureau. When did 3M's Scotch Tape business take off? When a salesman, not the technical people, invented a handy desk-top dispenser for what had previously been a narrow-use industrial product.[39]

Attention to the human side of business also means recognizing the kinds of skills a business has. Does the firm have skills in marketing, innovation, production, or service? Caterpiller Tractor has achieved success based on production of high-quality machines and rapid service.[40] Digital Equipment made its reputation on innovation.[41] And Phillip Morris capitalizes on its strength as a marketing company.[42] Identifying areas of major strengths and weakness can thus be a major factor in competing successfully.

The difference between firms is not simply a question of technical skills but one of temperament. The entrepreneurial, innovative, investment temperament that was responsible for the early growth of Texas Instruments or Digital Equipment would not be suitable to the meticulous-product and service orientation of Caterpillar Tractor or Delta Airlines. AT&T, while successful as a regulated monopoly, has undergone extensive change to prepare for competition.

Both temperament and skills have great importance for successful merger strategies. Both Heublein and Phillip Morris saw themselves as marketing firms in 1970. Both bought beer companies on the expectation that their marketing skills could assure them of a large chunk of this quickly growing market. Phillip Morris, which had manufacturing experience in the cigarette industry, succeeded with Miller Beer. Heublein, which had no manufacturing experience, failed in its attempt to make Hamm's a national beer.[43]

The criticisms just described were graphically summarized by Peter Drucker when he warned about the mergers of the 1960s:

> I do not believe that one can manage a business by reports. I am a figures man . . . one of those people to whom figures talk. . . . That is all right if we have the understanding, the meaning and the perception. One must spend a great deal of time outside where the results are. . . . One has to look at markets, at customers, at society, and at knowledge, all of which are outside the business, to see what is really happening. That, reports will never tell you.
>
> At the really critical moment, when a business is in trouble—and I have never seen a business that is not in trouble sooner or later—there is a very high premium on understanding a business, and not just on calculating. So, the conglomerates make me very uneasy, because they put far too much trust in reports. Reports are very comforting to me; they tell me a great deal. But they have also misled me often enough to make me realize that unless I go out and gain understanding, I may be acting on yesterday, even though the information is up to date.[44]

THE ROLE OF STRATEGIC THEORY

Strategic investment theories did not start the merger wave of the mid-1970s. Nor did the critique of strategy in 1980 halt the merger movement. The megamerger wave continues. The popularity of strategic investment theory established a framework for discussing the benefits of diversification by acquisition and the benefits of particular acquisitions. The later disenchantment used that same framework as a target for ciricizing growth by merger. Although the popularity of strategic theories was never the primary factor, the theories often provided helpful advice to those who used them wisely.

BCG's investment theories served a very important role for businesses. They emphasized to the single-product firm the importance of considering future demand for its product. BCG also argued that a firm should not invest more capital in a product simply because it had been profitable in the past. The theory insisted that capital allocations be based on a prediction of future demands for products.

BCG broadened the point of view of managers of profitable firms in stagnant industries. It discouraged single-product firms from raising costs by overinvesting in marketing or research, and it encouraged these firms to move the profits they controlled to the manufacture of products consumers will want in the future.

Equally important, BCG told diversified firms that they should not operate their subsidiaries as independent businesses. A profitable division should not have an automatic claim to its earnings or a large share of total earnings. Central management should not allocate capital funds as a reward for past performance. Capital allocation should be based on a considered judgment about the investments needed to increase future earnings.

The presentation of BCG theories shook up the "business as usual" point of view. If successful firms are the repositories for most new investment capital, it is vital to the nation's economy that those firms move their excess retained earnings from stagnant businesses to products of the future. The BCG matrix dramatized the importance of reallocating capital by showing that it is possible and profitable to do so.

BCG's advice to businesses—that they reallocate profits—was particularly persuasive because the process seemed so simple. That was misleading. Throughout the 1970s there were those who warned that capital investment was much more complex than being number one in a product market. The GE matrix, for example, required much more detailed analysis. Professors Salter and Weinhold of the Harvard Business School, in their book *Diversification through Acquisition*, noted that most mergers did not improve profits. They too stressed the need for detailed analysis to make profitable acquisitions and investments.[45]

But a complete strategic investment analysis is very complex. James Brian Quinn of the Business School at Dartmouth found that large planning offices of corporations are difficult to integrate into either the investment decisions or the operational production decisions.[46] The assumptions on which the more sophisticated strategic theories rely are so numerous and so speculative they often fail to persuade anyone other than the individual doing the analysis.

One is left then with two impressions about the usefulness of strategic investment theories. First, the theories provide important advice to corporate managers in an economy that gives control of most new capital to existing firms: managers must, therefore, reallocate capital. Second, strategic theories have not and cannot provide automatic answers to investment questions. At best the process of strategic analysis can inform those making capital-allocation decisions. After presenting the many factors that will affect the prospects for a successful investment or acquisition, business strategists must leave the decisions to those who are directly responsible for managing the firm.

Businesses seem to have recognized these limits on strategic investment theory. They have not employed business strategy consultants to choose merger targets. Rather, they may have accepted, for example, the general principle of investing profits from mature products into growing product markets, but they are likely to use their own criteria to determine which products are mature and what companies are suitable takeover targets. Thus, for any acquisition managers may look to strategic theory for advice, but they are likely to be influenced by many other factors. Equally important are the practical consequences of the merger on the firm, the personal impact of the merger on the firm's executives, or the need of the firm to respond to changes in its legal, technological, or competitive environment. If strategic investment theory has provided encouragement and confidence to merge, these other factors have often had a more direct impact on specific merger decisions.

CHAPTER 9

PRACTICAL OBJECTIVES
OF MERGERS

If managers are pushed toward mergers by an overabundant cash flow or a desire to move into growth markets, their choices of merger targets are most eagerly justified in practical terms. Although executives commonly celebrate the "synergy" or "fit" of all acquisitions, those that accomplish practical ends are described in more specific terms which emphasize the bottom line—profits. For example, mergers within an industry can reduce production costs by using larger manufacturing facilities. The target can provide unique resources or exceptionally inexpensive resources. The resulting merged firm may then be able to take advantage of financial economies. Or the resulting firm may be more profitable because of increased monopoly power.

Corporate managers proudly proclaim any of these objectives except monopoly power (which would gain the attention of antitrust authorities). Declaration of specific merger benefits deflects suspicion among investors that the merger is an empire-building exercise by egocentric executives. The named benefits also demonstrate a firm's managerial competence to the corporate community at large.

When corporate survival and growth are translated into an effective acquisition program, managers answer two practical questions: First, what kinds of potentially profitable businesses can the firm manage successfully; and second, if a takeover premium is paid, is the additional cost likely to be offset by operational savings after

193

combining the operations? The first question deals with the concept of "fit," the second is frequently termed "synergy."

While these terms are often used in vague and inconsistent ways, they have core meanings that describe important aspects of merger transactions. The central assumption of "fit" is that firms have limited talents as well as limited resources. An acquisition fits and is likely to be successful if the acquiring firm has unused resources to manage the target and the talents required to succeed in the target's business. These criteria can be met if the firm is merely expanding by acquiring another firm that makes the same products. Presumably, the managers of the acquiring firm already understand the business and can supervise the enlarged production capacity. Acquiring firms are also likely to have the requisite managerial skills if the target manufactures related products made on the same machinery or uses the same distribution channels. In other words, if the target firm will exploit an existing but unused capacity of the acquiring firm, the acquisition "fits."

"Synergy" is the combination of two separate entities that operate more efficiently as one than would the sum of their separate efforts. So, for example, when two large firms merge it is usually not necessary to maintain the entire central staff of lawyers, accountants, and personnel officers. Sales representatives can also present complementary products of two formerly separate firms in a single visit to the same customers.

Fit and synergy are closely related ideas. If an acquisition is a good fit, then there are likely to be many possible synergies. If the acquiring firm understands the production process, the distribution process, or the customers of its target, it is usually because the firms are engaged in some common activities which act as the basis for synergies. Similarly, if many synergies are possible, it is more likely that the acquiring firm will understand the target well enough to manage it.

Ideally, a merger should build on the organizational strengths of the acquiring firm and employ its underutilized resources more fully. Unfortunately, this does not always occur. Heublein's acquisition of Hamm's beer, for example, was premised on the acquiring firm's expertise in marketing and distributing alcoholic beverages. While this expertise may have provided a basis for some synergies, the acquisition seems to have been a misfit because Heublein's lacked the production experience necessary to manage a successful beer.[1]

There is also the possibility of a negative synergy from mergers. For example, when Western Pacific sought to take over Houghton Mifflin, the publishing house's leading authors threatened to leave if the deal were consummated.[2]

Planning successful acquisitions involves a great deal of guesswork about corporate competence and future market conditions. Merger plans are also constrained by the availability of appropriate target firms. As a result, even carefully planned acquisition strategies depend on targets of opportunity. Bendix, under the direction of William Agee, for example, considered dozens of potential targets over a three-year period before its abortive attempt to buy RCA on the cheap or its boomeranged attack on Martin Marietta. Other acquisitions are simply targets of the moment, rationalized after the fact by unspecified synergies or very sketchy fits.

Instead of exploring the highly subjective concept of fit or attempting to distinguish strategic rationales from postacquisition rationalizations, this chapter focuses on more identifiable, practical elements of mergers. These tangible benefits are the building blocks of long-term investment strategies and the catalysts to strategic acquisitions. They are sometimes even the sole justification for a merger.

IT'S CHEAPER TO BUY THAN TO BUILD

Some firms are bargains. For any number of reasons the stock market may undervalue the shares of a firm. An alert investor can profit by buying shares at the reduced price. Some corporate acquisitions are simply that, targets of opportunity. Others are fortuitously inexpensive means of achieving strategic plans. Still others are costly mistakes.

Franco Modigliani, the noted financial economist, made news in 1979 by declaring that stock market prices were half their true value.[3] He claimed that the essentially flat Standard & Poor and Dow Jones averages (the former was around 100, while the latter stayed below 1,000 during the 1970s) had failed to reflect the inflation during that decade and ignored its effect on devaluing the debt of corporations. By his measurement almost every stock was a bargain.

This formula for success seems to have been overoptimistic. In the year following the August 1982 bull market, the Dow Jones average rose only to the mid-1,200s. Consequently, investors had to be more selective in order to make substantial profits.

But there have been undervalued firms. According to *Business Week*, Michael Metz and his colleagues at Oppenheimer & Company found, in 1982, 115 major companies "worth more dead than alive."[4] The shares of these firms—which included U.S. Steel, Armstrong Rubber, H. K. Porter, and Control Data—were selling for substantially less than the value of their assets. For example, when a share of H. K. Porter was selling at $48, its liquidation value and its book value were both estimated to be around $130 a share.

In such circumstances, some firms, such as Victor Posner's Sharon Steel, have sought to profit from buying bargains on the stock market. It is not surprising that their targets, U. V. Industries for example, have found it more profitable for shareholders to liquidate the firm rather than accept a modest takeover premium.[5]

The low value placed on well-known corporate shares reflects more than the firm's earnings in a recession. It also incorporates the stock market's evaluation of the firm's management and its prospects. That, in turn, is based largely on an evaluation of a firm's capital-investment plans. Capital-investment policies are usually a more critical factor than problematic liquidation estimates.

Capital-investment programs have a profound effect on corporate fortunes. Mesa Petroleum's 1983 takeover siege of Gulf Oil, for example, was based on a difference of opinion about what to do with the profits from Gulf's valuable, proven oil reserves. Gulf's management wanted to reinvest the profits by exploring for new oil. If successful, the value of Gulf would be greatly increased. The low value of Gulf's shares suggested that the stock market considered the costly exploration to be risky. Mesa Petroleum, therefore, sought to take over Gulf and pay shareholders the value of the existing rich reserves directly.

The debate between the managements of Mesa and Gulf over investment policy could be resolved only by hindsight. In the meantime, the stock market seemingly created a bargain, wherein Gulf shares sold for substantially less than either Gulf or Mesa believed Gulf's resources were worth. Mesa's takeover seige eventually resulted in the multibillion dollar oil mergers of 1984—Chevron's acquisition of Gulf, Texaco's acquisition of Getty Oil, and Mobil's acquisition of Superior Oil.

The stock market is also said to undervalue shares in solid, but dull, companies, because it may be too expensive for the market to ferret out information about small independent firms or divisions of large firms. This provides an opportunity for imaginative entrepreneurs—like California builder David Murdock. According to *Fortune:*

In a series of complex transactions involving a total net investment of a bit under $1.5 million, Murdock then pieced together a tile business that was soon earning more than that sum each year on revenues of between $15 million and $20 million. For $600,000 he acquired Huntington Tile, a Southern California manufacturer that lacked marketing outlets; he then paid $300,000 for several small distribution companies that were having trouble getting enough tile. Then for $850,000, he purchased Pomona Tile from National Gypsum. The deal turned out to be one of his shrewdest acquisitions. With Pomona Tile he got its $300,000 inventory of raw materials and nearly ten acres of unusual land surrounding the plant that he sold off for $700,000.[6]

Murdock's success with his tile venture also illustrates how a firm that has specific uses for the to-be-acquired facilities benefits from a more practical understanding of corporate values. Such a firm need not consider the liquidation value of the target or even the target's investment plans. Having decided to expand, it is relatively simple for an acquiring firm to compare the price of new machinery with the price of a target firm.

Business Week reported that Con Agra paid less than half of the replacement costs of its target's grain facilities when it bought Peavey Company in 1982 for $177 million.[7] By this purchase Con Agra moved from fourth place to become the largest flour miller in the United States. It also gained large new grain export terminals. The excellent price was due to a cyclical slump in the demand for American grain.

The bargain was compounded because Con Agra added facilities inexpensively without introducing more milling capacity into a market already suffering from unused facilities. Had Con Agra built new facilities, an even smaller percentage of industry capacity would have been utilized, and industry losses would have likely increased. Accordingly, the purchase of Peavey was probably better for the profitability of Con Agra and the industry in general, assuming its decision to expand was correct.

The benefits of buying over building are usually clear, but there can be disadvantages. Peavey, for example, had its grain mills located some distance from the major flour markets. Frequently, target firms do not have the most modern machinery with the lowest variable cost per unit produced. In the event of an unused capacity price war, the target might be unable to maintain its market share against more efficient firms. Or the target might have intractable quality, distribution, or personnel problems.

This latest merger wave began amid a stagnating economy and a depressed stock market. Inflation greatly increased replacement costs, and the recession lowered corporate earnings. The selling price of corporate shares made many firms appear to be bargains. Firms with a positive cash flow, therefore, have sought to exploit their buying power. Some have done well, but others have not. There are bargains, but it is still often difficult to predict when a firm is buying one.

PRODUCTION ECONOMIES

Larger firms have many advantages over their smaller competitors, because, as noted earlier, there are substantial savings possible from large-scale production. Larger equipment is proportionally less expensive to operate. Longer production runs allow firms to use more single-product, fixed machinery with less down time than is needed for multipurpose machinery. Multiple plants scattered throughout the country can lessen transportation costs and speed delivery.

Although these production economies continue to be important— for example, in mergers between concrete manufacturers, where transportation costs are high, and some beer mergers, where multiple facilities have lowered delivery costs—such economies are less characteristic of the recent merger wave. The megamergers discussed here have been between already major firms that obtained most economies from large-scale production prior to the merger. If some additional economies were possible from a merger of large firms competing in the same industry, it is likely that the merger would have been unlawful under the antitrust laws because it would also substantially reduce competition in the industry.

The few mergers between directly competing, large firms have been exceptions. In the economically troubled steel industry, for example, the Justice Department did not block the 1982 merger of LTV and Lykes Corporation.[8] The consolidation of their subsidiaries, Youngstown Sheet and Tube with Jones & Laughlin, formed the nation's third largest steel producer. Nor did the Justice Department prevent LTV from acquiring the fourth largest producer, Republic Steel, in 1984.[9] These mergers were permitted in order to bolster the competitiveness of the failing American steel industry. During the 1982 recession, American steel producers lost over $3 billion, and only one of the seven largest made any profit.[10] The new LTV Steel unit was expected to shut down inefficient plants and utilize only the newest facilities to compete with European and Far Eastern producers.

These steel mergers are unlike the earlier merger waves. The formation of Standard Oil, General Motors, or U.S. Steel at the beginning of this century resulted in giant enterprises that lowered their costs through greater production volume. In contrast, more recent steel mergers seek lower costs by eliminating inefficient facilities and reducing production.

Today, scale economies are more likely to be achieved through mergers with firms that are not direct competitors. Some production economies still can be achieved, for example, by manufacturing two products on one set of machinery. Deluxe Check Printers is a good example of this practice. Deluxe is the largest printer of personal checks in the United States, and it is an extremely profitable firm. Even after spending $90 million on plant modernization and a partial acquisition of a printer manufacturer, it had no debt and almost $70 million in cash assets. But it faces obsolescence of these plants if, as has been predicted, checks give way to debit cards and other electronic fund-transfer systems. To guard against this and to maintain growth, Deluxe has entered the business-form market. It expects to use its rapid turnaround printing capacity, developed for checks, to attract small businesses that need limited runs of forms. Custom-made business forms will utilize Deluxe's current capacities more fully and thereby lower its production costs.[11]

OVERHEAD ECONOMIES

Even more typical of current mergers are nonproduction economies, such as those involving overhead, advertising, or distribution costs.

With regard to overhead savings, one central staff can establish personnel rules or financial reporting standards for several sets of subsidiaries. Larger pension funds do not demand a larger staff of investment advisors.

Spectacular advantages in advertising can also be gained through a merger. A firm with a nationally sold product can afford to advertise in ways that would be prohibitive for a regional firm, since costs of advertising to the better known firm are spread over many more sales.

Both Phillip Morris (in its promotion of Miller beers) and Procter & Gamble (in its promotion of Folger coffees) have advertised extensively on national television. Their regional and local competitors simply cannot hope to duplicate such exposure of their own products. The result, in part, of these aggressive advertising campaigns by national firms has been to eliminate numerous local breweries and coffee makers.[12]

Larger firms may also make multiple use of a brand name in their advertising. Seagram's introduction of its club soda and soft drinks in 1983, for example, benefited from the reputation Seagram had already established through its line of alcoholic drinks. When any of the Seagram brand products are featured, all gain exposure.[13]

Another advertising economy available to the large, multiproduct firm is to feature more than one product in a single format. Coca-Cola can, after its purchase of Columbia Pictures, encourage moviemakers to feature Coke or Tab where scripts require use of soft drinks.

There are, of course, some risks in linking products. If one Seagram product receives negative publicity, all may suffer a sales decline. Or the quality of Columbia Pictures may suffer if soft-drink executives interfere with a director's judgment and insist that Coca-Cola be featured in the movies they help finance.

Equal in importance to advertising and overhead economies are the marketing or distribution economies. Success in business often depends on marketing products where they are convenient to potential consumers. A firm that has established effective distribution channels for one product may be able to use these same channels to promote other products. Deluxe, for example, promoted its new customized business forms through banks that already sold Deluxe checks to their depositors.

Marketing efficiencies are frequently at the core of strategic acqui-sition programs. Acquisitions of products that use the same distri-bution channels can benefit from great savings in sales and promo-tion staffs. At the same time, the acquisition of a firm is unlikely to be challenged by antitrust authorities simply because the products can be distributed together.

Many firms have, therefore, pursued acquisition policies based on marketing similarities. The Paper Mate division of the Gillette Com-pany, for example, bought Liquid Paper Company for $47 million in 1979 to broaden its sales from pens to general office supplies. The large, pen sales-force was expected to be effective in promoting the growing market for correctable typewriter ribbons manufactured by Liquid Paper.[14]

Similarly, Frito-Lay's dedicated sales and delivery staff was ex-pected to provide an opportunity for promoting cookie sales after its acquisition of Grandma's bakery. Frito-Lay employs 10,000 sales-men who deliver perishable salty snack products to 300,000 retail stores. This rapid distribution system had the capacity to distribute profitably a cookie that is moist and has a short shelf life. The result-ing fresh-baked tasting cookie can command a premium price over most cookies with a longer shelf life.[15]

The opportunities presented by production, advertising, or mar-keting economies are real, and the realization of these synergies has been the driving force behind many acquisition programs. It should be noted, however, that by themselves, economies or synergies do not determine the profitability of an acquisition. The acquiring firm must not pay too much for the target company; it must be able to manage the target, and consumers must want the product. However attractive the theoretical integration of two firms may look, its effects on profitability must be proven.

IDENTIFYING UNIQUE VALUES OF RESOURCES

Quite apart from market value, particular resources may have special importance to an acquiring firm. The needs or the skills of an acquir-ing firm can make the personnel or the physical or technological resources of a target firm uniquely valuable. Exploitation of these resources is a hallmark of careful strategic planning.

Roy Rogers Restaurants, for example, paid $49 million in 1982 for Gino's, a chain of 360 fast-food outlets, even though it did not plan to continue any of the stores under the Gino's name or format. Roy Rogers, a division of the Marriott Corporation, possessed adequate development capital, but it faced significant barriers to expansion in the already crowded fast-food industry. The acquisition of Gino's provided a means of overcoming those barriers.

Good managers are critical to maintaining Roy Rogers' quality image and efficient operation. And because managers with sufficient experience are difficult to find in large numbers and training new managers is a slow and risky process, Roy Rogers solved this problem by retaining all of Gino's regional, area, and store managers.[16]

A good location is also critical to the success of fast-food restaurants. When expanding into built-up areas, though, the most desirable locations are usually occupied. Because Gino's already had restaurants in the geographical areas where Roy Rogers sought to expand, Roy Rogers was able to obtain prime locations by simply converting the Gino's outlets.

It is also common, however, for acquiring firms to replace the target managers with its own executives. Stroh's purchase of Schlitz is a dramatic example. For many years Schlitz was the nation's second largest beer company after Anheuser-Busch, maker of Budweiser. However, after the promotional campaigns that followed Phillip Morris's acquisition of Miller beer, Schlitz fell to a distant third. Despite efficient, modern breweries and a national distribution network, it had problems maintaining quality. Although its low-price brand, Old Milwaukee, and Schlitz Malt Liquor were leaders in their respective market segments, the Schlitz premium brand slipped badly. Because of the escalation in marketing costs, promoted by the Miller/Budweiser advertising war, Schlitz began to lose money.

Stroh's fortunes were almost the reverse. It was, in 1979, a Detroit-based brewer, eighth in the national standings, with a strong regional brand. Despite its strengths, it faced serious problems in the wake of the Miller/Budweiser battle for market share. Stroh tried to fight back by expanding its sales, but the marketing and brewing economies of the larger firms posed formidable competitive barriers.

The 1981 acquisition of Schlitz provided Stroh with an ideal opportunity. Buying Schlitz gave Stroh immediate access to a national distribution network. The network itself would become more efficient by the addition of Stroh's strong premium, super premium, and light beers. According to *Fortune*, Stroh expected that "synergies between the two companies should save at least $50 million pretax in administrative costs, commodity purchasing, shipping charges, and most of all, marketing expenses."[17]

The key to Stroh's success will depend on matching the managerial and brewing skills of Stroh with the physical resources of Schlitz. When little Stroh approached big Schlitz with an offer, Schlitz countered by offering to buy Stroh. The product fit and economies of scale would have been identical, but the Schlitz management had already shown itself unable to match Budweiser and Miller. Stroh, however, was able to convince the Morgan Guaranty Bank and the Crocker National Bank that they could make the merger work. In April 1982, with a loan of $340 million from the banks, Stroh made a successful tender offer for Schlitz.

Takeovers that are premised on turning around the failing fortunes of a target, such as Stroh's acquisition of Schlitz, are notoriously risky however. Phillip Morris's success with Miller Beer has not been matched by its results for 7-Up. Colgate-Palmolive bought the weak Helena Rubenstein cosmetics company in 1973 for $142 million and sold it for $20 million in 1980.[18]

Acquisitions can also have a critical competitive value: Buying is quicker than building. For example, Exxon's purchase of Reliance Electric was premised on a match between Exxon's technological breakthrough in electric motors and Reliance's expertise in the manufacture, distribution, and sale of electric motors. By buying a large company, Exxon positioned itself to exploit the new technology even if that technology did not receive patent protection. The great manufacturing capacity of Reliance would have enabled Exxon to bring large quantities of the new motor to market more quickly. This kind of jump on the competition could have established Exxon as a dominant manufacturer of electric motors. Had Reliance Electric been a better buy and had the new motor been practical, the acquisition might have been brilliant.

FINANCIAL SYNERGIES

Financial synergies can increase profits in two ways. They lower the cost to the firm of new capital, or they reduce the taxes the firm pays on its earnings. Sometimes a tax synergy will do both at the same time.

Financially based mergers have been widespread in the mega-merger wave. The popularity of such mergers can be explained more by a need to invest excess profits, than any need to develop the acquiring firms' existing businesses. The consequence has been the formation of business institutions whose parts may have little relation to one another. The sole common characteristic of the subsidiaries may be that they submit annual reports to the same board of directors. The acquiring firms have the authority to direct policy, integrate operations, and comingle capital, but typically they do less.

For reasons of management efficiency, morale, and a lack of expertise in operating the target, an acquiring firm often makes no changes in the management of the target, or it may replace only the target's financial officers. Thereafter, the acquiring firm is likely to limit its role to setting return-on-investment targets for the subsidiary and reviewing annual long-term capital-investment plans. Should the subsidiary fail to perform as planned, the financially focused acquiring firm is more likely to divest the business than try to improve its performance.

The hallmarks of the financially based merger are the absence of efforts by the acquiring firm to alter the internal operations of the target or to integrate them with the operations of other subsidiaries. Regardless of statements to the contrary, many mergers have as their only plausible benefit a financial synergy. United Technologies, for example, claims synergies for its operations. But what, apart from the "technology" idea, integrates the operations of its Pratt & Whitney jet engines, Otis elevators, Carrier air conditioners, or Sikorsky helicopters? Perhaps a more reliable clue to the nature of United Technologies is the tiny central staff maintained by chief executive officer Harry Gray. Consider Gray's statement of the firm's acquisition policy:

> We start off by saying that, number one, there's got to be a technology match between our area of interest and the company that we're interested in acquiring.
> Number two . . . we want it to be a market leader and profitable. . . .
> Three, we'd like to have a competent management.
> The fourth [criterion] is that the acquired company must have in-house development capability for its products as well as in-house marketing capability.

[W]e try not to go about changing the successful formula that built the company in the first place. . . .

One last thought on acquisitions. We neve go for a turnaround situation. I think that's about the worst news there is. Maybe somebody else can do that but we can't. We don't have a stable of management experts who are ready to go in and do everything better than the people who built the business.[19]

The synergies, if any, at United Technologies seem most likely to be financial. In general, firms are forthright about the financial synergies of their mergers. They do not hide the tax or other financial motives. They proudly parade the savings in taxes as lessened costs of capital.

Tax Synergies

There are two basic kinds of tax benefits to be gained from mergers: tax savings that result from the way the acquisition is structured, and tax savings that result from the operation of the two firms as a merged entity. Benefits can be split in any proportion between the acquiring firm and the target shareholders.

The taxability of the sale or exchange of shares, can be enormously important to shareholders, especially owner-managed family firms. Successfully managed family firms sometimes face significant tax problems if the founder wishes to retire. If the corporation pays the owner after retirement, the payments will be treated as salary or dividends and taxed at ordinary income rates.

If, instead, the firm is sold to a large firm whose shares are publicly traded, the founder can choose from a number of lower tax deals. The founder may decide to trade ownership for cash, in which case the founder will be taxed at the lower capital-gains rates on the amount the founder's investment in the firm has increased. Or the founder may choose to defer or avoid any income tax consequences from the sale by accepting payment in stock of the acquiring firm. He or she will be taxed on the increase in value only on the shares that are sold during the taxpayer's lifetime. The gain on other shares will escape income tax liability entirely. So the choice will depend on the founder's needs or investment desires.

The amount of tax savings at issue can be very substantial where a founder has built a large enterprise over a long period of time by reinvesting profits. The potential difference in tax dollars is frequently a major factor in bargaining over the sale price. In part, this is because the ability to redepreciate a target's assets depends on whether the sale was taxable to the target's shareholders. But fundamentally, the bargaining takes place because the tax savings are, in effect, a subsidy that both buyer and seller want.

In large takeovers the influence of a deal's structure on shareholders is likely to be much less decisive, because shareholders have less say in large, widely held corporations. Moreover, the impact of a takeover is likely to vary greatly among shareholders paying different tax rates and having different gains on their shares. Finally, these differences can sometimes be accommodated by structuring the takeover so as to give shareholders a choice between payment in taxable cash or nontaxable shares. Consequently, the tax savings from consolidated operations tend to be more important than those from the sale.

Some tax benefits of corporate integration are obvious. The elimination of the tax on intercorporate dividends by a subsidiary is an automatic, if modest, savings. More important, and more complex, are the tax savings that result from skillfully matching the income of one firm with the tax deductions and credits of another firm.

Mergers that take advantage of tax-loss carryovers were frequently mentioned as motives in the 1960s. The scenario consisted of buying a company for less than the value of its tax losses and then deducting its losses from one's income.

Although the Tax Reform Act of 1969[20] narrowed the circumstances in which the merged firm can use the target's losses, the motive remains important to this day. *Business Week* reported in July 1980 the frenzied efforts of KMS Industries to find a profitable merger partner in order to obtain the tax benefit of $22 million in accumulated losses. KMS, a giant conglomerate of the 1960s, had almost gone bankrupt in the subsequent stock market collapse. It limped along making substantial but profitless investments in the area of fusion research during the 1970s. The urgent need for a merger partner was based on the fact that losses may be used to offset income earned by the corporation in the following five years only. By 1980 time was running out for KMS.[21]

Tax losses can also provide corporations with an inexpensive means for pursuing expansion strategies. Pantry Pride, a southeastern retailing chain, fit Supermarkets General's geographic plan to enter the Sunbelt states. Supermarkets General was attracted by Pantry

Pride's $280 million tax loss. *Business Week* quoted one analyst on the benefit of the merger to profitable Supermarkets General: "The earnings should free a large amount of cash that 'could be very nicely used toward helping Pantry Pride and Supermarkets General to expand without having to borrow significantly.' "[22]

Buying unprofitable firms with tax losses is often a risky venture, because the target may bring more headaches than it is worth. A more sophisticated version of this tax strategy was central to Bruce Henderson's strategic investment advice and has been followed in a number of mergers. The refined strategy advocated the merger of healthy, well-run firms—one firm with more deductions and tax credits than it can use, the other with more income than it can shelter from taxation.

The 1982 attempt by the Ryder truck rental company to take over Frank B. Hall & Company provides an apt illustration. The Economic Recovery Act of 1981[23] altered existing tax rules to permit extremely generous, rapid depreciation of the trucks and investment tax credits on the purchases of new capital equipment. The purpose was to reemploy American workers by encouraging corporations to spend more. The effect on Ryder, an expanding capital-intensive firm whose principal assets were its trucks, was to swamp it in unused credits and deductions. It, therefore, sought a merger target with high earnings and high (i.e., unsheltered) corporate tax liabilities.

Ryder chose Frank B. Hall, a major insurance brokerage firm, as a merger target. Successful financial firms such as Hall generate a stream of income but have few capital assets and therefore cannot avoid or defer taxation on their income. A combined firm would use the excess Ryder credits and deductions to defer taxes on the Hall income.

The tax synergy was so ideal that Hall thought of the same idea, but its management had no intention of becoming a subsidiary of another firm. Hall's target was, ironically, Jartran, Incorporated, a truck rental company started by Ryder founder, James Ryder, after he left that company. Hall speeded up efforts to acquire the truck rental company in order to block Ryder by creating an antitrust barrier to the takeover. In evaluating Hall's "show-stopper" lawsuit, the court confirmed the tax motive of the proposed mergers:

Both firms recognize that a truck rental company is a capital intensive business which generates investment tax credits and that an insurance brokerage firm is a service business which generates significant non-sheltered income. Both firms, independently, and not without reason, concluded that the merger of a truck rental firm and an insurance brokerage firm would be a good economic fit.[24]

The most notorious user of tax and financial strategies was Morley Thompson of ill-fated Baldwin-United. In a meteoric career Thompson transformed the world-famous piano manufacturer into a giant financial conglomerate. His controversial use of complex transactions to gain tax benefits was illustrated in 1980 when the corporation was forced to divest twelve Colorado banks.

Baldwin had to sell the banks to comply with the Bank Holding Companies Act,[25] but wanted to defer taxes on its very substantial profit. To do this, it transferred the banks to a limited partnership. As the limited partner, Baldwin terminated its control of the banks and satisfied the banking authorities. At the same time, it sold $180 million in warrant bonds in exchange for its interest in the partnership, but delayed the transfer of ownership rights for at least five years. *Fortune* magazine described the purpose of these conplex transactions:

> Baldwin still [in 1982] has not, literally speaking, sold the banks. that won't happen—and capital-gains taxes won't start to be incurred—until the warrants are exercised, a process that can't start before 1985 and then can drag on until 1995. Baldwin estimates that it's deferring $30 million in capital-gains taxes this way. If they're deferred an average of ten years and interest rates average 10%, that $30 million tax liability shrinks to just $11.6 million in today's dollars.[26]

Delayed payment of federal taxes by sophisticated or simple strategies transfers money that would have been paid to the U.S. Treasury back to corporations. Accelerated depreciation schedules allow the deferral of taxes on larger amounts of income for short periods of time. Investment tax credits also have a limited life. Nevertheless, taxes may be deferred forever if the firm acquires more firms and more assets which generate deductions and credits. These untaxed earnings are a larger pool of income that can be reinvested (or distributed), and they provide a lower cost of capital to the firm than would otherwise have been the case. For the firm, the bottom line is more profits at less cost from tax-based mergers.

Other Financial Synergies

Apart from minimizing tax liabilities, there are two additional financial objectives to merging. The first involves matching or blending cash flows in a way that maximizes profitable corporate growth. The second reduces a firm's cost of capital (debt and interest) by making the firm more stable or less risky.

Using the cash flow of one firm for the cash needs of another firm has been an important goal of many mergers. For a firm like Ryder, it is found money to fully utilize tax benefits. But it is often more important to managers to have internal cash flows to pay for an expansion than it is to earn tax benefits. If the corporation has to borrow money or sell new shares, the managers may be unable to pursue the project at all.

Convincing investors can be a slow, uncertain, and expensive process. And raising outside capital interferes with the ability of managers to make and carry out long-range plans. If the project requires some element of surprise—an advertising campaign, a new product, land or mineral development deals—the process of raising capital may alert competitors and give them an opportunity to steal or match the idea. Even if the idea is unlikely to be stolen, investors may require an unacceptably high return on their money because they consider the project risky. Or investor support may decline midway through the project and make completion impossible.

For these reasons, firms prefer secure internal sources of funding. Managers know more about the health of their businesses than they would be willing to share with members of the public; therefore, they may be the only ones positioned to judge the riskiness of the firm and its ventures. The firm using internal funds need not prematurely reveal competitively sensitive facts. It may, instead, assign the project a cost for its developmental capital that will be unaffected by market rates. In short, internal capital provides the opportunity for consistent, comprehensive long-range planning.

These benefits are not only important to cash-hungry expanding firms that want to avoid or reduce rising debt costs, like Ryder. They are also important to profitable firms with cash to invest. Supermarkets General would have benefited more by investing in Pantry Pride as a subsidiary than as a stock market investment. In addition to tax savings on intercorporate dividends, a firm like Supermarkets General could benefit from ownership because it would have more facts than an outsider would on which to decide whether or not Pantry Pride should expand. Furthermore, as a parent corporation, Supermarkets General would be in a position to require beneficial modifications to a capital-spending plan and would be able to monitor those modifications closely.

In addition to these planning benefits of matching cash flows, operational efficiencies are possible if one firm has large amounts of cash that must be continually invested and the other has continual cash needs. For example, one benefit that was supposed to flow from the Mobil acquisition of Marcor was a cash synergy. The credit division of Marcor's Montgomery Ward had a large and growing clientele. Marcor could not continually expand credit to its customers. This negative cash flow would preclude buying new goods to offer for sale. It had a choice of either selling the debt at a discount or borrowing money to cover it.

Mobil, as a parent of Marcor, could provide the cash so the firm could retain the entire financing profit. Furthermore, this provided a large, presumably safe and profitable investment for Mobil's plentiful cash flow. The same monitoring calculations that the parent performed on the subsidiary should suffice for merging their cash flows. But after a decade of losses with Marcor, the acquisition demonstrates the need for more than financial synergies.

Although firms might prefer to rely solely on internally generated capital because it is more controllable and cheaper, most firms also raise funds through long- or short-term debt. Some have argued that if any outside funds are raised, a firm's internal cost of capital, measured by expected return, will have to equal market rates, or the capital markets will refuse to fund the firm. The cost to the firm of borrowing money is related to the perceived risk involved. Firms have reduced this perception of risk, and therefore their cost of capital, through mergers.

Debt is a fixed expense, dividends are not; the former cannot be deferred in a bad month or a bad year, while the latter can be. So if a company has "too much" debt, it is only a matter of time before current income drops and the firm faces the ultimate risks of insolvency or bankruptcy. On a narrower level, the presence of risk is important to financial officers because it affects a firm's cost of doing business. The interest rates charged to a firm reflect the risk perceived by lenders that the borrower will be late in making payments or unable to pay at all.

This concern over risk has generated a model of profitable mergers based on modern financial theories. Salter and Weinhold describe this risk/return model in the following way:

> The risk/return model argues . . . that management strategies that lead to either stabilized cash flows relative to the level of the economy, growth in free cash flow, or improved investor confidence about future cash flows will tend to lead to reduced systematic risk and increased market value for the firm. . . . The most efficient strategies are those that "de-coup" business performance from that of the economy.[27]

Financial analysts quantify risk by a statistical process that compares, over time, the value of a firm's shares with the performance of the stock market as a whole. The model assumes the stock market correctly reflects the value of shares based on knowledge available and that all shares will offer an equal return. It predicts then that shares have high returns only to compensate for high risks and low returns for safe investments. Although the mathematics are complex and the methodology is open to question, the general thesis can be illustrated by example.

Consider the riskiness of two firms, one a producer of home canning equipment, the other a fast-food restaurant chain. Each firm has its own competition and each is affected by economic cycles. Fast-food companies benefit from full employment because consumers have less time to prepare food and more money to spend. The canning-equipment firms benefit when unemployment is higher because people have more time to can their own food and can save money doing it. Because they are sensitive to the economy, both these firms may be viewed as risky. However, if they merge they may be perceived as less risky. This would make the merged firm a better investment and thus eligible for less costly loans even though the competition both businesses face in their separate markets is unchanged by the merger.

There is an advantage to such diversification through mergers, but shareholders can reduce their risk—if that is their concern—more effectively by buying shares in several fast-food and several canning-equipment firms. If shareholders are risk-takers and more interested in profit potential, the merger may be a drag because complete success would require both businesses to be booming, something that is unlikely given their different appeals.

For the corporation and its managers, stability may be more important than greater profit potential. A more stable cash flow may result in a lower cost of capital and a more consistent program of corporate development. This could be the key to success for previously separate firms and give them a decisive advantage over competitors.

National Steel bought the United Financial Corporation of San Francisco in 1979 for $230 million. Why? *Fortune* magazine answered, "National needs to protect itself against the inherent cyclicality of its industry."[28] Borg-Warner, a major auto-parts manufacturer, has made large acquisitions in the protective-services and financial-services industries to lessen its dependence on auto sales. James Bere, its chairman, boasted during the 1982 recession: "We've come a long way in reducing our vulnerability to the big swings in our traditional manufacturing business."[29]

For even the nation's largest firms, perceived riskiness is a major economic factor. When the $2.4 million Dart Industries merged with Kraft in 1980, Dart obtained financial benefits for its expansion plans. According to *BusinessWeek*, "Kraft's AA credit rating (the Dart rating was A) would give the new company in excess of $1 billion of unused borrowing capacity."[30]

A Word about Monopoly Power

Monopoly power—the ability to raise prices and increase profits— presumably continues to be an objective of mergers between competitors. Unlike other objectives, however, it is difficult to detect because the antitrust laws deter blatantly anticompetitive mergers. As noted in Chapter 5, it is no longer possible to achieve a monopoly by buying out all competitors. Instead, current mergers, at most, facilitate anticompetitive activity by lessening the number of rivals in a particular industry. The remaining firms find it easier to pursue their mutual interests by raising prices when the actions of fewer firms need to be coordinated.

How many of these anticompetitive mergers actually occur is difficult to judge. Certainly, the incentive to gain monopoly profits remains. Numerous prosecutions against firms for rigging bids and other forms of price fixing demonstrate a continuing willingness of firms to engage in criminal conduct to obtain monopoly profits. Consequently, the limitation on anticompetitive mergers seems to depend on the antitrust laws and premerger screening procedures.

OBSERVATIONS

Practical objectives have thus played an important role in choosing merger targets. Wayne Boucher's panel of merger experts rated them highly in their scale of the most popular objectives in merging.[31] In undisputed first place, the panel selected undervaluation as the most significant motive behind the decision to merge. Also highly rated were two reasons for preferring mergers to growth by internal expansion: Acquisitions achieve growth "more rapidly" (rated second) and mergers "avoid risks of internal expansion" (rated fourth). In addition, the panel found "reducing dependence on a single product" (rated sixth) and "reducing seasonal or cyclical variations in the present business" (rated eighth) to be of importance. Of the motives discussed in this chapter, the panel discounted only the advantages to be attained from increased company size as a currently attractive merger objective.

The Boucher panel, composed of merger experts, had a professional interest in portraying ongoing mergers as prudent and sensible. Such mergers were for some their bread and butter. Even so, the panel's agreement on the importance of practical objectives masked disagreements on, for example, whether undervalued firms actually exist or whether they are merely illusions of chief executives. Nor were panel members all convinced that the practical objectives of mergers can be achieved.

These experts did agree that the mergers of the late 1970s were undertaken with more serious, more substantive business intentions than those of the 1960s, but they could not argue that present-day mergers were necessarily more successful. Indeed, economic studies have done little to vindicate the view that mergers, on average, have benefited acquiring firms. The practical objectives we have examined may be, therefore, as important as components of executives' perceptions as they are building blocks of successful growth strategies.

CHAPTER 10

THE CEO'S DECISION TO MERGE

There exists a suspicion that large corporate acquisitions are undertaken to satisfy the imperial aspirations of chief executive officers (CEOs). The suspicion is that the merger motivations of a Harold Geneen of ITT, a Charles Bludhorn of Gulf & Western, or a Harry Gray of United Technologies have been personal and not primarily for the purpose of increasing profits.

Whatever truth there is to these suspicions, CEOs are often encouraged to make acquisitions by forces unrelated to the further production of corporate profits: Growth is perceived by the business community as good. Firms and managers are pressured to keep up with other firms that are growing by merger. There are monetary and other rewards from mergers for executives of acquiring firms. Finally, there is the professional prestige attached to the chief executive officer who executes a successful merger. An acquisition is quintessentially an action of the CEO.

Of course, firms do not enjoy unlimited resources. They cannot buy other firms forever simply to satisfy the whims of managers. The meteoric career of Morley Thompson at Baldwin-United shows that the marketplace will discipline executives who build business empires on economic quicksand.[1]

The corrective capacities of the marketplace are not always swift or sure. It is, therefore, important to appreciate the context in which CEOs make merger decisions. These decisions, which are based on predictions about the future, cannot be deduced solely from facts. Henry Mintzberg of McGill University, for example, has argued the corporate decisions are basically nonrational. *Fortune* magazine characterized his conclusions:

> According to Mintzberg, the [CEO] pays lip service to systematic long range planning, elaborate tables of organization, and reliance on computers and esoteric quantitative techniques. . . . In reality he's a "holistic, intuitive thinker who revels in a climate of calculated chaos." Mintzberg portrays the [CEO] as working at an unrelenting pace, jumping from topic to topic, disposing of items in ten minutes or less, and "constantly relying on hunches to cope with problems far too complex for rational analysis."[2]

CEOs may be forced to rely on hunches, but their decisions (or hunches) also reflect the nature of their position in the corporate organization and the attitudes of the corporate community toward growth by merger. These can create a predisposition to acquire other firms regardless of personal ambitions.

THE ACTION OF A CHIEF EXECUTIVE

No act exemplifies the power held by a corporate chief executive more than the acquisition of a large firm. Such acquisitions are peculiarly the decision of CEOs rather than a collective decision of staff. CEOs must decide to merge. They must select the target. And they must set the price. The number of imponderables and the consequences of a large acquisition make it impossible for CEOs to delegate these decisions to others.

Most business decisions are proposed and implemented by the corporate staff. The development of a new product, the opening of a new factory, or the raising of new capital must be approved by chief executives, but rarely do they work out the details of a new project. Staff members will research its feasibility and bring back proposed methods of implementing it. The chief executive will then examine and critique the proposal. If approved, the project is likely to be implemented by the staff without day-to-day supervision by the chief executive.

It is rare when the chief executive of a large, established corporation engages in the substantive work of the firm. Edwin Land, head of the Polaroid Corporation, is a rare exception. Like many others, he developed the original products, polarized lenses and instant photography, but unlike most successful executives he has continued to be the driving force behind product development. He was also largely responsible for the successful development of instant color film thirty years later. Few chief executives, even if they were engineers or scientists, would have the current knowledge to make such contributions. And even if they had the expertise to operate new stores or supervise the building of new facilities, they would normally consider such responsibilities a poor use of their time.

As a consequence of their role as chief executives, CEOs review and approve actions to be taken by others on the corporation's behalf. Despite their power, they spend most of their time in meetings or immersed in reports, projections, and proposals, rather than executing actions. The management consulting firm of Booz-Allen & Hamilton found, for example, that chief executives spend 46 percent of their time in meetings and another 25 percent waiting for people or information.[3] When executives do perform publicly, their actions are often ceremonial: opening new facilities, addressing shareholders, and the like.

Mergers are different. One of Professor Boucher's panel of merger experts commented:

> Nothing is more fun than an acquisition as an escape from the boredom of day-to-day business. The urge to merge is to break from the routine, to deal with high rollers, to find challenges, to make quick tough decisions.[4]

Fun may be an exaggeration or perhaps a metaphor for the personal challenge required by an acquisition.

Wayne Boucher's panel included leading merger lawyers, investment bankers, business consultants, accountants and publicists as well as one chief executive officer. All of them had worked closely with CEOs in the midst of takeovers. One thing on which all of these experts agreed was the role of the chief executive in mergers:

> If a company is to be successful in its acquisition program, the CEO must be personally involved. Because of the importance of timing in these deals you need a negotiator who can cut through the red tape and make whatever concessions and accommodations may be necessary to close the deal. A deputy without authority won't do.[5]

The role is more than one of chief negotiator, and it frequently includes initiation of the merger itself. Even chief executives of large firms, which have sophisticated strategic planning departments, have chosen targets without assistance. The Shearson/American Express merger was, for example, put together by Salim Lewis who made a direct approach to the chief executives of both firms.[6]

The decision to buy is unlike other decisions chief executive officers must make because of its immediate consequences. The news of a large acquisition instantly alters both the target and the acquiring firms. The takeover plan assembles the disparate economic resources of the acquiring firm, which are then pledged to banks in return for the cash to undertake the acquisition. In this form the corporation's economic power transforms a previously independent organization into a subsidiary subject to the chief executive's direction.

The decision is unique because of the way it forces others—bankers, investors, and so forth—to measure the value of the acquiring firm. The larger amounts at issue in the transaction require a more critical evaluation of the firm's worth. Assets, obligations, and prospects are suddenly put on the line.

Equally on the line is the judgment of the chief executive officer. Investors and lenders will evaluate whether the CEO's bid will capture the target, whether the bid overvalues the target, and whether the acquiring firm can manage the target. If they disagree with the CEO, banks may refuse to lend and investors may desert the acquiring firm, causing its stock price to plummet. The decision to buy, then, becomes a referendum on the executive's past performance and future plans.

The executive's decision to buy can also instantly embellish the acquiring firm's reputation by the addition of a brilliant target. Investments in new products or in developing target firms often take years to mature and evaluate and thus do not bring on sudden recognition of a firm's business savvy. Chief executives who begin major investment projects frequently retire before the projects are even brought to fruition. An acquisition, for good or ill, can be completed in a short time.

Chief executives become identified with their firms' large acquisitions. Mergers are natural courses of action for chief executives who have risen by their own efforts, by being doers. When a firm possesses the resources to make an acquisition offer or an opportunity to acquire is presented, the CEO is by training and by disposition ready to act. As another participant in the Boucher panel said:

The ultimate motive always present is the need or drive to *do* something. The businessman, the conglomerator, is a builder. He is not in the business of dismembering or dismantling corporations.[7]

That disposition to act, as we shall see, can be reinforced by the attitudes of others and by the executive's own aspirations.

GROWTH IS GOOD

There was a wide consensus among the Boucher merger experts that growth is a sign of corporate health. One participant, for example, declared:

> Expansion is a natural tendency; the desire for more locations, more employees and a bigger bottom line. No businessman today would say that he doesn't want his firm to expand, that he wants to hold tight, that he wants to consolidate, that he is working on return.[8]

Another panel member suggested a different perspective on the "grow or die" syndrome:

> If you ignore new business development, you can become a target for acquisition. Some conservative firms, which have long records of paying dividends, now recognize this danger and see that they should be seeking out acquisitions. The longer this takes, the more valuable they become.[9]

Finally, one merger expert suggested that for many large firms the question of *not* buying does not arise.

> Conglomerates are in the business of acquisition. That is their style and their commitment. . . . [A] conglomerate must acquire or else people will ask, "What's wrong with them? Aren't they in business any longer?"[10]

Although some of the Boucher experts denied that the ideology of growth by merger required a never-ending series of corporate acquisitions, they offered no business motivation for limiting growth.

The perception that corporate growth is good is not based solely on ideology, however. Securities analysts, lenders, and other investors may look to acquisitions and growth as a sign of business vigor and health. Executives also reap many personal benefits from belonging to a larger, more diverse organization. As one Boucher expert said, "Companies measure themselves first in terms of sales growth and second in terms of profit."[11]

The benefits to executives who engage in large-scale mergers are sometimes intangible (more minions, more dominions, more prestige) and sometimes economic (larger firms offer more career opportunities and distribute higher pay). A firm that can buy and sell other firms is a powerful (and therefore desirable) institution to be associated with. If it also owns glamorous, such as high-tech, businesses, that prestige rubs off on all the top executives. One Boucher participant put the matter ironically: "Imagine the status of the CEO of Crud Industries when he informs his cronies at the country club that Crud now owns a movie studio or a model agency!"[12]

A larger corporation usually pays its executives more. As noted earlier, Nobel Prize-winning economist Herbert Simon explained the higher pay as a function of structure.[13] Bosses must make more money than their subordinates; therefore, heads of major organizations must make more money than heads of smaller firms with smaller hierarchies. Also, it is easier to pay the top executives of larger firms more money because the overhead is spread over a wider total revenue. Even if the rate of profit is not improved by merger, total profits are likely to be greater, so the percentage used to pay top executive salaries is likely to be less.

Acquisitions also open new career opportunities for the cadre of top executives who direct the central staff. They can move from the crowded corridors of power to run their own divisions. This experience of directing a division can add to credentials and open the path to a chief executive position.

Thus, corporate growth not only looks good from the outside as a sign of health, it may also confer real benefits on corporations and their managers. Consequently, the chief executive is likely to be encouraged to make an acquisition by subordinates and by attitudes in the business community. On the other hand, the critical factor in the merger decision can be the self-aggrandizing dreams of a corporate leader.

MEGALOMANIA

Boucher's experts were divided on the role of power and prestige as motives for mergers:

- The big real motivations are the drive for ego satisfaction, power and status. This doesn't mean erratic or unintelligible behavior. You can and do have cool, methodical, rational egomaniacs.

- True only in a minority of cases.

- To claim to be able to look 5–10 years ahead and see how the business will be doing is really just another indication the [power] motive is at play.

- [Ego satisfaction] might be a by-product of mergers in general, but not a motive on its own.

- [Power] *must* be a factor because there are so many stupid decisions. It often seems that executives are playing *Let's Make a Deal* and trying to guess what is behind curtains 1, 2 or 3.[14]

Is the following behavior delusional? A corporate chief executive adds businesses to an already huge and diverse enterprise. The executive already has earned more millions than he will spend. Or is the executive merely continuing the activities that have made him, his predecessors, and his firm successful? Are his acquisitions conditioned by habit and by the expectations of others?

Studies of corporate leaders have shown some of them to be surprisingly modest about their personal accomplishments and capacities. These executives view themselves as persons of unexceptional qualities who have succeeded through luck and dedication to the corporation. They believe they were made by the corporation, rather than the other way around.

Since the publication of David Reisman's *The Lonely Crowd*[15] and William White's *The Organization Man*[16] in the 1950s, it has been understood that organizations can shape the values of their members. To use Reisman's term, these "other directed" individuals are likely to adopt and implement the values of others. Korn/Ferry, the executive-recruiting firm, studied 3,600 senior executives in 1979, and its findings confirmed that successful executives are conventional individuals who attribute their success to hard work rather than personal talents.[17] And as Christopher Jencks's book *Inequality* emphasized, luck plays a major role in success.[18] Consequently, it should not be surprising when chief executives gratefully continue the company policies that help them to high offices.

Some of these "other directed" executives might well follow an acquisition path blazed by prior merger experience. For them, it may be the essence of selflessness to pursue corporate growth. Having achieved or even exceeded their personal goals, the dangers and difficulties of the acquisition process are undertaken solely for the benefit of the corporation and their successors. Bearing the tension and anxieties of takeover battles are the way these executives give thanks for their own good fortune. Even the use of palatial office suites and corporate jets may not reflect personal vanity but the glory of the conglomerate.

A Wall Street Journal/Gallup Organization survey of 780 chief executives suggested a high proportion of dedication in these executives. "Six in every 10 said they believe a business executive must make personal sacrifices to succeed, and 80 percent of those who professed that belief acknowledged that their family lives have suffered because of their careers."[19] One of the Boucher panel experts described the contemporary business environment in this way:

> To survive, major corporations in this country have developed a feudal character. They have become dukedoms, and management believes in them. The idea is to keep the business within the realm, not just the family. Some managers will make tremendous personal sacrifices to this end.[20]

Perhaps, but the dramas of corporate infighting and takeover contests also suggest that some corporate leaders are motivated by personal interests. William Agee's career at Bendix is a prime example. In *Fortune* magazine's view, Agee was unfaithful to his former boss and patron Michael Blumenthal when he removed Blumenthal's friends from the Bendix board. Agee was also alleged to have tried to deny Blumenthal the top position at Burroughs when Blumenthal left the Carter administration. Furthermore, Agee permitted his personal relationship with his protegee, Mary Cunningham, to disrupt the operations of the Bendix corporate headquarters. His promotions of Cunningham alienated him from other executives and resulted in the loss of the corporation's president and its vice president for planning. Finally, he pursued a takeover attempt against Martin Marietta even after it became apparent that the strategy was extremely dangerous to Bendix's survival as an independent entity.

Alternative explanations of Agee's behavior are possible—a chief executive must have the full support of his board of directors and he must pursue the course he thinks best, taking wisest counsel regardless of scandal mongers. Nevertheless, it is difficult to review Agee's tenure at Bendix and consider it completely free of personal considerations.

Nor does it seem likely that acquisition decisions of other executives are entirely free of personal motives. The heedlessness with which some takeover defenses are conducted is more consistent with the personal interests of corporate executives than with the economic interests of shareholders. The Pullman Corporation's sale of its "crown jewels" described earlier defeated the takeover attempt by McDermott, but could have stranded the corporation. During the defense of Conoco, Ralph Bailey made it clear to his lawyer, Joseph Flom, that he was unwilling to have the firm taken over by Seagram, regardless of the consequences. According to the *American Lawyer*, Flom said,

> But Ralph there may come a time when we're standing out there with just our shorts on and we have to make a deal.[21]

Bailey is reported to have replied:

> I don't care if we're standing out there bare-ass naked. No compromise. And anyone who doesn't agree should tell me so I can get someone else to do his job.[22]

Consider Rupert Murdoch's media empire, which was founded in Australia on a formula for increasing the circulation and revenues of newspapers. With more scandal, sex, and sports and less news, his "fun" papers became enormously successful. Their profits financed his purchase of the *Sun* and the *News of the World* in Britain and founded the *Star* in the United States.[23]

Had Murdoch continued this pattern it might be easy to argue he was merely exploiting a profitable business formula. But his vision is clearly grander than that. His News Corporation now also owns London's *Times* and the *Sunday Times*, as well as New York's *Village Voice*. While he has cut losses for these papers or made them marginally profitable, they have little potential as major moneymakers. Other motives must be at work.

Murdoch has now moved on to the purchase of television stations and satellite broadcast systems. His discussions with Ted Turner about creating a European satellite news network, like Turner's CNN, and his January 1984 bid for Warner Communications (with its vast film library) suggest an almost unlimited appetite for profitmaking ventures.

Grand visions can benefit organizations, even when they are generated by leaders who identify the organization with themselves. Armed with unlimited sites for the organization's potential, such leaders have sometimes exerted superhuman efforts on behalf of their institutions. Where corporate leaders have had charismatic qualities, they have sometimes inspired loyalty and dedication among employees.

Accordingly, the pursuit of personal interest or personal glory by an executive can benefit the corporation by creating a cohesive workforce and harnessing potential energies. At its best, such a volatile emotional base can serve a corporation well when constrained by a competitive marketplace and the exercise of reasoned judgment. But these restraints can not always be counted on. In a marketplace with so much uncertainty, a chief executive can be tempted to resolve all doubts under a self-serving vision.

Blaming managerial egotism for notoriously unprofitable mergers should not, however, be resorted to too eagerly. Mergers, like all other entrepreneurial decisions, contain a high element of risk. Managerial vision gives executives the confidence to commit hundreds of millions of dollars in the face of such uncertainty. Inevitably, such confidence will prove to have been unwarranted for some mergers.

This managerial confidence and the predisposition to act is an important element of economic progress. Without optimism, it is hard to imagine investments in research programs and new products. The willingness to take a chance has been responsible for raising our standard of living since the beginning of the industrial revolution. To be sure, a large corporate acquisition is frequently different from an investment in a new or untried product. The acquisition may not hold out the same potential for public benefit. In many instances, though, the line separating the two kinds of investment is unclear.

Moreover, it may not be possible to limit such optimism to one kind of investment. It may spill over and infect merger decisions. Perhaps, then, we should accept that a certain proportion mergers will be unwise if any are to be undertaken.

Even with these qualifications there is reason for concern about the personal element in merger decisionmaking. In the typically short tenure of a chief executive, a large merger is likely to be the most distinctive of an executive's accomplishments. It gives the illusion, if not the substance, of corporate growth, and the daring and the execution of a merger often is admired by the corporate community. For a manager who desires a personal monument, the large acquisition—the most personal decision of a chief executive—is an ideal project. But maybe too ideal. As American University president Richard Berenzden has warned, "Growth for its own sake is the ideology of the cancer cell."

THE MEGAMERGER WAVE

There was a stampede of large acquisitions and contested take-overs in the decade following Mobil's acquisition of Marcor and Inco's acquisition of ESB. Beginning with one or two individuals a stampede then feeds on itself. It ends only when the herd is exhausted or has its attention diverted.

The megamergers of the 1970s had their origin in long-term structural factors that predisposed profitable companies to buy totally unrelated firms. They were further encouraged by a series of changes in the business environment that made acquisitions cheaper and gave particular firms compelling reasons to merge. Once begun, the movement was pushed toward hysteria by some who proclaimed mergers as the only path to economic success, and by others who condemned mergers but became convinced that the choice was either to acquire or be acquired. Time has exhausted much of the frenzy, but the underlying structural and environmental factors encouraging mergers remain.

Chapter 11 identifies three forces that served to whip up merger activity: excess earnings with no outlets other than mergers; changes in the business environment; and the mob reaction to hostile take-overs. Chapter 12 examines the oil mergers that set the pace for much of this feverish activity. Chapter 13 reviews the very different mergers of financial companies. In contrast to other well-known megamergers, these have been friendly deals undertaken to achieve specific business objectives.

CHAPTER 11

ACQUISITION FEVER

Merger mania is what some in the business press called it,[1] but it was more like an infection that spread through the business community. First, one long-established, successful firm bought an entirely unrelated business, and then another firm did the same, and then another. Although merger activity attained epidemic proportions, separate causes of the illness for many firms and industries can be identified. Some of these were structural causes affecting all firms, like the tax incentive to retain earnings or the maturing of the economies of industrial nations. Other causes owed more to individual changes in the competitive dynamic, for example, laws affecting one industry but not others, or strategic moves by rival firms. Once these forces broke conventions of business behavior, the new mergers inspired both the business fantasies and fears that led to acquisition fever.

STRUCTURAL FORCES

Acquisition fever starts with a corporation's need to dispose of excess earnings. Chapter 7 noted that corporate outlets for large accumulations of earnings are restricted. Shareholders will, for tax reasons, object to direct distributions of profit, and for other reasons, to excessive compensation to employees. Investing in new businesses or passive investments, however, often involve unacceptable risks.

Consequently, large mergers are sometimes the logical solution for a successful firm with profits that cannot be reinvested in its existing businesses.

Antitrust laws usually prevent successful firms from merging with their large competitors. The firm, therefore, must choose its acquisition targets from other areas of business. Choosing unrelated firms altered the perspective of both the acquiring firm and its targets. For the acquiring firm, it removed any restraint on corporate growth; for the target firm, it meant that it could not predict when or why it would be targeted.

Income tax incentives and antitrust are long-term structural features of American enterprise. Tax laws have facilitated managerial desires to maintain and increase corporate resources, and powerful antitrust laws, since 1950, have pushed American firms to look beyond their industry for merger targets. Even so, the largest, most successful firms did not become active acquirers of unrelated firms until the mid-1970s.

Numerous factors can explain the delay. The post-World War II economic and population booms provided a rapidly growing U.S. market for expanding businesses through the 1960s. In addition, large American firms found new markets abroad as economies revived in Europe and Japan and developed in the Third World. Investments in new capacity at home and abroad regularly absorbed the retained earnings of successful companies.

Also, although large firms were run in the 1950s by professional managers, these managers were less likely to view unrelated mergers as desirable. Chief executive officers were not typically business school generalists who had specialized in finance or marketing. Most of their business training took place inside the companies they headed. These executives often succeeded on their intimate understanding of a particular business, and they had little reason to be confident of their ability to effectively control a diversified firm. They might even have questioned the appropriateness of having many sizeable, unrelated businesses within a single firm. Finally, an implicit ethic, restrained giant firms from buying other firms against the wishes of the latter's management.

The 1970s Business Environment

By the 1970s all this had changed. The "American Challenge" that worried Servan-Schreiber was over.[2] American firms were bumping into each other abroad as they reached the end of the world economic frontier. They also were running into and sometimes were being pushed around by European, Japanese, and Third World firms. Increasingly, they faced these foreign competitors on home ground. Consequently, traditional reinvestment of profits in expanded manufacturing capacity was no longer so automatic and frequently was thought to be unwise.

At the same time, a new generation of corporate leaders was taking office. They were more sophisticated in their managerial and financial techniques, more likely to have had formal educational training in business, and less likely to have had direct operational responsibilities. While these leaders had witnessed the debacles that followed the 1960s conglomerate takeovers, they could appreciate the financial potential of such mergers and had learned about uncivil takeover techniques.

So the stage was set by the early 1970s for successful firms to adopt a new attitude toward conglomerate acquisitions in general, and hostile takeovers in particular. If internal expansion was blocked, retained earnings needed to be invested elsewhere. The safest investment could be found in a going business that could absorb profits. If the object was to find good business investments, why limit the choice to those firms that wished to merge? Why not choose the best target regardless of the wishes of that firm's management? Why not, indeed!

The economic times cooperated to make takeovers especially attractive for profitable firms. During the 1970s, successive price increases by OPEC, in part, caused a combination of recession and inflation. This produced a flat price level in the stock market whose value was eroded by inflation. While corporate profits were down (depressing the price of corporate shares), the value of assets was rising as replacement costs soared with inflation. For the firm with cash, this presented a great opportunity to buy the assets at a bargain (assuming the targets and their assets would be competitive when the economy rebounded).

Bargain hunting is not a polite business, as shoppers at a Filene's basement sale can testify. Whatever proprieties had existed between acquiring firms and their targets fell before the onslaught of hostile tender offers.

Any doubts that the targets were bargains were not shared by the managers of the acquiring firms. They paid premiums of 50 percent, 75 percent, and more for their targets. Acquiring firms in the 1960s typically paid only 13 to 25 percent more than the price target shares had previously traded for on-the-stock exchanges.[3]

MERGERS AS A RESPONSE TO CHANGE

If the pursuit of profit infected firms with acquisition fever, the fear of the consequences of change inflamed the condition. The 1970s saw many changes that threatened large, established firms. Changes in laws, new developments in technology, the depletion of critical resources, changes in consumer preferences, and new strategic moves by competitors each altered the business environment for major industries. Either alone or in combination, these changes forced firms to respond if they were to maintain their success or, in some cases, if they were to survive at all. For some, mergers promised a path to survival.

Law

Numerous industries have been eliminated or threatened with extinction by regulatory action. DDT, red dye number two, and cyclamates are but three of the many products that have been banned by government. Profitable firms that suffered regulation of their products shifted their resources into other businesses, often through acquisitions, when the opportunity arose.

The cigarette industry is a leading example. Since the Surgeon General's report on smoking in 1964 and the ban on television advertising of cigarettes in 1971, the threat of more direct legal restrictions has been real. As a result, the major cigarette companies have diversified their holdings by acquisitions of unrelated industries.[4]

The leading legislative change of the late 1970s was deregulation. Deregulation in the finance and oil industries helped to promote mergers, as we shall see, but it had a more variable effect in the transportation sector.

In the bus and airline industries, existing firms faced a growing number of competitors as a result of deregulation. The intercity bus industry had been dominated by the very profitable Greyhound. With deregulation, however, many new firms started to offer intercity bus service, and by 1982 over 1,000 buslines had obtained authority to operate service between the forty-eight contiguous states.[5] These newer firms offered substantially cheaper fares by paying their drivers and other employees less than Greyhound did. In the fall of 1983 Greyhound demanded, and got, a rollback in their employees' wages. The public got lower fares and a greater choice of buslines.

Deregulation in the airline industry has also encouraged both the formation of new companies, and, at the same time, has bankrupted other firms (such as Braniff and Continental) or severely reduced their profits. Even the giant airlines did not escape enormous losses. In 1981 Pan American lost $122 million and Eastern lost $22 million. The airlines blamed the rise in oil prices (that is, jet fuel) caused by OPEC, the decline in passengers due to the 1981 recession, and the lower fares offered by new airlines. Deregulation had opened the airline industry to a host of new competitors, and because these newcomers paid employees lower wages, they could also charge customers lower prices.

Initially, it had been thought that deregulation might cause a spate of mergers, as major airlines bought up competitors to extend service. (U.S. Air had done this in the northeast prior to deregulation when mergers were more difficult.) The expectation seemed to be confirmed by the bidding contest for National Air Lines, in which Pan Am emerged victorious. But it soon became clear that merger was not an automatically successful strategy to pursue. For one thing, Pan Am's new National employees became entitled to the higher wages Pan Am paid its international employees.[6] Pan Am's strategy was not followed.

The advantages of more permissive merger rules were thus outweighed by the advantages of low wages. As in the bus industry, new airlines could begin operations at a lower cost than established lines with high salary structures. Mergers in the air carrier industry, if they included payment of a takeover premium, would have increased the disadvantage of established lines.

The lower fares offered by the new airlines, such as New York Air, caused Braniff to go out of business and others—notably Continental and Eastern—to plead for wage rollbacks.[7] This competitive pressure reduced earnings, which not only discouraged mergers, but caused a break-up of the holdings of diversified airlines. TWA sold its hotel chain, and Pan Am sold its building atop New York City's Grand Central Station.[8] (Whether deregulation produced better service for passengers or for smaller cities is a matter of some dispute.)

In contrast to the bus and airline industries, megamergers have been encouraged by railroad deregulation. The Chessie System (formed by previous mergers of the Chesapeake & Ohio, the Baltimore & Ohio, and the Louisville & Nashville) bought the Seaboard Coast Line in a 1980 deal worth $1 billion to form the CSX Corporation.[9] Union Pacific acquired the Missouri Pacific in 1982 for $900 million dollars.[10] Also in 1982, the Norfolk & Western merged with the Southern Railway in a $1.7 billion deal to form the Norfolk Southern Corporation.[11] In 1983 Santa Fe Industries merged with Southern Pacific in the biggest rail merger ever: The acquisition was valued at $2.3 billion.[12] The largest takeover prize of all, however, may be coming. Conrail (the freight successor to mergers of the Pennsylvania Railroad, the New York Central Systems, the New York, New Haven & Hartford, and others), which dominates rail transport in the northeast, is likely to be sold to one of the giant rail corporations.[13]

Deregulation has produced mergers, not new entrants, in the rail transport industries, and four reasons can be identified that account for this. Because there is more capacity for rail transport than demand, and because starting a railroad is prohibitively expensive, the costs of right of ways and laying track make completely new entrants unlikely. And despite decades of poor earnings, deregulation has increased the potential for railroad profits, especially for larger railroads. Finally, as in other industries, mergers by some railroads have forced competing railroads to merge.

The railroad mergers were encouraged by a series of deregulation acts that ended with the Staggers Rail Act of 1980.[14] Prior to the passage of these laws, mergers were permitted only if public interest *required* the transaction. For example, the 1968 Penn Central merger was allowed in order to save the companies involved from bankruptcy. Under the Staggers Act the Interstate Commerce Commission permits mergers if the "transportation benefits of consolidation outweigh the anticompetitive effects."[15] Since the act, the Interstate Commerce Commission has also increased the discretion of railroads to abandon uneconomic lines, to raise or lower fares, to compete with other forms of transportation, and to acquire trucking firms.

All of these measures have combined to make railroads more profitable and more efficient. Previously, the railroad industry was so balkanized that few shipments reached their destination traveling on only one line. According to Standard & Poor's Industry Analysis, this was uneconomic for the short-haul railroad.[16] Mergers could make such shipments profitable by eliminating the short haul. At the same time, if the merged firm eliminated duplicatory trackage and uneconomic lines, it could reduce its overhead. If these mergers also lessened competition the railroad might be able to raise its rates.

Furthermore, the formation of longer rail lines by merger pressured remaining competitors to merge. After its formation, CSX had through north-south trackage in the southeasterm states. In addition to creating some transport economies, the merger guaranteed that north-south shipments begun on the Chessie System would be continued on the Seaboard Coast Line. CSX could also try to attract north-south business originating on either the Norfolk & Western or the Southern Railway. Not surprisingly, the latter two lines merged to realize economies and to assure themselves of through traffic.

Technology

Some mergers are undertaken to exploit technological changes. Others are designed to exploit technical developments that bridge previously separate industries. Still others are ways of incorporating advances in existing industries.

Railroad mergers, for example, have also been promoted by technological developments connecting previously separate transportation modes. Santa Fe Industries has been a leader in utilizing these advances. Its "A" container makes rail transport economically accessible to shippers of bulk and packaged commodities that are located off Santa Fe's rail lines. Such an innovation promises to further "the transformation of the railroad industry from an independent transportation industry vying for freight with trucks and barges to but one segment in multimodal transportation systems."[17]

That transformation has encouraged other rail companies to develop similar capabilities and acquire linking facilities. Already, CSX has established a substantial trucking business through its CMX subsidiary. In addition, CSX acquired Texas Gas Resources in 1983 for $1 billion to obtain the latter's barge business. The combined rail, road, and water transportation company will have a great incentive to develop additional technologies to integrate its various operations.[18]

Other industries are trying to incorporate new product features or production processes through mergers. As we have moved from diode tubes to transistors to solid-state technology and silicon chips, computer components have become important to more industries. General Motors bought Electronic Data Systems in 1984 for $2.5 billion as part of a diversification plan. But it also plans to use EDS to improve its internal management systems.[19] To keep up or to catch up, firms have turned to merger transactions.

Some firms, though, have sought to avoid the consequences of technological change. They have used mergers as a way of getting out of their previously profitable businesses. RCA, Motorola, and Zenith, for example, have abandoned production of consumer electronics in the United States. Sale of American-brand radios and television sets is made possible only by production in foreign countries. Instead of competing on product innovation, some American firms have chosen to diversify by merger. RCA, for example, bought Hertz, the auto rental company, for $238 million in 1967 and paid $1.3 billion for CIT Financial in 1979.[20] Motorola has realigned its operations through mergers to become a computer-components company.[21]

Consumer Preferences

Changes in consumer preferences reflect many factors, including technology, demographics, and personal tastes. People quickly tire of bongo boards, hula hoops, pet rocks and cabbage patch dolls. Producers of ephemeral items understand the need to continually recapture the public imagination. Such firms require new ideas not additional firms. For them mergers are too slow or unnecessary.

Most firms, however, are subject to longer, more predictable trends, and these trends can create opportunities for profitable mergers. Successful companies must learn to quickly adapt to technological refinements demanded by consumers—automatic timers, fuel-injection systems, portable televisions, portable telephones, and so on. Even more predictable is the impact of demographic shifts in our society. For example, we have smaller families and more individuals live alone. We are better educated, more informed, and live longer lives. More of us are moving to the Sunbelt states and more of us speak Spanish.

Since the early 1970s, after the peak of the post-World War II baby boom, it was clear that demographic shifts would dramatically change consumer demands. The falling birth rate, a new health consciousness, and the mechanized kitchen threatened the baby food industry. This industry could reduce salt and sugar contents, but it could not reverse the birth rate. However, new opportunities for soft foods in small serving containers were emerging and would continue to grow with the "graying" of America. in addition, more adults of all ages live alone and more dual-career, childless couples frequent restaurants and buy foods packaged in smaller containers.

Some firms have tried to follow these demographic shifts through mergers. For example, successful liquor distillers such as Seagram and Hiram Walker have found hard liquor to be more attractive to an older generation of drinkers. Thus, they have tried to expand the appeal of their products by selling "light" (that is, less alcoholic) scotch or bourbon and by emphasizing mixed drinks.[22] But Seagram has taken a more direct approach by a series of major acquisitions of wine firms, including the $200 million acquisition of Taylor Wines from Coca-Cola.[23] Wine has enjoyed rising sales among the current younger adult population.

Critical Resources

The restricted availability of oil resources in the 1970s caused American automobile manufacturers to lose sales to foreign makers of more economical, smaller cars. Although probably prevented by the antitrust laws from merging, the big three American auto firms have sought other forms of integration with more efficient Japanese makers of smaller cars. Chrysler entered into a long-term supply contract with Mitsubishi to make the Dodge Colt and Plymouth Champ. Ford, producer of the largest selling small "world" car, nevertheless bought a major interest in Toyo-Kogyo, and General Motors will scrap its Chevette in favor of a joint venture with Toyota.

Much has been made of the quality and production-cost advantages of Japanese car manufacturers. However, the critical factor to Japan's success in this market was the rise in gasoline prices after the

Arab oil embargo in 1973. The change in price of this one resource drastically shifted American buying habits away from big cars.

Strategic Moves

Some strategic mergers require that competitors either follow suit or abandon the industry entirely. When CSX was formed, the Norfolk-Southern merger became inevitable. Neither Norfolk & Western nor Southern Railway could afford to lose access to so much north-south rail traffic without assuring themselves of a high proportion of the remainder.

If CSX's barge and truck ventures prove successful, Norfolk Southern may have to follow these strategic moves as well. On the other hand, given that there are many trucking firms, it may find enough customers without creating its own integrated trucking operation.

A firm may decide not to follow the strategic move and concede that it will be forced out of the industry in the long run. In the meantime, though, it can use profits to diversify into new industries. Liggett & Meyers, for example, did not try to match the competitive moves of Phillip Morris or R. J. Reynolds in the cigarette industry. Instead, it used all its resources to diversify out of cigarettes. The Penn Central company survives as a conglomerate even though its railroad operators went bankrupt. Even before its $6.6 billion acquisition of Marathon Oil, U.S. Steel was redeploying its assets outside the steel industry rather than matching the production technology of its foreign competitors.

Although mergers, like those in the rail industry, can be part of an aggressive business strategy, megamergers seem to have been more commonly a defensive means of avoiding problems in a successful corporation's dominant business. In some industries, like tobacco or liquor, the problems may be insoluble, but this is not necessarily true of others. The abandonment of segments of the consumer electronics, steel, or automobile industries in favor of unrelated acquisitions suggests fear is a stronger motive for mergers than new business opportunities. It is also true that the antitrust laws typically prevent mergers between large competitors in industries other than oil or railroading.

Whether it intends to get out or stay and fight, the problem for the competitor is to decide at an early point whether it must meet a strategic move with its own merger. The competitor cannot wait until the value of the move is fully established. If it waits too long, good firms may no longer be available for purchase or the price may be too high. So the decision to enter a new field by merger, if it is taken, will be taken without full knowledge of critical facts. Whenever a basic element of an industry changes—whether it is the legal environment, technological developments, the availability of vital resources, or consumer preferences—managers must evaluate the change and act.

It may be an exaggeration to characterize these mergers, these reactions to change, as the products of fear. Change is a natural spur to action. A basic change in the competitive structure requires a response. But whatever name is given to the motivating force, the rapid response is not a logical deduction. However calculated, such mergers are shots in the twilight.

MERGER FAD AND MERGER FRENZY

The heightened number of mergers in the 1970s could be viewed as a natural response to underlying economic forces and a changing business environment. But the feverish pace at which mergers, and especially megamergers, was more than an adaptation to a new environment. The concurrence of two phenomena seem to have been responsible for this overreaction. First, the new promise of profits through mergers was accepted overenthusiastically. Second, this overactivity produced waves of defensive mergers. These mergers added to the perception that mergers were profitable and that they were necessary to preserve independence. More mergers produced more urgency to merge.

Fads recur within the business community because so many decisions have to be made before complete facts are available. Vertical integration, international expansion, automation, quality circles, image advertising, and consumer hot lines have all had their moment as the best new idea for businesses to adopt. All make sense for some businesses at some time. And each has died out as a fad when more was learned about the appropriate limits to the usefulness of the new technique.

Strategic investment theory was a fad perfectly suited to the 1970s. With traditional investments in expanded capacity blocked for many successful firms, new avenues of profitable reinvestment had to be found. Despite the flawed mergers of the 1960s, diversification through acquisitions remained the most promising answer. Once it gained credibility, its attractiveness as a solution to pressing investment problems was irresistable to some firms.

The idea of strategic mergers as investments gained credibility in three ways. First, academic studies beginning in the mid-1970s supported the proposition that appropriate targets could be identified. Reports by the Strategic Planning Institute and explanations from Harvard Business School professors and the Boston Consulting Group were all in terms familiar to the new generation of financially trained chief executives. Second, the recession had set stock prices at such low levels that even very large companies looked like bargains. Third, the acquisitions at prices high above the stock market trading levels made by already proven managers of successful firms seemed to confirm that such mergers were wise.

Of course, there was little solid evidence that merger strategies could be pursued profitably, but that is the nature of good new ideas: Get in on the ground floor! Buy while there are still bargains! Buy before the prices go up! If you don't move quickly, you miss the boat!

Firms did act quickly. According to W. T. Grimm, there were 15 $100 million mergers in 1975. By 1977 the number of megamergers reached 41. In 1978 the number almost doubled to 80. It continued to climb, reaching 116 in 1982, and 200 in 1984.[24]

The average price paid for these acquisitions was substantially above the price at which the target's shares had traded. The average premium in the 1960s ranged between 13 percent and 25 percent, but after 1979 the takeovers averaged a premium of close to 50 percent.[25] In contested takeovers the premium could go much higher. For example, holders of Marathon Oil shares, which had been selling for less than $60, ultimately sold out to U.S. Steel for $125 a share. Shares of Babcock & Wilcox, which had traded at $34 a share, were finally sold for a winning bid of $65 a share.

It is small wonder then that sophisticated CEOs, like Bendix's William Agee or Seagram's Edgar Bronfman, wanted to participate. They sold off valuable assets for the explicit purpose of having the cash to make major acquisitions. Bronfman realized $2.3 billion in selling Texas Pacific Oil.[26] He also tried to acquire St. Joe Minerals and Conoco before Seagram ended up with a piece of Du Pont. Agee sold off a group of businesses to develop his own $500 million hope chest, and devoted countless hours to developing the acquisition strategy that ultimately led to the ill-fated attack on Martin Marietta.

It seemed as if some firms were just waiting in line for a target to become available. Allied Corporation's Hennesy, for example, had learned his acquisition trade at United Technologies while serving as Harry Gray's number two man. He failed in his offer to become a white knight for Marathon Oil, but his persistence eventually paid off: He was given the honor of rescuing the beleagured Bendix.[27] McDermott failed in its attempt to buy Pullman, but became the favorite of Babcock & Wilcox.

The fad was encouraged by success stories. Harry Gray put together United Technologies from already large and profitable companies. Phillip Morris was able to pump profits into its acquisition of Miller. British Petroleum's acquisition of Sohio was timed perfectly to cash in on the oil strike at Prudhoe Bay.

But it was a fad. The acquiring firms followed no readily repeatable formula, and the choice of targets was unpredictable.

The growing number of acquisitions and the continued unpredictability of the targets quickly led to a frenzied atmosphere in the business community. From the outset this merger wave was understood to be different. In 1978 *Fortune* quoted a merger professional: "It isn't the Louis Wolfsons who are doing it today. It's the establishment doing it to itself."[28]

It seemed as if no one was safe. These were hostile tender offers, not friendly deals. They were made by large, successful firms with vast financial resources. If any safety existed, it was probably in size. So defensive mergers competed with offensive mergers and added to the confusion.

There *was* a different character to this new wave of mergers. The percentage of cash offers was up from 32 percent in 1969 to 53 percent in 1979, and stock swaps were down from 60 percent in 1968 to 26 percent in 1979.[29]

Shareholders could not be expected to resist the cash premium of 50 percent or 100 percent over stock exchange trading prices. With the introduction of two-tier tender offers, even shareholders who believed the premiums were less than the corporation's true value could be stampeded into selling. Their belief in the value of the firm would be overwhelmed by the fear that other shareholders would sell a controlling interest to the acquiring firm. If that happened, the remaining shareholders would be paid off in a forced sale at the lower second-tier price.

The vulnerability of firms to takeovers was dramatized by the megamergers. Mergers like RCA's 1979 acquisition of CIT Financial for $1.3 billion or G.E.'s 1975 acquisition of Utah International for $1.9 billion emphasized the resources available to the new group of acquiring firms and the unrelatedness of their targets. When faced with a hostile tender offer from a giant corporation, smaller firms could not hope to escape. Their only option was to seek a white knight who would fashion a more palatable takeover deal.

Even failed takeover attempts pointed in directions that encouraged mergers. By acquisition a firm might grow to a less digestible size. By acquisition a firm could rid itself of attractive cash reserves. And by acquisition a firm could create antitrust conflicts.

In the early phase, it seemed that very large firms could stiff-arm direct takeover attempts. Mead Corporation fought off Occidental Petroleum's 1978 tender offer. McGraw-Hill defeated American Express's 1979 attempt. Both were billion dollar firms. Alteration to a lesser size did not seem as helpful. Carrier Corporation did not succeed in discouraging a $500 million bid by United Technologies by buying Jenn-Air for $82 million.[30]

Nevertheless, firms worth hundreds of millions of dollars continued to pursue other defensive mergers. Firms like Kennecott Copper and Hiram Walker eliminated liquid assets by merger. Kennecott, for example, paid over $500 million to acquire Carborundum, while Hiram Walker escaped an impending tender offer by the purchase of a $600 million oil property.

The only certain defense strategy to prevent a takeover is to take shares from holders who might be tempted to tender. Consequently, some managers have sought to protect their independence by buying out their shareholders before anyone else. In 1983, for example, three of the largest transactions were "going private" deals. Metromedia shareholders sold out for $1.5 billion, Wometco Enterprises for $810 million, and MGM/United Artists for $620 million.[31]

Sometimes offensive and defensive mergers came into conflict. United Technologies' offensive $700 million offer for Babcock & Wilcox was defeated by the intervention of a white knight, McDermott, which had entered the bidding in part to rid itself of attractive cash reserves.[32]

Not surprisingly, the sudden upsurge in merger activity produced strong and quick reactions in the corporate community. By the close of 1978, the first year in which the new merger wave was fully manifest, a survey of the National Association of Accountants showed 40 percent of the nation's largest firms felt themselves vulnerable to takeovers.[33] Even before this, Walter Kissinger, chairman of the Allen Group, argued in a *New York Times* op-ed piece that hostile takeovers were undesirable business practices.[34] William Cary, former chairman of the Securities and Exchange Commission, described the emergence of "financial" mergers that were not constrained in the ways industrial mergers had been.[35]

Senators Kennedy and Metzenbaum introduced legislation, "The Small and Independent Business Protection Act of 1979," to limit the largest mergers.[36] Although the bill did not progress in Congress to become legislation, it attracted support. Paul Samuelson, the Nobel Prize-winning economist, argued in *Newsweek* for serious consideration of the proposals the act contained,[37] and Harvard antitrust law expert Phillip Areeda, writing in the *Wall Street Journal*, supported the passage of the new law.[38] The *New York Times* supported an alternative legislative proposal formulated by the Federal Trade Commission.[39] As a group, however, the business community sided against these proposals and legislative efforts died.

The pace of megamergers, however, did not slacken in 1980. The dollar volume of mergers continued to increase until it peaked in 1981 at $82 billion. That mark was erased by the $122 billion total recorded in 1984. The number of $500 million deals increased from six in 1978 to sixteen in 1979 and to twenty-six in 1981. Even billion dollar deals became common, with four in 1980, twelve in 1981, and 18 in 1984.[40]

Only after spectacular takeover contests (and the general recognition in 1980 that the problems of American business were partially self-inflicted) did the corporate community seriously consider limiting merger activity. The critique of strategic investment theories discussed in Chapter 8 played a major role. But most sobering were the sequential contests for Conoco and Marathon Oil and the 1982 debacle at Bendix.

After the Bendix battle the corporate community conceded that mergers were getting out of hand. Consequently, they then supported the creation of the SEC's Advisory Committee on Tender

Offers discussed in Chapter 4. But the Advisory Committee recommendations were mild and dealt only with the takeover process (not the reasons behind takeovers). They remain unenacted, and megamergers continue.

Aftermania

The frenzy associated with the megamerger wave seems to have dissipated. What we have seen since 1983 may be a more enduring pattern of corporate behavior. Enough time has passed to demonstrate that mergers are not an automatic path to eternal profits. It also became evident that neither mergers nor size provides any guarantee against takeovers. This experience was open for all corporate managers to see by the close of 1982.

As the limitations on the usefulness of mergers were being recognized, the bargain acquisition (or the appearance of bargain stock prices) began to disappear in most industries. The August 1982 stock market boom raised the costs of takeovers. W. T. Grimm reported in January 1984 that as

> [the] price/earnings ratio paid for acquisitions in 1983 increased to 16.7 from 13.9 in 1982 ... the premium paid over market has dropped significantly to 37.7 percent in 1983 from 47.4 percent in 1982.[41]

These relatively higher prices may have discouraged some hostile tender offers, and tender offers have dropped in number. For the first time in ten years stock swaps outnumbered cash deals in 1983.

Even so, there is no indication that this wave of mergers is ending. The number of mergers counted by W. T. Grimm in 1984 set a ten-year high. Their total value was $122 billion, up from $73 billion in 1983 (and surpassing the previous record of $82.6 billion set in 1981). And, significantly, the number of $100 million mergers jumped to 200 in 1984.[42]

The 1984 rise in billion dollar deals was most dramatic. Led by the acquisition of oil companies—including the back-to-back record-breaking takeovers of Gulf Oil and Getty Oil—the number rose to eighteen. But the willingness to acquire at this level was not limited to the oil industry. In the $2 billion to $3 billion range, targets included the Carnation Company, Electronic Data Systems, Esmark, and the Continental Group.[43]

We can expect a continued stream of megamergers. This merger wave survived recession, inflation, stock market lows, and stock market highs. Many of these mergers will continue to be an outlet for excess corporate earnings, and they will be limited in size and direction only by the resources that the acquiring firms seek to deploy.

Another group of mergers can be expected in industries responding to changes in the business environment. Depending on the nature of these changes, the response may lead to consolidation mergers (within an industry), integration mergers (adding new resources to an industry), or diversification mergers (outside an industry).

Finally, there will always be mergers in pursuit of profit and other mergers to satisfy personal ambitions.

CHAPTER 12

OIL MERGERS

In 1977 *Fortune* magazine's list of largest industrial firms in the United States included oil companies as four of the top eight, ten of the top twenty, and seventeen of the top fifty.[1] It is thus not surprising that they have participated in many of the recent megamergers. Even with only average profits, these enormous oil companies have possessed the financial resources to pursue large-scale mergers.

However, size alone does not explain the prominent participation of oil companies in the merger wave. It does not explain why these firms have been involved as targets or as acquiring firms in two out of three of the twenty largest mergers between 1974 and 1982. The explanation for oil's disproportionate role lies in the changing fortunes of the industry. Large oil firms were first acquirers, then targets, and eventually both at the same time.

Beginning in the 1960s American oil firms were forced to reconsider the future of their industry. Since the early 1900s American oil companies had been the largest producers of oil in the world. But by the late 1960s it was evident that U.S. oil reserves were declining and American firms might lose their dominant position. At the same time, it appeared that oil itself might cease to be the world's primary energy source in the not-too-distant future.

American oil companies sought to adapt to these new conditions in three ways: by diversifying into future energy industries, by diversifying outside of energy industries, and by acquiring the remaining

247

reserves of oil. They pursued each of these strategies by acquisitions of firms and acquisitions of resources.

These acquisition strategies were made more complex for several reasons. Foremost among them were the changing relationships with foreign suppliers of oil. The 1973 Arab oil embargo and the creation of OPEC raised the price of crude oil and made supplies of it less dependable. This situation was aggravated by the Iranian revolution, the Iraq-Iran war, and the general political instability in the Middle East. Foreign developments also made secure U.S. oil reserves more valuable.

The U.S. government responded to these events with a series of policies that fitted together only roughly. The two primary objectives of these policies were to prevent oil companies from exploiting consumers by obtaining "unfair" profits on the scarce oil and to obtain secure sources of energy for the United States. A secondary set of objectives was designed to prevent the largest, fully integrated oil companies from using their economic advantages to dominate oil industries.

Giant vertically integrated oil companies were, therefore, restricted in the use of domestic oil reserves. To prevent these oil companies from gaining windfall profits, price controls were instituted, and to prevent the integrated oil companies from squeezing out independent refiners, a system mandating allocation of crude-oil production to smaller oil refiners was imposed. Nevertheless, the oil industry in general and the integrated firms in particular profited in 1974 after the oil embargo.

ENERGY DIVERSIFICATION ACQUISITIONS

The large oil firms were also the firms best positioned to benefit if the United States turned to alternative sources of energy. William Greider, a *Washington Post* columnist, explained:

If the early promises of nuclear power are ever fulfilled, uranium will be mined and milled, perhaps enriched and reprocessed, by oil companies.

If America shifts from oil to coal as its principal source of energy the importance of the oil companies will multiply—not shrink—because of their vast holdings in coal. In the not-so-distant future when new technology converts coal to gas or liquid fuel or even a gasoline substitute, oil companies will make it and market it from the ground to the gas station.

Oil shale, tar sands, geothermal power—oil companies have established futures in these sources, too.

And yes even in solar energy.[2]

In the 1960s Conoco bought Consolidation Coal, the second largest producer of coal, Occidental Petroleum bought Island Creek, the fourth largest, Sohio bought Old Ben, the thirteenth largest, and Gulf bought Pittsburg and Midway, the fifteenth largest.[3] During the early 1970s Standard Oil of California bought 20 percent of Amax, the third largest coal producer, and Ashland Oil acquired Arch Mineral, the seventh largest producer. Shell bought Seaway Coal, and Mobil bought Mt. Olive and Staunton Coal in 1977. Sohio substantially increased its coal reserves in 1981 when it purchased Kennecott Copper. Five of the ten companies with the largest holdings of coal reserves are oil companies, including Exxon and Kerr-McGee, who do not engage in major coal production.[4]

When federal oil-shale deposits were opened for development in 1974, the bidders were Gulf, Indiana Standard, Shell, and Occidental Petroleum, all major oil companies.[5] Moreover, as Kathleen O'Reilly, executive director of the Consumer Federation of America, told the Senate Judiciary Committee in 1979:

> The major oil companies have also been expanding into alternative forms of energy. Recently, Mobil and ARCO have entered the solar field with Mobil acquiring Tyco Labs and ARCO acquiring Solar Technology. Additionally, Shell acquired a major interest in Solar Energy Systems. Four oil companies, Shell, Union, Occidental and Burmah, own 90 percent of the only full-scale commercial geothermal plant in this country. Furthermore, virtually every other Federal geothermal lease is controlled by oil companies.[6]

Similarly, oil firms had become the major suppliers of nuclear fuel. By 1978, after the $500 million acquisition of Anaconda by Arco, five oil companies, Kerr-McGee, Arco, Exxon, Conoco, and Sohio, owned over 50 percent of the U.S. uranium-milling capacity. These firms, with another five oil companies, also owned about half of the proven reserves of uranium in the United States.[7]

If the United States was to turn to alternative energy sources, it, therefore, had to turn to the oil companies. This created a dilemma because new energy sources required large outlays of capital for development, as did the search for new sources of oil. How could gasoline consumers be protected and at the same time encourage oil companies to develop both kinds of energy resources?

Oil exploration was facilitated by lifting price controls on newly found oil and on oil that could not be recovered by conventional means. This made these more risky oil exploration ventures profitable as the world price for oil rose. Later, the oil profits and the funds for energy development were increased by the substitution of a windfall profits tax for price controls. In addition, specific kinds of energy development projects—synthetic fuels and oil-shale and tar-sands conversions—were subsidized by the Department of Energy.

Each of these actions increased oil company profits. These steps further entrenched the role of large oil companies in the oil industry (and the broader energy industry as well) because they received the subsidies and gained the experience in new technologies at government expense. Overall these actions have lessened America's dependence on foreign oil, although this seems to have been as much as a result of consumers' conservation efforts brought on by higher prices.

Despite price controls and new taxes, oil profits soared between 1972 and 1981. With the exception of 1976 and 1977 (both of which were also very good years for oil companies), net revenues of oil companies rose markedly. According to a 1982 Federal Trade Commission report, total funds for the sixteen largest oil firms grew from $11 billion in 1972, to $22 billion in 1978, to $50 billion in 1981.[8]

How were these funds going to be invested? The FTC warned in 1979 that if these profits were used to buy resources and firms in the energy industry, the major oil companies would quickly eliminate all their smaller competitors.[9] *Business Week* emphasized the consequences of trying to find investments:

> So flush is Exxon that it is "buying the pot at all the lease sales," complains one industry executive. Referring to lease sales ranging from the Baltimore Canyon two years ago, where Exxon bid $367 million, to the recent South Atlantic sale, where it was the high bidder at some $34.5 million, he adds, "I don't think they see anything more down there than we do. They're just trying to keep themselves busy."[10]

NONENERGY DIVERSIFICATION ACQUISITIONS

Had the oil companies limited their acquisitions to energy companies, their actions would have been predictable. Although such acquisitions would have swelled the merger totals, they would not have added to the general merger frenzy. But the acquisitions went beyond investment in the energy industry.

Nonenergy acquisitions were a convenient way to dispose of excess earnings. In 1979 *Forbes* magazine examined the reasons for Mobil's notorious acquisition of Marcor (Montgomery Ward and Container Corporation of America):

> [Mobil executive Lawrence] Woods contends it wasn't a choice between $1.5 billion for Marcor and $1.5 billion for energy development. Mobil doesn't have enough good projects, he says, that could justify another $1.5 billion. ... "I wish to hell we had enough good projects to put [the money] in," he says. "We've been throwing money at projects in the U.S. as fast as they come up."[11]

The need to find investment outlets was, therefore, an immediate motive for Mobil's nonenergy diversification. But *Business Week* offered a more fundamental long-term reason for such diversification:

> The overriding fact is that oil companies are exploiting a dwindling natural resource. How long the inevitable exhaustion can be put off is a matter of fierce debate, both within the industry and among government policymakers. But at some point the oil companies will certainly be doomed to a business that will grow sluggishly, at best.[12]

To symbolize its acceptance of this new reality, the Sun Oil Company (Sunoco) dropped the word oil and renamed itself Sun Company. According to *Fortune* magazine, Sun's decision to diversify was made in 1970 by its newly designated chief executive officer, H. Robert Sharbaugh. "Sharbaugh's basic premise is that the managerial skills required to run a large, fully integrated oil company like Sun do not apply to most other businesses."[13] So he made a series of small acquisitions to develop managerial skills and internal expertise in nonenergy businesses. These he hoped would prepare the firm for its inevitable move out of the oil business.

Other oil executives shared Sharbaugh's view, but most were less tentative about their acquisitions. Thornton Bradshaw, then president of Arco, for example, bought the Anaconda Copper Company for $700 million, and this action reflected the general impatience of many oil executives in 1978. Bradshaw remarked, "The oil business is going into a decline. . . . It can still be profitable, but it won't be fun anymore."[14] As *Business Week* put it: "Oilmen have . . . tremendous advantages over many other industries—from buggy whip manufacturer to anthracite coal diggers—who have seen their day come and go. One [advantage] is the vast reserve of oil and gas still in the ground. . . . And few other major industries have been so consistently profitable." [15]

This analysis paralleled the prescriptions of Bruce Henderson and the Boston Consulting Group: Take the profits from a mature or declining industry and invest them in new growing industries. One can quibble whether nuclear energy, coal, oil shale, or tar sands are industries of the future, but clearly that was the premise of these investments by oil companies. Oil turned out to be more plentiful than anticipated in the short run, and nuclear energy was raising more problems than it solved. Oil shale and synthetic fuels remained uneconomic. But hindsight does not contradict the design or purpose of these strategic investments of the 1960s and 1970s.

The nonenergy acquisitions of oil companies were also part of this overall investment strategy. Mobil did not buy Marcor because the latter was a weak competitor of Sears, Roebuck. To the contrary, the fortunes of Montgomery Ward had revived in the 1960s, and they looked very promising in the early 1970s.[16] It was reasonable to argue that with the availability of Mobil's vast economic resources, Montgomery Ward might continue to grow and even surpass Sears.

Exxon's acquisition of Reliance Electric was specifically designed to capture a market of the future. In its acquisition of Becton, Dickinson shares, Sun correctly predicted that the health industry would grow in the late 1970s. And the acquisitions of the nation's largest copper-mining companies by Arco, Standard (Indiana), and Sohio were premised on a prediction of general economic recovery.

In each case these ill-fated acquisitions were not a consequence of any lack of strategic intention. Rather, the failures were due to other factors, such as economic events beyond the control of the companies, poor choice of investment targets, and an inability to manage unfamiliar businesses. The pull of investment strategy may have been overwhelmed by the push of profits that had no investment outlets in the energy field.

Armed with their riches, oil companies made large acquisitions throughout the economy. The list in Table 12–1 includes the largest nonenergy acquisitions between 1974 and 1981.

Even so, the 1982 FTC oil merger study found that the major, fully integrated oil companies were timid acquirers in comparison to

Table 12-1.   Nonenergy Acquisitions by Oil Companies, 1974–1981.

Primary Year	Oil Company	Acquisition Price	Target	Industry
1974–76	Mobil	$1.6 billion	Marcor	Merchandising containers
1975	Chevron	$333 million	Amax	Mining
1976–77	Arco	$784 million	Anaconda	Nonferrous metals
1977	Union	$234 million	Molycorp	Rare earth
1977	Gulf	$455 million	Kewanee	Chemicals
1978	Sun	$293 million	Becton, Dickenson (34%)	Medical equipment
1979	Standard (Indiana)	$462 million	Cyprus Mines	Mining
1979	Exxon	$1.5 billion	Reliance	Electric motors
1980	Getty	$568 million	ERC Corp.	Insurance
1981	Sohio	$1.7 billion	Kennecott	Mining/ Manufacturing

Source: *Hearings before the Senate Judiciary Committee on S.1245*; and *Mergers in the Petroleum Industry*, FTC Report (September 1982).

a group of firms they described as "petroleum related." These were diversified firms with substantial petroleum holdings. Like the oil companies, they benefited from rising oil values during the 1970s. The FTC found that the major oil companies were much more likely to make large acquisitions than other large firms, but less likely than the "petroleum related" firms.[17] Perhaps these already diversified firms were more confident of their ability to manage unfamiliar businesses. Tenneco, for example, bought four nonenergy firms, including Monroe Auto Equipment and Philadelphia Life Insurance, between 1974 and 1978 for over $800 million. Occidental Petroleum was even more aggressive. Although it failed in its billion dollar bid to acquire Mead Corporation, other efforts succeeded, including the $791 million purchase of Iowa Beef Processors.

If lack of experience in operating diverse industries was the major restraint on oil companies making nonenergy acquisitions, this no longer seemed the case in the late 1970s. The combination of rising oil profits and experience with initial acquisitions might have generated more and more acquisitions by oil companies. The specter of rich oil conglomerates swooping down and gobbling up the rest of American industry momentarily transfixed political leaders.

Senate Judiciary Committee hearings were held in 1979 to consider two issues: How could oil companies be required to reinvest their growing profits in the development of new energy resources for the United States? And how could nonoil industries be protected from takeovers by oil companies? The Consumer Federation of America's Kathleen O'Reilly warned about the latter:

> What do IBM, GE, Chrysler, ITT and U.S. Steel have in common? Among other things, that none of them is unaffordably beyond the economic grasp of the major oil companies. . . . Exxon, Mobil and Texaco had more sales and assets in 1978 than the collective sales and assets of the second 500 manufacturing firms in the United States. . . . The 16 largest oil companies had a sufficient cash flow in 1978 to purchase almost all of the stockholders' equity of the top 50 retailing firms (including Sears, J. C. Penny and Safeway), all of the top 50 transportation firms (including TWA, American and Pan Am) and all of the top 50 diversified financial companies (including Aetna and American Express).[18]

But it didn't happen. Perhaps the hearings, in addition to feeding the frenzy, warned oil companies of the public sentiment against nonenergy acquisitions. Perhaps oil companies realized that their nonenergy acquisitions had not been successful. In any case, soon after 1979 large oil companies began to be among the hunted.

OIL ACQUISITIONS

Beginning in 1979 with the $3.6 billion acquisition of Belridge Oil by Shell, megamergers became more identified with takeovers *of* oil firms rather than with takeovers *by* oil firms. This kind acquisition was not remarkable. Large oil companies regularly acquired small oil companies or oil and gas properties of other companies throughout the 1960s and 1970s. But such acquisitions were typically in the $50 million to $200 million range.

The most noted feature of the Belridge acquisition, therefore, was its size. In 1979 $3.6 billion was the largest acquisition ever made (a record soon to be shattered). This willingness to spend on a scale previously unmatched brought a whole new class of firms within the category of potential targets.

Cheap Oil Reserves

Equally remarkable, however, were the reasons Shell was willing to pay such a high premium for Belridge. Oil reserves that had previously been only marginally economic became very valuable because of the 1979 rise in world oil prices. American oil resources became particularly valuable after the 1979 Iranian revolution and the subsequent Iraq-Iran war.

Shell justified paying a fifteenfold premium over Belridge's 1970 value for two major reasons. Shell expected that its better technology would enable it to recover Belridge's heavy-crude reserves more economically. With rising world prices and decontrol of American prices on heavy crude these reserves were bound to be more valuable. In addition, Belridge had potentially huge reserves of oil located at depths previously unexplored. Shell expected technology and oil prices to make these reserves accessible.[19]

Shell was betting in the short run that OPEC would maintain its price and in the long run that dwindling world supplies and foreign political instability would make U.S. oil reserves uniquely valuable. The collapse of OPEC or big new oil strikes would have made that bet a loser. Shell was not alone: The Sun Company made the same bet.

Sun bought the Texas Pacific Oil Company in 1980 from Seagram for $2.3 billion. After the SEC forced it to disgorge its 34 percent holding of Becton, Dickenson (a health-products company), Sun dropped Robert Sharbaugh and his diversification strategy. The *Wall Street Journal* offered the following analysis of the decision by Sun's new CEO, Theodore Burtis:

> [W]ith Sun's profit soaring during the past few quarters—1979 net income rose 69% from the year earlier to $700 million—the nation's tenth largest oil company has the cash and financial strength to make a purchase of stunning proportions.[20]

Sun wanted the proven oil reserves to replenish its declining stocks of domestic oil. It also obtained millions of acres of unexplored properties.

Sun, like Shell, was especially well positioned to profit from these acquisitions. It had the expertise to recover additional oil from Texas Pacific's many depleted wells. Furthermore, Congress imposed lower windfall taxes on recoveries from these unused wells and also on recoveries from heavy crude and newly discovered oil. The wealthy oil companies had the resources and personnel to implement untried methods to recover these more profitable categories of crude oil.

These economies of scale led other major firms to make contemporaneous, though smaller, acquisitions. For example: Mobil bought General Crude from International Paper for $800 million in 1979 and Trans Ocean Oil from Esmark for $720 million in 1980; Getty Oil paid $564 million for Reserve Oil in 1979; Phillips Petroleum purchased Great Basins Petroleum for $196 million in 1980; and Gulf paid $141 million for Amalgamated Bonanza Petroleum in 1979.

Bonanza is the right word. The seventeen acquisitions of oil companies listed in Table 12–2 were the largest oil mergers executed between 1979 and 1983. And they were not limited to sales of oil properties. The largest involved acquisitions of vertically integrated oil companies.

This rush to acquire American oil reserves is understandable. It was a function of the rise in world oil prices, the political stability of the United States, economies of scale in recovering oil, and a desire by owners of the American oil properties to cash in on their profits. Even foreign companies, such as France's Elf Aquataine and oil-rich Kuwait Petroleum made $2 billion acquisitions in the desirable American oil market. Australia's CSR Ltd. bought Delhi International in 1981 for a lesser amount—$591 million.

Oil Company Bargains?

The attractiveness of major American oil companies to buyers is a complicated matter. In theory, the increased value of these firms' oil reserves should have been reflected in higher prices for their publicly traded shares. In this case, however, the stock market did not work. Whatever the reason, stock markets have persisted in valuing oil shares below the value of reserves. For example, during the battle for Conoco in 1981 *Newsweek* published a list of twelve oil companies showing that the estimated value of their oil reserves exceeded

Table 12-2. Acquisitions of Oil Companies, 1979-1983.

Year	Target	Acquisition Price	Acquiring Firm
1979	Belridge	$3.6 billion	Shell
1979	General Crude	$800 million	Mobil
1979	Reserve	$560 million	Getty
1980	Texas Pacific	$2.3 billion	Sun
1980	McMoran	$2.3 billion	Freeport Minerals
1980	Trans Ocean	$720 million	Mobil
1981	Hudson Bay	$1.4 billion	Dome
1981	Conoco	$8.0 billion	Du Pont
1981	Marathon	$6.6 billion	U.S. Steel
1981	Texasfulf	$4.2 billion	Elf-Aquataine
1981	Santa Fe International	$2.4 billion	Kuwait Petroleum
1982	Cities Services	$4.1 billion	Occidental Petroleum
1983	El Paso	$1.2 billion	Burlington Northern
1983	General American	$1.1 billion	Phillips Petroleum
1983	CITGO	$990 million	Southland
1983	Belco Petroleum	$800 million	Internorth
1979-83	All Targets	$40.4 billion	All Acquirers

Sources: W.T. Grimm & Co., *Mergerstat Review, 1982*, pp. 6-10; "Deals of the Year," *Fortune*, for years cited; and *Mergers in the Petroleum Industry*, FTC Report (September 1982).

the market price of their shares (see Table 12-3). Getty, Marathon, Cities Services, and Gulf were all acquired later. Amid the Getty and Gulf takeovers, the *New York Times* published an updated list containing thirteen bargain oil firms, including Exxon, the nation's largest industrial firm. A partial listing appears in Table 12-4. It is small wonder, then, that oil companies have been thought by some to be bargains.

That share prices remained low seems to be a function of the special nature of the oil industry. Vertically integrated oil firms have operated on the basis that they should add to their reserves an

Table 12-3. Undervalued Oil Shares, 1981.

Oil Company	Market Price per Share	Value per Share
Getty Oil	$72	$250
Marathon Oil	68	210
Standard of Indiana	60	205
Standard of California	40	172
Arco	50	170
Cities Services	56	130
Phillips	45	130
Sun Company	40	130

Source: "Who's Next at the Altar," *Newsweek* (July 27, 1981): 54.

Table 12-4. Undervalued Oil Companies, 1983.

Oil Company	Market Price of Company (in billions)	Value of Oil Reserves (in billions)
Exxon	$33.5	$41.7
Arco	11.5	23.4
Standard of Indiana	15.2	30.3
Sun Company	5.2	8.4

Source: Michael Blumstein, "Buying vs. Exploring for Oil," *New York Times*, March 19, 1984, p. D-1.

amount equal to the amount of oil they use up, that is, the amount they refine and sell. So long as the costs of finding new oil reserves are roughly the same as the costs incurred in finding existing oil reserves the price of oil shares on the stock market will reflect the rising value of the oil firm's existing oil reserves.

If, as is now the case, new oil reserves are likely to be much more expensive to develop, then the stock market is faced with conflicting signals. The future scarcity of oil will immediately drive up prices and the value of existing supplies. Oil companies will earn high short-term profits on their old oil, and total assets will be revalued upward. At the same time, their projected costs of doing business, that is, finding new oil, will increase at a rate equal to or faster than (if price controls limit the rise in value of existing reserves) the rise in asset value. Consequently, the projected cost of discovery and recovering new oil may actually depress the value of shares of a vertically integrated oil company even if it is earning record profits and its assets are increasing in value.

Tying the costs of future development to the ballooning rewards of past development drags down the price of oil shares. The commitment to risky, costly future oil exploration will cause oil companies to sell for less than the value of their existing reserves.

This scenario makes sense only if the stock market correctly guesses the future of the oil industry. The market may be wrong; prices of oil may not rise greatly in the foreseeable future. Or if they do rise to a point where investment becomes uneconomic, managers of oil companies may not dissipate their profits by continuing to invest in oil.

There are a number of reasons why the stock market might have believed that shareholders of oil companies would never enjoy the benefits of high oil profits, even if they were sustained for a number of years. Most of those profits have been reinvested in oil exploration or new energy projects. Oil executives had described this exploration as a very expensive and highly speculative investment. While the odds overall may be reasonable, given the number of drilling projects and other ventures, shareholders may perceive the future as extremely risky.

Oil executives themselves may have exacerbated the pessimistic view that their firms will stay in oil too long and squander their profits in oil ventures in the responses executives made to criticism of nonenergy acquisitions. By claiming to have invested in every plausible energy venture, they lent credence to reports in the business press that giant oil firms were bidding up prices of oil leases to unreasonable levels.

Shareholders may also have believed that it would be impossible for most oil companies to successfully diversify out of the oil industry. They may have been concerned that too many of the oil company assets—drilling equipment, tankers, pipelines, and refineries— could not be converted or sold for other uses. They might have feared, too, that if the wealth of oil companies could be converted to cash, the companies were too big to be permitted to buy into other sectors of the economy. Shareholders had only to look at the dismal record of the largest oil firms in their diversification acquisitions to add to their worries.

Together these reasons may have accounted for oil shares trading at substantially below the value of existing oil reserves, even if the medium-range future for oil was good. So long as the value of existing reserves was tied to the future prospects of the industry, the low value would persist. However, if the value of reserves could be uncoupled from future prospects, the value of the shares would increase.

Making Oil Companies Valuable

The value of this decoupling was manifest in the acquisition prices of firms whose principal assets were oil reserve companies. It was also evident in Mobil's attempt to takeover Marathon. Mobil wanted Marathon's oil reserves, in particular, the Yates Field, not its refining capacity or marketing network. Mobil made this explicit in its amended takeover bid which would have turned over those assets to the Amarada Hess Oil Company.

Unlike a shareholder, Mobil's valuation of Marathon rested on the immediate cost of obtaining other oil reserves. From this perspective Marathon was a bargain for Mobil. In fact, seen this way, almost all oil companies were bargains to each other.

It was expected, therefore, that Mobil's purchase of Marathon would be followed by a series of acquisitions among the largest oil firms. But despite the best efforts of the FTC under the Reagan administration, such mergers were barred on antitrust grounds. The courts were more skeptical than the FTC of the competitive impact of these mergers, and for a time courts discouraged all such takeovers.

The negative value of coupled oil reserves, however, remained open for other companies to exploit. Nonenergy companies might have been able to exploit the medium-run prospects without being locked into the energy industry in the long run. The profit experiences of U.S. Steel and Du Pont were discouraging, though. They were perhaps the victims of poor timing. Having borrowed large sums at extremely high interest rates, they entered the oil industry just when OPEC was losing its grip and oil prices declined. In any case, no comparable attempts were made.

But this did not end the matter. T. Boone Pickens, Jr., of Mesa Petroleum figured out a way to decouple the assets of an integrated oil firm. He argued that shareholders of the largest firms would profit most if those companies placed their oil reserves in a royalty trust. The trust would then pay the shareholders the value of those reserves directly as oil was recovered. In other words, Pickens sought to break up integrated oil firms.

Not surprisingly, the managers of integrated firms resisted this idea. They argued, as they had in Congress when resisting price controls and windfall profits taxes, that they needed the profits to assure America of adequate and secure energy resources.

This defense, however relevant to national priorities, simply illustrated Pickens's stated fear that shareholders would never have the opportunity to enjoy the profits of their holdings. Pickens sought a way to benefit from his insight. In doing so he took a leaf from Carl Icahn's book of investment strategies.

Pickens, through his Mesa Petroleum Company and together with several associates, bought low-valued shares in Cities Services, General American Oil, Superior Oil, Phillips Petroleum, and Gulf Oil. Like Icahn before him, when incumbent management refused to follow his suggestions, Pickens sought control in order to force acceptance of his suggestions. And like Icahn, he has profited handsomely from his efforts.

In each case, Pickens's attempts were rewarded but not by a takeover or the implementation of his proposal. According to the *Wall Street Journal*, Pickens's drive to take over Cities Services netted him $40 million when that company was forced into a merger with Occidental Petroleum.[21] His attempt on General American resulted in a merger with Phillips Petroleum and a $45 million profit. Superior Oil bought back his 3 percent stake for a $32 million premium before it was bought by Mobil. And the takeover of Gulf by Chevron earned him over $550 million.[22]

Pickens was not alone in pursuing this strategy. Bass Brothers Enterprises, for example, began buying shares of Texaco, and by March 1984 it had accumulated almost 10 percent of Texaco's shares. This was enough to convince the management of Texaco that it was threatened with a takeover.

For $1.25 billion dollars Texaco bought out Bass Brothers and its associates. The $250 million profit to Bass Brothers was given in exchange for their agreement not to buy additional Texaco shares for ten years. Bass Brothers also agreed to vote its remaining shares in support of the current management during that period.[23]

The Dilemma for Big Oil

Actions by the Bass Brothers and Boone Pickens emphasized the precarious posture of all oil firms. So long as shares remained valued at less than the selling price of their reserves eveh the largest industrial firm in the world, Exxon, was vulnerable to a takeover bid. Almost as dangerous to the largest firms were the consequences of takeovers of middle-sized oil firms. They were being forced into mergers (at bargain prices for known oil reserves) with slightly larger firms. These mergers would create new giant competitors with enormous and relatively cheap oil reserves.

Under these circumstances it was inevitable that the oil firms would challenge Judge Manos's 1981 decision that restrained Mobil from buying Marathon. The occasion for the challenge was dissension among the managers of Getty Oil and the heirs of J. Paul Getty. Initially, it appeared that the dissatisfaction would be resolved by a sale of the corporation to a middle-sized oil company, Pennzoil. At the last minute (or according to the *American Lawyer*, possibly a little later) Texaco grabbed the deal at a higher price—$10 billion.[24]

Led by Joseph Flom's firm, Texaco broke through the Mobil antitrust barrier. The different outcome was less a function of the skill of Skadden, Arps and more a function of the parties to the deal. Getty was a "friendly" merger (apart from the chagrin expressed at Pennzoil), and all Getty suitors were oil companies. None, other than the government, was positioned to argue an antitrust violation, and the government was not inclined to block this merger. In contrast, Marathon had premised its defense on a show-stopping antitrust lawsuit which was buttressed by seeking a nonenergy white knight, U.S. Steel.

The different partners to the acquisition of Getty gave the FTC the key role it had sought in the Marathon merger. At the time of that merger, the FTC had argued that the merger should be permitted if specified marketing, refining, and transportation facilities were divested. (The conditions would have been acceptable to Mobil.) The FTC's antitrust concerns were that the merger would reduce competition by giving Mobil an unduly large share of certain local gasoline markets. The FTC was not concerned that the merger might lessen competition among producers of crude oil.

The FTC took an identical position with regard to the merger of Getty and Texaco. The acquisition would require divestiture of some facilities, but Texaco could keep all the oil reserves. With no opposition, the views of the FTC prevailed.

The record $10.1 billion acquisition of Getty was topped within two months and started an avalanche of purchases. Standard Oil of California (now Chevron) acquired Gulf Oil for a new record of $13.3 billion. Gulf, fourth largest oil firm in the United States, under seige by Boone Pickens, sought refuge with its white knight, Chevron, the fifth largest oil firm. If you add the $1.2 billion Texaco paid Bass Brothers, the $5.2 billion Royal Dutch/Shell paid to complete its control of Shell Oil (U.S.), and the $5.7 billion Mobil paid for Superior Oil, the acquisition of oil shares in the first two months of 1984 amounted to $35.5 billion.

Thirty-five billion dollars is almost 90 percent of the total paid for all other large oil companies since the purchase of Belridge Oil in 1979. During those five years $40 billion was spent to acquire seventeen firms. After two months of 1984, it looked as if that record would be exceeded in a single year (see Table 12–5).

Predictably, some members of Congress reacted negatively to these mergers and the FTC's acquiescence to them. Senator Metzenbaum, a leader in the 1979 move by the Senate Judiciary Committee to limit oil mergers, again called for restrictions: "These mergers are almost obscene. They have absolutely no redeeming social or economic

Table 12–5. Acquisitions of Oil Companies, First Six Months of 1984.

Target	Acquiring Company	Estimated Acquisition Value (in millions)
Gulf	Chevron	$13,300
Getty	Texaco	10,125
Superior	Mobil	5,700
Shell	Royal Dutch/Shell	5,500
Bass Brothers	Texaco	1,200

Source: "Leading Deals and Deal Makers in the First Half of This Year," *New York Times*, July 3, 1984, p. D–6.

value. They don't make sense as a matter of national energy or anti-trust policy.[25]

Senator Metzenbaum's first point—concern about American energy reserves—struck a resounding note. J. Bennett Johnston, a traditional friend of oil firms and ranking Democrat on the Senate Energy Committee, echoed Metzenbaum's concern and introduced legislation:

> It is our intention to stop them dead in their tracks—Pickens, [Chevron], everybody. It seems to me decidedly not in the public interest to use up the nation's credit to create windfall profits and thereby divert funds from more useful endeavors such as drilling for more oil.[26]

The Chevron merger, however, had demonstrated the difficulty of eliminating such mergers in a way that satisfied national energy concerns. Gulf was under seige by Pickens. Once Pickens had raised $877.5 million, Gulf was left with only limited options. It could have acceded to Pickens's request and placed its oil reserves in a royalty trust. This might have eliminated the takeover incentive, but it would also have denied Gulf (and the nation) the use of those funds for exploration of new oil.

Gulf could have bought out Pickens, as Texaco did Bass Brothers, or used Martin Marietta's Pac-Man strategy and bought Pickens's company, Mesa Petroleum. Either seems an unsatisfactory response, like paying off a blackmailer. Even if the first attacker is stopped, any number of other persons can pursue the strategy so long as the company remains undervalued, as the St. Regis Corporation found out after it paid off Sir James Goldsmith in January 1984. St. Regis then faced successive takeover bids by the Loews Corporation and Rupert Murdoch in the following six months.

A more effective strategy is to raise the price of the firm above its liquidation value. If, for example, the giant oil firms could convince the market that they are well run and will not invest good profits in bad exploration ventures, their prices ought to rise. Unfortunately, for managers of the oil companies, they were unable to do that. Indeed, the *Wall Street Journal* reported that Gulf became vulnerable initially because it had been a poorly run oil company.[27]

No doubt the oil industry defenses in congressional hearings throughout the 1970s also contributed to the low valuation of oil company shares. Oil companies could not credibly argue for a high per-share price when they were being deprived, through price controls and taxes, of profits they claimed were necessary to cover rising exploration costs. Nor was the oil company defense of their diversifying acquisitions helpful. By arguing in Congress that oil firms were buying nonenergy companies because they were already funding even marginally reasonable energy development projects, they implied that the companies were ploughing back profits to satisfy national concerns about energy even at the expense of shareholder profits.

Another way of raising prices is for a firm to buy back its shares from those individuals who place a low value on them. In an extreme case—when all shareholders have a low opinion of a firm's management—the only way to safety is a leveraged buyout, taking the company private.

The Gulf board of directors turned down a leveraged buyout package put together by the firm of Kohlberg, Kravis, Roberts even though the buyout bid was higher than Chevron's.[28] Perhaps the board doubted whether the firm could function with so much debt. Had it succeeded it would have been almost ten times the size of the next largest "going-private" transaction, the $1.5 billion leveraged buyout of Metromedia.[29]

When the stock market values shares at less than the liquidation value of a corporation, it is a sign that the shareholders have lost confidence in management. The undervaluation is an invitation to a proxy fight or a takeover bid. Oil stocks had been undervalued for a long time before the invitation to buy or contest the management of giant oil firms was acted upon.

Was the oil industry as a whole poorly managed? Or is it possible that investors reacted pessimistically because they were uncertain and confused about the prospects of the industry? Did the oil companies become victims of a misunderstanding and investor group psychology?

If they became victims, oil executives have themselves to blame as much as anyone. Their nonenergy and energy acquisitions contributed to the new attitude among executives toward takeovers. Beginning in 1974 with the hostile acquisition of Marcor by Mobil, oil companies set the trend in the size of mergers, unfriendly deals, and the unpredictability of targets. Their mergers, as much as those of any industry, helped support the belief that businesses are just cash flows that can be mixed and managed by any good executive with financial training. The low value accorded oil stocks was at least partly due to poor prospects announced by oil executives.

With the Getty deal, Texaco seems to have set a new low in the conduct surrounding takeover bargaining. It entered the bidding after the Getty board of directors had approved a deal with Pennzoil.[30] With the acquisition of Gulf, Chevron set a new high in acquisition prices. The buyout of Bass Brothers' shares in Texaco seems to prove that no firm is too large to be taken over and no firm is too small to do the taking over.

Considering their role, it is hard to have sympathy for oil executives who feared takeovers. But what of the public interest? Is the recent history of oil takeovers the sign of a properly functioning stock market?

The consequences of takeovers are sometimes good, but not always. There is no reason, for example, to believe that America's energy needs would have been furthered if Gulf had established a royalty trust or if it had taken itself private. But then, there is no reason to believe that the sale of Gulf to Chevron will enhance the nation's energy resources either.

Like mergers in other business sectors, oil mergers possess characteristics that distinguish them from the overall megamerger wave. Oil mergers have had their own dynamic. The combination of current profits and the inevitable long-term decline of the industry led oil companies to experiment with diversification acquisitions. The relatively low price of shares in oil firms led to takeovers of oil firms.

The mergers resulting from the circumstances of specific oil companies changed the process by which takeover decisions were made for all industries. By 1982 the general merger frenzy had peaked, but the logic of the new takeover strategies was ready to start a new round of mergers within the oil industry. The temptation of low prices for oil shares was not resisted.

C H A P T E R 13

FINANCIAL COMPANY MERGERS

L ike mergers in the oil industry, acquisitions made by financial companies have been based on an industry dynamic. This once rigidly segmented industry is quickly being transformed by mergers and internal developments into a more homogeneous set of competitors as the distinctions between bankers, brokers, pension funds, and insurance companies are broken down. The transformation has been promoted by changing economic conditions, technological innovations, and new business opportunities.

THE TRADITIONAL FINANCIAL INDUSTRY

The financial industry in the United States was segmented by the Glass-Steagall Act in 1933.[1] Pitt and Williams have explained the reason for the act's divorcement of banking from the securities industry:

In 1932, Senator Carter Glass of Virginia surveyed the wreckage of the nation's banking system and collapsed stock market and concluded that the role of banks in the securities markets, and particularly the activities of bank securities affiliates, had made one of the "greatest contributions to the unprecedented disaster which has caused this almost incurable depression. . . . The Senate Banking and Currency Committee chronicled the abuses of banks and their securities affiliates, commenting that these affiliates had "devote[d]

themselves in many cases to perilous underwriting operations, stock speculation and maintaining a market for the banks' own stock often largely with the
resources of the parent bank."[2]

As a result of Glass-Steagall, commercial banks and other depository institutions were prohibited from engaging in investment banking activities such as underwriting, distributing, or dealing in securities.

Banks and savings institutions were also restricted by other federal and state rules. These established reserve requirements, investment limitations, and ceilings on the interest they could pay to depositors or charge to borrowers. In addition, states imposed rules that restricted entry into the banking business and limited the number of branches an institution was permitted to operate.

Other financial institutions, such as insurance companies, pension funds, and mutual funds, have been subject to similar state or federal regulation. These regulations are intended to limit the opportunities for self-dealing by institution managers and to protect the beneficiaries from speculative investments.

The securities industry itself became subject to regulation, but the rules that applied to it were more limited. Securities laws required, principally, disclosure of facts about investments and potential conflicts of interest among managers.

These labyrinthine rules, however, provided some advantages to each kind of financial institution. Commercial banks were favored by permission to grant depositors check-writing privileges and by authority to make business loans. Savings institutions were forbidden from making commercial loans, but had an advantage in attracting deposits because they were allowed to pay a higher interst rate than commercial banks.

Despite this legal separation of the financial industries, there continued to be overlaps among the activities of firms operating in different segments. While investment bankers underwrite and market corporate stocks and bonds, commercial banks buy corporate securities through their trust departments and arrange for loans to those same companies using their depositors' funds. Insurance policies, such as variable annuities, are often difficult to distinguish from some securities investments, which, in turn, resemble some bank savings certificates.

By recombining financial activities it is possible that a financial institution will engage in the conflicting interests that the Glass-

Steagall Act was designed to prohibit. To guard against the possibility of banks investing in new business ventures and acquisitions, the activities of financial institutions have been subject to approval by the Comptroller of the Currency, the Federal Reserve Board, and other agencies. As a result, mergers between firms in different segments were generally outlawed, and many mergers within segments were unlikely to receive government approval.

In the forty years following the passage of the Glass-Steagall Act, each financial segment developed separately and prospered. With insured accounts and a virtual monopoly on checking services, commercial banks had little trouble attracting depositors. The giant money-center banks increased their share of that market by offering convenience in the form of ubiquitous branch offices. When permitted, savings institutions also expanded their offices to lure depositors. As testimony to their profitability, the thrift institutions gave away irons, toasters, glassware, and televisions to new customers. Brokerage firms also fared well in an economy that grew almost consistently from the end of World War II through the 1960s. Seemingly, each segment enjoyed adequate opportunities for growth without testing the limits of its authority.

THE FORCES OF FINANCIAL CHANGE

In the 1970s the settled structure of financial industries changed. As each segment suffered economic reverses, each turned to provinces previously occupied by others. Eventually, the distinctions between segments blurred.

The key change for the financial industries was the end of the sustained growth in the American economy that had followed World War II. The deep and extended recession after the Vietnam War contrasted sharply with the milder recessions that had accompanied the economic growth of the preceding twenty-five years. The consequence of this recession, which was exacerbated by the OPEC oil-price increases, profoundly affected the American financial community and the world economy.

The recession occurred at a time when economic learning was increasing. The public, like the new generation of corporate managers, was becoming more sensitive to the workings of the economy. Employees, for example, demanded cost-of-living clauses attached to their wage rates. Growing numbers of retirees wanted assurances that they would benefit from their pension plans.

Stagflation, the name given to the 1970s' persistent recession, made obvious the costs and values of financial services even to those who had no formal economic training. Rising prices and inflation increased everyone's expenses and reduced the value of savings. By raising prices, inflation also contributed to a slowing of the economy which required greater use of less valuable savings and widespread use of increasingly expensive borrowings. As a consequence, the public demanded a better return on its money. Throughout the 1970s it became obvious the public was not getting it from traditional financial companies.

Brokerage Firms

Stock market investments which had sold as a sure hedge against inflation were a disaster in the 1970s. The Dow Jones average neared 1,000 in the 1969 boom stock market. During the 1970s it briefly broke through the 1,000 mark three times, only to fall back to substantially lower levels. Only the 1982 bull market seemed to firmly raise the market above 1,000. Between 1969 and 1982 the consumer price index increased over 200 percent. In other words, inflation had reduced the value of stock investments by two-thirds.[3]

The consequences for brokerage firms and their investment banking houses were severe. Individuals did not want to buy existing corporate shares or new issues of corporate securities. Large sums of investment money disappeared due to the recession, and other large sums were poised to leave the stock market entirely when other investments appeared.

Eventually, the investment banking houses sought to recoup these investment funds by creating money-market funds which competed with banks for demand-deposit accounts. By 1981 the money-market funds had attracted $175 billion. Merrill Lynch's money funds alone accounted for $36 billion, or more than the deposits of any American bank.[4]

Unless they adapted to changing conditions, many brokerage firms would go broke. Established firms found that they were challenged by new, low-cost discount brokers, and the industry was forced to abandon fixed commissions on shares traded.

Savings Institutions

The high interest rates of the 1970s had a disastrous impact on savings institutions. When annual inflation exceeded the rate of interest these institutions were legally permitted to pay, it was obvious that a passbook savings account was a losing proposition. It ceased to be an investment at all.

If thrift institutions offered anything, it was a service. Just as their safety deposit boxes provided a place to keep valuable papers and jewels, the federally insured savings accounts offered a secure place to store money. During the 1970s money, unlike tangibles, was losing value while stored.

The right to offer interest bearing checking (NOW) accounts helped savings institutions compete for depositor accounts. This innovative financial service offered by thrift institutions was at the expense of commercial banks' monopoly on check writing. The advantage gained by this new authority, though, was insufficient to protect the thrifts from record-breaking interest rates—over 20 percent annually—in the late 1970s.

Savings institutions became insolvent when they were forced to offer higher interest rates (to attract deposits) than they were earning on their investments. They derived their income, in large part, from long-term home mortgage loans. Because most of these loans were old, homeowners had obtained them at low interest rates. The thrifts had thereby obtained an assured, but low, income on the funds placed with them by their depositors. These depositors, however, could withdraw funds at any time and increasingly did so as interest rates rose. Consequently, to maintain deposits to cover their mortgages the thrifts had to raise the interest rates they paid. They were eventually to pay more to attract money than they were earning from it on their loans.

Commercial Banks

At the same time, the large, money-center commercial banks were facing problems of their own. Although they had a smaller proportion of unprofitable long-term low-interest loans, they were victims of the worldwide economic decline. Money-center banks earned their profits from large loans to the U.S. Treasury, businesses, and foreign governments. These loans had initially been especially profitable, but those profits quickly turned to losses when debtors were unable to repay.

Commercial loans can be profitable because a large amount of money is committed to a single transaction. The paperwork and credit checks are much less expensive, per dollar loaned, than automobile and other consumer loans. Their soundness, however, rests on business success. Consequently, even the higher rates available for commercial loans did not compensate for the bakruptcies of W. T. Grant, Penn Central, Railway Express, the Penn Square Bank of Oklahoma, and hosts of smaller firms in the 1970s and 1980s.

Rising bankruptcies hurt all commercial banks. But the money-center banks were particularly affected by even more lucrative loans to developing countries. These loans were committed in huge blocks (hence the very low transaction costs) and were not subject to any limitations on interest rates. Unfortunately, the world economic decline and the rise in oil prices hurt the less developed countries most and, thus, their creditors.

By 1983, according to the *New York Times*, the top ten American banks had loaned over $40 billion to Mexico, Brazil, Venezuela, and other Third World countries.[5] The worldwide recession made these loans questionable. The loans represented an average of 10 percent of their total outstanding loans. Citicorp alone had lent almost $10 billion. Overall, these loans exceeded the total shareholders' equity in all ten banks. If the Third World economy collapsed, so would the money-center banks in the United States.

The vulnerability of foreign loans led some money-center banks to reconsider consumer banking. Citicorp, for example, made a major commitment to shift its portfolio to consumer banking. On one side, it moved to reduce the cost of servicing individual depositors by re-placing tellers with automated teller machines (ATMs). On the other side, Citicorp entered nationwide consumer lending by becoming the largest distributor for Visa and Master Card.

Citicorp expects ATMs to attract new deposits at a reasonable cost. According to *Fortune*:

> Citicorp calculates that the average cost of a teller transaction is $1.27, com-pared with 55 cents for a machine transaction. If you double the customer volume of a brick and mortar branch you need about twice as much staff; with ATMs increased volume generates a far more modest rise in costs. And electronic systems are less sensitive to inflation.[6]

By 1984 Citicorp had installed over 550 machines at 270 locations around New York City. The *Washington Post* reported the success of this strategy:

> Largely because of the ubiquitous nature of the machinery, Citicorp has increased its share of deposits in New York City from 3 percent to almost 10 percent [in one] year. Three-quarters of all cash withdrawals made by the bank's customers occur at the [ATM] locations.[7]

In addition to being the leading issuer of Visa and Master Cards, Citicorp owns and issues the Diner's Card and the Washington-based Choice card. This gives Citicorp access to millions of customers for their consumer loan business.

Insurance Companies and Pension Funds

The insurance industry was also affected by the developments of the 1970s. As the public became more sophisticated in economic matters, the value of the industry's profitable whole-life policies was increasingly subject to doubt. States like New York, Connecticut, and Massachusetts offered low-cost savings-bank life insurance as pressure was put on the industry to provide policies with more competitive investment values.

The push in the direction of investment value put insurance-premium dollars in competition with retirement programs and more speculative investments. Retirement programs came into their own with the passage of ERISA (the Employee Retirement Income Security Act) and the introduction of IRAs (individual retirement accounts). The former created enormous new free-standing institutions that invested fully funded corporate pensions. The latter—a tax subsidy to individuals who saved for retirement—created a new business opportunity, IRAs, that all financial institutions were quick to offer.

THE NEW FINANCIAL ENTITY

As of 1985, the Glass-Steagall Act remains in effect. Nevertheless, the financial community is moving toward comprehensive financial corporations with nationwide scope. These corporations are expected to be much larger than existing institutions and more profitable. And they are being formed through mergers.

This new kind of financial entity is expected to offer, under one roof, check-writing privileges, interest on funds deposited, investment advice, brokerage services, insurance and retirement plans, nationwide credit and cash cards, personal and auto loans, home mortgage loans, and real estate services. In addition, the entity will offer a full range of services to business and governments, including, commercial loans, the underwriting of new issues of government and corporate securities, the marketing of new securities, and reinsurance. To provide these services the entity will have to employ an enormous staff of financial specialists nationwide. In addition, it will have to establish a national data-processing and telecommunications network to transact business and coordinate its myriad operations.

Despite the continuing restrictions of the Glass-Steagall Act, firms from different industries have made major commitments to creating more comprehensive financial entities. Citicorp (the nation's largest bankholding company), Bank of America (the nation's largest bank), Merrill Lynch (the nation's largest brokerage firm), Sears (the nation's largest retailer), Prudential (the nation's largest insurance company), and American Express (the nation's largest travel service firm), had by 1984 all established themselves in several segments of the financial industry. Each was struggling, in its own way, to create the first nationwide, comprehensive financial institution.

Sears has been a pioneer in designing an integrated financial institution. Although Sears was best known as a retailer and catalog sales company, it had accumulated major financial-service businesses before its chairman, Edward Telling, announced in 1981, "Our goal is to become the largest consumer-oriented financial service entity."[8] Sears already owned the Allstate property, casualty and life insurance companies which drew over $6 billion in annual revenues; Allstate Savings & Loan, a California thrift institution with 100 branch offices and $3 billion in assets; Allstate Enterprise Mortgage Corporation, servicing $1.4 billion in mortgages; and PMI, a $9 billion mortgage insurance corporation and, with 40 million holders of Sears credit cards, the nation's largest credit-card operation. The Allstate insurance companies alone accounted for over half of Sears' profits in the three years leading up to the 1981 announcement.

Telling's announcement was prompted by Sears' proposed takeover of Dean Witter Reynolds, the nation's fifth largest stock brokerage firm, and Coldwell, Banker, the nation's largest real estate broker. These two acquisitions, totaling $800 million, and a plan to offer a money-market fund invested in government securities formed the backbone of the new consumer financial services. The initial idea was for Sears to offer counter service for these new products as it had done successfully with Allstate insurance. According to *Business Week:*

> The company's 859 stores could double as full scale financial service branches. . . . This network of outlets "outnumbers the four largest bank holding companies combined."
>
> At the same time, Sears' in-house data base on consumer credit, by far the biggest of its kind, will become the nucleus for the carefully targeted selling of loans, stocks and other instruments.[9]

By 1983 *Business Week* was reporting that the in-store financial-services concept was working and the various segments were being integrated profitably:

> After 10 months, Dean Witter brokers are piling up almost four times as many new accounts in the [in-store] centers as at its other offices in the same cities. . . .
>
> The brokerage firm has fared [well] with its Sears Money Market Savings Account, which is actually a deposit with Allstate Savings and Loan. . . . The first in a series of the new Sears Tax-Exempt Investment Trust, introduced in May, was clearly a hit. . . . [T]he $20 million offering sold out practically overnight.[10]

The magazine went on to quote one competitor's concern: "Sears is eliminating the middleman up and down the line, so each profit they internalize puts them a step ahead."[11]

The potential now for internalization and integration is thus much greater. Coldwell, Banker is aided in selling houses by being able to provide mortgage money and mortgage insurance. The homeowners' casualty and life insurance companies are helped by access to new homeowners. The resulting credit records of homeowners and the records of Sears credit-card holders provide Dean Witter with financial profiles of good potential customers.

To make this integration work, Sears will have to have an unparalleled communications and data-processing capability. According to *Business Week*, by 1983 Sears was already the largest customer of both AT&T and IBM, with annual data-processing expenditures of $500 million.[12]

Others are also designing comprehensive financial-services institutions. American Express, for example, has undertaken a strategy similar to Sears'. Its traditional sources of income had been in traveler's checks (from which it profits on the sale of the checks and the use of the purchaser's money until the checks are redeemed), credit cards (for which it charges an annual fee and earns interest on borrowings), and various travel-related services. In 1968 American Express acquired Fireman's Fund insurance companies for $500 million, and in 1981 it acquired Shearson Loeb Roades for $900 million. Both acquisitions have been supplemented by smaller acquisitions of insurance corporations and regional brokerage firms, which provided new customer contacts and, importantly, additional trained staff. Its 1984 acquisition of Lehman Brothers Kuhn Loeb for $360 million made Shearson Lehman/American Express the second largest investment-banking firm in the United States, after Merrill Lynch.[13]

American Express's largest step was taken in 1983 when it acquired Investors Diversified Services (IDS) for $1 billion. This provided American Express with a trained national sales force with which to attract individual investments. Like Sears, American Express can use its data-processing capabilities to generate new investment customers and quickly measure credit worthiness.

Prudential's 1981 acquisition of the Bache brokerage firm for $385 million was also an attempt to make better use of financial information and attract customers by offering a fuller line of financial services.[14] Bank of America's 1982 acquisition of Charles Schwab, the nation's largest discount broker, was yet another effort to broaden financial services[15] and thus earn new customers.

The most daring plans have been undertaken by Merrill Lynch and Citicorp. Each, from its own vantage point, is challenging the restrictions imposed by the Glass-Steagall Act.

Merrill Lynch has broadened its brokerage and investment-banking businesses to compete with commercial banks for depository dollars and for commercial loans. It has also entered the real estate business (Merrill Lynch Realty), which is second in size only to Sears' Coldwell, Banker. As of December 1982, its Family Life Insurance Company had $8.3 billion worth of life insurance in force.[16]

Merrill Lynch's most powerful magnet for deposits has been its Cash Management Account (CMA). According to *Fortune*, the CMA is open to anyone who "deposits" $20,000 in cash or securities

A customer can write checks against his account and each month gets a bank-like statement reporting all his transactions. He may take out margin loans against the securities in his account. If he is instead blessed with cash, it will be swept automatically into the CMA Money Trust, there to earn market rates of interest.[17]

Although *Fortune* doubts that these accounts are directly profitable to Merrill Lynch, the side-effects of the CMA may make it worthwhile: "It discourages customers from taking their business to discounters, and it chains account executives to the firm since they cannot expect to take CMA-happy customers with them if they leave."[18]

Merrill Lynch has also established a Capital Resources subsidiary that offers commercial loans to businesses. Although forbidden by the Glass-Steagall Act from loaning funds deposited in CMAs or other Merrill Lynch money funds, Merrill Lynch can and has sold long-term bonds specifically to finance these loans. Nevertheless, Merrill Lynch expects to exploit a synergy in its loan operations that cannot be matched by commercial banks. *Fortune* describes the advantage:

Merrill Lynch is likely to have a relationship with, say, a maker of television-studio equipment in Chicago. In a typical example the manufacturer can't complete the sale to a customer in Little Rock because the customer is short of cash. A commercial bank in Chicago is likely to be aware of the manufacturer's dilemma as well. But Merrill Lynch also has a relationship with the customer because its office in Little Rock manages his investment portfolio.[19]

Unlike its major competitors, Merrill Lynch has not relied heavily on acquisitions to expand its financial services. Rather, it has chosen internal development, hiring key executives where needed, to start new ventures. For example, the Capital Resources unit's lending expertise was enhanced by hiring Donald Rudlett, a senior vice president of Citibank, and Richard Hanson, a senior vice president at the Chase Manhattan Bank.[20]

Merrill Lynch's reliance on hiring people rather than buying firms may be a result of its experience in 1978 after buying the White Weld brokerage firm for $50 million. Financial firms' most valuable assets are usually the skill of their employees and the trust of their clientele. Because the two are closely connected there is a danger that if the employees leave, so will the customers. Many White Weld executives left as soon as that firm was bought by Merrill Lynch.[21]

Other firms have, therefore, taken great care in financial mergers to retain skilled executives. Bank of America has made it attractive for Charles Schwab to continue to direct its discount brokerage operations by offering him profit sharing. Executive retention systems were also a major factor in Phibro's $500 million acquisition of Salomon Brothers.[22]

Citicorp responded to the challenge posed by Merrill Lynch frequently by acquisitions. To save failing thrift institutions, for example, the Federal Reserve permitted Citicorp to buy troubled savings and loans in California, Florida, and Illinois, thereby enlarging Citicorp's base for accepting deposits and its network of cash-withdrawal machines. Its effort to match Merrill Lynch's entry into insurance by buying the American State Bank of Rapid City, South Dakota, was rejected, though, by regulatory authorities in January 1984. Citicorp has benefited from other regulatory changes, however. Regulation Q, which limited the interest payments banks may pay on deposits, was lifted, and this eliminated the big advantage brokerage firms had had in their money-market funds.

In addition to offering its own money fund, Citicorp is also supplying what *Business Week* described as a mutual fund for its IRA customers:

> Customers now have a choice of investing in a pool of common stocks, a balanced mix of equities and bonds, income generating securities or short-term money market instruments all as part of the bank's normal fiduciary duties.[23]

Normal or not, it brings Citibank's services closer to a full-service financial institution.

The movement toward national financial institutions has not been limited to the biggest or the largest firms. Manufacturers Hanover made its bid for nationwide status in 1984 with its $1.5 billion acquisition of CIT Financial Corporation from RCA.[24] The Dreyfus Corporation moved from money funds to the banking business after acquiring the Lincoln State Bank in New Jersey. It successfully escaped federal regulatory limits by restricting the bank's activities to consumer lending and by selling all of its commercial loans.[25]

Nor has the transformation of the financial industry been confined to the emergence of nationwide institutions with full lines of financial services. Quite apart from the forced takeovers of failing thrifts, local and regional banking mergers and joint ventures have become common. These firms are cooperating to offer fuller financial services in order to capitalize on larger scale economies in data processing, automatic teller machines, and other technological developments. They are, thereby, challenging the developing national financial companies.

Financial mergers in the 1980s have been very different from the horizontal mergers of competing oil firms or the conglomerate mergers of unrelated firms that are typical of most megamergers. They have not served as outlets for excess profits. Instead, financial mergers have been part of a creative process that is transforming a set of related industries. The courage to undertake such large acquisitions may derive from the shift in general attitude toward megamergers, but the objectives in the financial industry have been more focused, immediate, and practical.

Even the nature of the deals has been different. The takeovers have been almost universally friendly. American Express, Sears, Bank of America, and Phibro have all made stock a major component of compensation. The use of stock reflects a shared sense that, as partners, the resulting firm will be more profitable, and that executives of the acquired firm are instrumental to the future success of the corporation.

These have not been marked concerns of the mergers examined in previous chapters. Shares of acquiring firms have tended to fall rather than rise as a result of most acquisitions. And the premise of most conglomerate mergers has been that unique skills are not needed to operate acquired firms. However plausible that thinking might be for other industries, it does not hold in the financial industry, where the product is employee skills. Mergers in the financial industries have not been conducted as a patternless frenzy of buying. They are clearly planned to achieve specific operational objectives.

To be sure, no one could know whether the objective of a national comprehensive financial institution would be attained. Facts were incomplete at the time these acquisitions were made. No one could know which of the many new institutional designs would turn out to be most efficient, which would be profitable and lasting.

Part of the industry's final shape will be determined by federal and state regulation. There are those who believe that evolving unregulated financial institutions threaten to reopen the dangers of general bankruptcy that the Glass-Steagall Act was intended to prevent. Bevis Longstreth, a commissioner of the Securities and Exchange Commission, has argued several points on this very issue:

> 1) Market discipline can only assure soundness in an environment where institutions are permitted to fail. 2) The links among financial intermediaries are often too extensive to prevent one failure from setting off others. 3) Therefore, the consequences of failures often impose unacceptable costs to our financial system. 4) Thus, to assure soundness a new system of government regulation is needed—a system broad enough to encompass all financial intermediaries and flexible enough to enable forces of full disclosure and market discipline to do their share of the job.[26]

Perhaps the rush to merge among financial firms will prove ultimately unwise, but at least these mergers have been made in light of the lessons learned from the flawed acquisitions of the 1970s. Financial mergers, unlike those in other industries, do not assume managerial omnicompetence. If these mergers were undertaken with optimism, that optimism was tempered by a recognition that they would succeed only through follow-up efforts on the part of management. Financial firms have not relied on supposed synergies; they have worked to create them.

PART FIVE

THE CONSEQUENCES OF MERGERS

What do we as a society gain from megamergers? Will mergers make the economy more, or less, efficient? Will they alter the political balance of power or the role of the individual in our society? These are fair questions to ask, but answers are difficult to come by. It is even too soon to know if these mergers will be more profitable than their predecessors in earlier waves. (There is, at present, no basis for believing so.) To discuss these questions we must build from theories and from studies of previous merger waves. With their help we can see the issues more clearly, even if the answers remain debatable.

Building from theory to fact is always a tricky business. The task is especially difficult because the effects of mergers discussed here are projected from generalizations about mergers and corporate behavior that are themselves the subject of debate. Different generalizations, not surprisingly, beget different conclusions. The following chapters, therefore, reflect both the uncertain state of our current knowledge and some of the diversity of viewpoints.

Chapter 14 considers whether mergers are likely to further the concentration of economic power in the United States. Economic concentration is quite high in the United States (about fifty firms control a quarter of the nation's business assets), and mergers can increase that concentration. Chapter 5 showed that fear of economic power in the hands of too few led Congress to pass the strongly anti-merger Celler-Kefauver Act of 1950. Since that time, there has been a significant rise in concentrated assets in the manufacturing sector. This helped to rekindle fears of increased concentration as a result of megamergers in the late 1970s. Chapter 14 concludes, however, that the possibility of greatly augmented economic concentration by merger is remote because at least half of American business assets are too dispersed to be centralized by merger.

Chapter 15 considers another major issue in policy debates: whether mergers improve the overall business efficiency of our society by replacing poor managers with good managers. The pursuit of improved efficiency has been a major building block in Chicago School arguments that securities and antitrust laws are unnecessary or over restrictive. The efficiency theory is an interesting one and doubtless describes many mergers, but the chapter concludes that its benefits are less in evidence than some have maintained.

Chapter 16 discusses the overall effects of mergers on America's economy. While quite a number of these effects may be considered beneficial, harmful aspects to the megamerger wave also can be identified. We have no means to calculate which predominate.

Having reviewed these economic issues, the final chapter turns to the question of corporate power. Corporate power has been at the center of legislative debates about mergers for a century. Large corporate size does not fit the small-town, self-sufficient, independent ideals on which this country was founded. Consequently, large mergers invariably provoke calls for restrictions on the practice of mergers or on the corporate size resulting from them.

Fear of corporate size has created a dilemma for Congress. We have not, so far, been willing to risk losing the economic benefits that accrue from corporate expansion or a flourishing free-market system. And we do not believe government officials or anyone else has the foresight to successfully predict which among the many mergers will be beneficial. But we do not want large firms to continue to grow by merger. The laws Congress has passed are numerous but narrowly drawn. Chapter 17 discusses the basis of our fears regarding corporate size, how corporate power has affected debate on merger restrictions, and the proposals that have been advanced to set direct limitations on corporate growth by mergers.

CHAPTER 14

MERGERS AND THE CONCENTRATION OF ECONOMIC POWER

During the conglomerate merger wave of the 1960s, humorist Art Buchwald wrote a column that so impressed a Supreme Court Justice he appended it to his dissenting opinion in an antitrust case.[1] The premise of Buchwald's column was that all companies west of the Mississippi had merged to form one corporation and all companies east had merged to form another. The two conglomerates— Samson and Delilah—were seeking antitrust permission to merge. Each time a wave of mergers occurs two perennial questions are raised: Where will it all end? And will the entire economy be swallowed up by a few giant corporations?

Economic power in America could become dramatically more concentrated in the years ahead, but that does not seem likely. The factors favoring an increase in aggregate concentration (the extent to which total business assets are concentrated in the hands of a few businesses) are balanced by factors that inhibit such concentration. In the past forty years large businesses have grown through merger and other measures, but they have not increased their total share of the nation's stock of business assets, which has also grown.

The emergence of the nation's largest firms as both acquirers and targets and the popularization of hostile tender offers have enlarged the scope and impact of mergers. Even so, the barriers to increasing aggregate concentration are formidable. First, the assets not controlled by the largest 100 firms are so dispersed, it would take a huge number of mergers to further concentration. Second, there is reason to believe that if such mergers did occur, the resulting firms would grow in size and diversity to a point where they would sacrifice efficiency and thus squander the competitive advantage that made them big.

One aspect of efficiency—the ability to innovate—is most affected by organizational size. Giant firms are not as innovative and do not adopt innovations as readily as their more rapidly growing smaller rivals. Innovation has been the key to the growth of our economy:

> Historically . . . output has grown at an annual rate of 1.5 percent. Robert M. Solow estimated that 81 percent of this increase, or about a 1.2 percent annual productivity growth rate, was attributable to technological change and the upgrading of the quality of the labor force. . . . Edward Denison estimated that technological change alone accounted for 36 percent.[2]

Consequently, the faster growth of smaller, more innovative firms has been able to offset established concentrations of economic power.

NUMERICAL OBSTACLES TO INCREASED CONCENTRATION

The growth of firms in the United States, frequently with the aid of mergers, has not kept pace with the economy. Table 14-1 shows that despite the merger boom of the 1960s the share of assets controlled by the largest nonfinancial firms in the United States actually declined slightly. Professor Lawrence White of New York University's

Table 14-1. Percentage of Total Nonfinancial Assets Owned by the 400 Largest Nonfinancial Firms.

Group	1958	1963	1967	1972	1975
Largest 50	24.4%	24.4%	24.5%	23.4%	23.3%
Largest 100	32.1	32.7	32.0	30.7	30.6
Largest 200	41.1	40.5	41.2	39.9	39.5
Largest 400	49.5	48.9	50.0	48.8	48.6

Source: *Hearings before the Senate Judiciary Committee on S.600,* 96th Cong., 1st sess., March/April 1979, Serial No. 96-26, part 1, statement of Alfred F. Dougherty, Jr., p. 146.

Graduate School of Business found a similar pattern in financial industries. The share of deposits held by the fifty largest banks declined from 38 percent in the early and mid-1960s, to 35 percent in 1974, and to 31 percent in 1978. The fifty largest life insurance companies had 83 percent of the insurance in force in 1960, but only 73 percent in 1970. By 1979 this figure had fallen below 70 percent.[3] Only in the manufacturing sector, which has been shrinking as a proportion of overall economic activity did the share of the largest firms experience growth. But most studies place the greater part of that increase before the 1960s merger wave.

There is no doubt that giant firms have grown substantially. Using constant dollars, Table 14-2 illustrates the proliferation of very large firms during the last thirty years. From the mid-1950s to the mid-1970s the number of firms with assets of $10 billion increased fivefold, and the number of billion dollar firms tripled. Firms employing more than 50,000 workers also increased over this time period: from thirty-two in 1958, to fifty-one in 1967, to seventy-nine in 1979.[4]

But as with assets, the increasing number of workers employed by large firms has been outpaced by the economy. Between 1969 and 1976 two of every three new jobs in the economy were to be found in small businesses.[5] Furthermore, in 1977, when the megamerger wave was gathering force, the *Fortune* 500 corporations employed over 15 million workers out of a total workforce of 101 million.[6] But during the height of the wave, when the workforce had expanded to 112 million, employment at *Fortune's* leading corporations had dropped to 14 million workers.[7]

Less rapidly growing large firms have tried to maintain their size relative to the economy by acquisition of rapidly growing firms.

Table 14-2. Number of Industrial Firms with Assets of Over $1 Billion (*using constant 1977 dollars*).

Year	$10 Billion	$5 Billion	$2 Billion	$1 Billion
1955	2	8	23	65
1965	5	16	46	101
1977	12	26	93	193

Source: *Hearings before the Senate Judiciary Committee on S.600,* statement of Alfred F. Dougherty, Jr., p. 148.

Fortune reported in 1978 that the sales and assets of its first set of 500 companies increased more quickly than those of its second 500 because of acquisition targets drawn from the top 500.[8] (Between 1970 and 1977 alone, firms in the top 500 acquired a total of 86 companies from the *Fortune* 1000.)[9] Economic studies by the late John McGowan and by Lee Preston of the State University of New York (Buffalo) confirmed that without these giant mergers aggregate concentration would have declined in the 1960s.[10]

The proliferation of megamergers may have increased the role of mergers in maintaining economic concentration, but it would require an even more massive wave of takeovers to dramatically affect the share of assets controlled by the nation's largest firms. The obstacle is the distribution of assets. After the largest 50 firms, business size declines rapidly. As Table 14–1 reveals, the top 50 firms have almost as many assets as the next 350. Consequently, it is hard to find enough large acquisitions to affect aggregate concentration substantially.

Even the 5 largest oil mergers of the 1980s—the combined assets of Gulf ($20 billion), Conoco ($11 billion), Getty ($9 billion), Marathon ($6 billion), and Superior Oil ($5.7 billion)—affect the aggregate share of the top 50 only slightly and the top 500 firms hardly at all. Together, these 5 firms had assets of $52 billion. Their disappearance from *Fortune*'s list of largest industrial firms means they will be replaced in the top 50 by much smaller firms, namely those that were previously numbered 51 to 55 on the list (not including Superior Oil). In 1982 those firms were Amax, Coca-Cola, W. R. Grace, and Beatrice, with combined assets of only $25 billion. The *Fortune* 500 list would be augmented even less by the addition of numbers 501–505 which in 1982 had combined assets of $1.5 billion.

The share of the top 10 or 20 firms can, therefore, be affected by megamergers, but after the top 500 firms an explosion of mergers would be required to have any noticeable affect on aggregate concentration. A firm would have to buy hundreds of smaller companies to match the size of even one top 50 firm.

We can probably agree then with Lawrence White's conclusion that at historical levels of merger activity statistics "indicate that, despite the merger waves, aggregate concentration has not been increasing in the United States"[11] and is unlikely to increase in the future.

FUNCTIONAL BARRIERS TO
INCREASED CONCENTRATION

But suppose there were an explosion of merger activity. Suppose the nation's largest firms went on a buying binge. Would this cause a sustained shift in aggregate concentration?

The question is not entirely fanciful. Large firms have undertaken massive acquisition programs of relatively small firms. Gulf & Western, for example, grew from a single-product firm in 1958, with annual sales of $8.4 million and 500 employees, to a $4 billion company with 100,000 employees in 1977 by acquiring over 100 companies.[12] Other firms could choose to emulate this behavior, which would, at least temporarily, further aggregate concentration.

Indeed, we have seen, on a reduced scale, such a pattern during the recent megamerger wave. Extremely large firms in oil, cigarettes, steel, and finance have all been making major shifts in their holdings through mergers.

Had the megamerger trend achieved grander proportions, Professor White's numbers would not have provided much guidance on the longer ranging effects of such heightened activity. We would then need a theory to describe the consequences of mergers on acquiring firms, that is, a theory that explained whether acquisitions help firms to grow faster than the rest of the economy.

Table 14-1 provides some suggestions for such a theory. The table presents the share of assets held by the largest 400 nonfinancial firms in the United States. The table shows that the share of the top 50 firms declined from 24.4 percent in 1958 to 23.3 percent in 1975, or a drop of 4.5 percent. The share of the top 100 firms fell by a similar percentage, but the top 200 dropped by only 3.9 percent, and the top 400 firms a scant 1.8 percent. Over this almost twenty-year period the smaller firms in the top 400 had grown faster than the larger ones.

The natural implication of these figures imply that large firms are losing ground to smaller firms because the former are less efficient. The numbers suggest that firms grow initially because they are efficient and profitable. They then use those profits to continue growing, even though this makes them less efficient. The implication is similar to the Peter Principle: Corporations continue to grow until they become so inefficient they can no longer compete with the faster growing, though smaller, firms. If this is correct, then an explosion of merger activity would produce a temporary surge in aggregate concentration followed by a decline as large firms lose the competitive race to smaller rivals.

This theory has its drawbacks, however. To be persuasive it must also explain why the largest firms in an industry—for example, General Motors, General Electric, Kodak, Coca-Cola, Seagram, and R. J. Reynolds—are commonly among the most profitable. Although Bruce Henderson's experience-curve claim that larger size results in greater efficiency now seems exaggerated, the converse has certainly not been proven.

It is possible, using economic and organization theories, to piece together an explanation that reconciles these seemingly contrary indications of the relationship between size and efficiency.

The explanation, in brief, is that firms become large because they are efficient. Either through insight or luck, they have developed a successful business formula. This accounts for their size, profitability, and excess earnings. In order to implement this formula in a large organization, the business must adopt fairly rigid internal procedures and bureaucratic rules. This leads to efficient production, but it also inhibits the firm from adapting to shifting competitive conditions. Consequently, the successful firm loses market share to smaller, more adaptive companies when competitive conditions change.

Nor can the successful firm avoid its decline by acquisition of rapidly growing target firms. The same bureaucratic rigidity, which is to some degree inherent in giant organizations, makes it difficult for the large firm to operate its faster growing acquisitions as efficiently as competing firms that remain independent. The villain is not size itself but complexity. When an organization becomes too complex—when its information circuits are overloaded—it sacrifices some degree of efficiency.

Organization theory teaches that bureaucratic structures have both strengths and weaknesses. The analysis described here stresses the weaknesses that can lead diversified firms to grow less quickly than smaller firms. The analysis rests on three major points: Size and diversity generate complexity which must be controlled to maintain efficient operation of a company; complexity can be controlled, but only at the expense of certain kinds of efficiency; and the type of efficiency sacrificed has its greatest impact on long-run corporate growth.

The first building block of our explanation must be a brief examination of the complexity of organizations. Theodore Caplow has demonstrated that as the size of an organization increases, the number of relationships between members of that organization can increase much more rapidly than members are added.[13] Depending upon the nature of these relationships, even a small organization can become very complex. Consider a group in which all individuals must relate to all others as pairs. Caplow's numbers show that the number of pairings rises dramatically upon the addition of members:

Size of Group:	2	3	4	5	6
Number of Pairs:	1	3	6	10	15

If however, each individual in the group must relate to all the other members both singly (i.e., as pairs) and also as members of subgroups, then the number of possible relationships grows even faster:

Size of Group:	2	3	4	5	6
Number of Relationships:	1	6	22	65	171

This variety of relationships is a source of strength for even small companies. Differing talents and viewpoints of members can be combined to achieve a great many objectives. But even small groups do not consider how to divide up tasks each time they get together. Instead, they sacrifice some of the rich variety of their resources and adopt routine procedures.

Business organizations establish routine procedures precisely to avoid complex relationships. To keep the organization manageable, businesses limit the duties and responsibilities of employees, even though this may waste talent. Nevertheless, some complexity of relationships is unavoidable in order to accomplish business objectives:

1. The activities of the employees must be assigned to accomplish routine work.
2. The employees must cooperate enough to permit the accomplishment of routine work.
3. The organization must be able to adjust if one or more individuals is absent.
4. The organization must know how many products it is manufacturing and how many it can manufacture to plan its sales programs.

5. The organization must know how it can improve its production processes to match the efficiency of its competitors.

Some of these relationships can be dictated by central managers, others can be delegated to lower level managers but some require interaction between all levels of a business bureaucracy. A foreman can be delegated responsibility to reassign employees during absences. To know the production capacity of a business can be more complex. It is determined by the physical limits of both machinery and employees, and by employee work motivation. The last is influenced by the interaction of many work and non-work factors.

Much more complex is the process that will improve production methods. For example, quality circles (discussions among production employees) have been shown to be an effective source of ideas for better production methods, presumably because production employees work most directly and continuously on them. But to make the circles a fruitful source the employees must desire to help the business, must believe their suggestions will be taken seriously and must believe they will not be harmed by an innovation which eliminated their jobs. Furthermore, there must be engineers to translate the ideas into machines. The suggested projects must be included in capital spending proposals. The suggestions must be compared with suggestions from other quality circles and technological developments at rival firms and elsewhere.

Carnegie Mellon's organization theorists, James March and Herbert Simon, have noted that new choices, like those generated by quality circles create large amounts of information, with high components of uncertainty, which require a great deal of feedback and cooperation among managers and employees.[14] If an organization maintains too many such efforts, managers are unable to absorb the information required to make decisions. Organizational efficiency is therefore limited by the capacity of managers to process information.

March's later work with his colleague Richard Cyert used this insight to understand how firms deal with the problem of organizational complexity. They found that businesses facing a new problem "search in the neighborhood of the problem symptom and reach in the neighborhood of the current alternative."[15] Any broader search would be objectionable because it could initiate a costly or endless inquiry into the problem to be solved. A radically different solution might create new unknown even more difficult problems for the organization. In order to retain control over their organizations, therefore, managers tend to limit the kinds of information they will consider. Or, as Nobel Prize-winning economist, Kenneth Arrow, put it: "The very pursuit of efficiency may lead to rigidity and unresponsiveness to further change."[16]

These conclusions provide a basis for our second level of analysis: Larger businesses are forced to create inefficiencies to reduce complexities and make themselves more manageable. Harvard Business School's Harvey Leibenstein developed the theory or "x-inefficiency," which illustrates how such necessarily narrowed procedures of an organization can decrease employee motivation and therefore lower productivity. He suggested that x-inefficiency commonly accounts for productivity differences of up to 50 percent.[17]

The assembly line provides a good example of how structure limits efficient production. The line, however well designed to minimize effort, cannot work faster than its slowest members. Smaller, less interdependent work units would not have the same vulnerability to inefficiency, because smaller units can more easily accommodate individual variations in skills. Leibenstein concluded:

> Other things equal, the larger the group size . . . the more inflexible the group effort position and the more difficult it is to introduce what may be deemed desirable changes [and] the greater the degree to which the group can contribute the x-inefficiency in production.
>
> Group size can frequently be lowered by splitting the group into successively smaller units. However, this is likely to increase the production of communication and incentive transmission [problems] between units.[18]

Oliver Williamson, the University of Pennsylvania's institutional economist, has suggested, building on the work of Alfred Chandler, that the large firm successfully solves many of these organizational problems of size through adoption of the multidivisional structure. This structure reduces the size of operational units by granting autonomy to line managers in day-to-day operations (as Leibenstein suggests is necessary) but retains authority for longer term decisions with central management.[19]

Nevertheless, in one critical area at least, Williamson conceded the superiority of smaller firms: innovation. Reviewing the work of Hamberg,[20] Jewkes,[21] and others, he concluded that major inventions are produced primarily outside large corporations. This view was confirmed by Kamien and Schwartz's exhaustive National Science Foundation study in 1975.[22]

Williamson also concluded that the few large firms that have produced numerous innovations, such as Du Pont, have contributed primarily technical improvements rather than basic inventions. He reported that the large firm is more likely to attract and employ persons who search for these kinds of inventions. This finding conforms to Cyert and March's observation of the narrow searches large organizations are forced to make to answer their problems.

Distrust of fundamental change is the basis for our final level of analysis. Because innovation is the key to long-term economic growth, large firms that are inhibited from adopting innovations are doomed to grow more slowly.

The corporation's emphasis on technological refinements rather than revolutionary breakthroughs may also explain the seemingly inconsistent evidence showing that larger firms display lower costs and earn greater profits. This attitude toward innovation can explain how large firms could have lower costs and change lower prices yet lose market share to small firms.

California Institute of Technology's Burton Klein has contributed a distinction which helps explain this anomaly. He posits two kinds of efficiency: static and dynamic.[23] Static efficiency occurs when an organization functions at its capacity. Dynamic efficiency refers to the active search for new solutions to replace existing technologies. Klein's description of resistance to technological change within a large, successful firm is consistent with Leibenstein's theory of x-inefficiency. Thus,

> it can be predicted that once the vice presidents learn of the prospective change, [the threatened department heads] will oppose it; and that the more loyal, devoted and efficient they are the stronger will be their opposition.[24]

Klein stressed that "static" success is likely to inhibit the large firm from embracing the "dynamic" technological opportunity. Even when the new technology becomes a commercial reality, the older, more refined product may retain, albeit temporarily, a cost advantage. Those who have prospered by developing the refinements on the product may argue for continued reliance on a proven record, blinded by past successes to both the potential of the new technology and the limits on the old. Klein pointed out, for example, that while leaders in radio tubes—GE, RCA, and Sylvania—entered the semiconductor business, their contributions to the new industry were smaller and slower in coming than newly formed businesses like Texas Instruments.[25]

Where an industry experiences little technological change, large firms are likely to benefit from their greater static efficiency. So, for example, R. J. Reynolds' tobacco products, Coca-Cola's soft drinks, and Seagram's liquors have dominated their respective industries for decades. Even in industries where technological change is important but slow in development, the large firm may be able to use its profits to support appropriate research or acquire and copy innovations. General Motors and Kodak have long maintained their positions in the American automobile and film markets. But even these giants have faltered when the technological pace quicked. Kodak has yet to catch Polaroid's instant photography or Xerox's photocopying products, and GM is trying to learn from Toyota how to make small front-wheel-drive cars.

Where the technological change is more fundamental to the industry—as with GE or RCA and computers—the dominant firms typically lack the necessary dynamic efficiency. They cannot innovate on their own or adopt the innovations of others quickly enough to compete and are forced to yield the field to newcomers.[26]

The rule is not invariable, though. Both Du Pont and IBM have maintained their preeminence despite great technological strides in their industries. But their dynamic efficiency is the exception. Klein's review of fifty industries showed that in none of them were the largest firms responsible for major invention.[27]

At any given time, therefore, one might expect the largest firm to have the lowest costs and highest profits based on past success. That success may, however, predispose the firm to resist, discount, or overlook the new technology that will replace its product or production process. Consequently, at some point the largest firms will grow less quickly than their smaller rivals.

Williamson suggested an alternative scenario:

> An efficient procedure by which to introduce new products is for the initial development and market testing to be performed by independent inventors and small firms (perhaps new entrants) in an industry, the successful developments then to be acquired, possibly by licensing or merger, for subsequent marketing by a large multidivisional enterprise.[28]

If Williamson were correct about the most efficient development of new technologies and industries, we should expect multidivisional firms to show some overall increase in their control of the economy. But the trends in aggregate concentration, however slight, are in the opposite direction.

So are other characteristics of merged firms. Dennis Mueller's study of acquisitions between 1950 and 1972 concluded that target companies achieved smaller market shares as a result of being acquired. When compared with similar firms that remained independent, the acquired firms grew less quickly. He estimated cumulative losses in market share from the time of acquisition in 1950 through 1972 to average 42 percent of original market share for conglomerate mergers and at least a 20 percent loss for horizontal mergers. In other words, the merged firm increased its assets and revenues as a result of the acquisition, but the acquired business entity was likely to grow more slowly than it would have had it not been acquired.[29]

David Birch and his associates at the Massachusetts Institute of Technology have reached a similar conclusion by measuring the rate at which firms add new employees. They found that firms employed more workers as a result of acquisitions and that some resulting firms continued to exceed the average rate at which firms added employees. But when the growth rate of the resulting firm was matched with firms that had been growing as fast as the targets, the comparable firms that remained independent grew at a faster rate.[30]

The implications of Birch's findings are twofold. Successful firms can increase their growth rate by acquiring rapidly growing firms, however, they cannot count on growing as fast as comparable firms that remain independent. Consequently, the larger acquiring firm will continue to lose ground to the most rapidly growing firms. Williamson's scenario for acquiring innovative firms appears, in this light, as a means by which large firms can slow their decline, not as a means to promote efficient growth.

Of course, no one knows exactly at what size or with what divisional structure firms lose efficiency through complexity. Surely the effect is individual. Some managers—such as the legendary Geneen of ITT—may be capable of superhuman feats. And some managers may be able to effectively operate certain kinds of firms in combination but have grave difficulties with others. Heublein's poor experience with Hamm's beer and Kentucky Fried Chicken contrasts with its many other more successful ventures.[31] Consequently, it is not possible to generalize about the effect of one particular acquisition of even our largest, most diverse businesses. At some point however, any firm can be overwhelmed by the complexity of the decisions it must make.

Whether our largest firms have already reached a size and diversity that ceases to allow efficiency is a matter of conjecture. The aggregate-concentration data and studies by Mueller and Birch on merged firms are consistent, though, with the view that, on average, giant firms have passed the point of efficient operation. Their failure to keep pace with growth of the economy and its fastest growing firms suggests lesser efficiency.

However, other factors may be just as important, if not more so. Major firms may be less flexible because their procedures have been established for too long a time. Or having achieved success, firms may relax and not try as hard. Either of these suggestions fits the aggregate-concentration data as well as the efficiency theory. The slight decline in aggregate concentration could be because the largest firms have not tried as hard as smaller firms, or because the largest firms are fighting a rearguard battle against growing inefficiency. If these explanations carry any validity, we might view large firms as sleepy but still powerful and capable of growth if roused. Under a charismatic leader or severe competitive pressure they again might gain in growth and up their overall efficiency.

While these alternatives seem plausible, they do not explain the merger findings of Mueller and Birch that considered mergers of large and small firms. Nor does the "sleepy giant" theory conform to casual observations about the capacity of large firms to manage their acquisitions. Exxon's purchase of Reliance, Mobil's purchase of Marcor, and Kennecott's purchase of Carborundum each suggest the supreme difficulty of integrating complex enterprises.

Regardless of the efficiency of current firms, it seems unlikely that the enormous number of mergers required to increase aggregate concentration could be undertaken without a loss of efficiency. Such an unprecedented wave of mergers would create corporations of unparalleled diversity that would be impossible to operate efficiently. The formulation of an annual capital budget for hundreds of firms in different industries would alone pose formidable problems. The coordination and integration of activities in such firms to achieve synergies would require the exponential growth in relationships described by Caplow. And most firms would quickly be caught short by the inherent limits on information processing described by March and Simon.

Perhaps it is the recognition of these limits or the questionable success of acquisition programs that has led large firms to be more modest in their merger strategies. If so, that is another reason mergers are unlikely to extend the concentration of economic power.

Observations

Corporate ownership of assets is only one way to concentrate economic power. Agreements between companies—such as cartels—can also centralize this power. Fear of such relationships led Congress in 1914 to forbid corporate directors from sitting on the board of competing firms. But as Edward S. Herman, Wharton finance professor at the University of Pennsylvania, has detailed in his book *Corporate Control, Corporate Power*, many other, less formal relationships can lead to concerted economic action.[32] Links between firms based on partial ownership, personal contacts, and common bankers or business consultants can all extend the concentration caused by mergers.

While the largest 50, 100, or 400 firms are unlikely to greatly increase their control over the economy by mergers, they currently control a high proportion. Between 1960 and 1979 the number of corporations filing tax returns grew from 1.1 million to 2.5 million and total (nonfinancial) corporate assets grew from $630 billion in 1960 to $3,668 billion in 1980. During this period the largest 50 firms maintained control over almost one-quarter of the total assets of this rising economy.

The share of economic resources in the hands of the 400 largest firms has been maintained in part by mergers and that share could be consolidated significantly. Although we will not have a merger between Art Buchwald's Samson and Delilah, who sought control of the entire economy, we could conceivably see mergers among the 400 firms who, taken together, represent almost half the nation's economy.

We do not have good measures of the relative efficiencies (static or dynamic) between large and small firms. The aggregate-concentration figures, which have shown only a slight decline in the assets of the largest firms, suggest the disparities are not great. If, as the Birch study suggested, some of this size is maintained by buying rapidly growing target firms, the inefficiencies may be somewhat larger. If Birch and others with similar findings are correct, then mergers enable large firms to keep and enhance their economic power after their efficiency has declined.

THE PERPETUAL MERGER MACHINE:
A TAX DIGRESSION

Is economic concentration determined solely by the relative efficiency of large businesses? In the late 1970s the staff of the Federal Trade Commission found what seemed to be a perpetual merger machine: a bias in the tax laws. The analysis maintained that tax laws subsidize both mergers and the operation of a firm after a merger, thereby encouraging more mergers and concentrations of economic power. The analysis was not completed because the project was abandoned with the change of presidential administrations in 1981. As a consequence, there is no estimate of the magnitude of the tax advantages the FTC identified.

These tax advantages, discussed earlier in the context of individual acquisitions, take on a different aspect when their impact on the competitive structure of America's economy is considered. Because it is difficult to choose appropriate targets, tax advantages may or may not make a particular acquisition profitable. However, if target firms are, on balance, no worse off financially than other firms in the economy and the tax laws provide an advantage to acquiring firms, then, overall, acquiring firms should have a competitive advantage. Acquiring firms should be able to buy out or outcompete their rivals. That they have not is a further indication of the inefficiency, on average, of merged firms.

Former Assistant Director of the FTC's Bureau of Competition, Albert Foer, summarized the staff's tentative conclusions for the House Ways and Means Committee:

> Because of the tax laws, larger diversified firms tend to have lower costs of doing business than smaller, newer, single line firms.

> The structure of tax laws tends to encourage large diversified firms to acquire profitable (or potentially profitable) smaller, newer, single line firms, among others, by effectively subsidizing the acquisition.[33]

The combined effect of the tax laws, Foer said, was to "create artificial tendencies toward economic concentration."[34]

Lower Operating Costs

The FTC staff believed there was evidence that diversified firms are more likely to benefit from lower operating costs than newly organized competitors because of two tax factors: Newly organized firms raise their initial capital from fully taxed savings, and they possess no current income against which to deduct their current tax credits and deductions.

Consider the following:

> In 1981 Business A is formed as a newly organized corporation. It has to raise $1 million in capital to pay for its initial equipment and to obtain operating capital. It raises the money by selling shares to, for example, individuals who pay 20 percent of their income in taxes. Despite unexpected great success selling its product, Business A fails to show a profit because of the expenses of advertising, costs of training employees, depreciation, and so on. Consequently, the firm must raise more operating capital each year for five years.

> In the same year, Business B is formed as a newly organized (or acquired) division of a profitable firm. It is in the same business as A, but obtains all its capital from its parent corporation.

The capital contributions to Business A are likely to be more expensive. Because the purchasers of shares in Business A were taxed 20 percent on their income, they had to earn $1.25 million to buy $1 million worth of shares. Business B, however, if it has matched its income from its currently profitable division through its overall tax credits and deductions, will escape all taxes and be able to invest $1 million from earnings of $1 million.

Business B will have lower costs of doing business because it can immediately reduce what would be tax payments to the full extent of its deductible expenses and tax credits. Suppose in the first year both businesses each had deductible expenses and tax credits equal to $400,000. The profitable corporation operating Business B would have its tax burden reduced $400,000 for 1981. Business B can keep and reinvest this amount of money tax-free in the following year. Business A will not have the use of this money until it earns profits. And even if it earns that amount in 1982, the deductions will then be worth less. The 20 percent rate of inflation in 1981 means that in 1982, Business A will be able to buy $80,000 less in products or services.

This $80,000 is irretrievably lost to the new business, and the more years it takes to balance its earnings and deductions, the less value the deductions will have. It is as if one company is given a tax refund for expenses and the other is not. Clearly, the one receiving a refund has more income, or relatively lower expenses, than the one that receives little or no refund.

While the diversified firm that has the benefit of the earlier deductions will have higher taxable income in later years, this is not necessarily a problem. First, it will have had the tax-free use of the money in the meantime, and, second, it can further delay taxes by acquiring additional new businesses or expanding old ones.

Merger Incentives

The FTC also believed there was evidence that a profitable firm can be worth more sold to another corporation than it is to its shareholders. This apparent anomaly was also attributed to tax law.

The value of a firm is, according to financial theory, the discounted value of the firm's future stream of earnings. To place those earnings in the hands of shareholders, however, the firm must be willing to part with some of its assets. Shareholders will be taxed at ordinary rates on the dividends declared. A growing firm is likely to need to retain its earnings, and its shareholders are unlikely to desire distribution at high tax rates.

An acquisition can solve these problems, because the acquiring firm can use its excess profits to pay off the target shareholders. The integrity of the target's assets is retained. It also pays the shareholders in a transaction that will be taxed at lower capital-gains rates.

The difference in taxes paid by the target shareholder (on income from the sale of shares rather than from a dividend) helps the acquiring firms pay for the takeover. Suppose the accumulated earnings of a business were $1 million. If shareholders paid a 50 percent income tax on this amount, distributed as dividends, then the value of the company to them is really $500,000. If instead the $1 million were paid by the acquiring firm, the 20 percent maximum capital-gains tax would result in the shareholders receiving $800,000. The

$300,000 is, in effect, a subsidy from the U.S. Treasury favoring a takeover.

But the acquiring firm need not pay all the $300,000 to the shareholders. If the acquiring firm pays $800,000 to the shareholders (taxed at the 20% rate), they will receive a total, after tax, of $640,000, or a $140,000 premium due to the lower tax rate. At the same time, the acquiring firm obtains a million dollar firm for $800,000. This subsidy adds to the competitive advantage of the acquiring firm over the shareholders of a single-business rival who had a higher cost of capital to begin with. So tax law can favor both the takeover of profitable firms and the subsequent operation of a target by a diversified firm with well-balanced deductions.

The tax-rate differential between ordinary income payable on dividends and capital gains applicable to sale of shares can also make a firm with substantial retained earnings vulnerable to a takeover. The acquiring firm can use the target's own assets to pay for the transaction. This partial liquidation of a target appears to have been part of Du Pont's strategy in acquiring Conoco.

But the tax advantages of acquiring rapidly growing firms has special importance for aggregate concentration. New, rapidly growing firms are the ones most likely to disperse economic concentration. Their products and services develop new industries and are responsible for most of the nation's economic growth. In doing so, they dilute the economic power of existing firms.

New, rapidly growing firms are also the ones likely to be at the greatest tax, and therefore competitive, disadvantage. Their shareholders are the ones who can benefit most from takeovers. Their tax deductions and credits are also the most beneficial to established firms armed with profits to be disposed of.

The logic of the tax structure suggested by the FTC staff is a powerful bias in favor of increasing aggregate concentration. Already, successful firms with excess profits have an incentive to buy growth industries to shelter their profits. The successful firm can operate a growth business with a smaller tax burden than their newly organized competitors. The result should be that successful firms ought to grow at least as fast as the healthiest sectors of the economy. And given their advantage in acquiring profitable firms from individual shareholders, they should increasingly concentrate the economic resources of the United States.

Instead, it appears that mergers have prevented erosion of the economic power of the nation's largest firms. Tax advantages, in fact, may have provided artificial support for some mergers that would otherwise have been uneconomical. Mergers may have actually slowed American economic development by encouraging the acquisition of firms that would have grown faster as independents. Because we do not know the true magnitude of these tax advantages, however, it is impossible to estimate just how much they have contributed to the maintenance of current aggregate-concentration levels.

CHAPTER 15

THE MERGER MARKET
FOR CORPORATE CONTROL

The subject of mergers generates heated political debate. Some observers passionately argue that mergers centralize economic power and thereby undermine our democratic institutions. Others, with equal enthusiasm, counter that mergers, and particularly the ever-present threat of takeover, represent a fountain of youth for American business. Chapter 14 suggested limits to the first argument; this chapter will focus on limits to the second.

THE TAKEOVER THEORY

In the 1930s Adloph Berle and Gardiner Means asserted that large American firms had ceased to be controlled by their owners and had fallen under the domination of managers.[1] Because shares of these firms were so widely dispersed, it was impractical for shareholders to oppose management. Consequently, except in extreme cases, corporate executives operated without interference from shareholders. Shareholders were more likely to sell their shares than attempt to displace management in a proxy fight.

Berle and Means raised a fundamental question: What *requires* corporate executives to act on behalf of shareholders rather than their own personal interests? To be sure shareholder lawsuits can prevent fraud and other gross abuses, but does anything actually encourage

303

managers to do their best to make a corporation profitable and share-holders rich?

Initial answers to this question were unconvincing. If a large firm were run badly, some suggested, its rivals would drive it out of business and the managers would lose their jobs. (What would make those management-controlled firms try harder was still unclear.) Furthermore, because managers typically are also shareholders, they benefit if the corporation is profitable. (Of course, managers will benefit more if they pay themselves higher salaries, rather than share those profits as dividends.)

In 1963 a British economist, Robin Marris, suggested a more direct constraint on managers. The threat of mergers, and specifically hostile takeovers, could act to discipline lazy or inept managers.[2] Marris argued that since the value of shares in a poorly run firm eventually fall, bargain-priced shares will attract other firms that can operate the mismanaged firm more profitably. To avoid takeovers, and thus any risks to their jobs, managers must behave to prevent the value of shares from falling.

The value of shares in a poorly run firm drops because shareholders have no way of replacing the managers. Inept managers are likely to remain in control, therefore, those shareholders who sell cannot obtain a high price for their shares. Consequently, they are glad to sell to a buyer who values the firm more highly because a new owner can install more competent management.

Other firms are likely to be the first to perceive the unfulfilled potential of a mismanaged firm. They are also likely either to employ a staff of competent managers ready to be installed in the target firm or to possess the skills needed to find more competent managers. Given the tax incentive to retain corporate earnings, corporations are one of the few institutions with the economic resources to finance a large takeover.

Takeovers, then, can serve two important functions in our economy. First, they replace inept managers with abler ones. Second, and most important, they threaten all corporate managers who do not act in behalf of shareholders.

Shortly after Marris announced his theory of takeovers, Henry Manne promoted a similar theory.[3] Although the takeover mechanism in the two theories operated in identical fashion, the circumstances in which takeovers were presumed to occur were very different. Manne claimed that takeovers solved the theoretical problem of managerial control posed by Berle and Means. He believed takeovers forced managers to be efficient and maximize shareholder profits. Marris, on the other hand, was more skeptical of the threat of takeovers as a constraint on managers.[4]

Marris is among a group of economists who draw insights about the behavior of firms from organization theorists, social psychologists, and political scientists. This group believes that corporate behavior is the result of a multitude of interpersonal and structural factors, including the competitive pressures exerted by other firms. While competition is viewed as ultimately the most important economic factor, the pace of competition is greatly affected by a combination of personal and institutional ingredients.

Manne, a strict price theorist, believes that competition determines or ought to determine all corporate actions. Personal interactions are influential only when government action permits corporations to escape the discipline of competition. He believes businesses that make "mistakes" are rapidly "disciplined" by the market. That is, a business that makes a mistake will lose the competitive race and fold or be taken over.

The above views disagree on how fast and how frequently the market reacts to mistakes and what happens in the meantime. Take, for example, the 1977 acquisition of the Carborundum Corporation by Kennecott Copper. We know that a widely held company such as Carborundum is unlikely to be able to resist a takeover attempt, so we make no initial assumptions about the effectiveness of Carborundum's management. Perhaps Carborundum simply suffered from unforseeable bad luck. Or perhaps Kennecott needed to invest the $809 million it realized on the sale of Peabody Coal to avoid becoming a takeover target itself.

In any case, the merger was not a success. *Business Week* ran a feature article detailing "How Kennecott has Mismanaged Carborundum."[5] So even if we assume that in 1977 Carborundum was poorly run, the situation was not improved by a takeover. Indeed, the reverse seems to have been the case.

In 1981 Sohio bought Kennecott for $1.7 billion. Perhaps this was punishment for Kennecott's poor management of Carborundum. Sohio itself had been taken over by British Petroleum (BP) in 1970. Since the opening of the Prudhoe Bay oil field, Sohio, a major partner, had become cash rich. Perhaps BP was simply seeking a place to invest a large chunk of excess earnings. Perhaps BP was following an oil industry acquisition fad for copper. In 1977 Arco had bought Anaconda Copper for over $700 million; in 1979 Standard Oil of Indiana bought the Cyprus Mines copper company for over $400 million; and in 1975, for $350 million, Chevron bought 20 percent of Amax and later tried to obtain control of it. It is hard to tell which of these possibilities is most likely.

In the meantime, what happened to Carborundum? Had it been made more efficient? Are its needs likely to be better understood by the BP or Sohio directors when it reports as a subsidiary of a subsidiary? Will the performance of Carborundum drag down Sohio so that it and BP become takeover candidates? Or will the failure to improve Carborundum be lost in the much larger revenues of Sohio? Was the poor performance of Carborundum already rationalized in the low price Sohio paid for Kennecott, and, as a consequence, is there no longer any pressure on Sohio to improve Carborundum? *Fortune* rated Sohio/Kennecott as one of the seven least successful mergers of the decade because of the depression in the copper industry.[6] Does this mean the problems of Carborundum are now forgotten?

This example suggests that while the threat of a takeover can encourage managers to behave efficiently, takeovers can happen for a number of other reasons. It also suggests that such mergers can decrease or at least fail to improve efficiency for long periods of time. The effect of mergers on corporate efficiency is a central issue for the Williams Act and other securities laws. It is also central to debates on antitrust policy. If Henry Manne were right in claiming that most takeovers encourage efficiency, then we should promote mergers. As a matter of public policy, we should remove legal obstacles to their accomplishment. If, on the other hand, takeovers are less predictable, and, on average, do not improve efficiency, then there may be reason to legislatively restrict mergers to improve efficiency or encourage other socially desired ends.

This is part of a larger debate about the role of government regulation in the economy. Does the economy regulate itself better than the government can? Or, in the case of mergers, does an unfettered market for corporate control work better than a regulated market? For the moment, our inquiry does not require such prescriptive judgments.

The question addressed here is how well does the merger market for corporate control work and what are the limitations on its effectiveness. To consider this, the chapter explores two perspectives: do circumstances encourage the takeover of poorly run firms, and have acquiring firms improved the performance of target firms?

THE TAKEOVER MARKETPLACE

Ideally, the marketplace for takeovers should be dominated by firms that (1) want to fix up targets and possess the skills to do it, (2) can identify improvable targets, and (3) have the financial resources to undertake acquisitions. Judged by these criteria, the marketplace is far from ideal.

The Master Fixers

Judging by business periodicals, few large firms claim to be experts in revitalizing poorly run firms. In contrast there are numerous articles describing how a divestiture, rather than an acquisition, saved a troubled business. When *Fortune* asked, "Who buys corporate losers?" its answer was, in general, individuals buy and fix up divisions of large corporations that were losers.[7]

The comments of Harry Gray quoted earlier deserve repeating in this context.

> We [United Technologies] never go for a turnaround situation. I think that's about the worst news there is. Maybe somebody can do that but we can't. We don't have a stable of management experts who are ready to go in and do everything better than the people who build the business.[8]

Royal Little, founder of Textron, one of the 1960s' giant conglomerates, was even more direct: "I never thought Textron was competent to take over any company and straighten things out. It's fantastic the number of things you can do that don't work."[9]

Of course, acquiring firms often have plans to alter the operation of their targets. They commonly establish stricter financial controls and new reporting requirements. They also may decide to integrate the operations of the target with those of other divisions. Such takeover plans are usually premised on retaining the strength of the target. Weak operations are likely to be sold or eliminated altogether, rather than fixed. The acquiring firm may add a new dimension to a target's operations, but it typically does not go in with major repairs in mind.

So, for example, when Phillip Morris buys Miller, it does not expect to help Miller brew, bottle, or distribute beer. Phillip Morris's contributions were money and marketing skills from its cigarette division. Parent corporations usually presumes the target's business operations to be basically sound.

The stories of corporate turnarounds are very different, and the Hart Ski Company is a good illustration. Its founders sold the successful company to Beatrice Foods in 1968 for $7.5 million. Beatrice installed new managers and spent lavishly to develop its new subsidiary. But by 1977 Beatrice had lost over $7.5 million on Hart. It then resold the ski division to a group including the son of one of the founders for $1.3 million. In their first year the new owners made a profit. *Fortune* magazine commented on this irony:

> The wipeouts of the Seventies cast additional doubt on that once popular theory that a good conglomerate can manage anything. The ski business is an odd segment of industry that is better left to people who understand it, who care deeply about it and who are willing to have a less predictable bottom line than most big corporations will tolerate.[10]

The ski business is not alone in needing managers who understand their industry segment. The managers of the American Safety Razor Company bought their division from Phillip Morris, which had given up on that industry. These managers were able to locate industrial and private-label razor segments which have made their now independent firm profitable.[11] Victor Kiam made himself a television celebrity and earned a fortune turning around the Remington Shaver Company, which had lost $30 million under the Sperry Corporation.[12] And Charles Lazarus performed a miracle worthy of his name when the profits from his independently run subsidiary—Toys "Я" Us—paid off the debts of its bankrupt parent corporation, Interstate Stores, in 1978.[13] Frank Nicholas and his partners bought Beech Nut baby foods in 1973 from Squibb for $16 million, then resold it for $35 million to Nestle in 1979 after developing a line of "natural" baby foods.[14]

Individual entrepreneurs are not necessarily better at running businesses than divisional managers. The large yearly total of small business failures is testimony to the fallibility of individuals. But a different mode of doing business sometimes permits the individual to succeed where a large firm does not.

Where fundamental change is necessary to save a business, the smaller firm may be more adaptable for reasons of organizational structure, as discussed in Chapter 14. Since larger firms tend to resist innovations, they may be less quick to adapt to altered competitive conditions. The small firm may not be constrained by considerations of bureaucratic fairness and needn't worry that if one division is changed other divisions may feel threatened (or, depending on the change, demand an equal opportunity). Information on operations and market conditions is more direct.

Kiam reduced overhead by $2 million his first week by firing seventy executives at Remington. Had Sperry done the same, able executives in other divisions might have left (fearing similar actions) and thereby upset the operations of those divisions.[15]

The undoing of the Hart Ski business at Beatrice was blamed on the failure to understand the details of the ski industry and the appointment of managers with no ski experience. With dozens of businesses to manage the central staff at Beatrice could not possibly understand the specifics of the ski and other sporting-goods industries. They had to rely on financial reports and data submitted by their managers. They lacked the knowledge required to pick able managers.

Phillip Morris may have understood the potential scope of selling safety razors for personal use. However, understanding of smaller but still profitable submarkets, such as window scrapers, may have presented complexities to decisionmaking it was either unwilling or unable to face.

In testimony before the House Committee on Small Businesses, community representatives complained that local businesses had failed after being taken over because they were mismanaged. One comment, about Draper Looms in Hopedale, Massachusetts, was typical of the opinions expressed before the committee: "They [Draper's acquirer] made a valiant attempt to run a business they knew nothing about and took the business down and us with them."[16]

The individuals who take over failing divisions have no monopoly on good ideas—indeed, at American Safety Razor the new owners were former divisional managers. It is the freedom to implement insights that made the difference.

But neither on-the-spot management nor flexibility alone can guarantee that managerial insights will be correct or successful. If Frank Nicholas's first idea for Beech Nut, which didn't work, had been his last, he would have been considered a quixotic character trying to revive faded glories. His story lives, like Victor Kiam's and Charles Lazarus's, because he eventually defied the odds. He saved, he revitalized, a failing company.

Such rescues are not limited to individual entrepreneuers, but the successes of large firms have a different flavor. Despite initial doubts, LTV seems to have made a success of its acquisition of troubled Youngstown Sheet & Tube. Stroh is thought to have a good chance of reviving Schlitz. What is notable about these mergers is that the acquiring firms were already in the same business as their targets, and both mergers offered the real possibility of reducing expenses through consolidation. In addition, these acquiring firms had proven expertise in the manufacturing and marketing of their targets' products.

These two large firm rescue stories are unlike the typical large acquisition where the target manufactures unrelated products. Rescues by large firms seem to depend on the acquiring firm's preexisting expertise in the targets industry. Consider, Chrysler was turned around when it faced bankruptcy by former Ford executive Lee Iaccoca, not a management consultant. Like Chrysler these revived large firms have been able to make radical changes in the operation of the target because the desperate need for change was obvious to its employees from its prior poor performance. In other words, the source of these successes parallels that of the small entrepreneur: expertise and flexibility.

In contrast, efforts to rescue unrelated companies, like Colgate-Palmolive's $142 million takeover of troubled Helena Rubenstein, have frequently resulted in frustration and losses. After seven years Colgate sold the firm for $20 million.[17]

Diversified firms do not fit the profile of successful revitalizers. They generally lack the expertise needed to evaluate fundamental changes in a target's existing approaches to business and more often prefer to buy after a firm has been revitalized. Mobil's purchase of Montgomery Ward followed the latter's successful reorganization (by managers hired from Sears) in the 1960s.[18] Nestle did not buy Beech Nut baby foods at the bargain price offered by Squibb; rather, it waited and paid over twice that amount to Frank Nicholas after he had turned the company around.[19] Once a turnaround has been made, the large firm expects its resources and reporting systems to enable it to expand and manage the target.

Finding Improvable Targets

For those firms that want to acquire and fix up poorly run businesses, appropriate targets can be difficult to find. Takeover theory presumes that when share prices fall, potential buyers will be able to discern if the lowered prices are due to bad management which can be improved. Share prices are, however, neither infallible evaluators nor clear indicators of corporate health.

Of course, if the stock market sets share prices at too low a level, an acquiring firm will not object to obtaining a bargain. If, however, the shares have declined but remain too high, the acquiring firm is likely to lose money. Even if the target firm is correctly evaluated, the acquiring firm that pays a premium is likely to suffer losses if the decline is not reversible through better management. Consequently, the acquiring firm is at risk unless it can correctly determine what the share prices mean.

The acquiring firm has the same information as other investors in the stock market. Information on the industry (availability of resources, prospects for market growth, strength of competitors) is derived from many sources of varying reliability. Information on the company is available from annual reports on assets, liabilities, and earnings, and these are usually supplemented by more detailed, voluntary disclosures by the company.

If only one company in an industry has declining earnings and a shrinking market share, it may be reasonable to assume that poor management is a root cause. Share prices are also likely to decline, but how is a prospective acquiring firm to know if they have declined enough? Statements by managers of troubled firms tend to be over-optimistic about the company's prospects, if only to protect the value of their personally held shares.

It is therefore necessary that these selective disclosures be weighed against public reports, but open records have little to reveal concerning the quality of internal management or the competitive potential of a firm. In addition, even the more objective numbers contained in an annual report may be misleading. Penn Central maintained its dividends almost up until the time it went bankrupt.[20] Consequently, the effect, if any, of voluntary disclosures is likely to bias the share price above its true value.

Nor does the acquiring firm necessarily have any basis for assuming that better management would reverse the problems of a company. The decline in the target's fortunes may be due to factors neither its management nor any successors are likely to understand or be able to correct. Success may owe to factors impossible to duplicate, such as image, secret know-how, or even luck. Once in position, it may be impossible to displace the more successful firms by improving management because buyers may not be price-sensitive. Customers may, for example, prefer to stay with a proven company than try a cheaper product if familiarity and reliability are important to them.

Intimate knowledge of a business is therefore required to learn these and other critical factors. Sometimes during negotiations for a friendly takeover an acquiring firm will discover these details with the cooperation of the target. However, even then it generally is not to the advantage of the target's management to stress these competitive limitations, because the acquisition price may be lowered. Exxon was surprised, for example, after its friendly deal with Reliance Electric to find that Reliance was worth substantially less than the $1.5 billion Exxon paid for it.[21]

In a hostile takeover, of course, it is certainly not in the interest of the target to explain its precise competitive posture. Although a target is likely to claim that its shares are undervalued by both the stock market and the prospective acquirer, the information it discloses is again likely to push the price toward overvaluation.

The lack of reliable information and the natural tendency to overinflate stock prices is likely to deter firms from making acquisitions premised on a revitalization of the target. This seems especially probable for hostile takeovers which are surrounded by the greatest secrecy.

The difficulty of acquiring accurate information on a target in the case of a hostile takeover has unfortunate implications for the role of mergers in improving efficiency. It is the corporation headed by executives who refuse to compete hard that ought to be targeted for takeover. Unfortunately, the various claims of these executives make it hard to distinguish between the lazy firms and firms that are doing as well as possible (i.e., firms that cannot be improved) or firms whose low price is due solely to temporary bad luck (i.e., firms that could improve given time).

Consequently, fewer firms are likely to decide to improve targets through takeovers because of the great risk of making mistakes. Managers are therefore less likely to fear takeovers because of poor performance and more likely to fear takeover for other reasons. They may as a consequence direct their efforts to avoiding takeovers for these other reasons and concentrate less on corporate efficiency.

The effects of takeovers often compound these informational problems. After it has disappeared into a diversified firm, the performance of the target is hard to measure because corporations are not required to report individual product earnings. With our rudimentary, segmental reporting system of corporate earnings, it is not surprising that large firms are able to effectively conceal their declining condition through conventions of accounting for substantial periods of time.

It is particularly troubling that diversified firms may be the least disciplined by the market for corporate control because they are the ones most free of competitive forces. They can subsidize their failures in one business with the profits from another, whereas, under like circumstances, a single-product firm would be either driven to improve its efficiency or go out of business. Hidden within the reports of a diversified firm, such failings may go entirely undetected by the public and even skilled observers.

Given the scarcity of accurate information for predicting the future of poorly run firms, it is not surprising that many of the success stories concern managers who acquire their divisions and develop them as independent companies. As divisional managers, they had information that typically an outsider could not have obtained. They, as insiders, have the critical information to evaluate whether or not a business can be rescued.

Given the paucity of information about most businesses, the occasions when a business will be recognized as improvable are limited. We should not expect, therefore, that the price of corporate shares will operate as a tight discipline on the efficiency of corporate managers. It is also likely that by the time managers can no longer hide their poor performance many firms will be beyond rescue.

Acquiring Firms

The merger market for corporate control could promote efficiency more effectively if acquiring firms were better suited to operate their targets. Unfortunately, there is little reason to believe that firms enter the takeover market because of their operating skills. Previous chapters have made plain the fact that firms acquire primarily to relieve themselves of earnings that they cannot invest elsewhere. Consequently, even if acquiring firms chose the targets they can manage best, they may not be able to match the performance of the target's managers, much less provide the "best" management.

Such a pessimistic prognosis for takeovers may seem unwarranted given that acquiring firms, in general, have proven themselves to be successful. Why shouldn't the competence of the managers be reflected in the successful operation of a new division? There is no reason to doubt that successful takeovers are possible. Nevertheless, there are reasons to doubt that the basis for success is automatically or even customarily transferable.

An acquiring firm is likely to need a set of skills to operate the unrelated business of a target that the acquiring firm has never developed, or the operating skills of the acquiring firm may have atrophied. Indeed, Harvard business professor Theodore Levitt has argued that the typical reason a firm considers its market to be declining is because it has lost the imagination and competitive edge that was responsible for its initial success.[22] Were the firm more skilled, it might find better investments in new applications for the products it has always made and knows best. Unimaginative acquiring firms have little to offer to target businesses, however poorly the targets were managed.

Perhaps more typical are firms that have retained their competitive skills—such as R. J. Reynolds or Coca-Cola—that are forced into the takeover market because expansion within their industry is blocked by legal restrictions or competitive dynamics. Neither of these companies has been able to find appropriate targets that even approach the profitability of their primary businesses. Nor have the special skills of these firms provided similar magic for their targets. Coca-Cola gave up on its wine business when it sold out to Seagram. It is now trying the movie business with Columbia Pictures. Reynolds has persisted with its acquisitions, but none has been a notable success.[23]

Even assuming these firms chose from among targets available at a reasonable price, management may still not be successful. One of the lessons business learned again in the late 1970s is that good management is not a generic skill. It is a combination of many factors, including a profound understanding of the business a company has undertaken. Thus, we cannot expect acquiring firms to provide their unrelated targets with the fundamental elements for success.

This does not mean that all or most mergers are doomed to failure. Many, like Phillip Morris's acquisition of Miller or McDermott's acquisition of Babcock & Wilcox will be successful. But chances of success are improved when the basic elements making for success predate the merger.

THE EFFECTS OF CONSOLIDATION

Henry Manne would argue that neither intention nor talent are the true test of the takeover market. He believes that the market operates independent of managerial wishes by disciplining those who disregard efficient behavior. Regardless of intentions, firms that make unwise acquisitions will be punished and those that succeed in improving their targets will be rewarded. Manne would also argue that if, on average, firms perform better after mergers, then the takeover market promotes efficiency.

This hypothesis, like the theory of takeovers itself, is plausible enough to consider seriously. Despite obvious obstacles to increasing efficiency through takeovers, there might be other unknown factors that tilt the overall consequences toward economic benefits. Consequently this section reviews efforts to measure whether mergers have, on average, improved efficiency.

There is a distressingly large number of studies on the efficiency of mergers. Unlike other social science issues, where academics disdain to retread the path of their rivals, merger studies have proliferated. Their great number is testimony both to the inconclusiveness of the methodologies and to the monetary support the research has attracted.

The studies have been divided by methodologies and conclusions. Economists from the Chicago School have generally found support for Manne's hypothesis, while other economists have found neither evidence of economic gains nor evidence of losses as a result of mergers. Virtually all studies have been criticized for methodological shortcomings.

Stock Market Studies

Yale Brozen, J. Fred Weston, George Benston, Michael Bradley, and Greg Jarrell and others have concluded that, on balance, mergers promote efficiency.[24] These Chicago School economists all rely on stock market studies that measure the value of the acquiring firm before and after acquisitions. If the acquiring firm pays a premium for the target and the acquiring firm's shares do not fall in value after an acquisition (or fall an amount less than the premium), the merger, they believe, must have increased the value of the consolidated firm over the value of the two firms separately. Consider the following example:

> Suppose Firm A's shares are selling for a total of $1 million and Firm B's for $10 million. If after B takes over A for $2 million the shares of B sell for $9.5 million, then the merger is considered to have increased efficiency.

Had efficiency not increased, Chicago School economists reason, the payment of $2 million for a company worth only $1 million would have depressed the value of Firm B to $9 million. Their studies consider irrelevant the fact that acquiring firms typically lose money on mergers.

Stock market studies are tricky because share prices vary so much. Many such studies have been criticized for measuring corporate value using inappropriate time periods. Measurements taken too close to mergers tend to reflect expectations of investors about the mergers rather than effects, measurements taken too far distant from mergers are likely to be more influenced by factors other than mergers. But there are more fundamental problems with stock market studies. As *Wall Street Week's* Louis Rukeyser is fond of saying, "The stock market has predicted nine of the last five recessions!"

Reliance on the stock market as proof of efficiency presupposes that the market accurately values all stocks (not just most of them) or that no one can systematically identify stocks that are under- or overvalued. If it is possible to identify undervalued shares, then the payment of a premium does not require greater efficiencies to prevent losses to acquiring firms. In the example above, if Firm A was worth $1.9 million but valued by the stock market at only $1 million, then the after-purchase value of $9.5 million of Firm B indicates that the consolidated value of the two firms fell by $400,000 (assuming all the other valuations were accurate).

The possibility of undervalued targets is important because undervaluation was listed by the Boucher merger experts as the most important criterion in target selection.[25] If the increased value from consolidation reflects only the acquisition of bargains, then the takeover market has no claim to promoting production efficiency.

That the stock market makes identifiable errors in valuation seems quite possible. The Value Line Investment Survey, for example, has consistently identified shares that are undervalued. Although many of its choices are wrong, on average the survey's assessments have been more accurate than the market's.[26] If the survey can locate a bargain, there is no reason acquiring firms shouldn't also be able to find them. Identifiable stock market valuation "errors" not only call into doubt the Chicago School interpretation that mergers have increased efficiency, they also cast doubt on stock market studies in general.

Moreover Dennis Mueller has criticized the results of Chicago School stock market studies that compare the percent of price decline for acquiring firms with the percent of price rise for target firms. He argues that these comparisons greatly underestimate the total losses to shareholders of acquiring firms by ignoring the fact that target firms are much smaller.[27] Also, stock market studies, such as Michael Firth's, have shown no efficiency gain at all.[28]

Stock market studies seem, therefore, a slender reed on which to hang the contention that mergers improve efficiency. Even if the claim were more consistently substantiated, the fact that acquiring firms generally lose money on acquisitions raises troubling issues. What are we to think of the efficiency orientation of managers who, more often than not, make unprofitable acquisitions? Are we to believe that they form the foundation of a system that encourages efficiency?

Other Studies

Other studies are more direct in concept. They have attempted to compare how firms would have performed had they remained separate with how firms have actually fared after merging. The problem is to establish how firms would have performed had they remained separate. Results of these studies generally show no efficiency gains.

Dennis Mueller, Keith Cowling, and others have tried to solve this problem by matching the acquired and acquiring firms with similar firms that remained independent.[29] This solution is also attacked as methodologically flawed. It has been objected that the choice of matched firms is subjective and the use of accounting data to measure profitability is unreliable.

These criticisms would carry more weight if Mueller and Cowling based their conclusions on a single test. But they do not. Mueller, for example, uses tests of profitability, growth rates, and price/earning ratios to come to his conclusion about American mergers. He also integrates his own findings with cross-national comparisons and studies of United States mergers that use other methodologies.

Neither these studies nor others have presented evidence of a decisive effect on mergers. The results range from mild increases in efficiency to small inhibitions. Overall, the results of empirical studies seem to be either neutral or inconclusive.

Other Considerations

Because all studies assume merging and nonmerging firms compete on an equal footing, they may underestimate (or overestimate) the efficiency of merged firms. If, for example, large firms have access to cheaper capital because of retained earnings and defects in the capital markets or if the tax laws favor acquiring firms, then the failure of merged firms to perform better is further evidence of inefficiency.

However, if the conditions of competition are unequal, the takeover incentives may be altered. Albert Foer explained the implications the FTC staff drew from the tax analysis described earlier:

> The apparently successful or emerging firm is the ideal takeover target. The acquiring firm can buy at capital gains rates the ordinary income expectations of the target's shareholders. In addition, the acquiring firm can deduct unused expense carryovers and credits against its income which were diminishing in the target's hands. Furthermore, it can operate the emerging firm at a lower cost due to tax laws by currently deducting in full its expenses and credits and by its (arguably) lower cost of capital due to retained earnings.
>
> *If this profile is accurate* and accounts for a substantial number of acquisitions, it has fundamental significance for competition policy. . . . *It stands*

on its head the conventional wisdom about the market for corporate control by creating an incentive for taking over able managers rather than poor managers.[30] (Emphasis added.)

Finally, it is important to recognize that none of the studies discussed above has attempted to measure the efficiency of megamergers. These larger mergers represent takeovers of those firms Berle and Means considered most insulated from stockholder control. The efficiency consequences of these takeovers therefore seem most important.

The one study of megamergers, so far, was performed by *Fortune* magazine. *Fortune* set out to determine whether the firms making the ten largest acquisitions of 1971 would have performed better in the following decade had they remained separate. Most of the results, as in other studies, were mixed. The *Fortune* study showed some firms did better together, but others did not. However, one finding was consistent: "Most of the acquisitions produced appalling low returns . . . and none of them matched the 13.8% median return for all the companies in the *Fortune* 500."

The implication that large diversified firms are generally less efficient is consistent with studies showing that conglomerates tend to be less profitable.[32] This suggests that megamergers may decrease rather than increase efficiency.

OBSERVATIONS

One consequence of megamergers has been to make takeovers easier. We no longer need rely solely on large corporations to "discipline" management-controlled firms. Despite the securities and antitrust premerger restrictions enacted in the past twenty years, it has become easier to mount a takeover attack. Carl Icahn, T. Boone Pickens, and the Bass Brothers have all proven that smaller firms, groups, and individuals can raise the money needed to finance a takeover.

But more takeovers is not demonstrably better. Dennis Mueller has commented:

Over the last two decades there have been more than 20,000 mergers in the United States and a proportionally higher number in the United Kingdom. A reading of the [Chicago] economics literature would lead one to believe that the bulk of these were to remove bad managers and improve the flow of capital in the economy. A reading of the conclusions of most empirical studies of mergers would lead one to believe that mergers had indeed had this effect. Yet after a generation of unprecedented efficiency-enhancing merger activity, both the U.S. and U.K. economies are at a standstill, each has lost ground in world product markets, productivity increases have ground to a halt.[33]

Mueller concedes the possibility that things might have been worse without the mergers but resists the conclusion that they have been of significant help.

Even if mergers themselves have decreased efficiency on average, the potential for takeovers may have had a salutory effect. Independent firms realize they are more vulnerable to takeover if the value of their shares drops. Their managers may respond to this constraint regardless of the effects of mergers on efficiency. We have, as yet, no studies that consider this particular issue.

What we know about mergers leads us to believe that mergers are rarely undertaken to increase efficiency and, in general, have little impact on efficiency. Most mergers are undertaken for less risky reasons.

The problem raised by Berle and Means remains: There is no strict discipline placed on the managers of widely held firms. The merger market for corporate control is but one of many looser constraints on managers. Along with the possibility of proxy fights, shareholder lawsuits, and the common interests of managers and shareholders, the threat of takeovers encourages managers to act on behalf of their shareholders, that is, to be more efficient.

CHAPTER 16

ECONOMIC FUNCTIONS
OF MERGERS

We do not know how to measure the overall value of mega-mergers. At best we can describe their probable impact on our competitive system. This impact is rather complex since competition between firms is more intricate than the tidy economic model described by price theory. Some corporate actions that would be senseless or harmful in the simpler world of economic theory may actually promote competition, while others, theoretically harmless, may undermine it. In practice, megamergers can reward entrepreneurs, improve overall company performance, intensify competition, redirect capital from stagnant industries, and create new industries. Many of these are vital functions of our economic system, but as we shall see similar mergers can also disrupt that system.

REWARDING ENTREPRENEURS
AND INVESTORS

The man with the better mousetrap has been the ideal of the American economy. Even today, in a business world dominated by large corporations, individual innovators are thought to be the wellspring of economic progress. They, with the support of financial backers, explore unproven ideas that lay the foundation of new industries. This innovativeness and willingness to undertake financially risky projects presupposes a system that will reward such efforts.

Some entrepreneurs are compensated by the financial rewards they receive as their businesses grow and prosper, but others have no interest in pursuing businesses once they are established. They want to move on to other matters. For them, mergers offer a solution.

The opportunity to sell businesses can act as a powerful inducement to start a new business, fix up an old one, or invest in either. Venture-capital companies specialize in financing new projects with the intention of selling out. The new or refurbished business strengthens the economy with fresh ideas and revitalized competitors.

Selling out also frees owners to return to matters they are most skilled at. The inventor is not necessarily best suited to promoting and developing a business, and even the executive who turns around a failing business may not have the talent or patience to administer that business over the longer run. In addition, the economy will benefit if these individuals return to the innovation or renovation process.

Selling out is even more critical to encouraging investment in untried projects. These investments are made almost exclusively for the purpose of financial rewards. Even after the business has proven itself, it may be years before it can pay out profits. The very success of the business may require reinvestment of all earnings to forestell competitors who would seek to satisfy the increasing demand created by a new product. Selling out provides risk-taking investors with a quick return on their capital and, for some, the resources to fund other venture-capital projects.

Selling out does not necessarily involve mergers. A small company, like Genentech or Apple Computers, can sell its shares to the public. But for many companies that lack a glamorous technology (like genetic engineering or computers), a public offering may be unfeasible. For them mergers are the most likely method of sale.

Although the takeover of innovative firms can serve important economic purposes, megamergers rarely perform these functions. The sale of a small innovative company is very different from R. J. Reynolds's billion dollar purchase of the multiproduct Heublein company. The small, but growing, company may need financial resources that are only available through mergers because it is unknown in the capital markets. Its investors may be locked in until the firm is sold. A publicly traded company such as Heublein faced no such difficulties. Its financial soundness was continually monitored, and investors had a ready market for their shares.

Furthermore, the takeover of a publicly held company is subject to special abuses. Because shareholders are many and do not know one another, they are susceptible to a stampede by two-tier tender offers and other tactics. As a result, shareholders of public companies may feel forced to sell their shares for less than they believe the shares are worth. In contrast, shareholders in closely held companies have rights to fair treatment that may not apply to larger corporations.[1]

In addition, the acquisition of a conglomerate like Heublein by an already diversified corporation like R. J. Reynolds further obscures the "signals of capitalism." The efficiency of our economy requires that executives be able to monitor the performance of other firms. The performance will, for example, signal other firms to enter a new business where high profits are being made. This entry of additional firms benefits consumers by increasing the supply of the product, offering the variety of other brands, and encouraging price competition, and gives successful firms a reason to control costs and innovate. Because corporations are not required to itemize sales or earnings according to each line of business they are in, the performance of individual products is obscured. As a result, R. J. Reynolds may be able to earn monopoly profits while consumers are left with fewer choices and higher prices.

Consolidated annual reports may also mask the poor performance of a failing business. Instead of being eliminated by competition or being taken over by more efficient competitors, the business may persist, contributing to inefficient overcapacity in an industry. Healthier firms may thereby have higher costs due to underutilization of their capacities.

Megamergers have had a limited role in rewarding entrepreneurs. Frank Nicholas's rescue of Beech Nut baby foods was no doubt premised on resale to a company like Nestle. If the $35 million Nestle paid can be considered a megamerger, then that takeover is one example. The $3.6 billion sale of Belridge Oil to Shell also rewarded its venture capitalists. But the typical target of a megamerger is not owned and operated by a small group. The target is more commonly a widely held firm with readily transferable shares, rather than a firm owned by an innovative entrepreneur.

Typically, it is investors, not entrepreneurs, who benefit most from megamergers. These investors normally have no relation to the managers of the company. Thus, the public benefit, if any, from such takeovers is to correct (through arbitrage) the stock market valuation of the target firm. This revaluation rewards investors who are then free to spend their profits.

The overall economy gets little direct benefit from this transfer of money. If the former shareholders reinvest their money, it is likely to be in other shares traded on the stock exchange, not in the purchase of new issues of securities. Thus, the immediate effect is to transfer money from corporations that might invest in new productive capacity or research to shareholders whose investments rarely reach the capital account of any corporation.

The theoretical benefit of revaluation lies in a stock market that can more accurately value businesses. This, in turn, allows firms to obtain capital from the banks and the securities markets at fairer rates. To believe that this indirect valuation process performs a public service, we must also believe that the stock market does value corporations accurately and that those who invest new capital, principally financial institutions, rely on these market valuations. We must also ignore the fact that takeovers make further valuations more difficult by obscuring subsequent industry performance.

Regardless of their effects on the capital markets, megamergers can provide potentially important benefits for our economic system. We have plenty of diversified firms in need of renovation. While large firms have avoided taking over corporate turkeys, individuals and small groups have been more daring. Using the takeover techniques pioneered by Carl Icahn and T. Boone Pickens, a new breed of corporate revitalizers could develop who buy poorly run large firms for the sole purpose of selling them.

The profit potential from reselling targets in pieces has already been recognized. Bendix's attempted takeover of RCA and Sharon Steel's assault on UV Industries were both premised on the profit that could be made by selling the constituent businesses of these conglomerate targets.[2] These new acquirers could gain their reward from the transfer of the target's businesses to better managers. (After successfully avoiding takeovers, both of these firms effectively conceded their managerial shortcomings by subsequent divestitures: RCA sold its large CIT financial division and UV Industries sold all of its businesses.)

Entrepreneurs lured by the prospects of larger resale profits may entertain more ambitious plans for poorly managed larger firms. Like Victor Kiam at Remington Shaver, they may ruthlessly prune their acquisitions to shape them up. As new owners not committed to established bureaucratic structures, they may have greater flexibility to integrate previously separate operations.

To be sure, such takeovers are a gamble. We have seen, however, individuals are more willing to take such risks than established firms. Now that takeover financing has become more available to small groups, we may see them buying larger firms in the coming years with the express intent of turning them around for resale.

IMPROVING BUSINESSES

As Chapter 15 indicated, megamergers are rarely undertaken with the principal purpose of rescuing a target from failure. Nor do megamergers commonly combine firms in similar businesses, thus producing efficiencies. Nevertheless, regardless of intent, takeovers can and do result in the improved performance of the consolidated firm. Whether or not megamergers generally tend toward improving companies is still a matter of debate, but in individual cases large-scale takeovers have led to more productive companies producing better goods or services at cheaper prices.

Consider, for example, McDermott's rescue of Babcock & Wilcox from United Technologies' hostile offer. The acquisition was undertaken to lessen McDermott's vulnerability by depleting its large cash reserves. While this may seem a less than ideal reason for a merger, *Fortune* reported that the results have been excellent.[3] McDermott benefited from the less cyclical cash flow of Babcock & Wilcox, and the latter gained from McDermott's decentralized decisionmaking and cash-management systems. The cash-management system, which required operating divisions to include cost of capital (specifically, interest costs), revealed unprofitable practices which, when eliminated, boosted earnings.

The takeover of Babcock & Wilcox illustrates that not only specific skills—such as Phillip Morris' marketing talents—but also general managerial skill can improve the performance of a merged company. Structural strengths and managerial insights may not help every merger, but for some acquisitions they supply the missing element to make a business profitable.

The McDermott/Babcock & Wilcox merger also illustrates another benefit of consolidation: a more stable cash flow. In a perfect economic market internally generated capital would be available for no lower cost than external capital from the sale of securities or loans. Thus, the cost of capital would be unaffected by a more stable cash flow. But in a business world characterized by uncertainty and less than complete information, a firm that understands its own capacities better than outsiders can invest retained capital on the basis of more accurate, less costly information.

Of course, the internal allocation of capital is also subject to unprofitable, noneconomic pressures that are less common in the financial markets. The personal satisfactions of managing the largest (or most glamorous) corporation or having plush corporate headquarters are lesser attractions to investors. The capital markets are likely to stick more closely to purely economic criteria.

If corporations were more constrained by competition, if corporate executives were more rational in their economic thinking, and if information on successful business practices were more freely available, the potential improvements from corporate takeovers would be fewer in number. In the absence of this more ideal economic world, consolidations can benefit the merging firms. They can result in net benefits even if the mergers decrease efficiency in other ways.

INTENSIFYING COMPETITION

Burton Klein has called competition the "hidden foot" of capitalism.[4] While Adam Smith's "invisible hand" directs businessmen to satisfy consumer demands with the promise of profits, Klein believes only the threat of a kick in the pants makes them take risks and work hard. The fear of competitive extinction can overcome even the inertia of a large bureaucratic organization. Thus, megamergers that intensify competition can be a source of continuing strength for our economy.

The importance of vigorous competition to economic vitality is clear. Even Japanese economic growth, which has been held out as a paradigm of the virtues of cooperation, has had hard competition at its core. The Japanese coordination of government and industry and cooperation among workers has existed in the context of highly competitive industries.

The spectacularly successful automobile and electronics industries in Japan faced a double set of competitors in the beginning. To establish themselves they had to first earn a place in the crowded Japanese market. Toyota, for example, has many domestic competitors—including Nissan, Mitsubichi, Toyo Kogyo, Honda and Fugi—more than General Motors. Similarly, Hitachi electronics business faces stiff competition from Matsushita, Sony, Toshiba, Mitsubishi, Sanyo, Sharp, and Nippon Electric in their domestic market. Second, to enter the American market these firms had to produce goods sufficiently low in cost to remain competitive after the expense of shipping the products across the Pacific.

In fact, the competitive barriers were even more formidable, because Japan was to import most of its raw materials. Firms had to absorb the cost of shipping these raw materials (frequently from the United States) and earn enough foreign currencies from exports to buy materials for its domestic and export markets. Given these conditions, if the Japanese firms were to exist at all, they had to be very productive.

To replicate the intensity of the Japanese experience we need more and more evenly matched competitors. Megamergers can do this by creating stronger rivals to dominant firms. The acquisition of American Motors by Renault, for example, made possible the development of the Alliance, according to *Motor Trend* magazine the 1983 "car of the year." Stronger rivalries do not always improve the competitive process, however.

Certainly, there are examples of large acquisitions where an acquiring firm has increased competition. Procter & Gamble's acquisition of Folgers created a serious national rival to General Foods' Maxwell House coffee. Phillip Morris's acquisition of Miller enabled the latter company to compete with Budweiser for the title "king of beers." And Coca-Cola's acquisition of Taylor Wines was intended to challenge the wineries of Ernest and Julio Gallo.

But increased rivalry in these industries have raised more questions than they answer about the competitive effects of mergers. In both coffee and beer the increased market share of the challengers has come almost exclusively at the expense of local competitors, many of whom have gone out of business.[5] Moreover, in neither industry has the result of this competition been to lower prices for consumers. In the beer industry, quite the opposite has occurred, where Miller Lite and its imitators sell at premium prices even though they are cheaper to produce than regular beer. The number of brand coffees available has also been reduced. The consumer benefits from increased competition is, therefore, more questionable than might first appear.

If these newcomers had succeeded by selling better tasting products, their victories might be less open to question. It has been argued, however, that the key to their success has been in lower advertising costs, not better flavor or even lower production costs.[6] A national brand can spread the cost of advertising over a larger number of sales and thereby reduce the advertising cost per unit sold. These advertising-cost differentials, it is argued, favor large competitors but do not benefit the competitive process, and hence, consumers.

In addition, it has been suggested that large acquiring firms can engage in activities that are even more destructive to competition. When it expanded into new local and regional markets, Folgers, for example, attracted customers by distributing discount coupons. Maxwell House and local coffee makers had to match the coupon offer even if it meant losing money on sales.[7] The consequences for regional firms that typically have no other revenues could be bankruptcy. In other words, diversified national firms have the potential to drive regional firms out of business by cross-subsidizing their local discounting operations with coffee profits from other areas or with profits from their parent corporation. The temporary lower prices could then be replaced after eliminating local competitors with higher consumer prices.

William James Adams, a University of Michigan economist, has argued that acquisitions such as Procter & Gamble's purchase of Folgers have a special potential to lessen competition.[8] The firm Procter & Gamble faces in its coffee market, General Foods, also operates in many other industries where Procter & Gamble sells products. As a consequence, Procter & Gamble will fear retaliation on its weaker product lines if it pursues coffee strategies that General Foods considers overaggressive. So, for example, Procter & Gamble may refrain from lowering prices, which would reduce nationwide profits for both firms, or using other competitive tactics which seriously threaten General Foods market share (as opposed to the shares of regional coffee makers).

In contrast, neither Anheuser-Busch, the owners of Budweiser, nor the Gallo wineries, have any reasons for competitive reticence. Beer and wine are their primary businesses, and therefore any attack on these products is tantamount to war. They have both responded to the challenge by aggressively competing for an expanded market share and by moving into new premium-wine and quality-beer markets.

So the tendency of megamergers, which create diversified firms, may not always be to strengthen the hidden foot of capitalism. In some circumstances, acquisitions as more likely to shackle competition.

REDIRECTING CAPITAL FROM
STAGNANT INDUSTRIES

In an ideal capital market all profits would be returned immediately to the market. Businesses wishing to make further capital outlays would then compete on equal terms for funds. But our capital markets are far from ideal. Profits are not distributed, in part, because of managerial preferences and tax consequences. Information on projects is difficult to share in a competitive market, and distributing profits and collecting new capital are costly transactions. Under these circumstances it is sometimes better if a firm with profits earned from a stagnant industry invests them in a growing business.

This conclusion is a practical one not necessarily a preferred result. Certainly the largest acquisitions of firms in declining industries have not had a distinguished record of success. The oil, cigarette, or liquor industries have not shown a great talent for earning profits in other businesses. However, as managers in these industries appear intent on keeping control over their profits, it is perhaps better that they not reinvest them in their current businesses. Further investments in the liquor or cigarette business would most likely raise costs (e.g., by increasing advertising expenses) for all firms without improving the product or augmenting corporate profits. Compared with such misguided competitive zeal, almost any other kind of investment would be better.

Other imperfections in the capital markets—problems gathering accurate information and transaction costs—provide somewhat less persuasive reasons for industries to undertake megamergers. There are, for example, at least two kinds of problems when information is shared in a competitive market. First, the investor may be unable to determine whether the business seeking capital is lying. Second, the business seeking capital may lose its advantage if its disclosures to potential investors are revealed to competitors.

These information problems are partially solved if matters are kept to a single corporation's internal capital-allocation process. Executives are less likely to lie (exaggerate) before a board of directors because their board has more direct disciplinary powers than investors. Directors should also be a more trustworthy recipient of the information because of legal restraints, and because they will benefit from the success of the project. Business information problems are, in any case, less acute for large corporations. Through a course of dealing, corporations can often establish their credibility and learn whom they can trust.

Similarly, transaction costs disbursing dividends and raising new capital, while substantial, are more likely to be barriers for smaller firms. Large corporations routinely disburse dividends and raise money in the capital markets. Increasing the amounts should not alter their costs appreciably. And even if transaction costs did raise the price of new capital, the economy as a whole might be better off. There is no reason to think that capital markets are more likely to make worse investments than the oil, cigarette, and liquor industries have made.

The nation's economy could, however, be hurt if all profits were distributed, because the capital available for productive investment might be reduced. Currently the greatest proportion of savings that become investments in new productive capacity are made by corporations with retained earnings.

If all profits were distributed, some might never make it back to corporate coffers. A large chunk would be taken in as taxes on dividends. Another chunk would be spent on personal consumption. And a further chunk would be used to bid up prices in speculative investments in the real estate, stock, and commodity markets.

In this costly and imperfect economic world, then, there are some benefits to reallocations of capital within a corporation that are not available in the public markets for capital.

CREATING NEW INDUSTRIES

In principle, the strongest argument in favor of megamergers is that takeovers can create new industries. Until recently this argument was only theoretical. No new industries had been established by the consolidation of previously separate, but already giant, firms. Now it appears that the emerging nationwide financial institutions may be such an industry.

There are ways other than by merger for a comprehensive financial institution to develop, but it is possible that such ways are too difficult, unreasonably costly, or simply unnecessarily slow. If, for example, the cost advantage of new institutions simultaneously requires nationwide credit profiles, full investment services, and large collections of funds to lend, then mergers may be the only way to prove economic viability.

If we were to bar the kind of mergers we have so far witnessed in the financial industry, we risk preventing the development of more productive business organizations. The evolution of the financial industry illustrates that the resulting firms, although larger, may be more efficient and more attuned to the needs and desires of consumers. They may offer more service for less money. In short, they may be more competitive.

Of course, giant, integrated, nationwide financial institutions may not be the most desirable of organizational structures. It may be that the computer revolution will make smaller, independent, specialized financial firms that draw on centralized data sources (such as Visa or Master Card) and that have access to national investment markets (such as the stock exchanges) will prove to be more efficient. We will not know which provides better service unless we permit both to develop.

OBSERVATIONS

In assessing the value of takeovers we must weigh not only the contradictory potential of megamergers. We must also factor in the direct and indirect costs of these takeovers. In 1983 the fees of investment bankers for the top twenty deals amounted to over $100 million.[9] Antitrust litigation costs have been estimated at $75 million a year.[10] To that must be added the expenses of securities litigation and the value of the time that corporate executives and others spent on the transaction. In addition, there are pretakeover costs incurred by the hundreds of firms that never become targets—altering by-laws, hiring investment bankers and lawyers, hours spent planning defenses, and so on. Finally, there are the financial and psychological costs of takeovers—depressed morale, administrative adjustments, and the higher earnings needed to recoup the premium price paid for the acquisition.

It comes as no surprise to those who follow corporate acquisitions that the economy pays a high price for merger activity. But just as hope springs eternal for managers of acquiring firms, the competitive economy is institutionally optimistic. Even if today's mergers are unprofitable, it is assumed that managers learn from the mistakes of their predecessors. Tomorrow's managers will make wiser, more productive mergers.

In an economy characterized by uncertainty and imperfect data, learning must be based on experience. There is no more dramatic lesson than the spectacular failures of others. Exxon's $600 million mistake, Mobil's, Hiram Walker's, Baldwin's, and Kennecott's, are all important examples of what not to do.

But finding right answers cannot be deduced. That requires even more groping in an uncertain business world. Having identified successful mergers, like Phillip Morris/Miller or Sears/Dean Witter, managers must try to determine what made them work. In trying to emulate such triumphs more mistakes will be made. And even when mergers are profitable (neither Miller nor Dean Witter have reached that point), we always have a responsibility to ask whether the private profit also benefits the public.

CHAPTER 17

MERGER POLICY

M egamergers make us uncomfortable. They remind us how big corporations have become and how few checks there are on the power of corporate chief executives. Giant corporations, which provide us with the benefits of mass production and mass-marketing techniques, do not fit the egalitarian ideal of our society. Their size dwarfs all other private institutions. Takeovers which instantly enlarge corporate size unavoidably illustrate the unparalleled power of corporate managers.

Despite our discomfort we have chosen not to regulate corporate size, or ban mergers, or permit only those mergers that are beneficial to society. The laws that make some acquisitions illegal (if they will reduce competition or if they are achieved unfairly) leave it to the corporate community to decide which other mergers will occur. We rely on a self-adjusting system to select transactions that will benefit society.

The central issue for merger policy has been to obtain the benefits of large organizations and, at the same time, preserve the self-regulating character of our economic system. The key to progress and efficiency under this system is the free interaction of private enterprises with relatively equal access to resources. Since the emergence of the multidivisional corporation in the late nineteenth century, however, large firm size has been interpreted as a threat to that economic system and to other self regulating systems in our society. Historian

Richard Hofstadter found the public's early response to large size through antitrust had three kinds of goals.

> The first were economic; . . . economic efficiency would be produced by competition. . . . The second class was political; the antitrust principle was intended to block private accumulations of power and protect democratic government. The third was social and moral; the competitive process was believed to be a kind of disciplinary machinery for the development of character. . . .[1]

Congress has been reluctant to closely restrict mergers for fear it would damage the freedom necessary to our economic system. Merger statutes have, therefore, been written and implemented narrowly to protect the economic rights of competing firms, consumers, and investors. It was assumed that these laws would also respond to more general concerns about the growth of big business.

The Sherman Antitrust Act of 1890, the Clayton Antitrust and Federal Trade Commission Acts of 1914, the Celler-Kefauver Amendments of 1950, the Williams Act of 1968, the Tax Reform Act of 1969, and the Hart-Scott-Rodino Act of 1976 were each congressional reactions to fears about unregulated corporate expansion. In each of these statutes Congress chose to address leading characteristics of the then current merger wave. They dealt with immediate threats such as unfair takeover tactics, monopoly profits, unjust business dealings, reduced competition, or the narrowing of entrepreneurial opportunity. Any further regulation was left to the internal workings of the marketplace.

The laws have largely satisfied their initial objectives. The Sherman Act eventually eliminated the blatantly coercive takeover tactics used by Standard Oil and other trusts. The Celler-Kefauver Amendments drastically reduced mergers between direct competitors. The 1969 Tax Reform Act lowered the tax subsidy for takeovers wherein shareholders were paid by issuing new debt. The Williams Act and the Hart-Scott-Rodino Act have ended the "Saturday night special" surprise takeovers. If these laws did not put an end to the merger waves, they were successful in preventing repetitions of the more characteristic abuses.

Nevertheless, large firms have always been able to find new ways to grow by merger. When that growth was perceived to be part of a merger wave, that perception has generated renewed pressure for legislation.

Since the very large takeovers of the late 1970s, there have been several attempts to add to the existing legislation. The reason is not hard to discover. The fifty largest corporations control an immense proportion of American business resources—almost one-quarter of the total assets held by all nonfinancial corporations.[2] Mergers between these huge enterprises threaten to further consolidate these already centralized resources.

This chapter considers how future merger policies might integrate the concerns generated by megamergers. It begins by examining the distinctive powers exercised by a large corporation and how these powers are augmented by further growth. It then describes how these powers have influenced the development of policy during the megamerger wave. Finally, the chapter reviews proposals that address current concerns yet continue to permit business executives to decide what combinations of businesses should be formed.

POLITICAL POWER AND MANAGERIAL POWER

Large corporations no longer enforce their will, as Carnegie did at the Homestead steelworks, with a private army of Pinkertons or by blatant bribery of Congress and state legislatures. Nevertheless, their political and social influence remains pervasive. That influence is determined, in large part, by the sheer size of the corporation.

Megamergers enhance the power of a corporation in two ways. Acquisitions enlarge the impact of managers' decisions to include more businesses, more employees, more customers, and more communities. Mergers also increase corporate resources, thus making feasible actions which smaller corporations could not undertake. The growth of already large firms raises concerns that they will become centers of disproportionate power in a society that is premised on diversity and decentralized power. Such large organizations could disrupt the balance of our political system and do blur the distinction between private decisions and public policy.

Political Power

Since 1787, when Madison wrote his *Federalist Papers*, it has become an article of faith that America's political system requires a dispersion of power. Too much centralization threatens to permit the domination of our political institutions.

Although they have no votes, corporations play a significant role in our political process, one that has been recognized and protected by the Supreme Court.[3] They can influence decisions by mobilizing influential people and by contributing substantial sums of money. Larger firms are, therefore, more able and more likely to engage in political activities effectively.

Nonetheless, in the 1950s and 1960s some insisted that big business occupied neither a favored nor a powerful political position. For example, when President Eisenhower's nominee for Secretary of Defense, General Motors executive Charles Wilson, told the Senate he believed "what was good for our country was good for General Motors, and vice versa,"[4] he created a public uproar. The "what's good for General Motors is good for the country" attitude was not politically acceptable.

At this time, it was also argued that corporations that did engage in political activity were likely to be on opposite sides of issues. Adolph Berle, writing in the mid-1950s, observed, "There is no high factor of unity when several hundred corporations in different lines of business are involved."[5] Consequently, whatever power business possessed was likely to cancel itself out.

At the close of the 1960s, University of California (Berkeley) Business School professor Edwin Epstein provided an extensive list of reasons why the political influence of corporations was not commensurate with their resources.[6] Two reasons acted as especially important limitations. First, there were well-organized groups of labor unions, farmers, and consumers who had countervailing political power; and second, the public did not like big business and distrusted proposals it supported. Epstein concluded:

> Corporate managers have eschewed general political leadership and have concerned themselves with limited politics for limited purposes. . . . Indeed, excessive political activity on the part of a corporate manager is looked upon somewhat askance by his professional colleagues.[7]

The Watergate revelations of laundered money for President Richard Nixon's 1972 reelection campaign and Dita Beard's disclosures about the campaign contributions that ITT made allegedly in exchange for the Justice Department's dropping of an antimerger lawsuit suggest that corporate influence on politics has been continuous, if not always visible.[8] In any case, after the establishment of the

Equal Employment Opportunity Commission, the Environmental Protection Administration, the Occupational Health and Safety Administration, and the Consumer Safety Products Commission, big business became more active and open in its attempts to influence political decisions. In 1972 *Business Week* estimated that 800 of the nation's largest 1,000 firms had lobbying operations in Washington.[9]

Perhaps most notable was the organization of the Business Round-table. Unlike the national Chamber of Commerce or the National Association of Manufacturers, membership in this trade association was limited to 190 large firms and required the personal participation of their chief executive officers. Michael Pertschuk, then chairman of the Federal Trade Commission, explained his view of the organization's significance at a 1979 Antitrust Seminar sponsored by Time, Incorporated:

> Surely the emergence of the Business Roundtable as the preeminent lobbying institution explodes [any] images of political paralysis or diffidence on the part of corporate managers. . . . [It] signifies . . . political activism as a first priority of the corporate managers. Indeed the visibility and direct personal involvement of the chief executive officers remove any shadow of a doubt that aggressive political activity has become not only respectable, but the hallmark of a corporate leader.[10]

An indication of the very large firm's alertness to opportunities for political influence was their more rapid formation of political action committees (PACs). A decade after the publication of his book arguing the limits of corporate influence, Epstein recorded how the nation's largest firms were quickest to take advantage of their rights to organize PACs. By 1979 63 percent of the top 100 *Fortune* firms had PACs, whereas 55 percent of the top 200, one-third of the top 500, and only one-fifth of the *Fortune* 1000 had similar organizations.[11]

Large corporations enjoy unique advantages in influencing political decisionmakers. The individual interests of these corporations can support lobbying activities that other firms could only undertake as part of a group. Large firms can also draw upon and coordinate more diverse elements to argue for their interests. The bigger scale of their lobbying permits specialization and continuity that makes their lobbying more effective.

Large firms overcome a major obstacle to influencing political decisions by undertaking their own lobbying activities. For smaller firms, lobbying must be done in groups. While each small firm benefits from the concerted effort, there is a tendency for members of industry groups to pay out as little as possible in order to obtain a "free ride" on the contributions of others. Because each firm hopes the others will subsidize the lobbying, it is often difficult to maintain support for such trade associations.

Even when this financial obstacle is overcome, there are the additional difficulties of coordinating lobbying through trade associations. As Robert Pitofsky, former FTC commissioner and later dean of the Georgetown University Law School, explained:

> The contention that groups of firms are the equivalent of a single firm in organizing to achieve political goals [flies] in the face of what we know about firm behavior in an analogous area—namely cartel organization. We know that given a large number of participants, different levels of efficiency and capacity and different outlooks about the rewards of vigorous competition or cautious cooperation, cartels are notoriously difficult to organize and maintain. In the absence of contrary evidence one might reasonably expect that . . . commitment to a single set of political goals . . . should be easier to organize, coordinate and maintain when relatively few political and economic interests need to be consulted.[12]

The diversified firm can also more easily justify the expense of an independent lobbying organization. As Columbia University law professor Harlan Blake has pointed out:

> A single product firm, operating directly or through a trade association has relatively few possible pay-offs over which to amortize large investments in lobbying or political good will. A conglomerate's many divisions, however, deal with every important agency of government, and the number of possible pay-offs is much greater.[13]

Having decided to lobby, the large firm with its own lobbying division knows it must provide financial support.

The large firm also has coordination advantages. It can resolve differing points of view within the organization and present a united front, which can be impossible for a trade association. A restriction on Japanese imports, for example, might favor northeastern manufacturing plants but hurt west-coast importing, assembling, and distributing facilities. Only if both groups of facilities were owned by a single firm would a united position favoring trade restrictions be likely.

Diversified corporations can enforce a more exceptional kind of coordination, too, by enlisting the support of executives of subsidiary corporations whose businesses have no direct interest in the matter at issue. Their personal influence or seeming disinterest provide an additional dimension to lobbying efforts.

The greatest advantages of the large diversified firm in lobbying, however, lie in a full-time lobbying organization and the size of the resources on which it can draw. Political scientist Robert Salisbury has described the advantages of the full time professional lobbying operation: "[M]ore time is devoted to developing research materials [and] negotiating coalitions of support within and outside decisional bodies. . . . [T]he more professional the lobbying the more symbiotic the relation between lobbyist and decision maker."[14] Knowing who is important, who is friendly, and what information political decisionmakers will consider makes lobbying much more efficient.

Being heard, gaining access to political decisionmakers, amid a heated political controversy can be critical. Senator Phillip Hart of Michigan described the relationship between size and political access in this way: "When a major corporation from a state wants to discuss something with its political representatives you can be sure it will be heard. When that same company operates in thirty states it will be heard thirty times."[15] In testimony before the Senate Judiciary Committee, then director of the FTC's Bureau of Competition Alfred Dougherty further illustrated Senator Hart's statement:

[A] large firm can often mobilize enormous and diverse resources to dramatize the importance of its message. General Motors sent a letter to 1.3 million shareholders, 13,000 dealers and 19,000 suppliers asking them to support its eventually successful campaign to postpone safety and emissions standards. Similarly, when ITT attempted to merge with the ABC network in 1968, according to one report, 300 congressmen and senators complained to the Antitrust Division about its intervention at the FCC in opposition to the merger. This is not altogether surprising since ITT has 265 subsidiary corporations; over 200,000 shareholders; over 400,000 employees; and operates in every state.[16]

This base of political influence is automatically expanded in the case of megamergers. Directly or indirectly, politicians can be made to understand that an "unfriendly" vote will result in no political contributions, or harm to their constituents. Constituents can be made to suffer by the closure of facilities if the political climate from a particular area is unfriendly.

Of course, access does not always determine political decisions. General Motors only delayed the new automobile standards. ITT not only was prevented from acquiring ABC, it was also forced to sell two of its major acquisitions. So Epstein's observations may still be true that assertion of political power by big businesses is of limited value and can backfire when it is blatant.

More skillful lobbying might have prevented some of these issues from becoming political controversies. Matthew Crenson's study, *The Un-Politics of Air Pollution*, concluded that the economic importance of U.S. Steel deterred the cities of Gary and East Chicago from even considering strong antipollution actions. Although this kind of dominance may seem unlikely on the national political scene, Yale political economist Charles Lindblom argues that a similar phenomenon operates at all levels:

> Any government official who understands the requirements of his position and the responsibilities that market-oriented systems throw on businessmen will therefore grant them a privileged position. He does not have to be bribed, duped or pressured to do so. Nor does he have to be an uncritical admirer of businessmen to do so. He simply understands, as is plain to see, that public affairs in market-oriented systems are in the hands of two groups of leaders, government and business, who must collaborate and that, to make the system work, government leadership must often defer to business leadership.[17]

In other words, at some corporate size Charlie Wilson's dictum holds true. Consider the aid the American automobile industry received when faced with a serious Japanese challenge. The United States negotiated import restrictions on the very grounds that what was good for General Motors was good for the United States. Smaller firms in a smaller industry might have had to accept the consequences of competition.

There is no doubt that size gave General Motors and ITT unique advantages. As continuing players in the political process they and other large firms are bound to learn how to use these resources more skillfully. As they do, we move further away from the political balance Madison described in *Federalist* No. 10.

Managerial Power

We distrust the power of corporate managers because it violates basic expectations of how our society ought to work. Corporate executives control the destinies of other people. They exercise this power, but in practice they are responsible only to themselves. The incongruity of these private officials exercising public functions is made more acute by megamergers which magnify that unresponsible private power.

Individual responsibility is a core idea in American society. It rests on values favoring personal liberty and beliefs about the dynamics of American culture, politics, and economics. We believe our society will function better if individuals act wisely and that they will act more wisely if they must face the consequences of their actions. We also believe the harm an individual suffers from the consequences of an unwise action is more than outweighed by the lessons to the individual and to society about the foolishness of such actions.

This idea applies to our political debates, our artistic expressions, our styles and fads, as well as to our economic system. We expect that individuals acting on their own will discover new concepts. If a concept is better, it will be copied, and the whole of society may benefit from the insight. If the new concept is wrong or simply unpopular, it will cause little harm to anyone other than the individual who freely tried it out. The penalties suffered by that individual are thought to be a small price to promote the dynamic of progress. University of California, Berkeley political scientist Aaron Wildavsky has emphasized the survival value of this diversity:

> Diversity is also treasured. Since the main hypothesis of democracy is that we are likely to be mistaken, diverse sources of ideas are cultivated to provide new and competitive hypotheses.[18]

The judgment about the benefits of the dynamic is a practical one. It is premised on actions by individuals or small groups who affect only themselves. That premise is violated by the very nature of a large modern corporation. For example, miscalculations by managers can throw thousands of individuals out of work and disrupt the economic foundations of entire communities. This power to affect others so vitally is more commonly expected to be reserved for government.

Despite the discontinuity, we normally ignore the public character of large corporations. If a business fails, we do not rescue it on the grounds that the diversity of our society will provide other opportunities for those harmed. But where society may not be able to absorb the consequences of bankruptcy, their public character cannot be ignored and the organization is rescued.

In recent years we have seen a number of government bailouts: Lockheed, Chrysler, the City of New York, the railroad business of Penn Central, and the Continental Illinois Bank and Trust Company. The significance of these rescues is not, as some have argued, the elimination of the incentive for managers of large organizations to behave responsibly; they are punished by the need for rescue. Rather, it is the open admission that these very large institutions have lost their predominantly private or local character.

The threat of bankruptcy merely forces society to act on its recognition that these are public institutions because their failure would affect so many people. But that public character exists prior to bankruptcy. It is inherent in the capital-investment decisions of large corporations, their research and marketing decisions, their employment practices, their plant and office locations, and their charity contributions. The widespread impact of their decisions makes for their public character.

Large corporations have generally conceded the public nature of their decisions. Clifton Garvin, chairman of the board at Exxon, the nation's largest industrial firm, spoke for many when he said:

> Corporations are part of the life of the communities in which they do business. Their operations affect not only the economic and physical well-being of such communities, but the social and cultural environment as well. Consequently, corporations carry responsibility well beyond conducting their primary business.[19]

This responsibility for others is contrary to the underlying model of our society, where individuals influence each other by example, not by direction. And this responsibility is an unavoidable consequence of corporate size. Charles Lindblom has written perceptively on the discretion corporate managers must have in exercising these responsibilities:

> Even under highly competitive conditions corporate executives . . . cannot unerringly find one correct solution to their complex problems. Since they cannot, they have to exercise discretion. Even in principle there is no least-

cost solution to a complex problem. . . . Inescapably, corporate executives find delegated decisions to be in their hands with no guidance from popular control, not even pressure toward least cost.[20]

The power exercised by managers in diversified firms is often plain to even the most casual observer. When Greyhound obtained wage concessions from its bus drivers, it did not open its books and put the union president on its board of directors (as failing Chrysler did) or seek the protection of the bankruptcy courts (as Continental Air Lines did). Greyhound made its wage position clear and reminded its workers that bus transportation represented only a small portion of the corporation's earnings.

Takeovers can be a traumatic experience for entire communities, who are accustomed to local ownership. Robert Stern and Howard Aldrich report:

> The presence of large absentee-owned firms [can] reduce civic spirit, defined [here] as "widespread participation in civic affairs. . . ." Such activity was traditionally the province of the independent middle class businessman. He benefited from the contacts in government, community growth and infrastructure investments. In contrast the welfare of large corporations does not depend on personal local contacts.[21]

The more national perspective of large firms also erodes the economic base of the community because resident managers are less likely to look for local suppliers to support the enterprise.[22] As a consequence, communities lose the organizational diversity needed to generate or attract other businesses, and become even more hostage to the decisions of distant corporate managers.

If the business fails after takeover, the local community is bound to blame this on corporate managers who were so removed that "they didn't understand the business and didn't have time to learn it."[23]

Even if the business succeeds, the fact of takeover can be traumatic. New bosses must be pleased, and their interests must be learned and satisfied. All because of a stock transaction using other people's money!

Berle and Means's description of the power of the corporate executive in the 1930s is still an accurate portrayal of today's managers:

> The economic power in the hands of the few persons who control a giant corporation is a tremendous force which can harm or benefit a multitude of individuals, affect whole districts, shift the currents of trade, bring ruin to one community and prosperity to another. The organizations which they control

have passed far beyond the realm of private enterprise—they have become more nearly social institutions.[24]

Even when exercised with the greatest care and best of intentions, managerial discretion raises fundamental problems. Who gave corporate executives the right to make decisions on product safety or on research that will affect millions of people? How can individuals who disagree with the decisions effectively promote alternatives? The executives of the modern corporation are an oligarchy that coopts its successors. Shareholders play little role in this process. Unions, suppliers, and customers are too dispersed or share too few interests to have a major impact on most corporate policies. As a consequence, opposition must focus on governmental action.

Government does have the power to oppose the will of corporate managers, but it is not suited to running businesses. Its officials have no secret knowledge about the best technological choices to make or the most suitable personnel practices. Consequently, although government enforces important public values, its intervention tends to be limited, clumsy, and, ironically, subject to influence by those it is supposed to regulate.

For the most part, the large corporation is regulated by its managers who are responsible only to themselves. The structure of the corporation centralizes power over its resources into the hands of a very few individuals. Megamergers instantly magnify the scale of these resources controlled by those individuals. This distant, unresponsible power of corporate managers over the future of others has been a major concern of merger policy since its inception and remains so. The more concentrated the power of those individuals become, the less we resemble our ideal of a self-regulating society that leads by example.

The Corporate View

From the perspective of the corporate manager, the question of power looks very different. As chief executives, they often find themselves confronted with more demands than they can possibly satisfy. The CEO must satisfy consumers, employees, shareholders, communities and politicians. If consumers don't buy, the corporation collapses. If employees don't perform, the corporation loses its competitive edge. If shareholders don't record better earnings, the cost of capital will rise. If the local hospital, art gallery, theatre, or zoo receive no donation, the corporation will be accused of greed. If executives are "bad" citizens, politicians will make the corporation's life miserable by enforcing any of a vast and confusing array of federal, state, and local laws, or by passing new ones.

The distrust and fear must be particularly grating to large corporations that bring higher wages and more enlightened personnel standards to what had been backward enterprises run by provincial business barons. Lindblom tells us, for example, "ten major coal mining companies run by coal companies showed a record, for one period, of over 40 injuries and deaths per man hours worked compared with less than 7 for mines operated by steel companies."[25] Even megamergers within the same industry can bring such benefits. The acquisition of National Airlines by Pan Am resulted in raising the pay and benefits of National employees to the Pan Am level. Frequently, acquiring firms add capital to enlarge businesses. Certainly they do not buy businesses with the intent of ruining them.

As for the vaunted political power of the large corporation, executives often find themselves hemmed in on every side. Not only are the corporation's actions followed in detail by the media, they are always mistrusted. Further, because the corporation is a continuing player with diverse interests, it must always be building coalitions and arranging compromises. It cannot, like single-interest lobbies such as truckers, right-to-lifers, or environmentalists, apply a single litmus test of political loyalty. The corporation must keep in mind the more general goals of economic, social, and political stability. It must be as concerned with the overall health of the economy as with its own special advantages if it is to have a market for its products.

And the corporate executives who fail at any of their tasks have no reason to rest easy. If they disappoint their research people, their marketing executives, or their production managers, executives may be left with massive resignations by their most talented employees. If that happens, executives may inflame a normally docile board of directors and be replaced. Even in an oligarchy nobody likes a loser.

The harassed corporate executive's perspective is surely accurate, but it reinforces rather than contradicts the view of others. Large corporations make decisions that directly affect the public. Corporate executives are neither elected nor trained for this public role; they are only indirectly accountable, and then only when they have been very unlucky or strayed beyond wide bounds of permissible behavior. It is not surprising, therefore, that the public resents or fears megamergers that add to the resources controlled by large corporations and further swell the power of their managers.

POLICY BATTLEGROUNDS

Each new effort to enact merger restrictions has been sparked by a very large merger or a group of mergers. There were several such efforts during the megamerger wave. These legislative initiatives posed a strategic problem for corporations that opposed them. The corporations were not only mistrusted in any of the claims they made, there was actually little they could say on their own behalf. As a consequence, the large corporations have financed surrogates to explain, in their expert opinions, why mergers are good for the economy even if they don't help acquiring firms.

If the facts of megamergers had been different, the corporations might have made their own defense. If they could have pointed to dozens of mergers that brought to market products that smaller, inventive firms could not produce or distribute commercially, or if they could have shown that prices declined as a result of mergers, or even if they could have shown that profits rose, corporations might have been able to make some credible arguments. However, the most recent experience with mergers was the discredited conglomerate merger wave of the 1960s. That suggested mergers are unprofitable.

A corporate executive could hardly be expected to testify, "You don't need to worry about my acquisitions, Senator. The more I buy the sooner I will be bankrupt." The argument cast in that form fails because it makes a fool of the chief executive officer and provides legal grounds for the executive's removal from office. Furthermore, while not entirely believable when stated by the corporate manager, if it were true, the projected bankruptcy would provide yet another reason to ban the merger.

These same facts, however, provide the foundation for a more elegant argument when made by disinterested experts. They could argue, even if the executives could not, that the test of merger efficiency was not corporate profitability. They could argue, in the Henry Manne tradition, that even an unprofitable merger improved efficiency if the acquiring firm's share declined in value an amount less than the premium paid over the selling price of the target's shares prior to the takeover. Moreover, the fact that the mergers were not notably successful could be reflected in other statistics showing that acquiring firms were not increasingly dominating the economy.

As a tactical matter, this line of argument is nothing short of brilliant. First, the basic point is simple, direct, and positive. "Mergers improve efficiency" is a point anyone can understand. Its implications for policy are clear: More mergers are better. Second, the proof of the point could not be debated in Congress because the proof methodology is conceptually obscure and mathematically sophisticated. Merely understanding the proof criteria—decline in value of acquiring firm equals less than premium paid for target—is especially difficult because its logic is counterintuitive. Normally, we expect a decline in corporate value to reflect inefficiency. How could a legislator argue against the conclusions if that legislator couldn't even understand the theory? If the theory *were* grasped, the legislator could not expect to critique the econometric equations which often use hundreds of stock market quotations to prove efficiency. Clearly, this is a matter for experts, and legislators can only draw implications from experts' findings.

Using aggregate stock market statistics served another purpose. It diverted attention from the individual mergers that had turned out badly. No corporate chief executives had to be embarrassed by miscalculations made in paying too much for a target. Indeed, given the complexity of the proof, there was no reason for experts to dwell on numbers indicating that overall mergers were unprofitable. It was better, clearer, to emphasize the conclusion: Mergers increased efficiency.

Expert opinion then is the defensive strategy of choice for big business in debates on merger policy. They have used it in legislative hearings and elsewhere when they have had the opportunity.

There have been several major policy battlegrounds during the megamerger wave, and three of them offer a good illustration of the strategies adopted by big business. First, early in the wave there were a series of hearings before the Antitrust Subcommittee of the Senate Judiciary Committee. Second, there was the Securities and Exchange Commission's Advisory Committee on Tender Offers following the Bendix/Martin Marietta takeover battle. Third, the Senate held debates following the Texaco/Getty and Chevron/Gulf acquisitons.

Although big business was able to dominate the outcome of each of these, recurrent battles have shown that the sentiment against corporate growth by mergers is constant.

The Victory Strategy

In July and September of 1978 Senator Edward Kennedy, then chairman of the Antitrust Subcommittee of the Judiciary Commmittee, held hearings on the accelerating wave of large mergers. In the course of those hearings, he was told by representatives of both the Federal Trade Commission and the Department of Justice that such mergers could not be stopped under existing laws. He invited both agencies to submit proposals for new legislation to cover the large conglomerate mergers.

Hearings on new legislation were scheduled for early spring of 1979, and representatives of the business community were invited to testify. The FTC and the Department of Justice were to present the legislative proposals. Senator Kennedy, Senator Metzenbaum, and others were to introduce a bill of their own.

The Department of Justice proposal would have discouraged conglomerate mergers by reversing the burden of proof in antitrust cases. Any firm that made a large acquisition would have been required to prove that the merger would improve competition. The proposal submitted by the FTC staff permitted large mergers but would have required a simultaneous divestiture of business operations equal in size to the acquisition target. The bill introduced by Senators Kennedy and Metzenbaum—"The Small and Independent Business Protection Act of 1979"—combined aspects of both the Justice Department and the FTC proposals for acquisitions of $350 million firms, and added a flat ban on mergers between firms that separately possessed assets in excess of $2 million.[26]

Members of the Carter administration argued there were too many mergers for the wrong reasons. They believed the costs of waging takeover battles was excessive, the disruption of managerial resources was debilitating, and even the preparation of takeover defense plans was enormously wasteful.

Harold Williams, former chairman of the Securities and Exchange Commission, claimed the $100 billion used in takeovers during 1978 and 1979 should have been put into productive investment.[27] Robert Reich, former director of policy planning at the Federal Trade Commission, condemned the mergers as a form of "paper entrepreneurialism."[28] F. M. Scherer, a leading industrial-organization economist, may have summarized this critique best:

> [These] mergers do little or nothing on average to enhance industrial efficiency. . . . If a single sweeping generalization must be rendered, they are a deadly serious but preponderantly sterile managerial ego game.[29]

The prospect of new restrictive merger legislation was taken seriously by the business community. A Democratic, liberal, activist Congress, with the backing of Jimmy Carter, seemed likely to put through the legislation. The Business Roundtable set defeat of the legislation as its number one priority.

The strategy of the Roundtable was devised by its attorney, Ira Millstein. Millstein had the ideal background for the job. He was the senior antitrust partner at the New York law firm of Weil, Gotshal & Manges, outgoing chairman of the Antitrust Section of the American Bar Association, and a cofounder of Columbia University's Center for Law and Economic Studies. He was, therefore, intimately familiar with both the antitrust bar and the work of academics on antitrust issues.

His personal testimony before the Antitrust Subcommittee was limited to a Business Roundtable-sponsored panel that addressed the political and social effects of mergers. Included on the panel was Edwin Epstein, who testified that political science literature had established no correlation between corporate size and political power. Millstein's own conclusion was, if anything, even more modest: "The bill's apparent predicate—that large firms . . . vest in the hands of private groups undue discretionary power—is not supportable, at least at this time."[30] He therefore urged more study before passing legislation on these grounds. (Millstein also happened to be conducting a study of the political power issue under the auspices of the Columbia center and later published a book entitled *The Limits of Corporate Power*.)[31]

The other panels of experts that Millstein coordinated with the National Association of Manufacturers, the Chamber of Commerce, and the American Petroleum Institute were less self-effacing. In all, they presented the testimony of fifteen experts who added four points to those made by Millstein and Epstein. First, there is no trend toward concentration of economic power. Second, American corporations will be at a disadvantage if they cannot merge and foreign firms can. Third, the merger market for corporate control improves efficiency. And fourth, the proposed statutes were poorly drafted, using new terms that would take years to define.

The phalanx of experts testifying in five separate panels included distinguished Chicago School economists and law professors such as Richard Posner, Kenneth Dam and Yale Brozen of the University of Chicago, J. Fred. Weston of UCLA, William Baxter of Stanford, and George Benston of the University of Rochester. These and the other business witnesses received expenses and often a fee from the business groups.

In the course of the hearings, Senator Metzenbaum questioned the witnesses about their relationships with the sponsoring groups. For example:

> Mr. Benston: Excuse me, Senator, I am not representing the Business Roundtable.
> Senator Metzenbaum: . . . Is the Business Roundtable paying your expenses?
> Mr. Benston: yes sir.
> Senator Metzenbaum: Are they paying you a fee?
> Mr. Benston: Yes sir.
> Senator Metzenbaum: And you say you are not a witness for the Business Roundtable?
> Mr. Benston: Absolutely . . . I am representing myself to the extent I have expertise and knowledge and independent judgment.
>
>   There are probably things in this statement which someone will disagree with. I have not cleared it with any one . . . nor has anyone told me what to say or how to say it.[32]

Professor Benston's rejection of any implication that he had trimmed his views for purposes of testifying at the hearing is surely correct. His prior views on the issues were well known and perfectly consistent with his testimony. J. Fred Weston's presentation on the effects of mergers for the U.S. Department of Commerce later in 1979 was consistent with his testimony for the Business Roundtable. Betty Bock's testimony on economic concentration merely summarized her decade of work at the Conference Board, (a business supported research organization).

On the other hand, it is equally certain that the Business Roundtable chose George Benston because of his known views, rather than because of his independence. Business groups have cultivated and promoted academic points of view congenial to their own. Paying Professor Benston for his testimony and then publishing it under the auspices of the American Enterprise Institute is but one example of that support.[33]

An outstanding example of business support for congenial academic viewpoints is Henry Manne's Law and Economics Center. The center has followed Manne from the University of Rochester to the University of Miami and is currently with him at Emory University. It has an ambitious objective — to educate federal judges, law professors, and economists about the proper relationship between government and business. In simplistic terms the message delivered at the Law and Economic Center by its leading teachers, UCLA economists Armen Alchain, Harold Demsetz, and Benjamin Klein, is: No regulation is good regulation. The message is paid for by big business.

Over 100 of the nation's largest corporations help finance the Law and Economics Center's activities through annual contributions. The "Center's general policy of not seeking permanent endowment funds"[34] reflects its free-market philosophy, which denies the existence of a "free lunch" and espouses the exchange of value for money. The value business receives includes subsidized education for American judges and law professors.

By 1979, when 20 percent of the federal bench had gone through the program, questions were raised (and then dropped) about the propriety of judges accepting a "free" education in economics from big business. The same questions could have been raised about the generation of law professors who have gone through the Center's program, or about the government antitrust lawyers and business-press reporters who have been the target of a similar program taught by Alchain, Demsetz, and Klein under the auspices of UCLA's Institute for Contemporary Studies. These targeted groups are the key formulators or implementors of antitrust and regulatory policy and the prime molders of attitudes toward government regulation. For many members of these groups, the distinctive view of economics and the economic consequences of regulation presented by these Chicago School economists is the only formal training in economics they will ever receive.

How effective these general educational programs or more focused efforts such as testimony are is open to dispute. The Small and Independent Business Protection Act of 1979" never even made it out of the committee. The votes were not there. The Energy Antimonopoly Act of 1979," a similar bill introduced by Senators Kennedy and Metzenbaum after Exxon bought Reliance Corporation for $1.6 million, met a similar end.

Why did these bills fail to attract support? Perhaps the Senate was persuaded by Professor Dam (subsequently appointed Undersecretary of State by President Reagan) that American automobile companies would be unable to compete with the much smaller foreign rivals he named—Volvo, Volkswagen, Renault, Datsun, and Toyota—if American firms were forbidden to merge.[35] Perhaps the Senate was persuaded by Professor Brozen that "assets are being moved from poor management to good management in the typical acquisition."[36] Perhaps the Senate was persuaded to wait for Millstein's study of the political power of large firms. Or perhaps doubts were raised about the economic testimony of witnesses supporting the legislation. Given the stagnation of American industry and the growth of foreign competition by 1979, Congress may have been unwilling to pass legislation that had any possibility, however remote, of slowing the American economy.

In any case, despite the presumptively antibusiness character of Congress, no legislation passed. Whatever its precise role, the expert witness strategy seems to have helped. It also kept the discussion away from the embarrassingly poor record of acquiring firms. In the end, the megamerger wave rolled on.

Policy Debates Among Victors

With the election of Ronald Reagan to the presidency and a Republican majority in the Senate, the business community probably expected few problems with mergers. Spectacular mergers, however, generate their own debates and no megamerger has been more of a spectacle than Bendix's attempt to take over Martin Marietta. The ensuing debate about takeover tactics in the SEC's Advisory Committee on Tender Offers mentioned in Chapter 4 was especially notable in one respect: None of the participants, with the possible exception of former Supreme Court Justice Arthur Goldberg, was concerned about growth by merger. Instead, their primary concern was to ensure that the takeover process presented an appearance of fairness to the investing public.

The advisory committee, dominated by merger professionals, recommended that the Williams Act rules be modified to guarantee shareholders an opportunity to study competing bids before their tendering options expire. It also advised that significant limitations be placed on certain dubious aspects of takeover battles, such as payment of greenmail to would-be acquirers or providing golden parachutes to corporate executives. Although the committee would not forbid the most pernicious tactics that undermine the bidding process, such as two-tier tender offers and lockups, the recommendations would establish a more dignified pace for billion-dollar takeover contests and would match the weapons of competing bidders and target corporations more evenly.

In this setting, the role of the Chicago School was independent of and adverse to the position of big business. The Chicago School, in the persons of Frank Easterbrook and Greg Jarrell (later appointed chief economist of the SEC during the Reagan administration), took the position, in a dissent almost as long as the committee report, that takeovers were good because they will improve management. Easterbrook and Jarrell would prohibit the target firm from almost any defensive action, but would permit golden parachutes to reduce target management's personal incentives to prevent takeovers. By eliminating the restraints of securities laws, they intentionally would help the first bidder to become the only bidder. To encourage such takeovers they want to reward first bidders who have invested in identifying "mismanaged" target firms. The benefit of encouraging such takeovers—they presumably expect and desire a much larger number than currently exists—is to be more efficiency. If another firm is a better manager of the target than the first bidder, the targets can be resold or taken over by more efficient managers in subsequent transactions. Eventually, only the most fit corporations would remain.

However useful that free-market model of corporate interaction might be in debates with antibusiness zealots, it held no attraction for the representatives of business in discussions among themselves. These business representatives recognized substantial differences among mergers. Some are good, others are bad. They believed that managers of target firms have a right or even a duty to resist takeovers to protect the interests of their shareholders. They also believed that an extended bidding process between competing firms would produce a fairer result for shareholders and a better chance of finding a more able acquiring firm.

More fundamentally, they disagreed about the role of government in the economy. The business executives believed that government intervention can improve the marketplace. They were particularly sensitive to the need to retain the confidence of shareholders by having the government guarantee the fairness of the takeover process.

As Kenneth Arrow winner of the 1972 Nobel Prize in Economics has pointed out, such concerns are not accounted for in Chicago School price theory.

> [I]n a strictly technical and objective sense, the price system does not always work. You simply cannot price certain things. . . . Consider . . . trust among people. Now trust has a very important pragmatic value, if nothing else. Trust is an important lubricant of a social system. It is extremely efficient; it saves a lot of trouble to have a fair degree of reliance on other people's word. Unfortunately this is not a commodity which can be bought very easily. If you have to buy it, you already have some doubts about what you've bought. Trust and similar values, loyalty or truth-telling, are examples of what the economists would call "externalities." They are goods, they are commodities; they have real, practical, economic value; they increase the efficiency of the system, enable you to produce more goods or more of whatever values you hold in high esteem. But they are not commodities for which trade on the open market is technically possible or even meaningful.[37]

Business is a continuing game in which all players must have confidence in the underlying process. The representatives of the corporate community on the advisory committee recognized that only an arbiter outside the market system can provide the basis for that confidence — the government.

The Challenge of the Phoenix

Why, after refusing the "Small and Independent Business Protection Act of 1979," did Wall Street believe the Senate would pass an antimerger bill in 1984? Wall Street knows that any number of antimerger bills can be killed, but the sentiment against megamergers remains. With the ashes of previous bills new ones are written.

To be sure, the megamergers that set off the legislative action had set new records—first, Texaco's $10 billion bid for Getty, then,

Chevron's (Standard Oil of California as it was then known) $13 billion bid for Gulf, and finally during the debates Mobil's lesser $6 billion bid for Superior Oil. Even so, the belief that Congress would pass an antimerger law in 1984 seems remarkable. Consider the circumstances:

1. President Reagan had made deregulation of business a major goal of his administration;
2. Attorney General William French Smith had said, with specific reference to antitrust policy, that his department did not believe big was bad;
3. The Senate was solidly controlled by a Republican majority; and
4. The FTC was applying existing antitrust laws to these transactions and had already required Texaco to make substantial divestitures of oil facilities as a condition of approving the merger with Getty.

Furthermore, neither the parties to the mergers executed by Texaco, Getty, Chevron, and Gulf, nor the precipitators, like T. Boone Pickens, were in favor of the legislation. To the contrary. They all lobbied hard against legislation that would have stopped large oil companies from buying smaller ones.

Senator J. Bennett Johnston's introduction of the oil merger moratorium bill was less surprising than the warm reception it received by his Senate colleagues. Johnston, the conservative Louisiana Democrat and ranking minority member of the Energy and Natural Resources Committee, was a noted friend of oil companies, but his constituents were the smaller independent oil firms, not the giant integrated firms that were doing the buying. These smaller oil firms have been traditional supporters of the Democratic Party, and they were worried by the consolidations of larger firms.[38]

Senator Johnston's introduction of the bill and its Democratic support are explainable, but the cracks in Republican opposition to it are harder to understand. According to the *American Lawyer*, there was a clear majority in favor of doing something about the oil mergers.[39] Only the most determined efforts by the oil firms and the Republican Senate leadership prevented that "something" from being the adoption of Johnston's proposal.

Because the legislation was aimed at particular takeovers, the corporations could not use disinterested surrogates to argue their case.

Instead, they launched a massive campaign using the personal influence of many of Washington's most skilled lobbyists. The campaign
began when Johnston's first attempt in attaching his bill to legislation pending before the Senate failed by only six votes.

The surprisingly close margin alerted Lynn Coleman of Skadden,
Arps that the deal his firm had negotiated for Texaco to buy Getty
might come apart. Again according to the *American Lawyer*, Coleman, a former general counsel and deputy secretary of the Department of Energy, called his friend Johnston and argued that it would
be unfair to include the Texaco/Getty deal in the legislation on the
grounds that Texaco (and Getty) had had no notice that Congress
might object. Johnston is reported to have agreed.

On March 6, Senator Johnston issued his ultimatum. He intended
to "stop them dead in their tracks—Pickens, [Chevron], everybody."
Carla Hills, a former cabinet officer in the Ford administration, was
asked to check out for Chevron whether or not its merger with Gulf
was in jeopardy. Hills, at that time the Washington-based partner of a
Los Angeles law firm and a member of the Chevron board of directors, reported back that there, indeed, was trouble.

Within two days Chevron drafted a team of experienced political
infighters. The team was coordinated by a Washington lawyer, William Van Ness, who had ten-years experience as counsel to the Senate Energy Committee under Henry Jackson. He was aided by lobbyist Charls Walker, deputy secretary of the Treasury in the Nixon Administration who helped persuade Majority Leader Howard Baker to
fight the bill. Another lobbying firm, Parry and Romani, was brought
in to persuade its former bosses, Republican Senators Hatch and
DeConcini. Richard Richards, another Washington lawyer and Republican National Committee chairman from 1981 to 1983, worked
with the Senate Republican leadership to get the White House to
openly oppose the Johnston bill.[40]

By Monday, March 12, the presidents of Chevron and Gulf,
George Keller and James Lee, added their presence to the fight in
Washington. They argued their own case: The merger was not anti-
competitive; it would not reduce oil exploration. John Gutfreund,
Gulf's investment banker at Salomon Brothers, went to plead the
case personally with Senator Johnson. Johnston turned him down,
as he had earlier turned down a similar plea from T. Boone Pickens.
(Pickens's group, which had failed to take over Gulf, stood to make
$780 million from the Chevron deal.)

While voting on the Johnston bill was delayed (by the Senate debate on a school prayer amendment), the political process continued. Senator Johnston directed his staff to make sure that the bill did not include the Texaco/Getty deal and did protect the Texas Eastern Corporation, a Houston-based independent oil firm. Lynn Coleman from Skadden, Arps was invited to help a Johnston staffer rewrite the bill. So was Ky Ewing, former deputy assistant attorney general for antitrust in the Carter administration. His firm, Vinson & Elkins, represented Texas Eastern.

By March 19, Senator Johnston was persuaded to change the bill again, this time to exempt all pending mergers (including Chevron/ Gulf and Mobil/Superior).[41] According to the *American Lawyer*, both Russell Long, the senior senator from Louisiana, and Edwin Edwards, its governor, urged him to do so; and Johnston learned that some of the investors in the Pickens group were Louisiana oil people who stood to lose money if the merger fell through.

When it was announced that the bill would be prospective, the now targetless proposal gained, rather than lost, support. Apparently, senators had been deluged by phone calls from thousands of shareholders (in Getty, Gulf, and Superior Oil) who would lose money if the transactions were stopped. By making the bill apply only to future transactions, it now seemed to be unstoppable.

Why was there so much sentiment to pass a bill? The specific concerns about monopoly power and energy policy had been answered by Keller and Lee. In any case, the record breaking Chevron/Gulf transaction would no longer have been covered by the bill. So the issue was not Texaco/Getty, Chevron/Gulf or Mobil/Superior. Rather, it was the trend. It seems to have been the old fear of growth without limit. For that the prospective bill provided protection.

The Republican leadership still opposed the bill and sought a way to stop it. At the last moment, March 28, Robert Dole found a suitable alternative. Rather than a moratorium on large oil mergers, the Senate would put firms on notice that in the following ninety days the Senate would consider permanent antimerger legislation. Any new legislation would be made retroactive to March 28. Thus, any merger begun during that ninety-day period might be undone by Congress. The legislation was referred to Senator Dole's Finance Committee on the grounds that the tax laws provided the basis for large takeovers. That killed the Johnston bill.

RESPONSIVE POLICIES

Because the decision to grow by merger is not based on the dynamics of any business, corporate size is limited only by managerial choice. And although the market might discipline foolish growth, such corrections are made long after targets are brought to ruin by mismanagement. Even with mismanagement, corporate failure can be avoided if the government can be persuaded to provide the firm's business a protected status by tariffs or other subsidies. In the meantime, the unreviewed decisions of the corporation's managers determine the future for communities, corporate shareholders, consumers and many thousands of employees. Megamergers can therefore disrupt the competitive, intellectual, social and political diversity which is the strength of our society.

The objective of merger policy has been to limit the growth of large firms without replacing the unreviewable, centralized power of corporate executives with the even more centralized power of government officials. Even assuming government were adequately controlled by the electoral process and knew enough to make sensible business decisions, the further centralization of authority would diminish the diversity and competitive rivalry that are thought to be the sources of American efficiency and innovation.

Merger policy can accomplish its objective either by restraining the size of corporations to preserve a broader distribution of power or by limiting the power of large firms. Only an unlikely and radical reconfiguration of the tax laws could accomplish the former without seriously disrupting the private decisionmaking process. The latter, limiting corporate power, is more feasible but requires a patchwork quilt of regulations which can only address some major concerns. In the past, we have chosen the quilt rather than attempt to establish an ideal multitude of small firms. In the future we are likely to do the same.

Restoring the Ideal

There is little doubt that the number of megamergers and even corporate size could be reduced by changing existing tax laws. If the tax incentive to retain earnings were eliminated, corporations would not accumulate excess earnings. Robert Hatfield, then chairman of the

Continental Group and spokesman for the Business Roundtable, said as much in the hearings on the "Small and Independent Business Protection Act of 1979."[42] University of Rochester economist, George Benston has also blamed tax laws for the run of megamergers.[43]

In 1962 Milton Friedman declared, "The corporate tax should be abolished." And he went on:

> Whether this is done or not, corporations should be required to attribute the individual stockholders earnings which are not paid out as dividends. . . . The individual stockholder should then be required to report the attributed but undistributed earnings on his tax return as well as the dividend. Corporations would still be free to plough back as much as they wish, but they would have no incentive to do so except the proper incentive that they could earn more internally than the stockholder could earn externally. *Few measures would do more to invigorate capital markets, to stimulate enterprise and to promote effective competition.*[44] (Emphasis added.)

Given this seemingly widespread and longstanding agreement on the desirability of a basic reform of the tax laws, why has the current structure persisted? One might expect, for example, that Senator Dole's 1984 alternative merger-study bill, which replaced Senator Johnston's oil merger moratorium, would have resulted in a bill from the Senate Finance Committee. However, despite general agreement that any of the proposed reforms would reduce retained earnings, there is a companion concern that these earnings, which form the bulk of new capital, would be lost to corporate investment if the funds became available to shareholders. They might spend the money on personal consumption items. That loss of investment capital would reduce overall economic activity.

There are other tax reform strategies that encourage neither retention nor personal consumption. For example, if the current tax structure were modified to eliminate the personal income tax on dividends that were reinvested, then the capital-formation incentive would remain. But unless there were complex further limitations, those reinvested dividends might end up in the stock market or in real estate. In either case, the effect would be to bid up the price of existing goods rather than pay for new business capacity. Retained earnings available for investment would become speculative investments in the secondary securities markets.

Careful drafting might produce a tax law with the desired result, and if it did it would represent a radical shift in the way American firms do business. This modified tax structure, if successful, would result in firms disgorging their annual earnings and going to the capital markets each year for money to fund the following year's projects. While limiting unnecessary corporate growth and increasing the mobility of capital, this arrangement would also reduce the ability of corporations to engage in long-term planning and make projects requiring secrecy or surprise more difficult. Thus, real investment opportunities might decline. In the face of such uncertainty it is not surprising that Congress has been reluctant to attempt the fundamental reform that has met with so much theoretical acceptance.

And business executives of major corporations, like former Business Roundtable chairman Robert Hatfield, are unlikely to favor such tax reform. They would stand to lose direct control over the investment of retained earnings, and their planning process would be disrupted.

Even shareholders would have little to gain immediately from such tax reform. Their annual investment task would become more complex because they would have to reinvest a greater portion of their savings. The investments themselves would be limited to new and presumably more speculative securities issues.

Only the newer, smaller corporations that receive less than their "fair" share of capital under the current system are likely to be direct beneficiaries of reform. But growth companies might be unwilling to trade the security of their current earnings for the possibility of attracting larger amounts of new capital. Their energies and skills are likely to be needed internally and the firm could be at an informational disadvantage in the capital markets. That same external disadvantage handicaps other growth firms that might press for tax reform in the political process.

It is unlikely that Congress will attempt to establish an Adam Smithian world of small competitors. However attractive in theory the prospect of dismantling big business is risky and lacks a strong political constituency.

PATCHWORK POLICIES

If we continue to rely on the interaction of individuals and organizations to produce economic, social, and political decisions, that interaction would be improved by preventing managers of large organizations from exerting undue power. There is no neat or simple way to restrict such power because corporations and other large organizations operate in so many different contexts. The few restrictions discussed below are therefore strategies designed to enhance or reinforce the self-regulating character of our society.

Takeover Tactics

Takeover rules have improved greatly as a result of the Williams Act and the Hart-Scott-Rodino Act, but they remain a disgrace. There is simply no reason to permit the managers of either acquiring firms or target firms to manipulate the bidding process. Although these managers have gained undisputed control of large corporations, the shareholders are still the owners. Their right to decide when or if they will sell that ownership should not be subject to coercive tactics.

Two-tier tender offers and lockups are inherently manipulative tactics. As the discussion in Part I made clear, two-tier tender offers can force shareholders to sell out for less than the holders believe the shares are worth, and lockup tactics prevent fair bids by rival acquiring firms by limiting the value of the target to them. These kinds of tactics can be pursued by executives because of the enormous corporate resources at their disposal. They should be barred from using those resources to defeat rights of shareholders.

The SEC's Advisory Committee on Tender Offers refused to forbid either lockups or two-tier offers. No doubt it recognized that, theoretically, these tactics can prevent a full and free bidding contest. The committee's recommendations, however, were justified by experience, not theory.

From their experience as investment bankers, merger lawyers, risk arbitrageurs, and white knights, they concluded that without the enticement of the crown jewels in a lockup agreement white knights are unlikely to appear, so there will be no bidding. As a practical matter the shareholders will suffer because the first bid will win. Therefore, even if a second round of bidding is discouraged by the lockup, the shareholders will at least get the benefit of one competing bid.

The committee may also have been concerned that legal prohibitions against lockup agreements are unrealistically technical rules to impose on a target management in the middle of a takeover battle.

Once the board of directors of a target firm has established its objectives, corporate managers must act quickly with the resources at hand to implement them. To ask that managers do more than act in the firm's best interest within the confines of the business-judgment rule may seem unrealistic to experienced takeover lawyers like Flom and Lipton.

The committee may be correct in thinking that shareholders will usually benefit from the use of lockups, but their use is still contrary to the more general objectives of the Williams Act and other securities laws. Lockups undermine the integrity of the stock market process by taking the valuation of the target firm out of the hands of the marketplace and the shareholders. There is no obvious need for such tactics to entice bidders—U.S. Steel, for example, pursued its bid for Marathon even after it lost its lockup. The benefits of lockups ought to be more carefully demonstrated.

Instead of recommending the prohibition of front-end-loaded, two-tier offers, the SEC's committee suggested that tender offers for less than all shares be open for two weeks longer than offers for all outstanding shares. Such rules might be advantageous to a rival bidder with a one-tier offer, but they would have no impact on the more usual cases in which there is either only one bidder or the competing bidders are also making two-tier offers. With competing two-tier offers, the shareholders would still be subject to stampeding, even if they believe the offer is unfairly low, in order to avoid being caught in the second tier.

Although the committee listed reasons why a firm might want to acquire less than all of a target's shares, none of these reasons justifies an explicit or implicit two-tier tender offer. None explains why the committee refused to eliminate the fear of second tier by guaranteeing at least equal payment to minority shareholders in a federal appraisal process. Perhaps the members felt federal action to be unnecessary. In a *Wall Street Journal* preview of 1983 merger tactics, Arthur Fleischer was quoted as advising potential target firms to adopt corporate-charter provisions protecting minority shareholders against payment of lesser amounts in a second-tier freezeout.[45]

Although Fleischer's recommendation is presented as a "shark repellent" antitakeover provision, it also has the effect of permitting shareholders to vote freely for or against a tender offer. With a guaranteed price for their shares they can afford to tender only when they believe the offer is fair, not simply because they do not want to risk being frozen out at an unfair price. This kind of provision might dampen the takeover business, but it also seems fundamental to an equitable stock market. It is disturbing and inconsistent with the idea of a free market for shareholders to be forced to sell shares for less than they believe the shares are worth.

Takeover Incentives

The structure of the takeover market is unsound. Information about potential targets, especially firms that are too diverse to be managed effectively, is insufficiently available to encourage a vigorous take-over market. The firms most active in megamergers are not those most likely to improve business. And we need a takeover market with stronger incentives to improve efficiency.

Public reporting of earnings by individual lines of business might enable the market to work more effectively. Where it appeared that firms were becoming too complex to be managed effectively, a Carl Icahn, a T. Boone Pickens, or a Victor Posner might be willing to buy the firm and break it up into more profitable units. Or a Victor Kiam might offer to buy the divisions that the diversified firm could not run successfully. Both of these would encourage corporations to re-main at their most efficient size.

Another mechanism to discourage corporate growth was proposed by the FTC staff at the hearings on the "Small and Independent Business Protection Act of 1979." Its so-called cap and spinoff pro-posal would have required very large firms to divest themselves of businesses equal in size to those they were acquiring.[46] In other words, no growth by merger. A firm could trade in its business by merger, but it could not grow. Large firms would no longer acquire simply because they had no other use for their earnings. They would have to decide they could manage the target firms better than some of their existing businesses.

The solution offered by the FTC staff, though, is not perfect, because it might prevent the emergence of useful new forms of larger business enterprises like the national financial organizations. It also might encourage firms to overinvest in existing businesses rather than divest any resources.

Although surely in need of refinement the cap and spinoff propo-sal is a major breakthrough toward merger regulation because its test of efficiency is self-administered. Unlike a government restriction permitting only those mergers that improved efficiency, this proposal does not require governmental officials to make speculative business judgments. Corporations would continue to decide what businesses they can manage best without any government review.

The cap and spinoff proposal would not even limit corporate size. It would only put an end to limitless corporate expansion that is the product of executive intention but not bound by the dynamics of any business. It would require a corporate reason for megamergers other than growth for its own sake.

Corporate Power

Corporate power and the fear of corporate power increase with the size of corporations. Merger policy, through the antitrust laws, has never addressed the concern with size directly. Megamergers, which comply with those laws, have made antitrust largely irrelevant. We, therefore, need more direct limitations on the growth and exercise of corporate power.

The cap and spinoff proposal offers some help in this matter. It prevents the instantaneous leap in corporate size that seems to provoke the greatest fears. It could be applied only to the combination of those largest firms—the top 50, 100, or 200, for example—that already control a large proportion of the nation's resources. That would prevent any sudden radical shift in distribution of power in our society.

The political influence of the large firm, however, needs to be limited more directly. But that must be done as part of a general reform of campaign spending. As matters currently stand, the rules controlling PACs diminish the direct power of merging firms by eliminating one of their PACs.

The great question raised by Berle and Means in the 1930s—to whom are corporate executives responsible?—remains unaddressed by self-regulating proposals. Ralph Nader, Mark Green, and others have argued for detailed regulation of large corporations through federal chartering.[47] Like Henry Simons's earlier proposals, the Nader/Green plans impose significant restrictions on corporate freedom. Unlike Simons, however, they do not advocate a radical reduction in firm size to a point where a market consists solely of small firms needing no regulation.

Others, like William Norris, chief executive officer of Control Data Corporation, have sought to alter the basis of the problem by reinvolving shareholders in corporate decisionmaking. Norris would require any large merger to be approved by a vote of the shareholders of both the acquiring and the target firms.[48] Prior to that vote Norris would require the acquiring firm to submit a statement of its plans for the target that would spell out in detail what effects the takeover would have on the target shareholders, employees, local suppliers, local philanthropic contributions, product improvements, quality of service, and so forth. Norris claims his plan is not an exercise in nostalgia. He believes shareholders can and would exercise their votes responsibly.

Observations

These approaches to merger policy are not likely to be adopted in the immediate future. Congress seems to have lost confidence in its ability to legislate. It has become preoccupied with economic growth, but doubtful of its ability to intervene in helpful ways. As a consequence, we are apt to see more megamergers.

But pressures for merger legislation are not going to disappear. Public opinion polls consistently show that Americans believe corporations have become too big and too powerful. A 1979 survey, for instance, reported that half the public seldom believes business leaders, and 70 percent believes that business has too much influence over government.[49] Although there is little sentiment to dismember existing large corporations, megamergers have clearly reawakened an underlying fear and distrust of corporate power.

A special concern about corporate power is raised by the mergers of large media companies. When Capital Cities takes over the American Broadcasting Company, Gannett adds to its chain of 124 newspapers, S. I. Newhouse buys the *New Yorker* or Rupert Murdoch acquires the *Times* of London or the *Village Voice* the acquisitions invariably remind the public that the direct influence of the media is for sale to anyone with enough money. While media conglomerates generally have refrained from imposing editorial policy on their subsidiaries, there is nothing but their judgment to stop them from doing so. Consequently the attempt by Senator Jesse Helms and the conservative Fairness in Media group to take over CBS and change Dan Rather's Evening News was viewed by many as frightening or dangerous. The fact is we have no laws that prevent the acquisition of large companies.

Perhaps because it is difficult to strike the right balance, merger laws have often had long gestation periods. In the 1920s and throughout the 1930s and 1940s, the Federal Trade Commission advocated making two changes in the antitrust laws: covering mergers by acquisition of corporate assets and requiring corporations to notify the antitrust enforcement agencies of an intention to merge prior to completing the transaction.[50] The "asset loophole" was closed in 1950 by the Celler-Kefauver Act. In 1976, the Hart-Scott-Rodino Act gave the FTC and the Justice Department premerger notification authority.

We can expect more merger legislation.

MORE MEGAMERGERS

If we lived in the age of reptiles, this book would probably be about dinosaurs. Megamergers, like the dinosaurs before them, are interesting because of their great size and how that size affects their environment.

Megamergers have transformed the business landscape. Once a questionable business device of upstart, empire-building executives, takeovers have now become accepted business practice for successful, established firms. The consequence is that today no firm is immune from takeover. Forces that promote megamergers, primarily the accumulation of excess profits, remain. Even if the fad and frenzy have faded, megamergers are not about to follow dinosaurs into extinction.

Although no longer considered to be a recipe for corporate success, megamergers and hostile tender offers are routine business tactics. If one firm identifies another as a profitable target, it will not be deterred by the fact that the target is larger or that its management will resist a takeover attempt. Banks and other members of the financial community are now accustomed to funding such David and Goliath takeover assaults.

Dexel Burnham Lambert's junk bond genius Michael Milken showed during the 1985 back-to-back takeover attempts on Phillips Petroleum by T. Boone Pickens and Carl Icahn just how much money is available to finance a giant acquisition. Although Pickens and Icahn were both paid off in greenmail, to make the Icahn attempt credible Milken had to persuade Phillips and the stock market that he could raise $4 billion to finance the takeover.[1]

Takeovers have increased the size and diversity of already large firms. They have centralized, inside a single corporate headquarters, decisions that were formerly made by independent, locally managed corporations. This continued centralization of economic resources has changed America.

Megamergers have shifted centers of business decisionmaking away from Buffalo, Syracuse, Utica, Worcester, Springfield, Scranton, Toledo, Dayton, and Youngstown. These cities, once the birthplace of new businesses and industries, have lost regenerative capacities as their economic life has come under the dominion of distant corporate heads. The diversity of opportunity they offered is not matched today by more specialized, innovative enclaves like Silicon Valley in California and Route 128 outside of Boston. We no longer have a multitude of cities with the fragmented economic structure that urbanologist Jane Jacobs identified as the source of progress in Western civilization.[2]

Ours is a more bureaucratic society. The vertically integrated, multidivisional firm of the turn of the century replaced the decisions of many small entrepreneurs within a single industry with the discipline of the corporate hierarchy. Those multidivisional firms competed against other integrated firms in their product markets for customers and in the financial markets for capital. Now, to a greater extent, the capital-allocation function takes place in the board room, rather than on Wall Street.

The trend toward decisionmaking within giant organizations means that these organizations must adapt to include the strengths of the structures they displace. We need new and better organization theories to operate these new corporations made up of unrelated business. They face enormous information barriers to sensible decisionmaking. They cannot adopt the oversimplistic BCG investment matrix nor can they use the complex GE market-attractiveness matrix. They must, therefore, discover new ways within the corporate structure to decentralize decisionmaking to manageable units.

As corporations become larger and more diverse in their holdings, they must also become more responsive if they are to avoid the fate of the dinosaur. They must be more sensitive to the individual aspirations and preferences of their employees and customers. They must nurture the diversity that produces innovative insights. Jobs must become more interesting and offer greater opportunity for workers if costs are to be contained and quality maintained to attract and hold customers.

These are not new concerns. Corporations have tried many steps in the past to address them. Consumer hot lines, quality circles, and profit centers are but a few examples. Megamergers have increased these concerns by making the ultimate decisionmakers even more remote.

There *are* indications that megamergers are producing some managerial insights. For example, an increasing proportion of mergers are divestitures. W. T. Grimm reported that the number rose from 666 in 1980 to 932 in 1983.[3] These divestitures indicate, if not an ability to operate the more complex diversified firm, at least a groping toward a more manageable constellation of businesses. Divestitures also indicate that corporate information-feedback systems are telling managers what businesses they cannot operate successfully.

A number of these divestitures are leveraged-buyout sales to divisional managers or to employees through employee stock ownership plans (ESOPs). Sales, such as Phillip Morris's divestiture of the American Safety Razor Company, reverse the trend toward concentrated economic power. They also provide the flexibility to return businesses to a more appropriate corporate size.

Billion dollar leveraged buyouts, however, pose their own problems. When Metromedia or City Investing go private, we lose sight of their performance and decisionmaking. By switching public equity holdings to debt, corporate managers become immune from takeovers and escape all of the reporting obligations of public corporations. Decisions with regional or national importance then can be made in secrecy, with accountability to no one other than the government. Government is not well suited to such an exclusive responsibility. It operates better as a supplement to private, self-regulating systems.

We can expect a continued parade of unrelated mergers since the structural forces that encourage them remain. The logic of the life cycle analysis and the problem of excess profits for firms in stagnant or declining industries persist. If corporations retain their earnings—and they are likely to do so—then they must find investments for them. Perhaps, like the Sun Company under Robert Sharbaugh, they will try to build managerial expertise through small acquisitions before committing large capital resources.

A planned shift of corporate resources may or may not be possible. Telegraphing moves may drive up acquisition prices or invite competing bidders. Profitable mergers are frequently fleeting opportunities that must be seized or foregone entirely.

The transitory basis of merger transactions makes them vulnerable to fads. The unavoidably incomplete information that supports an acquisition decision is frequently filled in by a new "theory." On April 3, 1984, shortly after the Texaco/Getty and Chevron/Gulf mergers demonstrated that oil firms were undervalued, the *New York Times* ran an article purporting to show that the film libraries of major entertainment firms were worth more than the market value of their shares.[4]

Was the valuation of film companies correct? The theory emerged from the Warner Communications buyback of its shares from Rupert Murdoch and a series of defensive maneuvers by the Disney Corporation. Even if those shares were undervalued, could the film companies have been obtained at a bargain price? Could the film libraries be sold at their estimated value?

Definitive answers to these and other questions are rarely available to managers of acquiring firms. The decision to acquire is therefore necessarily based on speculation. Like so many other aspects of human endeavor, in mergers it helps to be lucky.

We delegate corporate executives primary responsibility for the nation's economic decisions. They decide how to invest the capital of America. Mergers are one option. Acquisitions can provide a place to store excess earnings, an avenue to achieve personal ambitions, or a means to produce better products and services. The managers choose.

NOTES

PART I, INTRODUCTION

1. Tim Metz, "Mergers Expected to Stay Plentiful in 1983, but Will Be Less Exciting," *Wall Street Journal*, January 3, 1983, p. 5.
2. "Those Guns for Hire," *Time* (January 29, 1979): 44.

CHAPTER 1

1. W. T. Grimm & Co., *Mergerstat Review, 1982*, p. 49.
2. Judith H. McQuown, *Playing the Takeover Market* (New York: Seaview Books, 1982).
3. United States v. Chiarella, 445 U.S. 222, 224 (1980).
4. "Profits from Picking Merger Targets," *Business Week* (January 14, 1980): 101.
5. "Why Shell Bid So High For Tiny Belridge Oil," *Business Week* (October 15, 1979): 37–38.
6. Roy Rowan and Thomas Moore, "Behind the Lines in the Bendix War," *Fortune* (October 18, 1982): 156.
7. See, for example, Essex Universal Corp. v. Yates, 305 F.2d 572 (1962).
8. *In Re Caplan's Petition*, 20 A.D.2d 301 *aff'd men* 14 N.Y.2d 679 (1964).
9. "Roundtable: The Fine Art of Valuation," *Mergers and Acquisitions* 17 (Spring 1982): 28.
10. Martin Lipton, "Takeover Bids in the Target's Boardroom," *Business Lawyer* 35 (1979): 101.

CHAPTER 2

1. Duane Michals, "The Dealmakers," *Fortune* (January 24, 1983): 56.
2. "Roundtable: The Fine Art of Valuation," *Mergers and Acquisitions* 17 (Spring 1982): 25.
3. Stephen Adler, "First Boston's M & A Prodigy," *American Lawyer* (January 1983): 71.
4. Don Gussow, *The New Merger Game* (New York: AMACOM, 1978), pp. 115-16.
5. "How Inco's Cash Carried the Day," *Business Week* (August 3, 1974): 19-20.
6. Richard Phalon, *The Takeover Barons of Wall Street* (New York: Putnam, 1981).
7. Wellman v. Dickinson, 475 F. Supp. 783 (1979).
8. "Ira Harris: Chicago's Big Dealmaker," *Business Week* (June 25, 1979): 73.
9. Gary Hector, "Is Any Company Safe from Takeover?" *Fortune* (April 2, 1984): 20.
10. Robert Steyer, "Deals of the Year," *Fortune* (January 24, 1983): 48.
11. Adler, "First Boston's M & A Prodigy," p. 71.
12. Phalon, *The Takeover Barons*, p. 23.
13. Tim Metz, "Goldman Sachs Avoids Bitter Takeover Fights But Leads in Mergers," *Wall Street Journal*, December 3, 1982, p. 1.
14. Edward Meadows, "Deals of the Year," *Fortune* (January 25, 1982): 36.
15. Ibid.
16. Steven S. Anreder, "High Wire Finance: Leverage Buyouts Offer Plenty of Reward, Risk," *Barron's*, September 24, 1979, p. 4.
17. John D. Williams, "Forstman Little is Making a Name in the Leveraged-Buyout Business," *Wall Street Journal*, March 7, 1984, p. 33.
18. Meadows, "Deals of the Year," p. 40.
19. "Ira Harris," p. 74.
20. Ibid.
21. Peter W. Bernstein, "Profit Pressures On the Big Law Firms," *Fortune* (April 19, 1982): 91.
22. Martin Lipton and Erica Steinberger, *Takeovers and Freezeouts* (New York: Law Journal Seminars Press, 1979).
23. See Michael Keenan and Lawrence White (eds.), *Mergers and Acquisitions* (Lexington, Mass.: D.C. Heath and Co., 1982); and Wayne L. Boucher, *The Process of Conglomerate Mergers*, prepared for the Federal Trade Commission (June 1980).
24. Advisory Committee on Tender Offers, *Report of Recommendations*, U.S. Securities and Exchange Commission (Washington, D.C., July 8, 1983).
25. James C. Freund, *Anatomy of a Merger* (New York: Law Journal Seminars Press, 1975).

26. Stephen Axxin, Blaine Fogg, and Neal Stoll, *Acquisitions Under the Hart-Scott-Rodino Antitrust Improvement Act* (New York: Law Journal Seminars Press, 1979).

27. Bernstein, "Profit Pressures," p. 94.

28. Tim Metz, "Merger Masters: Outside Professionals Play an Increasing Role in Corporate Takeovers," *Wall Street Journal*, December 2, 1980, p. 1.

29. "Remit $20 Million," *Wall Street Journal*, August 19, 1981, p. 31.

30. Steven Brill, "Conoco: Great Plays and Errors in the Bar World Series," *American Lawyer* (November 1981): 47.

31. Bernstein, "Profit Pressures," p. 94.

32. Brill, "Conoco," p. 41.

33. Ibid.

34. Leslie Wayne, "The Corporate Raiders," *New York Times Magazine*, July 18, 1982, p. 51.

35. Texasgulf, Inc. v. Canadian Development Corp., 366 F. Supp. 374, 375 (1974).

36. Wellman v. Dickinson, 475 F. Supp. 783 (1979).

37. Racketeer Influenced and Corrupt Organizations Act: 18 U.S.C. §1961 *et seq.*

38. Brill, "Conoco," p. 41.

39. Mobil Corp. v. Marathon Oil Co., 669 F.2d 366 (1981). See also Paul Blustein and Dean Rotbart, "Court Rulings on U.S. Steel and Mobil May Change Merger Game, Slow Oil Takeovers," *Wall Street Journal*, January 7, 1982, p. 23.

40. Wayne, "The Corporation Raiders," p. 51.

41. Phalon, *The Takeover Barons.*

42. "PR Exec Specializes in 'Takeover' News," *Editor and Publisher* (August 23, 1980): 24.

43. Wellman v. Dickinson, 475 F. Supp. 783 (1979).

44. Louis Kraar, "Seagram's Sober System for Buying Big," *Fortune* (May 18, 1981): 57.

45. "Business Bulletin," *Wall Street Journal*, March 20, 1980, p. 1.

46. Daniel Hertzberg and Tim Metz, "Merger Boom Finds Bank Loans Plentiful," *Wall Street Journal*, July 14, 1981, p. 2.

47. Robert A. Bennett, "Chase and Citibank Help Raise Billions in Takeover Stakes," *New York Times*, July 14, 1981, p. D-6.

48. G. Christian Hill, "Lloyd's Offers U.S. Concerns Insurance for Costs of Fighting Takeovers," *Wall Street Journal*, May 12, 1980, p. 14; and Tim Metz, "Outside Professionals Play an Increasing Role in Corporate Takeovers," *Wall Street Journal*, December 2, 1980, p. 1.

49. Eleanor Johnson Tracy, "A Killing in Babcock & Wilcox," *Fortune* (October 1977): 266.

50. Margaret Laws, "Risk and Reward," *Barron's*, November 30, 1981, p. 9.

51. Priscilla S. Meyer, "Cancelled Poll of McGraw-Hill Holders Signals End to American Express Bid," *Wall Street Journal*, February 26, 1979, p. 11.

52. Lee Smith, "The High Rollers of First Boston," *Fortune* (September 6, 1982): 55.

53. "An Anxiety Attack over Delay in Gulf's Deal," *Business Week* (August 16, 1982): 27.

54. Richard Vilkin, "Advising Risk Arbitrageurs Challenges M & A Lawyers," *Legal Times of Washington*, June 1, 1981, p. 28.

55. "It was Click, Click, Click," *Fortune* (August 27, 1979): 13.

56. Tracy, "A Killing at Babcock & Wilcox," p. 269.

57. Mary Greenebaum, "Tips for Takeover Targets' Stockholders," *Fortune* (December 28, 1981): 109.

58. Robert J. Cole, "Arbitrage: What to do if Caught in Merger Battles," *Personal Investing* 83 (1961).

59. Meyer, "Cancelled Poll of McGraw-Hill Holders," p. 11.

60. Ibid.

61. Stanley Ginsberg, "Sitting Ducks," *Forbes* (April 14, 1980): 115.

62. Ibid.

63. Tim Metz, "Icahn's 'Scare 'em' Strategy Faces a Big Test in Fight Over Dan River," *Wall Street Journal*, November 17, 1982, p. 33.

64. Susie Gharib Nazem, "Marshall Field's Too Successful Strategy," *Fortune* (March 22, 1982): 81.

65. "Let Us Now Consider Carl Icahn," *Wall Street Journal*, December 22, 1983, p. 14.

66. Paul Blustein, Tim Carrington, and Tim Metz, "Takeover Tips," *Wall Street Journal*, February 13, 1981, p. 1.

67. Phalon, *The Takeover Barons*.

68. "Ex-Broker and Father all Barred by SEC from Insider Trading on Takeover Data," *Wall Street Journal*, February 23, 1981, p. 4.

69. "Former Navy Official Pleads Guilty to Trades of Stock on Inside Data," *Wall Street Journal*, September 7, 1982, p. 41.

70. Richard L. Hudson, "SEC Goes After Santa Fe Insiders But Light Penalties Draw Criticism," *Wall Street Journal*, November 23, 1982, p. 35.

71. Leslie Wayne, "Inside Trading by Outsiders," *New York Times*, May 27, 1984, p. C-1; Andy Pasztor, "Thayer Enters Plea of Guilty in Trading Cases," *Wall Street Journal*, March 5, 1985, p. 4.

72. Arthur Keown and John Pinkerton, "Merger Announcements and Insider Trading Activity: An Empirical Investigation," *Journal of Finance* 36 (1981): 855.

73. Securities and Exchange Act, Section 10(b), 15 U.S.C. §78; Rule 10b-5 (17 CFR 240.10b-5).

74. Rule 14e-3 (17 CFR 240.14e-3).

75. Hudson, "SEC Goes After Santa Fe Insiders."

76. Arthur M. Louis, "The Unwinnable War on Insider Trading," *Fortune* (July 13, 1981): 78.

77. Ibid.

78. Henry Manne, "Defense of Insider Trading," *Harvard Business Review* 44 (November/December 1966): 113.

79. Ibid.

CHAPTER 3

1. Samuel L. Hayes and Russell A. Taussig, "Tactics of Cash Takeover Bids," *Harvard Business Review* (March/April 1967): 135.

2. W. T. Grimm & Co., *Mergerstat Review, 1982*, pp. 50, 70, 71.

3. The Williams Act: 15 U.S.C. §§78m; 82 Stat. 454 (1968).

4. SEC Regulations 17 CFR 240 (1984).

5. Pro Rata Rule, Securities Exchange Act Release No. 34–19336, 47 Federal Register 57679 (December 28, 1982).

6. Eleanor Johnson Tracy, "A Killing in Babcock & Wilcox," *Fortune* (October 1977): 268.

7. Ibid.

8. Mobil Corp. v. Marathon Oil Co., 669 F.2d 366 (1981).

9. Ibid.

10. Hart-Scott-Rodino Antitrust Improvement Act of 1976: 90 Stat. 1383 (1976).

11. Third Annual Hart-Scott-Rodino Report of the Federal Trade Commission to Congress (1979).

12. Hayes and Taussig, "Tactics of Cash Takeover Bids," p. 143.

13. Klaus v. Hi-Shear Corporation, 528 F.2d 225 (1975).

14. Kenneth Labich, "How Jimmy Lee Let Gulf's Shareholders Win Big," *Fortune* (April 2, 1984): 23.

15. Matthew Josephson, *The Robber Barons* (New York: Harcourt, Brace & World, Inc., 1962), pp. 122–25.

16. Peter W. Bernstein, "A Company That's Worth More Dead than Alive," *Fortune* (February 26, 1979): 42.

17. Tracy, "A Killing in Babcock & Wilcox," p. 267.

18. Panter v. Marshall Field & Co., 486 F. Supp. 1168, 1194–5 (1980).

19. Stephen A. Hochman and Oscar D. Folger, "Deflecting Takeovers: Charter and By-Law Techniques," *Business Lawyer* 34 (1979): 537.

20. Edgar v. Mite Corp., 457 U.S. 624 (1982).

21. Paul Blustein, "More Companies Use 'the Lockup' to Ward off Unfriendly Takeovers," *Wall Street Journal*, January 28, 1981, p. 31.

22. Wienberger v. UOP Inc., 457 A.2d 701 (Delaware 1983).

23. Melvin A. Eisenberg, "The Legal Roles of Shareholders and Management in Modern Corporate Decision Making," *California Law Review* 57 (1969): 85–86.

24. Berwald v. Mission Development Co., 185 A.2d 480 (1962).
25. "A Fight No One Can Afford," *Business Week* (September 27, 1982): 99.
26. Singer v. Magnavox Co., 380 A.2d 969 (1977).
27. Ibid.

CHAPTER 4

1. John McDonald, *The Game of Business* (Garden City, N.Y.: Archor Press/ Doubleday, 1977), pp. 367–70.
2. Lee Smith, "The Making of the Megamerger," *Fortune* (September 7, 1981): 58.
3. Julie Salamon, "Staid Bank Trust Departments Jarred by Rapid-Fire Bids in War for Conoco," *Wall Street Journal*, August 3, 1981, p. 8.
4. Steven Brill, "Conoco: Great Plays and Errors in the Bar's World Series," *American Lawyer* (November 1981): 39.
5. Smith, "The Making of the Megamerger," p. 61.
6. Brill, "Conoco," p. 41.
7. Ibid.
8. Smith, "The Making of the Megamerger," p. 64.
9. Conoco Inc. v. Seagram Co., Ltd., 517 F. Supp. 1299, 1303 (1981).
10. Albert A. Foer, "Merger Wars," *Multinational Monitor* (January 1982): 9.
11. Tim Metz, "The Conoco Chase," *Wall Street Journal*, August 6, 1981, p. 1.
12. Quoted by Brill, "Conoco," p. 49.
13. Ibid.
14. Metz, "The Conoco Chase," p. 1.
15. "Du Pont: Straining to Pay the Price of its Conoco Victory," *Business Week* (May 10, 1982): 61.
16. Louis Kraar, "Seagram Tightens its Grip on Du Pont," *Fortune* (November 16, 1981): 78.
17. Dean Rotbart, "Marathon Oil Co. Stock Spurts 9.5% On Takeover Talks," *Wall Street Journal*, July 10, 1981, p. 2.
18. "Who's Next at the Altar," *Newsweek* (July 27, 1981): 54.
19. "Marathon Oil Directors Review Industry Mergers," *Wall Street Journal*, July 23, 1981, p. 2.
20. Henry F. Myers, "Mobil's Marathon Loss, Its Second in 6 Months, Is Tied to Its Blunders," *Wall Street Journal*, January 8, 1982, p. 1.
21. Ibid.
22. Paul Blustein and Dean Rotbart, "Court Rulings on U.S. Steel and Mobil may Change Merger Game, Slow Oil Takeovers," *Wall Street Journal*, January 7, 1982, p. 23.
23. Mobil Corp. v. Marathon Oil Co., 669 F.2d 366 (1981).
24. Blustein and Rotbart, "Court Rulings on U.S. Steel and Mobil," p. 23.
25. Paul Blustein, Stan Crock, and Mark Dodosh, "FTC Opposes Mobil Takeover of Marathon Oil," *Wall Street Journal*, December 9, 1981, p. 3.

26. Radol v. Thomas, 556 F. Supp. 586 (1983).

27. Hugh D. Menzies, "The Boardroom Battle at Bendix," *Fortune* (January 11, 1982): 54.

28. "RCA may be Run Out of Time," *Business Week* (March 22, 1982): 30.

29. Eleanor Johnson Tracy, "Unwelcome: Bendix's Pass at RCA," *Fortune* (April 5, 1982): 8.

30. Roy Rowan and Thomas Moore, "Behind the Lines in the Bendix War," *Fortune* (October 18, 1982): 158.

31. Connie Bruck, "Inside the Bendix Fiasco," *American Lawyer* (February 1983): 35.

32. Frank H. Menaker, "The Brass Ring," *The Advocate*, Washington College of Law, American University (Spring 1983): 7.

33. Ibid.

34. Ibid.

35. "Bendix Can only Profit from its Marietta Bid," *Business Week* (September 13, 1982): 37.

36. John Koten and John D. Williams, "Bendix-Martin Marietta Battle Pits Resolved Agee Against Shrewd Gray," *Wall Street Journal*, September 9, 1982, p. 29.

37. Bruck, "Inside the Bendix Fiasco."

38. Ibid.

39. Thomas C. Schelling, *The Strategy of Conflict* (Cambridge, Mass.: Harvard University Press, 1960), p. 24.

40. Rowan and Moore, "Behind the Lines," p. 158.

41. Rowan and Moore, "Behind the Lines," and Bruck, "Inside the Bendix Fiasco."

42. Martin Marietta Corp. v. Bendix Corp., 549 F. Supp. 623, 633 (1982).

43. Robert Steyer, "Deals of the Year," *Fortune* (January 24, 1983): 48.

44. See, for example, Barnaby J. Feder, "For Allied, Gains May Take Time," *New York Times*, September 27, 1982, p. D-1; John Holusha, "New Roles for Bendix and Agee," *New York Times*, September 27, 1982, p. D-1; Peter Behr and Mark Potts, "Agee and the Prospect of Defeat," *Washington Post*, September 12, 1982, p. H-1; and Mark Potts, "The Clash of the Corporate Titans," *Washington Post*, September 26, 1982, p. G-1.

CHAPTER 5

1. Albert A. Foer, "Merger Wars," *Multinational Monitor* (January 1982): 9.

2. Greyhound's bus transportation revenues in 1981 accounted for $1 billion out of a total of $5 billion in annual earnings (*Moody's Transportation Manual [1982]*, p. 2,059).

3. Rush Loving, Jr., "The Penn Central Bankruptcy Express," *Fortune* (August 1970): 104.

4. Betsy Morris and Marj Charlier, "Esmark Accepts Sweetened Beatrice Bid; Option is given for Swift/Hunt-Wesson," *Wall Street Journal*, May 25, 1984, p. 3.
5. Sherman Antitrust Act: 15 U.S.C. §1 *et seq.* (1890).
6. Congressional Record, Vol. 21, p. 2,457 (1890).
7. Ibid., p. 2,460.
8. Richard Hofstadter, "What Happened to the Antitrust Movement," in *The Paranoid Style of American Politics* (New York: Alfred A. Knopf, 1965), p. 196.
9. Matthew Josephson, *The Robber Barons* (New York: Harcourt, Brace & World, Inc., 1962), p. 118–19.
10. Robert H. Lande, "Wealth Transfers as the Original and Primary Concern of Antitrust: The Efficiency Interpretation Challenged," *Hastings Law Journal* 34 (1982): 65.
11. See Richard Hofstadter, *The Age of Reform* (New York: Random House, 1955); William Letwin, *Law and Economic Policy in America* (New York: Random House, 1965); and Hans Thorelli, *Federal Antitrust Policy* (Baltimore: Johns Hopkins Press, 1955).
12. Lande, "Wealth Transfers," p. 99.
13. Congressional Record, Vol. 21, p. 4,100 (1890).
14. Ibid., p. 3,146.
15. Gabriel Kolko, *The Triumph of Conservatism* (1963).
16. Hofstadter, "What Happened to the Antitrust Movement," p. 197.
17. Clayton Antitrust Act: 15 U.S.C. §12 *et seq.* (1914).
18. Federal Trade Commission Act: 15 U.S.C. §42 *et seq.* (1914).
19. Federal Trade Commission v. Western Meat Co., 272 U.S. 554 (1926).
20. Brown Shoe Co. v. United States, 370 U.S. 294, 314 (1962).
21. Richard Hofstadter, *The Age of Reform* (1955), p. 227.
22. See Federal Trade Commission v. Eastman Kodak, 274 U.S. 619 (1927), and Arrow-Hart & Hegemen Electric Co. v. Federal Trade Commission, 291 U.S. 587 (1934).
23. Louis Galambos, *The Public Image of Big Business in America, 1880–1940* (Baltimore: Johns Hopkins University Press, 1975), p. 264.
24. Celler-Kefauver Act of 1950: 64 Stat. 1,125 (1950).
25. Congressional Record, Vol. 95, p. 11,486 (1949).
26. Congressional Record, Vol. 96, p. 16,452 (1950).
27. *FTC Report on the Merger Movement: A Summary Report* V (1968), p. 68.
28. 370 U.S. 294 (1962).
29. Ibid., p. 315.
30. Ibid., pp. 317–18.
31. Ibid., p. 317.
32. Ibid., pp. 320–21.

33. United States v. Von's Grocery Co., 384 U.S. 270 (1966).

34. F. M. Scherer, *Industrial Market Structure and Economic Performance* (Boston: Houghton Mifflin, 1980), p. 124.

35. *Final Report and Recommendations of the Temporary National Economic Committee*, S. Doc. No. 35, 77th Cong., 1st session, 38 (1941).

36. Hofstadter, "What Happened to the Antitrust Movement," p. 233.

37. 370 U.S. 294, 323 (1962).

38. Derek C. Bok, "Section 7 of the Clayton Act and the Merging of Law and Economics," *Harvard Law Review* 74 (1960): 226.

39. *Task Force on Antitrust Policy Report (The Neal Report)*, reprinted in *BNA Antitrust and Trade Regulation Report*, No. 411 (May 27, 1969), part 2.

40. U.S. Department of Justice, "Merger Guidelines," Paragraph 3 (May 1968).

41. Ernst F. Schumacher, *Small Is Beautiful* (New York: Harper & Row, 1975).

42. *Task Force on Productivity and Competition*, reprinted in *BNA Antitrust and Trade Regulation Report*, No. 413 (June 10, 1969), pp. X1-X8.

43. *The Neal Report*, p. 6.

44. Joseph Bain, *Barriers to New Competition* (Cambridge, Mass.: Harvard University Press, 1956), and Bain, *Industrial Organization* (New York: John Wiley & Sons, 1968).

45. Richard Posner, "The Chicago School of Antitrust Analysis," *University of Pennsylvania Law Review* 127 (1979): 925.

46. Conference at Airlie House, Virginia: Harvey J. Goldschmid et al. (eds), *Industrial Concentration: The New Learning* (Boston: Little, Brown & Co., 1974).

47. Herbert Simon, *Administrative Behavior: A Study of Decisionmaking Processes in Administrative Organizations*, 3rd ed. (New York: The Free Press, 1976).

48. Robert H. Bork, "Legislative Intent and the Policy of the Sherman Act," *Journal of Law and Economics* 9 (1966): 7.

49. Robert H. Bork, *The Antitrust Paradox: A Policy at War with Itself* (New York: Basic Books, 1978).

50. Carl Kaysen and Donald F. Turner, *Antitrust Policy* (Cambridge, Mass.: Harvard University Press, 1960).

51. Phillip Areeda and Donald F. Turner, *Antitrust Law: Analysis of Antitrust Principles and Their Applications*, Vol. 1 (Boston: Little, Brown & Co., 1978), p. 23.

52. William Baxter, "How Government Cases Get Selected—Comments from Academe," *Antitrust Law Journal* 46 (1977): 588.

53. Richard A. Posner, "The Chicago School of Antitrust Analysis," *University of Pennsylvania Law Review* 127 (1979): 925.

54. Robert Pitofsky, "The Political Content of Antitrust," *University of Pennsylvania Law Review* 127 (1979): 1,051.

55. Robert Lande, "A Cost-Benefit Analysis of Electric Peakloan Pricing," *Public Utilities Fortnightly* 103 (1979): 9.

56. Lande, "Wealth Transfers."

57. Robert H. Lande and Alan A. Fisher, "Efficiency Considerations in Merger Enforcement," *California Law Review* 71 (1983): 1,580.

58. Robert Harris and Thomas Jorde, "Antitrust Market Definition: An Integrated Approach," *California Law Review* 72 (1983).

59. Michael Isikoff, "FTC Shifting Antitrust From Big Business to Novel Areas," *Washington Post*, June 18, 1984, p. G–1.

60. U.S. Department of Justice, *Merger Guidelines*, 47 Fed. Reg. 28493 (1982).

61. Paul Blustein, Stan Crock, and Mark Dodosh, "FTC Opposes Mobil Takeover of Marathon Oil," *Wall Street Journal*, December 9, 1981, p. 3.

62. Hency C. Simons, *Economic Policy for a Free Society* (Chicago: University of Chicago Press, 1948).

63. Ibid.

64. George Stigler, "The Case Against Big Business," *Fortune* (May 1952): 123.

65. Milton Friedman, *Capitalism and Freedom* (Chicago: University of Chicago Press, 1962).

66. See Lawrence Sullivan, "Antitrust, Microeconomics and Politics: Reflections on Some Recent Relationships," *California Law Review* 68 (1980): 1; Joseph Brodley, "Potential Competition Mergers: A Structural Synthesis," *Yale Law Journal* 87 (1977): 1; Brodley, "Limiting Conglomerate Mergers: The Need for Legislation," *Ohio State Law Journal* 40 (1979): 867; John Flynn, "Introduction, Antitrust Jurisprudence: A Symposium on the Economic, Political and Social Goals of Antitrust Policy," *University of Pennsylvania Law Review* 125 (1977): 1,182; Eleanor Fox, "Antitrust, Mergers, and the Supreme Court: The Politics of Section 7 of the Clayton Act," *Mercer Law Review* 26 (1975): 389; Fox, "The Modernization of Antitrust: A New Equilibrium," *Cornell Law Review* 66 (1981): 1,140; Louis Schwartz, "On the Uses of Economics: A Review of the Antitrust Treatises," *University of Pennsylvania Law Review* 128 (1979): 244; and Schwartz, "Justice and Other Non-Economic Goals of Antitrust," *University of Pennsylvania Law Review* 127 (1979): 1,076.

CHAPTER 6

1. Alfred D. Chandler, *The Visible Hand: The Managerial Revolution in American Business* (Cambridge, Mass: Belknap Press, 1977), p. 249.

2. Alfred D. Chandler, "The Coming of Oligopoly and its Meaning for Antitrust," in *National Competition Policy: Historian's Perspectives on Anti-*

trust and Government Business Relationships in U.S., FTC Publication (August 1981), p. 72.

3. Chandler, *The Visible Hand*, pp. 106–107.
4. Ibid.
5. Samuel Richardson Reid, *Merger, Managers and the Economy* (New York: McGraw-Hill, 1968), p. 46.
6. Chandler, "The Coming of Oligopoly," p. 73.
7. Ibid.
8. Matthew Josephson, *The Robber Barons* (New York: Harcourt, Brace & World, Inc., 1962), p. 429.
9. Jesse W. Markham, "Survey of the Evidence and Findings on Mergers," in *Business Concentration and Price Policy* (Princeton: Princeton University Press, 1955), pp. 163, 181.
10. Ibid., p. 152.
11. Chandler, "The Coming of Oligopoly," p. 923.
12. Markham, "Survey of the Evidence and Findings on Mergers," p. 166.
13. Frederick Lewis Allen, *Only Yesterday* (New York: Bantam, 1959), p. 205.
14. *Mergers in Industry: A Study of Certain Aspects of Industrial Concentration* (New York: National Industrial Conference Board, Inc., 1929).
15. Reid, *Mergers, Managers and the Economy*, pp. 63–64.
16. George J. Stigler, "Monopoly and Oligopoly by Merger," *American Economic Review* 40 (May 1950): 31.
17. Markham, "Survey of the Evidence and Findings on Mergers," p. 171.
18. Ibid., p. 181.
19. Peter O. Steiner, *Mergers: Motives, Effects, Policies* (Ann Arbor: University of Michigan Press, 1975), pp. 206–207.
20. Ibid., Table 1–3, p. 14.
21. Ibid., Table 5–2, p. 104.
22. Lewis Beman, "What We Learned From the Great Merger Frenzy," *Fortune* (April 1973): 70.

PART III, INTRODUCTION

1. Willard Carlton, Robert Harris, and John Steward, "An Empirical Study of Merger Motives," prepared for the Federal Trade Commission (December 1980).
2. Wayne L. Boucher, "The Process of Conglomerate Mergers," prepared for the Federal Trade Commission (June 1980).

CHAPTER 7

1. Alfred Chandler, *The Visible Hand: The Managerial Revolution in American Business* (Cambridge, Mass.: Belknap Press, 1977), pp. 415–500.
2. Ibid., p. 387.

3. Dodge v. Ford Motor Co., 204 Mich. 459 (1919).

4. IRS Regulations, §1.537 2(b)(2).

5. Lester C. Thurow, *Dangerous Currents: The State of Economics* (New York: Random House, 1983), p. 147.

6. Digital Equipment Corporation, *Annual Reports* (1976, 1979, 1982).

7. Michael E. Porter, *Competitive Strategy: Techniques for Analyzing Industries and Competitors* (New York: McGraw-Hill, 1980), p. 91.

8. Robert H. Miles, *Coffin Nails and Corporate Strategies* (Englewood Cliffs, N.J.: Prentice-Hall, 1982).

9. *Moody's Industrial Manual* (1983), p. 3,318.

10. Shawn Tully, "The Man Who Scored Coca-Columbia," *Fortune* (February 22, 1982): 73.

11. "Seagram Acquires Wine Spectrum," *New York Times*, November 8, 1983, p. D-4.

12. Robert A. Bennett, "A Bank, By Any Other Name . . . ," *New York Times*, December 27, 1981, p. III-1.

13. Urban C. Lehner and Laurie P. Cohen, "GM to Acquire EDS in Transaction Valued at as Much as $2.55 Billion," *Wall Street Journal*, June 29, 1984, p. 3.

14. Ibid.

15. Bayless Manning, "Book Review: The American Stockholder," *Yale Law Journal*, Vol. 67 (1958), p. 1,477.

16. Milton Friedman, *Capitalism and Freedom* (Chicago: University of Chicago Press, 1963), p. 130; and Bruce D. Henderson, *Henderson on Corporate Strategy* (Cambridge, Mass.: Belknap Press, 1979).

17. *Penn Central Annual Reports*, for years listed.

18. Jeremy Main, "Help and Hype in the New Products Game," *Fortune* (February 7, 1983): 60.

19. Vivienne Marquis and Patricia Haskell, *The Cheese Book* (New York: Simon and Schuster, 1965), pp. 23-24.

20. Miles, *Coffin Nails*.

21. Douglas Martin, "The Singular Power of a Giant Called Exxon," *New York Times*, May 9, 1982, p. III-1.

22. Lewis Beman, "Exxon's $600 Million Mistake," *Fortune* (October 19, 1981): 68.

23. "The $250 Million Disaster that Hit RCA," *Business Week* (September 25, 1971): 34.

24. John Koten and Laura Landro, "Bendix's Surprise Purchase of RCA, Stake May Pay Off Handsomely, Observers Say," *Wall Street Journal*, March 10, 1982, p. 2.

25. Ronald Alsop, "Du Pont Uses Innovative Methods in Struggle to Reduce Huge Debt," *Wall Street Journal*, November 26, 1982, p. 15; and Irwin

Ross, "How the Champs do Leveraged Buyouts," *Fortune* (January 23, 1984), p. 78.

26. Eleanor Johnson Tracy, "A Killing in Babcock & Wilcox," *Fortune* (October 1977): 266.

27. "Hiram Walker, Sheltering Its Liquor Income in Oil Exploration," *Business Week* (September 15, 1980): 80.

28. Robert J. Samuelson, "Can Any Good Come from Merger Turmoil?" *Washington Post*, June 20, 1984, p. F-1.

29. "How America's Top Moneymakers Fared in the Recession," *Business Week* (May 9, 1983): 84.

30. John Kenneth Galbraith, *Economics and the Public Purpose* (Boston: Houghton Mifflin, 1973), pp. 113-14.

31. Dale D. Buss, "UAW Endorses Rouge Steel Pact on Concessions," *Wall Street Journal*, September 19, 1983, p. 2.

32. Bryan Burrough, "Continental Air Official saw Chapter II as 'stock' Against Unions," *Wall Street Journal*, December 14, 1983, p. 10.

33. "How America's Top Moneymakers Fared," p. 84; and "Intel Engineers Resign to Design Own Company," *Wall Street Journal*, January 19, 1983, p. 20.

34. Wellman v. Dickinson, 475 F. Supp 804 (1979).

35. Richmond Television Corp. v. United States, 345 F.2d 907 (1965).

CHAPTER 8

1. Bruce D. Henderson, *Henderson on Corporate Strategy* (Cambridge, Mass.: Belknap Press, 1979).

2. Ibid., pp. 164-66.

3. "Managers who are no Longer Entrepreneurs," *Business Week* (June 30, 1980): 78.

4. Ibid.

5. Robert H. Miles, *Coffin Nails and Corporate Strategies* (Englewood Cliffs, N.J.: Prentice-Hall, 1982).

6. "Hiram Walker: Sheltering Its Liquor Income on Oil Exploration," *Business Week* (September 15, 1980): 80.

7. "An Oil Hangover for Hiram Walker," *Business Week* (February 22, 1982): 50.

8. Edward Morrison, "An Introduction to Four Business Strategy Models," in Edward Morrison and Richard Craswell, *Papers on Business Strategy and Antitrust*, Federal Trade Commission (September 1980), pp. 45-46.

9. Raymond Prescott, "Law of Growth in Forecasting Demand," *Journal of American Statistical Association* 18 (December 1922): 471.

10. Henderson, *Henderson on Corporate Strategy*, p. 82.

11. Ibid., p. 83.

12. See, for example, William J. Baumol et al., "Earnings Retention, New Capital and the Growth of the Firm," *Review of Economics and Statistics* 52 (November 1970): 345; and Henry G. Grabowski and Dennis C. Mueller, "Life-Cycle Effects on Corporate Returns on Retentions," *Review of Economics and Statistics* 57 (1975): 400.

13. Morrison, "Introduction to Four Business Strategy Models."

14. Kenneth R. Andrews, *The Concept of Corporate Strategy* (Homewood, Ill.: R. P. Irwin, 1971); and Michael E. Porter, *Competitive Strategy* (New York: The Free Press, 1980).

15. Henderson, *Henderson on Corporate Strategy*, p. 82.

16. F. M. Scherer, *Industrial Market Structure and Economic Performance* (Boston: Houghton Mifflin, 1980), p. 83.

17. "Worth It," *Forbes* (September 15, 1975): 24–25.

18. Robert Buzzell, Bradley Gale, and Ralph Sultan, "Market Share—A Key to Profitability," *Harvard Business Review* (January/February 1975): 98.

19. Lynn Adkins, "Don't Blame the System, Blame the Managers," *Dun's Review* (September 1980): 82.

20. William J. Abernathy and Robert H. Hayes, "Management Minus Invention," *New York Times*, August 20, 1980, p. D-2.

21. "Capitalism: Is it Working?" *Time* (April 21, 1980): 40.

22. "An Economic Dream in Peril," *Newsweek* (September 8, 1980): 50.

23. "Revitalizing the U.S. Economy," *Business Week* (June 30, 1980): 56.

24. Buzzell, Gale, and Sultan, "Market Share," p. 98.

25. John McDonald, *The Game of Business* (Garden City, N.Y.: Anchor Press/Doubleday, 1977), pp. 32–69.

26. Anne B. Fisher, "Winners (and Losers) from IBM's PC Jr.," *Fortune* (November 28, 1983): 44.

27. Robert Buzzell, "Are there 'Natural' Market Structures?" *Journal of Marketing* 45 (Winter 1981): 42.

28. Ibid.

29. William K. Hall, "Survival Strategies in a Hostile Environment," *Harvard Business Review* (September/October 1980): 75.

30. "For Executives of the 1980s, A Stress on Return," *Business Week* (June 1, 1981): 88.

31. Nariman K. Dhalla and Sonia Yuspeh, "Forget the Product Life Cycle Concept," *Harvard Business Review* (January/February 1976): 102.

32. Richard G. Hamermesh, M. Jack Anderson, and J. Elizabeth Harris, "Strategies for Low Market Share Businesses," *Harvard Business Review* (May/June 1978): 95.

33. Richard G. Hamermesh and Steven B. Silk, "How to Compete in Stagnant Industries," *Harvard Business Review* (September/October 1979): 161.

34. A. F. Hussey, "General Foods Perks Away: New Producers Help Push Earnings Toward $5.25 a Share," *Barron's*, August 20, 1979, pp. 39–40.

35. "An Onrush of Mopeds," *Business Week* (June 20, 1977): 33.

36. Hall, "Survival Strategies."

37. Theodore Levitt, "Marketing Myopia," *Harvard Business Review* (July/August 1960): 45.

38. Thomas J. Peters and Robert H. Waterman, Jr., *In Search of Excellence* (New York: Harper & Row, 1982).

39. Ibid., pp. 193–195.

40. "Caterpillar: Sticking to Basics to Stay Competitive," *Business Week* (May 4, 1981): 74.

41. "Corporate Culture," *Business Week* (October 27, 1980): 148.

42. Miles, *Coffin Nails and Corporate Strategies.*

43. Malcolm S. Salter and Wolf A. Weinhold, *Diversification through Acquisition* (New York: The Free Press, 1979), p. 138.

44. Peter F. Drucker, *Technology, Management and Society* (New York: Harper Colophon, 1970), pp. 95–96.

45. Salter and Weinhold, *Diversification through Acquisition*, p. 22.

46. James Brian Quinn, "Formulating Strategy One Step at a Time," *Journal of Business Strategy* (Winter 1981): 42.

CHAPTER 9

1. Malcolm S. Salter and Wolf A. Weinhold, *Diversification through Acquisition* (New York: The Free Press, 1979), p. 138.

2. "Firm Says Authors Miffed By a Possible Takeover," *Wall Street Journal*, April 19, 1978, p. 22.

3. Sanford Rose, "The Stock Market Should be Twice as High As It Is," *Fortune* (March 12, 1979): 138.

4. "Inside Wall Street: Bargains that are Better Dead Than Alive," *Business Week* (July 12, 1982): 68.

5. Peter W. Bernstein, "A Company That's Worth More Dead Than Alive," *Fortune* (February 26, 1979): 42.

6. John Quirt, "The Man Who Collects Companies," *Fortune* (March 26, 1979): 81.

7. "Did Con Agra Bite Off More Than It Can Chew?" *Business Week* (May 3, 1982): 35.

8. "An Antitrust About-Face on Republic and LTV," *Business Week* (April 2, 1984): 31-32; and Peter Behr, "LTV Seeks to Acquire Republic Steel," *Washington Post*, September 29, 1983, p. A–17.

9. Ibid.

10. Ibid.

11. "Deluxe Check Printers: Electronic Banking Pushes it Into Business Forms," *Business Week* (September 6, 1982): 103–104.

12. See statement of Dr. Willard F. Mueller, *Hearings on Acquisitions and Mergers by Conglomerates*, before the Senate Judiciary Committee, 95th

Congress, 2nd Sess., May 12, July 27, July 28, and September 21, 1978, pp. 85–91; and statement of Paul De Lima, *Hearings on S.600*, before the Senate Judiciary Committee, 96th Congress, 1st Sess., March/April 1979, part 1, pp. 345–52.

13. "Distillers Must Cope with a Sobering Future," *Business Week* (May 2, 1983): 112.

14. "Paper Mate's Broader Outlook," *Business Week* (January 28, 1980): 69.

15. Ann M. Morrison, "Cookies are Frito-Lays New Bag," *Fortune* (August 9, 1982): 66.

16. "Roy Rogers Trots to a Gallop: Gino's Purchase and New Advertising are Keys to Growth Strategy," *Restaurant & Institutions* (May 15, 1982): 4.

17. Ann M. Morrison, "Betting the Barn at Stroh," *Fortune* (May 31, 1982): 121.

18. Peter W. Bernstein, "Who Buys Corporate Losers?" *Fortune* (January 26, 1981): 61–62.

19. "Harry J. Gray: Thoughts on Acquisitions," *Financier* (November 1978): 36–37.

20. Tax Reform Act of 1969: 83 Stat. 487.

21. "KMS's Stormy Return to Mergers," *Business Week* (July 14, 1980): 84.

22. "Acquisitions: A Grocery Giant's Sunbelt Strategy," *Business Week* (March 1, 1982): 23.

23. Economic Recovery Tax Act of 1981: 95 Stat. 172.

24. Hall, Inc. v. Ryder Systems, Inc., No. 82 C–0092, N.D. Ill. (1981).

25. Bank Holding Companies Act: U.S.C. §1841, *et seq.*

26. Geoffrey Colvin, "The Smart Taxophobe at Baldwin-United," *Fortune* (March 8, 1982): 58.

27. Salter and Weinhold, *Diversification through Acquisition*, p. 106.

28. "In the News: Getting Away From the EPA," *Fortune* (April 9, 1979): 15.

29. "Borg-Warner: Expanding into Services is Helping to Beat the Recession," *Business Week* (August 16, 1982): 74.

30. "The Man Behind Kraft's Merger," *Business Week* (August 25, 1980): 76.

31. Wayne I. Boucher, *The Process of Conglomerate Mergers*, prepared for the Federal Trade Commission (June 1980), p. 35.

CHAPTER 10

1. Anne B. Fisher, "The Decade's Worst Mergers," *Fortune* (April 30, 1984): 270.

2. Roy Rowan, "Those Business Hunches are More than Blind Faith," *Fortune* (April 23, 1979): 110.

3. "Boss Productivity," *Wall Street Journal*, August 18, 1981, p. 1.

4. Wayne I. Boucher, *The Process of Conglomerate Merger*, prepared for the Federal Trade Commission (June 1980), p. 27.

5. Ibid., p. 124.

6. Edward Meadows, "Deals of the Year," *Fortune* (January 25, 1962): 36.

7. Boucher, *The Process of Conglomerate Merger*, p. 27.

8. Ibid., p. 12.

9. Ibid.

10. Ibid., p. 13.

11. Ibid., p. 12.

12. Ibid., p. 70.

13. Herbert Simon, "The Compensation of Executives," *Sociometry* (March 1957): 32.

14. Boucher, *The Process of Conglomerate Merger*, pp. 59–60.

15. David Reisman, *The Lonely Crowd* (New York: Yale University Press, 1950).

16. William H. White, Jr., *The Organization Man* (New York: Simon and Schuster, 1956).

17. "Organization Men Still Run the Show," *Newsweek* (June 18, 1979): 75.

18. Christopher Jencks, *Inequality* (New York: Basic Books, 1972).

19. Frank Allen, "Chief Executives Say Job Requires Many Personal and Family Sacrifices," *Wall Street Journal*, August 20, 1980, p. 21.

20. Boucher, *The Process of Conglomerate Merger*, p. 29.

21. Steven Brill, "Conoco: Great Plays and Errors in the Bar's World Series," *American Lawyer* (November 1981): 44.

22. Ibid., p. 46.

23. "Business as Usual," *The Economist* (January 31, 1981): 14–15; and Merrill Brown and Michael Schrage, "Two Adversaries: Proud, Self-Made and Different," *Washington Post*, February 12, 1984, p. G–1.

CHAPTER 11

1. Bruce Jacobs, "Holding Merger Maniacs at Bay," *Industry Week* (June 27, 1983): 24.

2. Jean Jacques Servan-Schreiber, *American Challenge* (New York: Athemeum, 1968).

3. W. T. Grimm & Co., *Mergerstat Review, 1982*, pp. 70–71.

4. *Moody's Industrial Manual* (1983), pp. 3,268, 3,318.

5. Agis Salpukas, "Decontrol's Bus Line Impact," *New York Times*, December 29, 1983, p. D–1.

6. "What the National Merger Did to Pan Am," *Business Week* (June 22, 1981): 86–88.

7. Richard B. Schmitt, "Braniff Filing Shows Unsecured Creditors Face Major Losses if Reorganization Fails," *Wall Street Journal*, July 6, 1982, p. 2; "Continental Air Seen Readying Plan to Cut $100 Million Costs," *Wall Street Journal*, January 18, 1982, p. 2; and Margaret Loeb, "Outlook for Eastern Air Appears Brighter Despite $34.4 Million Net Loss for Quarter," *Wall Street Journal*, October 10, 1983, p. 8.

8. "Stockholder Meeting Briefs," *Wall Street Journal*, October 12, 1979, p. 39; and "Pan Am to Sell New York Offices for $400 Million," *Wall Street Journal*, July 29, 1980, p. 3.

9. Howard Rudnitsky, "Done," *Forbes* (January 31, 1983): 90.

10. Robert Steyer, "Deals of the Year," *Fortune* (January 24, 1983): 48.

11. Ibid.

12. Bill Paul and Marilyn Chase, "Santa Fe, Southern Pacific Set Merger Valued at $5.2 Billion," *Wall Street Journal*, September 28, 1983, p. 3.

13. Agis Salpukas, "CSX Plans Close Look at Conrail," *New York Times*, January 12, 1984, p. D-1.

14. Staggers Rail Act of 1980: 84 Stat. 1,897.

15. "The Pacrail Decision, New Ground Rules for Mergers," *Railway Age* (November 29, 1982): 10.

16. *Standard & Poor's Industry Analysis* (July 1983): R16.

17. Ibid., p. R15.

18. Daniel P. Wiener, "Deals of the Year," *Fortune* (January 23, 1984): 55.

19. Urban C. Lehner and Laurie P. Cohen, "GM to Acquire EDS in Transaction Valued at as Much as $2.55 Billion," *Wall Street Journal*, June 29, 1984, p. 3.

20. "RCA Says Sales, Profits Continued High Pace in April—Acquisition of Hertz Voted," *Wall Street Journal*, May 3, 1967, p. 1; and Scott R. Schmedel and Priscilla S. Meyer, "RCA Corp. Set to Acquire CIT for $1.35 Billion," *Wall Street Journal*, August 20, 1979, p. 3.

21. "Motorola's New Strategy: Adding Computers to its Base in Electronics," *Business Week* (March 29, 1982): 128.

22. "Distillers Must Cope with a Sobering Future," *Business Week* (May 2, 1983): 110; and Norman A. Berg and Charles W. Hofer, *Heublein, Inc.*, Harvard Business School, 9-373-103 (Boston: Intercollegiate Case Clearing House, 1972), pp. 3, 4, 6.

23. "Seagram Acquires Wine Spectrum," *New York Times*, November 8, 1983, p. D-4.

24. W. T. Grimm & Co., *Mergerstat Review, 1982*.

25. Ibid., pp. 50, 71.

26. Louis Kraar, "Seagram's Sober System for Buying Big," *Fortune* (May 18, 1981): 57.

27. Peter W. Bernstein, "The Hennessy Hurricane Whips Through Allied Chemical," *Fortune* (December 17, 1979): 98.

28. A. F. Ehrbar, "Corporate Takeovers are Here to Stay," *Fortune* (May 8, 1978): 91.

29. W. T. Grimm & Co., *Mergerstat Review, 1982*, pp. 70-71.

30. "Carrier, United Technologies Set Terms for Merger," *Wall Street Journal*, April 2, 1979, p. 22.

31. W. T. Grimm & Co., Press Release, January 12, 1984.
32. Eleanor Johnson Tracy, "A Killing in Babcock & Wilcox," *Fortune* (October 1977): 268.
33. "Multicompanies," *Forbes* (January 8, 1979): 238.
34. "Against Forced Takeovers," *New York Times*, January 22, 1978, p. IV-19.
35. William L. Cary, "When Firms Merge," *New York Times*, June 23, 1978, p. A-25.
36. See *Hearings before the Senate Judiciary Committee on S.600*, 96th Cong., 1st Sess., March/April 1979, part 2, p. 471.
37. Paul A. Samuelson, "Kennedy's Antimerger Initiative," *Newsweek* (September 3, 1979): 56.
38. Phillip Areeda, "Kennedy's Anti-Oil Bill," *Wall Street Journal*, August 6, 1979, p. 10.
39. "Having it Both Ways on Mergers," *New York Times*, August 31, 1979, p. A-22.
40. W. T. Grimm & Co., *Mergerstat Review, 1982*, pp. 6-10, and Press Release, January 31, 1985.
41. W. T. Grimm & Co., Press Release, January 12, 1984, p. 1.
42. W. T. Grimm & Co., Press Release, January 31, 1985.
43. Ibid.

CHAPTER 12

1. *Fortune Double 500 Directory* (1978).
2. William Greider, "U.S. Oil Industry Stakes Out Role for the Future," *Washington Post*, May 22, 1977, p. 1.
3. *Keystone Coal Industry Manual* (1977).
4. Ibid.
5. "The New Diversification Oil Game," *Business Week* (April 24, 1978): 78.
6. *Hearings before the Senate Judiciary Committee on S.1245*, 96th Cong., 1st Sess., March/April 1979, Serial No. 96-29, part 1, p. 191.
7. Ibid., testimony of Duane Chapman, pp. 426, 430.
8. *Mergers in the Petroleum Industry*, Federal Trade Commission Report (September 1982), p. 82.
9. *Hearings before the Senate Judiciary Committee on S.1245*, testimony of Alfred F. Dougherty, Jr., p. 234.
10. "The New Diversification Oil Game."
11. Allan Sloan, "Mobil's Monkey," *Forbes* (June 11, 1979): 41.
12. "The New Diversification Oil Game," p. 76.
13. H. Menzies, "Why Sun is Educating Itself Out of Oil," *Fortune* (February 27, 1978): 42.
14. Ibid., p. 43.

15. "The New Diversification Oil Game," pp. 76–77.
16. John McDonald, *The Game of Business* (Garden City, N.Y.: Anchor Press/ Doubleday, 1975).
17. *Mergers in the Petroleum Industry*, p. 52.
18. *Hearings before Senate Judiciary Committee on S.1245*, statement of Kathleen O'Reilly, p. 189.
19. "Why Shell Bid so High for Tiny Belridge," *Business Week* (October 15, 1979): 37.
20. Paul Blustein, "Big Oil Finds Outlets Limited," *Wall Street Journal*, April 9, 1980, p. 1.
21. Charles F. McCoy and G. Christian Hill, "Pickens Likely to go Hunting with Gulf Profits," *Wall Street Journal*, March 7, 1984, p. 22.
22. "Leading Deals and Deal Makers in the First Half of This Year," *New York Times*, July 3, 1984, p. D–6.
23. Agis Salpukas, "Texaco to Buy Its Stock Back," *New York Times*, March 7, 1984, p. D–1.
24. Steven Brill, "Getty Games," *American Lawyer* (March 1981): 1.
25. Steven Greenhouse, "An Unsettling Shift in Big Oil," *New York Times*, March 11, 1984, p. III–1.
26. Ibid.
27. J. Ernest Beazley and Doron Levin, "Gulf's Failure to Take Bold Defensive Steps Set It Up for Takeover," *Wall Street Journal*, March 7, 1984, p. 1.
28. Kenneth Labich, "How Jimmy Lee Let Gulf's Shareholders Win Big," *Fortune* (April 2, 1984): 23.
29. Bill Abrams, "Metromedia Inc.'s Holders Approve $1.13 Billion Buyout," *Wall Street Journal*, June 21, 1984, p. 20; and Irwin Ross, "How the Champs Do Leveraged Buyouts," *Fortune* (January 23, 1984): 70.
30. "Texaco's Bid for Getty, A Record $9.89 Billion, Belies its Stodgy Image," *Wall Street Journal*, January 9, 1984, p. 1.

CHAPTER 13

1. The Glass-Steagall Act of 1933, 48 Stat. 162.
2. Harvey L. Pitt and Julie L. Williams, "The Glass-Steagall Act: Key issues for the Future of the Financial Industry, *Securities Regulation Law Journal* 11 (1983): 235–6.
3. *The Dow Jones-Irwin Business and Investment Almanac* (Homewood, Ill.: Dow Jones-Irwin, 1984), p. 254.
4. Carol Loomis, "The Fight for Financial Turf," *Fortune* (December 28, 1981): 54.
5. Alan Riding, "The New Latin Debt Crisis," *New York Times*, March 11, 1984, p. III–1.

6. Orin Kramer, "Winning Strategies for Interstate Banking," *Fortune* (September 19, 1983): 104.

7. Merrill Brown, "Citicorp Taking the Lead in High-Tech Finance," *Washington Post*, March 25, 1984, p. G-2.

8. Robert A. Bennett, "A Bank by Any other Name," *New York Times*, December 27, 1981, p. III-1.

9. "The New Sears," *Business Week* (November 16, 1981): 140.

10. "The Synergy Begins to Work for Sears' Financial Supermarket," *Business Week* (June 13, 1983): 116.

11. Ibid.

12. Ibid.

13. Gary Klott, "What Shearson Will Gain," *New York Times*, April 11, 1984, p. D-1.

14. "Your Friendly Broker, the PRU," *Fortune* (April 20, 1981): 15.

15. Gary Hector, "The Banks Invade Wall Street," *Fortune* (February 7, 1983): 44.

16. *Best's Insurance Reports: Life-Health* (1983), p. 698.

17. Loomis, "The Fight For Financial Turf," p. 56.

18. Ibid.

19. Lee Smith, "Merrill Lynch's Latest Bombshell for Bankers," *Fortune* (April 19, 1982): 67.

20. Ibid.

21. Lee Smith, "The Mauling Merrill Lynch Never Expected," *Fortune* (October 23, 1978): 78.

22. Tim Carrington, "Phibro Will Buy Salomon Brothers for $550 Million in Cash and Debt," *Wall Street Journal*, August 4, 1981, p. 2.

23. "Citibank's back door to a mutual fund," *Business Week* (March 7, 1983): 30-31.

24. James L. Rowe, Jr., "Manufacturers Nears National Status," *Washington Post*, March 18, 1984, p. F-1.

25. Gary Hector, "How Dreyfus Plans to Beat the Banks," *Fortune* (March 21, 1983): 64.

26. "Why Free Markets and Banks Don't Mix," *New York Times*, May 29, 1983, p. III-3.

CHAPTER 14

1. United States v. Pabst Brewing Co., 384 U.S. 546 (1966).

2. Jesse W. Markham, "Concentration: A Stimulus or Retardant to Innovation?" in Harvey J. Goldschmid et al., eds., *Industrial Concentration: The New Learning* (Boston: Little, Brown, 1974), p. 247.

3. Lawrence J. White, "Mergers and Aggregate Concentration," in Michael Keenan and Lawrence J. White, eds., *Mergers and Acquisitions* (Lexington, Mass.: D. C. Heath, 1982), p. 97.

4. *Hearings before the Senate Judiciary Committee on S.600*, 96th Cong., 1st Sess., March/April 1979, Serial No. 96–26, part 1, statement of Alfred F. Dougherty, Jr., p. 148.

5. Steve Lohr, "Small Business: Job Role Highlighted," *New York Times*, January 18, 1980, p. D-1.

6. *The 1978 Fortune Double Directory* (1978): 21.

7. Joan Campo, "The 500," *Fortune* (April 30, 1984): 295.

8. Stratford Sherman, "The Fortune Directory of the Second 500 Largest U.S. Industrial Corporations," *Fortune* (June 19, 1978): 171.

9. *Hearings before the Senate Judiciary Committee on S.600*, statement of Alfred F. Dougherty, Jr., p. 151.

10. See John McGowan, "The Effects of Alternative Antimerger Policies on the Size Distribution of Firms," *Yale Economic Essays* 423 (Fall 1969); and Lee Preston, "Giant Firms, Large Mergers and Concentration: Patterns and Policy Alternatives, 1954–1968," *Industrial Organization Review* 1 (1973): 35.

11. White, "Mergers and Aggregate Concentration," p. 98.

12. Gulf & Western Industries, Inc., Annual Report (1978).

13. Theodore Caplow, *Principles of Organization* (New York: Harcourt, Brace & World, 1964).

14. James March and Herbert Simon, *Organizations* (New York: John Wiley & Sons, 1958), p. 141.

15. Richard Cyertand and James March, *A Behavioral Theory of the Firm* (Englewood Cliffs, N.J.: Prentice-Hall, 1963).

16. Kenneth J. Arrow, *The Limits of Organization* (New York: W.W. Norton, 1974), p. 49.

17. Harvey Leibenstein, *Beyond Economic Man: A New Foundation for Microeconomics* (Cambridge, Mass.: Harvard University Press, 1976), p. 45.

18. Ibid., p. 134.

19. Oliver E. Williamson, *Markets and Hierarchies: Analysis and Antitrust Implications* (New York: MacMillan, 1975), p. 23.

20. D. Hamberg, "Invention in the Industrial Research Laboratory," *Journal of Political Economy* 71 (April 1963): 95.

21. John Jewkes, David Sawers, and Richard Stillerman, *The Sources of Inventions* (New York: W.W. Norton, 1969).

22. Morton Kamien and Nancy Schwartz, "Market Structure and Innovation: A Survey," *Journal of Economic Literature* 13 (1975): 1.

23. Burton H. Klein, *Dynamic Economics* (Cambridge, Mass.: Harvard University Press, 1977), p. 9.

24. Ibid., p. 58.

25. Ibid., pp. 128–29.

26. Ibid., p. 133.

27. Ibid.

28. Williamson, *Markets and Hierarchies*, pp. 205–206.
29. Dennis Mueller, "Mergers and Market Share," University of Maryland Working Paper (1983).
30. House Committee on Small Businesses, *Hearings on Conglomerate Mergers*, 96th Cong., 2nd Sess., statement of David Birch, February 12, 1980, p. 231.
31. Malcolm S. Salter and Wolf A. Weinhold, *Diversification through Acquisition* (New York: The Free Press, 1979), p. 138.
32. Edward S. Herman, *Corporate Control, Corporate Power* (New York: Twentieth Century Fund, 1981).
33. Subcommittee on Select Revenue Measures, Ways and Means Committee, U.S. House of Representatives, *Hearings on H. R. 6295*, June 4, 1982, statement of Albert Foer.
34. Ibid.

CHAPTER 15

1. Adolph A. Berle and Gardiner C. Means, *The Modern Corporation and Private Property* (New York: Harcourt, Brace & World, 1968).
2. Robin Marris, "A Model of the 'Managerial' Enterprise," *Quarterly Journal of Economics* 77 (May 1963): 185; and Marris, *The Economic Theory of "Managerial" Capitalism* (Cambridge, Mass.: The Free Press of Glencoe, 1964), ch. 2.
3. Henry Manne, "Mergers and the Market for Corporate Control," *Journal of Political Economy* 73 (April 1965): 110; and Manne, *Insider Trading and the Stock Market* (New York: The Free Press, 1966).
4. Marris, *The Economic Theory of "Managerial" Capitalism*, p. 54.
5. "How Kennecott has Mismanaged Carborundum," *Business Week* (May 23, 1983): 127.
6. Anne B. Fisher, "The Decade's Worst Mergers," *Fortune* (April 30, 1984): 262.
7. Peter W. Bernstein, "Who Buys Corporate Losers," *Fortune* (January 26, 1981): 60.
8. "Harry J. Gray: Thoughts on Acquisitions," *Financier* (November 1978): 36–37.
9. Bernstein, "Who Buys Corporate Losers."
10. Dick Griffin, "The Happy Divorce that Saved Hart Ski," *Fortune* (December 18, 1978): 86.
11. Bernstein, "Who Buys Corporate Losers," p. 62. Also, Case Study of American Safety Razor Company, in House Committee on Small Business, *Hearings on Conglomerate Mergers*, 96th Cong., 2nd Sess., January/February 1980, pp. 383, 408.
12. "Smooth Performance, Remington's Shaver Turnaround," *Fortune* (January 11, 1982): 11.

13. "Saving the Company that Acquired Him," *Business Week* (February 19, 1979): 47.

14. Bernstein, "Who Buys Corporate Losers," p. 65.

15. "Smooth Performance."

16. *Hearings on Conglomerate Mergers*, testimony of Bernard Stock, Administrative Coordinator to the Board of Selectmen, Town of Hopedale, Mass.

17. Bernstein, "Who Buys Corporate Losers," pp. 61–62.

18. Fisher, "The Decade's Worst Mergers."

19. Bernstein, "Who Buys Corporate Losers," p. 65.

20. Rush Loving, Jr., "The Penn Central Bankruptcy Express," *Fortune* (August 1970): 106.

21. Fisher, "The Decade's Worst Mergers," p. 263.

22. Theodore Levitt, "Marketing Myopia," *Harvard Business Review* (July 1960): 45.

23. See discussion of R. J. Reynolds's acquisitions in Chapter 7.

24. George Benston, *Conglomerate Mergers: Causes, Consequences, Remedies* (Washington, D.C.: American Enterprise Institute, 1980); J. F. Weston, "Industrial Concentration, Mergers and Growth," in *Mergers and Economic Efficiency* (U.S. Department of Commerce, 1980); statement of Yale Brozen, *Hearings before the Senate Judiciary Committee on S.600*, 96th Cong., 1st Sess., April 25, 1979, part 1, p. 419; Gregg Jarrell and Michael Bradley, "The Economic Effects of Federal and State Regulation of Cash Tender Offers," *Journal of Law and Economics* 23 (1980): 371.

26. Wayne I. Boucher, *The Process of Conglomerate Mergers*, prepared for the Federal Trade Commission (June 1980).

26. Daniel Seligman, "Can you Beat the Stock Market?" *Fortune* (December 26, 1983): 82.

27. Dennis C. Mueller, "Further Reflections on the Invisible Hand Theorem," in Peter Wiles and Guy Routh, eds., *Economics in Disarray* (Oxford: Basil Blackwell, 1984).

28. M. Firth, "The Profitability of Takeovers and Mergers," *Economic Journal* 89 (June 1979): 316.

29. Dennis C. Mueller, ed., *The Determinants and Effects of Mergers* (Cambridge, Mass.: O.G.&H. Publishers, 1980); Keith Cowling, et al., *Mergers and Economic Performance* (Cambridge, England: Cambridge University Press, 1979); and G. Meeks, *Disappointing Marriage: A Study of the Gains from Merger* (Cambridge, England: Cambridge University Press, 1977).

30. Subcommittee on Select Revenue Measures, Ways and Means Committee, U.S. House of Representatives, *Hearings on H.R. 6295*, June 4, 1982, statement of Albert A. Foer.

31. Arthur Louis, "The Bottom Line on Ten Big Mergers," *Fortune* (May 3, 1982): 88.

32. Richard P. Rumelt, *Strategy, Structure and Economic Performance* (Cambridge, Mass.: Harvard University Press, 1974); and J. Fred Weston and

Keith V. Smith, "Further Evaluation of Conglomerate Performance," *Journal of Business Research* 5 (1977).
33.   Dennis Mueller, "Further Reflections," p. 180.

CHAPTER 16

1.   Perlman v. Feldmann, 219 F.2d 173 (1954) (*cert. denied*, 349 U.S. 952 [1955]).
2.   "RCA May Have Run Out of Time," *Business Week* (March 22, 1982): 20; and Peter W. Bernstein, "A Company that's Worth More Dead than Alive," *Fortune* (February 26, 1979): 42.
3.   Shawn Tully, "The Mismatched Merger that Worked," *Fortune* (April 19, 1982): 166.
4.   Burton H. Klein, "The Role of Feedback in a Dynamically Stable Economic System," California Institute of Technology. (Unpublished.)
5.   House Committee on Small Businesses, *Hearings on Acquisitions and Mergers by Conglomerates before the Senate Judiciary Committee*, May, July, September 1978, statement of Dr. Willard F. Mueller, pp. 85–91; and *Hearings before the Senate Judiciary Committee on S.600*, 96th Cong., 1st Sess., March 30, 1979, part 1, statement of Paul DeLima, p. 351.
6.   *Hearings on S.600*, statement of DeLima, pp. 351, 709.
7.   Ibid., p. 350.
8.   William James Adams, "Market Structure and Corporate Power: The Horizontal Dominance Hypothesis Reconsidered," *Columbia Law Review* 74 (1974): 1,276.
9.   Daniel P. Wiener, "Deals of the Year," *Fortune* (January 23, 1984): 55–56.
10.   Alan A. Fisher and Robert H. Lande, "Efficiency Considerations in Merger Enforcement," *California Law Review* 71 (1983): 1,675.

CHAPTER 17

1.   Richard Hofstadter, "What Happened to the Antitrust Movement," in *The Paranoid Style of American Politics* (New York: Alfred A. Knopf, 1965), pp. 199–200.
2.   See Chapter 14, Table 14-1.
3.   First National Bank of Boston v. Bellotti, 435 U.S. 765 (1978).
4.   Eric F. Goldman, *The Crucial Decade—and After: America 1945–1960* (New York: Vintage Books, 1960), p. 239.
5.   Adolf Berle, *The American Economic Republic* (New York, Harcourt, Brace & World, 1963), p. 13.
6.   Edwin Epstein, *The Corporation in American Politics* (Englewood Cliffs, N.J.: Prentice-Hall, 1969).
7.   Ibid., p. 228.
8.   William Manchester, *The Glory and the Dream* (Boston: Little, Brown, 1974), p. 1,234.

9. "Why the Government Lobbyist is Necessary," *Business Week* (March 18, 1972): 63.

10. Reprinted in Michael Pertschuk and Kenneth Davidson, "What's Wrong with Conglomerate Mergers?" *Fordham Law Review* 48 (1979): 9.

11. Edwin Epstein, "Business and Labor in the American Electoral Process: A Policy Analysis of Federal Regulation—The Rise of Political Action Committees," Institute of Government Studies, University of California (Berkeley) Working Papers (1970), pp. 31-32.

12. Robert Pitofsky, "The Political Content of Antitrust," *University of Pennsylvania Law Review* 127 (1979): 1,055.

13. Harlan Blake, "Conglomerate Mergers and the Antitrust Laws," *Columbia Law Review* 73 (1973): 555.

14. Robert Salisbury, "Interest Groups," in Fred I. Greenstein and Nelson W. Polsby, eds., *Handbook of Political Science: Non-Governmental Politics* (Reading, Mass.: Addison-Wesley, 1975), p. 211-12.

15. Ralph Nader, Mark Green, and Joel Seligman, *Taming the Giant Corporation* (New York: W. W. Norton, 1976), p. 223.

16. *Hearings before the Senate Judiciary Committee on S.600*, 96th Cong., 1st Sess., March 8, 1979, part 1, statement of Alfred F. Dougherty, Jr., p. 201.

17. Charles E. Lindblom, *Politics and Markets* (New York: Basic Books, 1977), p. 175.

18. Aaron Wildavsky, "Changing Forward Versus Changing Back," 88 *Yale Law Journal* 217 at 233 (1978).

19. Clifton Garvin, "Exxon and the Arts," *Lamp* (1978): 10.

20. Lindblom, *Politics and Markets*, p. 155.

21. Robert Stern and Howard Aldrich, "The Effect of Absentee Firm Control on Local Community Welfare," in John J. Siegfried, ed., *The Economics of Firm Size, Market Structure and Social Performance* (Proceedings of a conference sponsored by the Bureau of Economics, Federal Trade Commission, July 1980), p. 165.

22. Ibid., pp. 168-69.

23. Testimony of John R. Baker, President, American Safety Razor Co., *Hearings on Conglomerate Mergers* before the House Small Business Committee, 96th Cong., 2nd Sess., January 31, 1980, p. 55.

24. Adolf A. Berle and Gardiner C. Means, *The Modern Corporation and Private Property* (New York: Harcourt, Brace & World, 1968), p. 46.

25. Lindblom, *Politics and Markets*, p. 154.

26. *Hearings on S.600*, March 8, 1979, opening statements of Senators Edward M. Kennedy and Howard M. Metzenbaum, pp. 1, 8.

27. Conglomerate Mergers—Their Effects on Small Business and Local Communities. Hearings before the House Committee on Small Business. 96th Cong., 2nd Sess., January/February 1980, p. 281.

28. Robert B. Reich, *The Next American Frontier* (New York: Penguin Books, 1983).

29. Testimony of F. M. Scherer. *Hearings before the Senate Judiciary Committee on S.600*, 96th Cong., 1st Sess., 1979.

30. *Hearings on S.600*, part 2, statement of Ira Millstein, p. 49.

31. Ira M. Millstein and Salem M. Katsh, *The Limits of Corporate Power* (New York: MacMillan, 1981).

32. *Hearings on S.600*, part 2, p. 292.

33. George Benston, *Conglomerate Mergers: Causes, Consequences, Remedies* (Washington, D.C.: American Enterprise Institute, 1980).

34. Law & Economics Center, *Year 5 Annual Report* for the Academic Year 1978-1979, p. 20.

35. *Hearings on S.600*, part 2, p. 416.

36. Ibid., p. 482.

37. Kenneth J. Arrow, *The Limits of Organization* (New York: W. W. Norton, 1974), pp. 22-23.

38. Elizabeth Drew, *Politics and Money* (New York: MacMillan, 1983).

39. Steven Brill, "The Ultimate Insiders' Game," *American Lawyer* (May 1984).

40. Ibid.

41. Ibid.

42. *Hearings on S.600*, part 2, statement of Robert Hatfield, p. 98.

43. Ibid., statement of George Benston, p. 293.

44. Milton Friedman, *Capitalism and Freedom* (Chicago: University of Chicago Press, 1962), p. 132.

45. Tim Metz, "Mergers Expected to Stay Plentiful in 1983 but will be Less Exciting," *Wall Street Journal*, January 3, 1983, p. 5.

46. *Hearings on S.600*, part 1, statement of Alfred F. Dougherty Jr., p. 129.

47. Ralph Nader, Mark Green, and Joel Seligman, *Taming the Giant Corporation* (New York: W. W. Norton, 1976).

48. *Hearings on S.600*, part 1, statement of William Norris, p. 44.

49. Yankelovich, Skelly and White, "Report to Leadership Participants on 1979 Findings on Corporate Priorities." (Mimeo, 1979.)

50. Brown Shoe Co. v. U.S., 370 U.S. 294, 312 at n. 25 (1962).

MORE MEGAMERGERS

1. Anthony Bianco, "How Drexel's Wunderkind Bankrolls the Raiders," *Business Week*, March 4, 1985, p. 90.

2. Jane Jacobs, *The Economy of Cities* (New York: Vintage, 1971).

3. W. T. Grimm & Co., *Mergerstat Review* (1983).

4. Sandra Salmans, "The Value of Film Libraries," *New York Times*, April 3, 1984, p. D-1.

BIBLIOGRAPHY

Andrews, Kenneth. *The Concept of Corporate Strategy.* Homewood, Ill.: R. P. Irwin, 1971.

Aranow, Edward; Herbert Einhorn; and George Berlstein. *Developments in Tender Offers for Corporate Control.* New York: Columbia University Press, 1977.

Areeda, Phillip, and Donald F. Turner. *Antitrust Law: Analysis of Antitrust Principles and Their Applications.* Boston: Little, Brown, 1978.

Arrow, Kenneth J. *The Limits of Organization.* New York: W.W. Norton, 1974.

Axxin, Stephen; Blaine Fogg; and Neal Stoll. *Acquisitions Under the Hart-Scott-Rodino Antitrust Improvement Act.* New York: Law Journal Seminars Press, 1979.

Bain, Joseph. *Barriers to New Competition.* Cambridge, Mass.: Harvard University Press, 1956.

Bain, Joseph. *Industrial Organization.* New York: John Wiley & Sons, 1974.

Benston, George. *Conglomerate Mergers: Causes, Consequences, Remedies.* Washington, D.C.: American Enterprise Institute, 1980.

Berle, Adolph A., and Gardiner C. Means. *The Modern Corporation and Private Property* New York: Harcourt, Brace & World, 1968.

Bork, Robert H. *The Antitrust Paradox: A Policy at War with Itself.* New York: Basic Books, 1978.

Brozen, Yale. *Concentration, Mergers and Public Policy.* New York: MacMillan, 1982.

Chandler, Alfred D., Jr. *Strategy and Structure: Chapters in the History of the American Industrial Enterprise.* Cambridge, Mass.: M.I.T. Press, 1962.

399

Chandler, Alfred D., Jr. *The Visible Hand: The Managerial Revolution in American Business.* Cambridge, Mass.: Belknap Press, 1977.

Cyert, Richard M., and James March. *A Behavioral Theory of the Firm.* Englewood Cliffs, N.J.: Prentice-Hall, 1963.

Drucker, Peter F. *Management: Tasks, Responsibilities, Practices.* New York: Harper, 1974.

Drucker, Peter F. *Technology, Management and Society.* New York: Harper Colophon, 1977.

Freund, James C. *Anatomy of a Merger.* New York: Law Journal Seminars Press, 1975.

Friedman, Milton. *Capitalism and Freedom.* Chicago: University of Chicago Press, 1962.

Galambos, Louis. *The Public Image of Big Business in America, 1880-1940.* Baltimore: Johns Hopkins University Press, 1975.

Galbraith, John Kenneth. *Economics and the Public Purpose.* Boston: Houghton Mifflin, 1973.

Goldschmid, Harvey J., et al. (eds.). *Industrial Concentration: The New Learning.* Boston: Little, Brown, 1974.

Gussow, Don. *The New Merger Game.* New York: Amacom, 1978.

Henderson, Bruce D. *Henderson on Corporate Strategy.* Cambridge, Mass.: Belknap Press, 1979.

Herman, Edward S. *Corporate Control, Corporate Power.* New York: Twentieth Century Fund, 1981.

Hofstadter, Richard. *The Age of Reform.* New York: Random House, 1955.

Hofstadter, Richard. *The Paranoid Style of American Politics.* New York: Alfred A. Knopf, 1965.

Josephson, Matthew. *The Robber Barons.* New York: Harcourt, Brace & World, 1962.

Kaysen, Carl, and Donald F. Turner. *Antitrust Policy.* Cambridge, Mass.: Harvard University Press, 1960.

Keenan, Michael, and Lawrence J. White (eds.). *Mergers and Acquisitions.* Lexington, Mass.: D.C. Heath, 1982.

Klein, Burton H. *Dynamic Economics.* Cambridge, Mass.: Harvard University Press, 1977.

Leibenstein, Harvey. *Beyond Economic Man: A New Foundation for Microeconomics.* Cambridge, Mass.: Harvard University Press, 1976.

Letwin, William. *Law and Economic Policy in America.* New York: Random House, 1965.

Lindblom, Charles E. *Politics and Markets.* New York: Basic Books, 1977.

Lipton, Martin, and Erica Steinberger. *Takeovers and Freezeouts.* New York: Law Journal Seminars Press, 1979.

Manne, Henry. *Insider Trading and the Stock Market.* New York: The Free Press, 1966.

March, James, and Herbert Simon. *Organizations.* New York: John Wiley & Sons, 1958.

Marris, Robin. *The Economic Theory of "Managerial" Capitalism.* Cambridge, Mass.: The Free Press of Glencoe, 1964.

Martin, David D. *Mergers and the Clayton Act.* Berkeley: University of California Press, 1959.

McDonald, John. *The Game of Business.* Garden City, N.Y.: Anchor Press/Doubleday, 1977.

McQuown, Judith H. *Playing the Takeover Market.* New York: Seaview Books, 1982.

Miles, Robert H. *Coffin Nails and Corporate Strategies.* Englewood Cliffs, N.J.: Prentice-Hall, 1982.

Mintz, Morton, and Jerry S. Cohen. *America, Inc.* New York: Delta Publishing, 1971.

Mueller, Dennis C., ed. *The Determinants and Effects of Mergers.* Cambridge, Mass.: O.G.&H. Publishers, 1980.

Nelson, Ralph L. *Merger Movements in American Industry, 1895-1956.* Princeton: Princeton University Press, 1959.

Peters, Thomas J., and Robert H. Waterman. *In Search of Excellence.* New York: Harper & Row, 1982.

Phalon, Richard. *The Takeover Barons of Wall Street.* New York: Putnam, 1981.

Porter, Michael E. *Competitive Strategy: Techniques for Analyzing Industries and Competitors.* New York: The Free Press, 1980.

Reid, Samuel Richardson. *Mergers, Managers and the Economy.* New York: McGraw-Hill, 1968.

Rumelt, Richard P. *Strategy, Structure and Economic Performance.* Cambridge, Mass.: Harvard University Press, 1974.

Salter, Malcolm S., and Wolf A. Weinhold. *Diversification through Acquisition: Strategies for Creating Wealth.* New York: The Free Press, 1979.

Schelling, Thomas C. *The Strategy of Conflict.* Cambridge, Mass.: Harvard University Press, 1960.

Scherer, F. M. *Industrial Market Structure and Economic Performance.* Boston: Houghton Mifflin, 1980.

Simon, Herbert. *Administrative Behavior: A Study of Decision-Making Processes in Administrative Organizations.* New York: The Free Press, 1976.

Simons, Henry C. *Economic Policy for a Free Society.* Chicago: University of Chicago Press, 1948.

Sobel, Robert. *The Rise and Fall of Conglomerate Kings.* New York: Stein and Day, 1984.

Steiner, Peter O. *Mergers: Motives, Effects, Policies.* Ann Arbor: University of Michigan Press, 1977.

Sullivan, Lawrence A. *Handbook of the Law of Antitrust.* St. Paul, Minn.: West Publishing, 1977.

Thorelli, Hans. *Federal Antitrust Policy.* Baltimore: Johns Hopkins University Press, 1954.

Williamson, Oliver E. *Markets and Hierarchies: Analysis and Antitrust Implications.* New York: MacMillan, 1975.

INDEX

403

ABOUT THE AUTHOR

Kenneth M. Davidson is presently a lawyer at the Federal Trade Commission. His articles on legal and economic subjects have appeared in the *Journal of Business Strategy*, the *California Law Review*, and other scholarly journals. Mr. Davidson's career has been evenly divided between government service with two federal agencies and the academic world where he was a law professor at three universities. He holds degrees from the University of Chicago, the University of Pennsylvania, and Yale University. *Megamergers* was written while he was teaching at the University of Maryland. The book draws, in part, on his experiences as Deputy Assistant Director for Special Projects at the Federal Trade Commission.